MONTAIGNE
IN MOTION

MONTAIGNE IN MOTION

Jean Starobinski

Translated by
Arthur Goldhammer

The University of Chicago Press
Chicago and London

Jean Starobinski, winner of the 1984 Balzan Prize,
is professor of French literature at the University
of Geneva. His numerous works have been translated
into English, German, Japanese, Italian, Spanish,
and Romanian. *Montaigne en mouvement,* the French
edition of this work, was awarded the Prix européen
de l'essai in 1982 by the Veillon Foundation of
Lausanne.

Arthur Goldhammer's recent translations include
Serge Guilbaut's *How New York Stole the Idea of
Modern Art* and Roland Mousnier's *The Institutions
of France under Absolute Monarchy, 1598–1789,*
volume 2.

This work was originally published as
Montaigne en mouvement, © Editions Gallimard,
1982.

THE UNIVERSITY OF CHICAGO PRESS, CHICAGO 60637
THE UNIVERSITY OF CHICAGO PRESS, LTD., LONDON

© 1985 by The University of Chicago
All rights reserved. Published 1985
Printed in the United States of America

94 93 92 91 90 89 88 87 86 85   5 4 3 2 1

LIBRARY OF CONGRESS CATALOGING IN PUBLICATION DATA

Starobinski, Jean.
  Montaigne in motion.

  Translation of: Montaigne en mouvement.
  Includes index.
  1. Montaigne, Michel de, 1533–1592. Essais. I. Title.
PQ1643.S7413   1985   844'.3   85-1026
ISBN 0-226-77129-6

Contents

Translator's preface

The translator into English of any work about Montaigne must acknowledge one paramount debt of gratitude: to Donald Frame, translator of the now standard edition of Montaigne's complete works (see chap. 1, n.1). All citations from Montaigne in the present work are taken from Frame's superb rendering. Occasionally it has been necessary to change a word or two in order to emphasize some connotation of the French singled out for commentary by Jean Starobinski; places where this was the case are indicated in the text or notes. Passages from Latin authors cited by Montaigne are given in English as in the Frame translation (which should be consulted for the sources of the English versions). Chronological indications marking the various layers of Montaigne's text as established by Pierre Villey are included here whenever Starobinski included them in the French. Certain words in citations from Montaigne have been italicized by Starobinski, usually to call attention to a word or passage that has been or will be the subject of commentary.

An English translation by John A. Gallucci of a somewhat altered version of part of chapter 4 appeared in *Yale French Studies* 64 (1983): 273–305. I found it useful to consult this version before making my own translation.

Arthur Goldhammer

Preface

In the beginning, Montaigne had to face the following question—a question that he himself posed: Once pessimistic philosophy has repudiated illusory appearances, what then? What remains to be discovered by an author who has denounced artifice and dissimulation on all sides? Will he be allowed to achieve the truth, being, and identiy in whose name he has deemed the veiled world unsatisfactory and bidden it farewell? If words, language, are indeed a "commodity so vulgar and so vile," how paradoxical it is to write a book, to try one's hand at a work of language! The *motion* that the present work will attempt to trace is that which, starting from the question raised above, encounters a paradox from which there is no easy escape.

I have attempted to follow the development of a philosophy that derives its impetus from an act of refusal. It is not my intention here to redo what others have already done, often quite well: to set forth Montaigne's ideas concerning universal change and flux, to organize propositions scattered throughout the *Essays* into a coherent philosophy, or to attempt to identify the concepts and attitudes which, at one stage or another of publication, were accorded a preeminent position in the work. The motion on which I have chosen to focus is that which animates the logical consequences of the original negation. While not indifferent to the question of how Montaigne's *Essays* evolved (a problem treated, in a work of fundamental importance, by Pierre Villey and subsequently explored in different ways by others), I felt that, for present purposes, it was possible to set this question aside.

Although this book does deal with many of the philosophical and stylistic problems raised by Montaigne's work, the reader should be forewarned that, unlike the works of Friedrich, Frame, and Sayce, the pages that follow are not intended to provide a synthetic account of Montaigne's life, thought, and style. It is not my intention to situate Montaigne in relation to his times or to recount the history of his work's reception. My only purpose is to trace the consequences—or series of consequences—of a specific act, which was both intellectual and existential in nature. I took a similar approach in an earlier book, devoted to Rousseau, whose work is in so many ways—as auto-biography, as pedagogy, as social and political theory—a response, at times a quite conscious response, to the *Essays* of Montaigne. From the outset, *Montaigne in Motion* was conceived as a complement to *Jean-Jacques Rousseau: la transparence et l'obstacle*. The point of these two parallel studies lies in the similarity of the actions that serve in each case as point of departure—the criticism of false appearances and their attendant evils—even though the ultimate outcomes are quite different: unable to attain true being, Montaigne acknowledges the legitimacy of appearance, whereas Rousseau, unreconciled, imagines that hostile clouds are gathering all around, in order to preserve his conviction that within his own heart transparency has found its last refuge.

The reader will no doubt have noticed that the question with which the present work begins is a perennial commonplace of moral rhetoric as well as an early version of the suspiciousness which, in one form or another, is characteristic of so many contemporary attitudes. It is, I trust, hardly necessary to state explicitly that the prevalence of such attitudes today is not without bearing on my decision to make the denunciation of lying the point of departure for my interpretation of my Montaigne. I have attended to what Montaigne says as closely as I am able, in the hope that, as far as possible, I might leave the first move up to him. But since I myself begin with a modern anxiety, and turn to Montaigne, in his text, for answers to this century's questions, I make no attempt to get around the fact that to study "Montaigne in motion" requires "moving into Montaigne," so that reflection on the text becomes intertwined or fused with the text itself. My reading is an interrogative one, whereby the critic attempts to clarify his own situation by interpreting, without doing violence to the specificity or remoteness of the text, a specimen of discourse drawn from the living past.

The consequences of skepticism in philosophy are of course three-fold: emphasis on the phenomenal (phenomenalism), attachment of extreme importance to the present moment, and reliance on the experience of the senses. Another consequence, among Christian philosophers, is fideism. All of this may be found in any history of philosophy. It might seem, then, that the final destination of Montaigne's philosophical adventure was fixed in advance. Such a schematic view, abstracting as it does from the quite personal character of Montaigne's journey toward an always elusive goal, would fail, however, to do justice to what is most valuable in the *Essays*. All the variations of a *chaconne* may be inferred from the first notes of the bass, yet the piece is not finished until all its developments are complete. The seven chapters of the present work may all be read as variations on the theme of a sophisticated return to the world of artifice and appearance repudiated at the outset. Weaving among themselves a complex harmony, these variations help to clarify the original theme as it is taken up and repeated by one voice after another: friendship, death, freedom, the body, love, language, and public life.

Montaigne has left a warning to his would-be commentators: "There is more concern with interpreting interpretations than with interpreting things, and there are more books about books than about any other subject: We do nothing but comment on one another. There are swarms of commentaries; authors are quite rare." More than that, Montaigne hoped to find an *adequate* reader, one who could imagine the *infinite essays* for which his book might serve as a pretext. This reader would take advantage of the author's collaborator, *fortune,* whose contribution is evident in those aspects of the book that *go beyond* (its author's) *conception and knowledge.* In writing this book I have tried both to respect Montaigne's warning and to avail myself of his license.

ONE

«And then, for whom are you writing?»

The indictment

The surrounding world is all lies and treachery. "Dissimulation is among the most notable qualities of this century. . . ."[1] [Deceit] maintains and feeds most of men's occupations."[2] People massacre one another under cover of noble pretexts which, in reality, merely mask base interests.

By accumulating such scattered observations, Montaigne develops an ancient theme, older than Plato, who first cast it in mythical form. Exploited by Stoics and Skeptics; developed by Boethius; given wide currency by various medieval authors, most notably John of Salisbury;[3] and repeatedly invoked by moralists and preachers, this is the theme of the world as theater, in which men do no more than play out their roles, speaking their lines and gesticulating like actors on a stage—until death decrees their final exit. This theme was at times employed to exalt the omnipotence of God, simultaneously author, director, and spectator of this vast production; on other occasions it was used to denounce the idle fictions in which gullible men allow themselves to believe. Montaigne does not fail to cite the words attributed to Petronius, "Mundus universus exercet histrioniam,"[4] later echoed within the walls of the Globe Theatre by melancholy Jaques in Shakespeare's *As You Like It:* "All the world's a stage, and all the men and women merely players."[5]

What Montaigne, in common with many of his contemporaries, uses this image to emphasize is the idea that the world, like a theater, creates illusions. It is a play of shadows that holds us in its grip. The grandeur of princes is pure theater: clever imitators are able to mimic majesty and win the respect of the populace. No less illusory are the wisdom extolled by the champions of prudence and the doctrines propounded by learned scholars. Everywhere there is *trumpery, knavery, affectation,* and *artifice.* "Yes, even the mask of greatness put on in our plays affects us and deludes us somewhat."[6] Everything is borrowed "for mask and show" in a cruel and futile display.[7] More from weakness than from malevolence, ordinary men are susceptible to this sort of deception. Prisoners of their imaginations, forgetful of themselves, they let themselves be gulled. They mistake the appearance for the essence. Both monarchs, for their bellicose purposes, and religious factions, through their propaganda, are perfectly capable of taking advantage of this human blindness. Both need credulous men, men easily swayed by opinion and ready to shed their own blood and the blood of others for the sake of the cause. "Any opinion is strong enough to make people espouse it at the price of life."[8] Wherever one looks, triumphant impostors and satisfied dupes are to be found. "I have in my time seen wonders in the undiscerning and prodigious ease with which people let their belief and hope be led and manipulated in whatever way has pleased and served their leaders, passing over a hundred mistakes one on top of the other, passing over phantasms and dreams."[9]

In denouncing the viciousness of false appearance, Montaigne is at one with the spirit of his age. Flattering the prevailing taste, he exploits a commonplace idea, which he varies and amplifies and embellishes with abundant citations and conceits. Yet through this commonplace he is in fact aiming at an aspect of contemporary reality on which the traditional antithesis of being and appearance bears more directly than at any other time in history. The wars through which the princes of Europe are seeking to augment their power (with the formation of the major European states still in the offing); the religious conflicts that threaten to undermine the very principle of authority (with the elevation of man's "inner conscience" to the position of supreme authority still looming on the horizon); and the ubiquitous violence, the constant danger that besets all men—all of these circumstances provide pressing reasons for dissimulation and deception; as a result, these have become generally accepted forms of behavior and are frequently taken as themes of literature. In this age of excess, the teachings associated with the ethical and religious tradition of *contemptus mundi* have been exaggerated: the temptations of this world are traps, the true goods lie elsewhere. Before long, the baroque theater would depict disillusionment (*desengaño*) as a moment of bitter grace, in which characters too long sunken in blindness would suddenly regain their sight.[10]

The world against which Montaigne levels a finger of accusation is a labyrinth in which the counterfeit passes for legal tender. Hypocrisy, far from being regarded as a mask that one must penetrate, is everywhere praised as "this new-fangled virtue of hypocrisy and dissimulation, which is so highly honored at present."[11] The juggling of offices and ranks is a scandal for all to behold. Anybody involved in public affairs is aware of what goes on and must, since everybody

2

is doing it, take steps at once to protect himself and remain on his guard. "Our truth of nowadays is not what is, but what others can be convinced of."[12] Duplicity and cunning are not discoveries that men make in time, but handles to the world available to anyone bold enough to grasp them. Men learn to dissimulate as they learn to talk, by listening to what is going on all around and mimicking what succeeds. Education is quickly acquired. Politics is defined, in principle, as ostentation, trickery, and ruse—wholly legitimate defenses against an enemy's ambush and the hazards of fortune. "Innocence itself could neither negotiate among us without dissimulation nor bargain without lying."[13] So little trouble is taken to hide a lie that lying has become the universally accepted convention. Concealment and duplicity are the common "form," the normal way of doing business—lying, at first tacitly tolerated, is now the general rule.

On the other hand, it is not uncommon in this verbose age to find false appearances being denounced. There were accepted formulas for decrying the universality of lying and for protesting one's own sincerity, one's willingness to engage in flattery, one's eagerness to tell the truth, however imprudent it might be. "Parrhesia" and protestations of sincerity or candor were devices commonly used by smooth talkers.[14] The rhetorical contrast between being and appearance, the topos according to which this world is the world of fraud and deception, were among the common tricks of the duplicitous. Hypocrites could deliver admirable speeches condemning hypocrisy. Anyone who saw profit in so doing could rail against deception, buttressed by innumerable citations, yet remain a character wearing a false mask, an actor in the ultimate role of disillusioned sage. The rules of dissimulation would have been incomplete had they not included among their recommended stratagems the refusal to dissimulate. The enemy of concealment is often just another stage device: the play becomes (or *appears* to become) believable because it includes a character who ostensibly refuses to believe in the appearances he encounters. In the baroque era this ultimate illusion was expressed symbolically by the play within a play. The actor defending himself against illusion takes on the status of a real being, thanks to the interplay of relative oppositions. The spectator believes that the actor is not on the stage because he denounces yet another stage. (And so it goes today with ideology, one of whose most effective diversionary tactics is the denunciation of ideology.[15]

Montaigne is obviously making use of this kind of rhetoric. Indeed, he goes it one better, drawing from the humanist tradition methapors of disloyalty and indictments of lying. But he does what he does with

3

a new seriousness and irony. He is to be believed when he insists on his veracity, when he declares that it "is painful for me to dissemble,"[16] or that "I have ordered myself to dare to say all that I dare to do,"[17] or when he tells how his "face" and "frankness"[18] have on several occasions saved his life. The traditional precepts find in him a ready welcome: for him, to live with an open heart is no mere turn of phrase but an injunction that he has no difficulty putting into practice. By the same token, the gate of his castle remains open to all comers.

Montaigne casts the net of his skepticism quite widely. Looking at the history of mankind, he determines that the consequences of sincerity and deception are quite unpredictable. "By diverse means we arrive at the same end," says the title of the very first essay in book 1. Unpredictability means that deception can never be certain of achieving its goals even in the world of *facts;* hence Montaigne decides in favor of that which the moral tradition has established, in *law,* as being of higher moral value: sincerity. Whatever the outcome of our actions (which outcome depends on God alone), Montaigne is in no doubt as to the correct moral choice: insistence on veracity remains his unvarying standard of judgment, his permanent criterion for criticizing morals and for governing his own behavior. This standard is, admittedly, a commonplace, but Montaigne's desire for originality is not so great that he rejects it. Such is his concern for honesty that it is untouched even by his recognition of the mutability of all things.

Montaigne shaped his response to the world-theater by drawing on the humanist tradition. If it is true that "most of our occupations are low comedy,"[19] should we laugh or cry? To the sorrowful compassion of Heraclitus Montaigne preferred its fabled opposite, the laughter of Democritus. This comparison heightens the contrast between the two positions and renders compromise less likely. Once again, we have every reason to believe that Montaigne wholeheartedly subscribes to the lesson that he draws from the traditional cultural stereotype:

> (A) Democritus and Heraclitus were two philosophers, of whom the first, finding the condition of man vain and ridiculous, never went out in public but with a mocking and laughing face; whereas Heraclitus, having pity and compassion on this same condition of ours, wore a face perpetually sad, and eyes filled with tears. . . . I prefer the first humor, not because it is pleasanter to laugh than to weep, but because it is more disdainful, and condemns us more than the other; and it seems to me that we can never

4

be despised as much as we deserve. . . . We are not so full
of evil as of inanity; we are not so wretched as we are
worthless.[20]

Here, Montaigne is temporarily adapting to his own purposes an
attitude that dates from the beginnings of philosophy: Democritus
laughs at the world's folly, but it grieves him just the same, and in
fact he exacerbates his melancholy by his relentless efforts to get at
the causes of the folly he mocks.[21] (Later, in 1621, Robert Burton
would publish his *Anatomy of Melancholy* under the pseudonym Democritus Minor, invoking the name of Montaigne among his precursors.) Hamlet repeats a line remarkably similar to one in the passage
of Montaigne cited above: "Use every man after his desert, and who
should escape whipping?"[22] And Freud mentions this verse from
Hamlet more than once, most notably in "Mourning and Melan-
cholia," where it is adduced as evidence for the clear-sightedness of
self-accusation on the part of the melancholic.[23] By what special privilege do such judgments of melancholy, more than other words, pass
down through the ages, linking the author who pronounces with the
reader who reads and pronounces in his turn? Should we conclude
that the propensity to quote (about which we shall have more to say
later on) is a consequence of the self-denigration of the melancholic?
Montaigne's excuse for the borrowings that serve him as embellishment is that he prefers to speak through the stronger voice of a
Seneca or a Plutarch. Citation, an avowal of weakness, shows a
marked predilection for the discourse of melancholy.

But Montaigne does not merely take seriously the lessons of the
masters of antiquity and try to live in accordance with precepts consecrated by tradition. He goes even further. When he casts his eyes
about him, he thinks he sees the end of the world: "Now let us turn
our eyes in all directions: everything is crumbling about us. . . . It
seems as if the very stars have ordained that we have lasted long
enough beyond the ordinary term. And this also weighs me down,
that the evil that most nearly threatens us is not an alteration in the
entire and solid mass, but its dissipation and disintegration, the worst
of our fears."[24] When everything seems to be in collapse, is it not time
time to remedy our dissatisfaction, to press our questioning with
ever-greater urgency, to arm ourselves with higher standards, to
shun every vanity (including even learned discourse on vanity), and
to bring to our defense every available resource of sophistication and
irony? Desire for independence becomes the main source of energy,
though this need not interfere with listening to the past or reading the
exemplary texts it provides.

Votive space

To have discerned so clearly the "banishment of truth,"[25] Montaigne must have formulated within himself a standard of candor and veracity which the world constantly disappointed. Would he have spoken so often of inconstancy and fraud had he not imagined a possibility of constancy and honesty, however vague his hope of living up to this standard may have been? To charge that the world is false presupposes belief in an opposite value: a truth situated elsewhere (whether in this world or out of it) which would authorize us to intervene in its name, to act as the prosecutors of falsehood. In denouncing the "prestige of appearance" Montaigne implicitly declares himself in favor of the unequivocal plenitude of true being.[26] But he knows this plenitude only through the force of his refusal to accept falsehood and deceit. At the moment he declares his opposition to the world, Montaigne cannot claim to possess any truth: he merely proclaims his hatred of "sham." The truth is the still-undiscovered positive implicit in the negation of proliferating evil; the truth has no fixed visage but is merely the unappeased energy that animates and arms the act of refusal.

The opposition between truth and falsehood initially has no way of manifesting itself other than through spatial figures. Skeptical refusal is expressed metaphorically in the act of standing aloof, abs-taining. Montaigne feels the need to create a private *place* for himself at a distance from the world—a place where he can make himself a spectator of human life and feel protected from all its pitfalls. If the world is a deceptive theater, one must not remain on the stage; instead, one must find a way to establish oneself elsewhere. To exile oneself from a world where truth has been banished is not really to go into exile. (And Montaigne expresses his astonishment that Socrates, who saw the "horribly corrupt laws" of Athens for what they were, did not choose to accept a "sentence of exile."[27])

The secession from the world thus figures as an inaugural act. It determines the site where Montaigne withdraws from the trade in deception; it establishes a frontier, consecrates a boundary line. The site in question is no abstract height: in Montaigne everything has substance. His separate place will be his tower library—a belvedere in the family manor which offers a commanding view of the surrounding countryside. It is no secret that Montaigne did not make this his permanent residence: he continued to devote much of his time to public affairs, to conciliatory negotiations. He did not shirk what he saw as his duty to the common weal. What mattered in his eyes was to have secured the *possibility* of occupying his own private territory, the possibility of withdrawing at any moment into absolute solitude, of quitting the game: the important thing was to establish a concrete as well as symbolic embodiment of the imagined distance between himself and the world, a place always ready to receive him whenever he felt the need; but he felt under no obligation to reside there permanently. Thus a hiatus was opened up between the gaze of the spectator and the agitation of mankind, a pure interval, which enabled Montaigne to perceive how the mass of men voluntarily choose bondage while he, each time he withdrew to his library, assured himself of a new liberty. He saw the shackles in which other men remained bound but felt his own fall away. For the first conquest is not knowledge but self-presence (*présence à soi*).

Now, this occupation of a place, this creation of a space inaccessible to the world's falsehood, also marks a caesura in time. To see this we have only to pay attention to the wording of the inscriptions that Montaigne had painted in 1571. A precise date is attached to the break in his life. A new era had begun, and it was important to situate it precisely in relation to both the collective time of Christendom (*Anno Christi 1571 . . . pridie cal. mart.*[28]) and his own biographical time (*aet. 38 . . . die suo natali*). Mention of his birthdate reinforces the idea of a voluntary *birth*. Time takes on a new origin and at the same moment acquires a new meaning: it is the limited lifespan that remains (*quantillum in tandem superabit decursi multa jam plus parte spatii*), the few days that will be added to the life already elapsed. A new law or rule comes into effect. Renewed attachments compensate for the detachment that is at once voluntary and involuntary. The new order is no longer that of *servitium* but that of *libertas*. Liberation goes hand in hand with constriction. A strict opposition emerges between the expressions of disgust and of desire to make a break (*servitii aulici et munerum publicorum pertaesus*) and the votive act which both consecrates and narrowly circumscribes the place of retreat (*libertati suae, tranquillitatique, et otio consecravit*). This place is metaphorically the "bosom of the learned Muses" (*doctarum virginum sinus*): the allusion, of course, is to the round shape of the library, to the walls that "in curving round"[29] hold the collection of works of poetry, philosophy, and history with which Montaigne wishes to surround himself. The images of withdrawal (*recessit*) and the hidden place (*dulces latebras*) coupled with the feminine figure of the Muses (Montaigne will later declare that he might well have preferred to have produced a child "by intercourse with the Muses [rather] than by intercourse with [his] wife"[30]) evoke for the modern reader the psychoanalytic concept of "regression" and all the ideas associated with it. When Montaigne

7

refers to tranquillity (*quietus* and later *tranquillitas*), security (*securus*), and repose (*otium*), it may seem that he is merely confirming the regressive nature of his desire. The house containing his library is, to be sure, the ancestral seat (*avitas sedes*) handed down through the male line, but this masculinity (associated with domanial property since 1477) is counterbalanced (so far as the psychoanalytic argument is concerned) by the feminine gender of the word *sedes* and by the predominance of feminine nouns in the list of terms consecrated by the inscription (*libertas* and *tranquillitas*; only *otium* is not feminine, but neuter!). But in all of this it is important to recognize, as Hugo Friedrich has shown, the traditional formulas of *otium cum litteris*, a "contemplative" variant of the humanist life, which was recommended after the more active path of *civic* humanism turned out to be impracticable or fraught with peril[31] (Montaigne, who diligently discharged his political duties, is proof that the two attitudes could alternate.) The inaugural inscription of 1571 should not be read primarily as a psychological document: it conforms to a cultural paradigm—impersonal and generalizable. One might, however, argue that in the present case the humanist tradition, by its exaltation of antiquity as a wellspring and source of nourishment and its justification of withdrawal into solitude (*sibi vivere*), placed at the disposal of Montaigne's desire ready-made formulas in which to pour his dissatisfaction, nostalgia, sublimations, and need for security: a full "instinctual" use of a coded language can be guessed at . . .

The inscription with which Montaigne dedicated his "library" to his liberty and personal tranquillity stood alongside another inscription (which for some time has been harder to decipher) dedicating the premises also to the memory of Montaigne's lost friend, Etienne de La Boétie.[32] The dedication to his departed "brother" is coupled with the dedication to himself: the library that Montaigne hoped to enjoy also held the books bequeathed to him by La Boétie. The *tranquillity* he hoped to relish in the second half of his life (that which links up with death) was to prolong and perpetuate his dialogue with his best friend. The time spent in the library is thus framed on either side by death: the death that awaits Montaigne himself, and the death that he survives. The role of *identity* is important in both perspectives. On behalf of La Boétie, Montaigne felt responsible for an image, a resemblance: he took care in editing his friend's works (1570–71) and took it upon himself to preserve, to transmit, whole and intact, his admired companion's likeness as he was in life.[33] The rule of identity is this: to lose nothing, to alter nothing, to wrest from death and time images that would otherwise be lost in oblivion and obscurity. (We

8

shall have to consider this point several more times in what follows.) On his own behalf, Montaigne hoped above all that by securing for himself repose, freedom, leisure, tranquillity, and security, he might escape the "mutation" and vain ceremony to which public life condemns those whom it subjugates: his purpose will be to live in dialogue with himself, faithful to his nature and to Nature in the larger sense, and thus to cease to go astray.

The question of identity

The dilemma (or crisis) to which the 1571 retreat provided a decisive response thus involved a choice of *identity*, of a stable relationship to oneself—in conscious opposition to the world and its theater of illusion.

It is customary to regard the first chapters that Montaigne wrote (between 1572 and 1574) as "impersonal" texts, in contrast to subsequent chapters which mark the entrance of the ego and of the desire to paint a self-portrait. It must be granted, however, that the "painting of the self" is merely a belated development of a philosophy that is from the first oriented toward personal life; the question of the ego is raised from the start. Montaigne first tried to answer it by traditional means, and it was because he found those means incapable of satisfying his expectations that he later adopted a different method, essaying a wholly different attitude.

One has only to read the texts of the first period to see that Montaigne is particularly susceptible to arguments from moral philosophy (of the Stoics as well as Epicurus) counseling self-reliance and self-possession. He repeats and paraphrases these arguments to himself, he rehearses them with variations—and what is more, he will continue to make them his own to the end of his days.

Reread, for example, the chapter entitled "Of solitude" (1:39), the argument of which is frequently echoed in other passages; what Montaigne is seeking is a place in this world which is truly his own, unlike other men who, allowing themselves to be carried away by their own imagination, presumption, or vanity, take leave of themselves, desert, in order to conquer imaginary honors or riches. Montaigne, in subscribing to this argument, includes himself in the collective *we* of the remonstrance: "Among our customary actions there is not one in a thousand that concerns ourselves. . . . Who is there that will not readily exchange health, rest, and life for reputation and glory, the most useless, worthless and false coin that is current among us?"[34] In this way we become subject to the power of other people's words. It is impatience, or the need to cut a striking figure on another stage,

9

that drives men to abandon their true place, thus giving rise to the comedy of the world with its proliferation of masks. For men arm themselves with the expressions and accoutrements that transport them, before the fact, into the chimerical future to which they aspire. And so inevitably a creature fallen prey to the temptations of the imagination is transformed into a man of deceit, a wearer of masks. Having bestowed false visages on all things, he cannot appear before them except concealed behind a mask or grimace. He is hypocritical because he is *alienated* (as a later vocabulary would have it): he has made his being dependent on opinion, esteem, on the *words* by which others (the "world," "society") confer "reputation" and "glory." (Rousseau's formulation of the first count in his indictment of society scarcely differs from this in its language.[35])

Everything that belongs to the order of the project, every anticipation in which the individual takes the future for granted, becomes suspect in the eyes of this morality, which holds that it is a culpable weakness for one to set one's sights *elsewhere*. Montaigne refers to this in the title of one of his early chapters (1:3): "Our feelings reach out beyond us." There he writes: "We are never at home, we are always beyond. Fear, desire, hope, project us toward the future."[36] This apothegm takes a negative view of the enthusiasm that causes us to transcend the present and reach out toward the future, an enthusiasm over which the shadow of uncertainty always hangs. Even the quality of providence comes in for criticism, for providence jeopardizes the individual's cohesion and constancy, which can only rest on a continuous *here* and *now*: providence presupposes a morality of *restraint* (in every sense of the word), which prevents man from dispersing himself and commits him to breviloquence, sententiousness, and, so far as the objects of desire are concerned, to *continence* (of which Montaigne will repeatedly insist he is incapable).

Withdrawal from desire: this is the universal error which Montaigne, following Seneca, stigmatizes, and from which he hopes to escape. "My professed principle . . . is to be wholly contained and established within myself."[37] He vows, or at any rate advises his readers, to resist the temptations that Pascal would later subsume under the synthetic noun *divertissement* (amusement):[38] "It is here in us, and not elsewhere, that the powers and actions of the soul should be considered.[39] . . . We must reserve a back shop all our own, entirely free, in which to establish our real liberty and our principal retreat and solitude."[40] To focus one's thoughts *here* (as opposed to elsewhere) is to bring the maximum possible attention to bear on the place actually inhabited by consciousness, on the identity assigned

10

thereto, and on the powers that are unlocked through this conversion to self (*conversion à soi-même*). (The animal's inability to foresee the future will thus become, for Montaigne, a claim to superiority.)

Effective teaching and healthy moral choice dictate unequivocal responses to a series of alternatives, all of which involve choosing between concentration and disintegration of the self. It is immediately obvious which alternative is correct as between *being* and *appearance*, *here* and *elsewhere*, *self* and *others*, *mine* and *alien*, *natural* and *artificial*, *spontaneous* and *learned*, *interior* and *exterior*, *profound* and *superficial*. Each of these antitheses contains, or resonates with, all the others. All are interchangeable or equivalent. The decision is taken in advance: the antitheses in question do not allow suspense or hesitation. All indicate a choice to be made, and advocate turning inward, regaining self-possession, autonomy, and autarchy.

What does philosophy's ancient teaching have to say?[41] That man, subjected to outside forces, squanders his being: he is passion and passivity, the pleasures he pursues disappoint him in the end, he dissipates his substance, his will flags, and he becomes a slave. Yet life regains its solidity and value to the extent that man is willing to plumb his inner depths and take refuge in the fortress of the self. To do so is to regain one's health, to recover one's natural vigor. Once he has gotten rid of all that is alien, man can enjoy his true strength, purely possessed. At one with himself, he forbids his energies to reach out toward a chimerical future or an external objective and thus prevents the self's substance from draining away. When he acts, he chooses a point of exertion as close as possible to the agent himself. In the limit, the ideal action will consist in total self-reflection, in the reaffirmation of a persistent identity and nothing else; turned back on itself, action does not extend beyond the limits of the *here* and *now*, but fills them, consolidates them, inhabits and possesses them in possessing itself, in pulling itself together. Now, here: this instant and this place will from now on be *contained* and preserved in the decision to be oneself and to belong only to oneself. Time and space are no longer endured as destructive forces but produced from within by the voluntary decision that affirms the *here* and *now* by its own decree. Thus consciousness may hope never to be distracted from the self. It husbands an unexpended reserve of energy that perpetuates itself from moment to moment, without aiming at anything other than itself and hence without seeking to invest anything outside itself. This action of the self on the self striving for completion must be wary of flattery and inducements from outside. One must remain constantly on one's guard, perpetually suspicious, ready to fend off any tempta-

11

tions that might distract the attention or drain energies needed for taming the self and defending it against its enemies. This suspicion extends even to the subject himself: solitude does not free us from our vices, weaknesses, or "concupiscences": "It is not enough to have gotten away from the crowd, it is not enough to move; we must get away from the gregarious instincts that are inside us; we must sequester ourselves and reappropriate ourselves."[42] This overinvestment in the ego ideal is not without peril for the ego itself, to use the language of contemporary psychology. Montaigne will make the point in his own way, however.

Montaigne's interpreters have in general been clearly aware of how this kind of "turning inward," derived from the teachings of the Greek and Latin philosophers, differed from that urged by Christian piety and especially by Augustinian preaching: the latter advised turning inward in order to heed the voice of God and submit to his judgment, internalizing the individual's submission to the transcendental. By contrast, the withdrawal desired by Montaigne has as its only purpose the discovery of a conversational mirror within oneself; it aims to restore full powers of judgment to the mortal individual, dividing the self between two equal powers and rejecting the claims of any outside authority. Although humanism and religion both recommend interior "conversation" and *reappropriation*, from the standpoint of the believer this is but a first step, to be followed by obedience to divine authority and the hope of salvation. For the humanist who has taken his distance from religion, the inner reappropriation, if successful, is sufficient unto itself. The solitude sanctioned by humanism is not to be confused with the traditional *vita contemplativa*, which in the religious scheme of things was opposed to the *vita activa*, or life in the world. The humanist attitude would later be denounced, by the moralists of Port-Royal and after them by Malebranche, as culpable self-indulgence. Montaigne was perfectly aware that his choice was not that of religious vocation. He begs pardon for this, offering weakness as his excuse while indicating his reverence for those capable of true devotion: "They set God before their eyes, an object infinite both in goodness and in power; in him the soul has the wherewithal to satisfy its desires abundantly in complete freedom. . . . And he who can really and constantly kindle his soul with the flame of that living faith and hope, builds himself in solitude a life that is voluptuous and delightful beyond any other kind of life."[43] But denial of the flesh and a radical rupture with the realities of the world Montaigne declares to be beyond his reach; while seeming to praise asceticism, he declares himself incapable of it:

"Wiser men, having a strong and vigorous soul, can make for themselves a wholly spiritual repose. But I, who have a commonplace
soul, must help support myself by bodily comforts."[44] At times he
shows himself more severe toward those who carry contempt for the
world to the point of "dissociating themselves from their bodies":
"They want to get out of themselves and escape from the man. That
is madness: instead of changing into angels they change into beasts;
instead of raising themselves, they lower themselves. These transcendental humors frighten me, like lofty and inaccessible places."[45] This
is to shatter life's recaptured unity: it is again to succumb to the evil of
exteriority, to stand "outside oneself." Montaigne saves his most vigorous disapproval for those who seem to break with the world only to
reform what they have abandoned and subject it even more strenuo-
usly to God's commandments, to which they claim to be privy: in
Montaigne's eyes such fanatics are themselves merely actors wearing
masks, the first victims of the opinions they wish to impose on
others.

If Montaigne opts for inward *identity*, for a stable and equal relationship of the segments of the self, he does so while continuing to
focus his gaze on the world, with which he maintains ties that do not
impair his self-possession. From the windows of his library he looks
out onto court and bailey. He intends to maintain as much *presence* in
the world as is compatible with his refusal of servitude (because the
freest personal existence includes the life of the flesh, and the body is
a "piece" of the world, a part of nature[46]).

By recapitulating in this way several of the major themes of ancient
moral philosophy, Montaigne is in fact taking up ambiguous arguments which can be used, in the name of speaking the whole truth,
on behalf of either commitment or withdrawal from commitment, action or the shunning of action. When he contrasts the solidity of *acts*
with the futility of *words*, he accepts the traditional moral teachings
and opts for acts. What Friedrich calls his "aristocratic pretensions"[47]
are thereby bolstered: a well-born gentlemen disdains to give prece-
dence to style, to eloquence, to the blandishments of cunning words
(see 1:51, "On the vanity of words"). In the moral order, the traditional antinomy *res/verba* militates in favor of the solidity of things
over the wind of rhetoric. But when it comes to the contrast between
the *inside* and the *outside*, which harks back to another traditional antithesis and moral injunction, he refuses to be dragged into action,
which belongs to the fradulent realm of the "outside": just a moment
ago I mentioned his views concerning those who opted for action in
their zeal to reform religious dogma or civil law, in the name of a truth

they claimed to possess. The only activity that does not deceive is the inner action of an individual: the activity of judging the world, or oneself. Ultimately it will be the action of which the ego is both source and target, an action expressed in terms of reflexive verbs: to essay oneself, to examine oneself, to paint oneself—*self-referential* movements to which we shall be paying particularly close attention in what follows. In the end, both words and acts regain their validity, but guaranteed by reflective consciousness and apathy. The identity that will finally be offered to us in the work of the self-portraitist is different from the identity that Montaigne originally sought in the strict and tacit equality between the segments of the self. Our task will be to follow Montaigne's progress from one concept of identity to the other. The *movement* that I shall try to describe is nothing other than the effort of a man who, starting from a concept of identity based on the principles of constancy, stability, and self-consistency (a goal that turns out to be impossible to achieve), begins to develop a new concept of identity without abandoning the original one, but nonetheless altering its content and meaning.

The theoretical life and the function of the example

The relation to the world that Montaigne initiated from his refuge of reading and repose was what the ancients called *theoria*, or the theoretical life, i.e., comprehension of the world as it offers itself to the contemplative gaze. In a passage added to the manuscript by Montaigne's own hand (subsequent to 1588) we find one of many classical *topoi* justifying *theoria*: "Our life, Pythagoras used to say, is like the great and populous assembly at the Olympic games. Some exercise their bodies to win glory in the games, others bring merchandise to sell for gain. There are some, and not the worst, who seek no other profit than to see how and why everything is done, and to be spectators of the life of other men in order to judge and regulate their own."[48] This is not merely a "chrie," or rehearsal of an *authorized* opinion, an opinion worthy of approval, but even more a statement of the attitude that Montaigne himself intends to adopt in the face of contemporary reality: "As I seldom read in histories of such commotions in other states without regretting that I could not be present to consider them better, so my curiosity makes me feel some satisfaction at seeing with my own eyes this notable spectacle of our public death, its symptoms and its form. And since I cannot retard it, I am glad to be destined to watch it and learn from it. Thus do we eagerly seek to recognize, even in shadow and in the fiction of the theaters, the representation of the tragic play of human fortune."[49]

14

Gazing upon the agitation of men absorbed by battles and interests of their own, the stationary spectator looks to the causes of things: his concern is to discover the *how* and the *why*, in order to satisfy his *curiosity*. This does not mean that he is disinterested, however; he can, if he wishes (and Montaigne seems to have so wished, at least when he began his work), strive to ensure that the truth revealed in the spectacle of the world is applied in his inner life. To succeed in this he must enlist the aid of his judgment (i.e., the intellectual act in which an individual looks at himself and compares himself with others) and his will (i.e., the formative or transformative act by which an individual *governs* his life).

The aim of the investigation, acutely pursued through the varied spectacle of human action, is to discover regular sequences, which will possess, in addition to explanatory value, direct or indirect *regulative* value. The fortune or misfortune of illustrious men may serve as models or warnings: even the errors of great men disclose principles of conduct and in so doing help to unify our moral lives. A moral truth perceived externally in its universal validity should be capable of being reexperienced internally in the same way; its efficacy should be apparent in the identity of its inner and outer forms, i.e., in the consistency and cohesiveness of the soul. The hope that animates this view is that mimetic fidelity will guarantee inner fidelity. Once the truth has been grasped by the contemplative gaze (i.e., *theoria*), it cannot be changed in any essential way, only repeated; hence the subject who has taken possession of the truth is himself assured of maintaining a stable identity. Internal continuity comes about as a result of fidelity to the external model. In particular, this is the function that the spectator ascribes to exemplary lives: an *exemplum*, or figure that stands apart (*ex-emplum*) and yet stimulates imitation and generalization, can help strengthen the individual through its unique virtue. An individual who constantly strives to resemble an exemplum that is in itself a marvel of constancy is actually striving to achieve an identity of his own. To live up to such a standard, or at least to begin to do so, it ought to be enough merely to *recall* the exemplum or its emblem, an effigy on a medal. The impersonal literature of adages and lessons will be effective to the extent that the reader puts all his personal energy into his response. But *histories* will be even more effective. We have only to fix our gaze upon examples so admirable that we cannot help rehearsing them within ourselves:

> Until you have made yourself such that you dare not trip
> up in your own presence, and until you feel both shame

and respect for yourself, (C) *let true ideals be kept before your mind* [Cicero], (A) keep ever in your mind Cato, Phocion, and Aristides, in whose presence even fools would hide their faults; make them *controllers* of all your intentions; if these intentions get off the track, your reverence for those men will set them right again. They will keep you in a fair way to be content with yourself, to borrow nothing except from yourself, to arrest your mind and fix it on definite and limited thoughts in which it may take pleasure; and, after understanding the true blessings, which we enjoy in so far as we understand them, to rest content with them, without any desire to prolong life and reputation. That is the counsel of true and natural philosophy, not of an ostentatious and talky philosophy like that of Pliny and Cicero.[50]

We must turn our eyes toward exemplary individuals so that we can in turn imagine their eyes fixed on us: under the *scrutiny* of those who are set over us much as teachers and parents are, we are assigned our private truth, we learn the act of reaffirmation that constitutes our personal identity, and we do so purely in confrontation with ourselves (*dans la pure présence à soi*).

The efficacy of the example depends in large part on its being a completed event; the image of moral perfection that it holds out is conjugated in the past perfect tense. The sharpness of its outline is associated with its remoteness in time. But the past of the example is for those devoted to it secretly inhabited by the future of the must-be. What the exemplary man *was* we must be in our turn, we *shall be* if we apply ourselves with all the energy at our disposal. For the exemplum, as I hardly need point out, is a preexisting cultural form that offers itself for us to emulate: the goal is to construct our own egos, to shape ourselves by surmounting all that is amorphous and vague in everyday life. It is to surround all that is soft and fluid in our "conditions and humors" with a firm outline copied from life in order to gather our substance together and cause it to solidify. A stamp is thus always impressed upon us. (La Boétie, Montaigne says, is a "soul of the old stamp."[51])

The imitation of the exemplum is a simulacrum, but a simulacrum that aims at identification. It is a role, but a role into which we must pour ourselves by allowing its law to inhabit us. We give ourselves over wholly to the formative power of the example. The latter, by giving us contour and firmness, at first seems either to rob us of our spontaneity or to oblige us to repress it. But before long the example has invaded us fully, pervaded our life. And our second spontaneity will then effortlessly carry out the acts required by the embodied model. To assimilate the exemplary lesson: such is the classical program of a pedagogy whose aim is to inculcate *norms* through imitation of great lives in which those norms have seen actualized. (This is a good point at which to measure the distance that separates the world of humanism from the contemporary cultural situation. In the humanist world, the example stands out against a horizon of achieved perfection—the ancient world; or else it offers itself in the form of a figure that is at once familiar and transcendent—Christ. By contrast, contemporary ideals—heroes, stars, charismatic figures, many of them ephemeral and interchangeable—are usually taken from the contemporary world itself; they are frequently subject to "manipulation," which, since exemplary figures are a powerful means of directing our desires, allows them to be exploited for economic and political ends.)

The ancient exemplum is a figure in a theater that has nothing to do with the theater of the world (*un théâtre absolu*); it is separated from our world as the "Italian stage" is separated from the hall: the exemplum speaks, it carries the force of an admirable maxim, it is simultaneously maxim and act. Even more: it judges us, for it determines the scale of values, the measuring rod against which our merits and demerits are gauged. Exemplary words and images are too powerful ever to vanish from memory. Their imprint is indelible: for the example, as we shall see more than once, is usually deployed in a memorable scene, in which we are offered the hero's words inextricably intertwined with his life and death. We shall be looking more closely in what follows at two important illustrations of this point: the death of La Boétie and the suicide of Cato.

The exception

It is not impossible, as has been asserted,[52] that Montaigne, when he began writing the *Essays*, set out in search of paradigms of many kinds (political, military, and moral) in an attempt to write a manual for the perfect gentleman. But his attention immediately turned, as Hugo Friedrich and Karlheinz Stierle have rightly pointed out,[53] to the exception that contradicts the paradigm, to discrepancies among the lessons implicit in the great exempla consecrated by tradition, and to the testimony of various writers that the same behavior may on one occasion yield good results and on another disaster. In considering many examples, Montaigne saw how setting one beside another may give rise to contradictions, to mutual destruction. No human act can claim to be a fixed model or universal rule: there are singular occurrences, remarkable events, and uncommon individuals worthy of our consideration. These do not lend themselves to imitation; and even supposing one wished to imitate them, they turn out to be inimitable, unsuitable as guides and protectors for our travels. Hence the past, like the contemporary world, offers a multitude of *facts* worthy of curiosity, yet none that can claim to exercise full authority over our lives. To be sure, these facts are far from equivalent to one another; some wear the aspect of good, others of evil, and in Montaigne the verdict of the moral conscience generally never wavers. As I said earlier, he never hesitates as to what is *inadmissible*. But it is one thing to ascribe a moral value to a famous act and another thing to see that act as a value capable of orienting our own action, as life's polar star, so to speak. In the final analysis, all exempla, no matter how noble, are treated as mere anecdotes (in the sense of "curious oddities" or, at most, "wonderful stories," certainly worth the effort of retelling). They testify only to their singular existence; such-and-such "occurred," according to witnesses worthy of being believed. Thus the only thing exemplified is that a possibility was in fact realized. Nothing is indicated but the occurrence of an event: sometimes quite unexpected or out of the ordinary and hence worthy of our admiration (*mirabilia*) but hardly of imitation. Manifesting their own uniqueness, exempla point to a world composed of unique, dissimilar entities, a world of diversity in which "fabulous testimony" deserves at least a hearing and perhaps full confidence. Each new event adduced as a specimen adds another dash of color to the picture of a motley world ruled by heterogeneity, variety, and contradiction, another patch to an enormous patchwork "of human capacity"[54]—contingent and devoid of normative authority.

No doubt Montaigne, who was in the habit of selecting and borrowing details—words and actions—from ancient books for use in his own, was acutely aware of how easily those details could be mobliized, altered, and permuted: he knew, in a word, how readily they could be decomposed into *passages,* with all the ambiguity implicit in the term. His reading of doxographers such as Stobeus encouraged him in this. No longer is the exemplum a fixed beacon shining above the vicissitudes of the corruptible world. It is simply a piece of this disorderly world, an instant in its ever-changing state, a figure of universal flux. With the passage of time and the harm done by repetition, the exemplum is stripped of its preeminence, its privileged permanence. The paradigmatic figure loses the universal authority invested in it and returns to the accidental existence of which it is henceforth just one more manifestation. The would-be rule dissolves and is reabsorbed in the irregularity of the phenomenal universe. By contrast, the spectacle of the historical and natural world, enriched in this (sixteenth) century by innumerable marvels reported from other continents, comes to seem inexhaustible and manifold: possibly insecurity gains the upper hand with the encyclopedic expansion of "tableaux" and "histories" which, despite many efforts to establish enduring systems of nomenclature and classification, refuse to conform to any irrefutable order and contribute to the breakdown of the traditional structures of knowledge. Monsters, sports of nature, claim the same rank as lawful forms, since nature, everywhere the same, cannot distinguish between her legitimate offspring and her bastards. Deviance is henceforth only one possibility among many: its scandalous aspects are abolished with the disappearance of an undisputed right path or goal. "Every example is lame,"[55] concludes Montaigne, after instructing us not to hobble ourselves before exemplary men.

Henceforth it becomes impossible to complete the circuit linking the external example to the inner constancy of individual identity. Man must take the risk of living without the protection afforded by the example. Montaigne will even carry this to the point of saying, of his own moral life, that it is "exemplary enough if you take its instruction in reverse."[56]

Division, monsters, and melancholy

To make oneself a spectator of the world and at the same time to examine oneself: the goal is unity, an orderly life. It is reappropriation. Paradoxically, however, the result is the opposite. Unity vanishes, and the order of the inner scene is destroyed.

How does this reversal come about? Suppose that what happens—to thought and speech—is an unforeseen consequence of the division that intervenes between the man who contemplates and the object that is contemplated.

Let us attempt to retrace the steps of the process.

From the first, comprehensive *theoria* has much in common with the doctrines of self-sufficiency and autarchy. It is not enough to observe the world as a spectacle, and yet too much to put oneself forward in the external world. One must become one's own theater. According to an injunction formulated by Seneca and stressed by Montaigne, "You and one companion are an adequate theater for each other, or you for yourself."[57] The division necessary to observation requires duality: duality at first accepted as a temporary condition—in the expectation of conscious unity, which will come to pass once the observed ego submits to the commandments of the observing ego and the spectator-ego is able to give full approbation to the spectacle-ego. But in Montaigne's attempt to put this injunction to the test, the self-contemplative division leads not to stability but to rapid proliferation, Doubling does not secure replication of *identity* but introduces difference, inaugurating the whole infinite series of the countable. A breach is opened, and multiplicity, limitless change, rushes in and takes over. The self, which had been its own theater, is taken over by a crowd of actors, who come not from outside but from within. (Admittedly, what is involved here is a trick of language: once the "I" becomes an object in the grammatical sense, nothing prevents each of its passions, ideas, etc., from acquiring the same quasi-autonomous objective status.) The stage fills with intruders: to control or rule it becomes a hopeless undertaking. Repose cannot be attained, as much as it may be desired. In an important passage (which constitutes the essential portion of the brief chapter 1:8, "Of idleness"), Montaigne recognizes that he did not reap all the benefit he expected initially from his retreat:

> (A) Lately when I retired to my home, determined so far as possible to bother about nothing except spending the little life I have left in rest and seclusion, it seemed to me I could do my mind no greater favor than to let it entertain itself in full idleness and stay and settle in itself, which I hoped it might do more easily now, having become weightier and riper with time. But I find—
> Ever idle hours breed wandering thoughts
> Lucan
> —that, on the contrary, like a runaway horse, it gives a hundred times more trouble than it took for others, and gives birth to so many chimeras and fantastic monsters, one after another, without order or purpose, that in order to contemplate their ineptitude and strangeness at my pleasure, I have begun to put them in writing, hoping in time to make my mind ashamed of itself.[58]

This is the first confidence that Montaigne offers concerning the origins of his book. What it took to get him started was a reversal of for and against, a malicious play of contraries. He hoped for calm in a secure setting ("stay and settle in itself"), and for a silent conversation with himself alone ("to let my mind entertain itself in full idleness"). Instead, he experienced a feverish disorder, a proliferation of worries. Rather than the full reality of an orderly life, he witnessed the birth of a swelling horde of monsters and unreal creatures. He then felt himself under an obligation to note them down, record them, put them in writing. He sought relief in the act of writing, in the book to be created. Since he had not, however, renounced the moral goal of inner edification, he had to make his *mind ashamed* of itself. The writer who says "I" in this text, who writes in the first-person singular, affirms that he is different from rather than identical to what he discovers within himself. The desired unity is thus deferred, postponed until later: the *runaway horse* must first be tamed, the naughty *mind* must be scolded as one scolds a child. The contemplative (theoretical) attitude is not thereby abolished; but the mind cannot offer itself sympathetic approval, since it finds itself in the presence of something alien, which resists identification ("in order to contemplate their ineptitude and strangeness at my pleasure").

Count up the number of occurrences of different persons (in the grammatical sense) on this page: their multiplicity is striking. He who says "I" or "me" observes and acts upon his "mind" (a distinct entity which functions grammatically as an indirect object). The mind in turn establishes a reflexive relationship with *itself* (which substitutes for the relation to others). What is more, this same mind gives birth to the unruly horde of monsters. And it is then toward this second set of offspring (the first being *my mind*) that the primary subject (*I*) resumes its contemplative attitude. Where can unity find refuge? On the one hand in the permanence of the primary subject, tireless witness of the escape from his mind and the series of monstrous progeny. And on the other hand in the final *writing*—the record which, in the continuity of its own space, must gather up the unreal and discontinuous plurality of *chimeras and fantastic monsters*. The *writing* and the voice that proffers the primary *I* tend increasingly to reinforce one another, as we shall see.

Another passage, this one concerned with the genesis of the *Essays*, needs to be considered along with those examined previously: the passage containing Montaigne's admission to Mme d'Estissac, at the beginning of the eighth chapter of book 2, "Of the affection of fathers for their children":

> It was a melancholy humor, and consequently a humor very hostile to my natural disposition, produced by the gloom of the solitude into which I had cast myself some years ago, that first put into my head this daydream of

21

meddling with writing. And then, finding myself entirely
destitute and void of any other matter, I presented myself
to myself for argument and subject.[59]

The explanation that Montaigne here proposes is no less important
than the preceding one. These two sentences set forth a chain of reasons. They establish a complex set of causes at the origin of the *Essays*, causes that operate both in time (*some years ago . . . first . . . then*)
and in a tripartite space, comprising the world (*the solitude into which I
had cast myself*), the body (*humor, head*), and the mind (*finding myself
entirely destitute and void*). Montaigne blames a physical disposition
and a disorder of "temperament" (*melancholy humor*), themselves
products of an emotional state (the *gloom* resulting from his temporary choice to lead a solitary life). Furthermore, his melancholy
humor is the cause of his *daydreaming* (which should be taken in a
strong sense, meaning delirium, folly, obsession), the precise equivalent of the "chimeras and fantastic monsters" of the previous text.
Thus we are confronted with a series of causes and effects, in which
modifications of the body and modifications of the mind mutually
determine one another. There is nothing to detain us in Montaigne's
(implicitly) proposed interpretation of the relationship between the
soul and the body, which conforms completely to the medical an-
thropology handed down by Galen and generally accepted in the sixteenth century. Galen's doctrine was a psychosomatic theory which
Montaigne, eager as he was to respect the "fraternal juncture" of soul
and body, had no difficulty approving, even though he had little faith
in the unverifiable deductions drawn from the theory by physicians.
He deemed it adequate in a general way as a basis for description and
assignment of causes.[60] Montaigne shared with many others of his
age the conviction that there is a close relation between solitude and
melancholy (one seeks solitude because one is melancholy, and conversely, one becomes melancholy as a result of leading a solitary life).
He was also familiar with the danger of melancholy inherent in intellectual pursuits (those of melancholy complexion will spend their
lives reading or writing books; those who devote themselves to literary works expose themselves to the danger of melancholy). And he
was not unaware that melancholy can have two contrary effects, pro-
ducing either brilliant inspiration or dull stupor.[61] He also knew that,
according to the most widely accepted medical ideas, the "atrabil-
ious" man was one who was suspicious, who shut himself up and
looked anxiously upon the world as a sinister comedy, a misanthrope
who believed himself surrounded by masked enemies.

22

In Renaissance physiology, melancholy (or atrabile) was, along with blood, bile, and phlegm, one of the four fundamental humors whose mixture determined an individual's temperament. A body whose humors were properly proportioned was an instrument that the soul could govern without too much difficulty. But any imbalance, especially any excess of bile (*choler*) or melancholy, allowed physical passion to gain the upper hand. When this happened, the individual's will was eclipsed and his behavior was governed, unbeknownst to him, by a material fatality. For what nature then compelled him to do he was no longer responsible. To blame melancholy, as Montaigne does (for putting *into my head this daydream of meddling with writing*), is to plead innocent of the crime of writing; it is to let it be known that one has not chosen to become a writer entirely of one's own free will; the reasons for the choice lie rather in the dark recesses of the body, in the most somber of the substances of which we are made. If we look carefully at the passage just cited, it becomes clear that the only voluntary act mentioned by Montaigne is the decision to live in solitude, into which he voluntarily *casts* himself. To what end? Recall the inscription that he had painted on the walls of his library: for Montaigne the choice of solitude was equivalent in intention to the choice of liberty. Disgusted (*pertaesus*) with public office, tired of servitude (*servitium*) in the Bordeaux Parlement, he believed that a solitary life would be a free life. But now we witness a reversal similar to that by which the plurality of monsters replaced the unity of virtue. Solitude is the cause of gloom and melancholy. The hope of liberty evaporates: one must endure the effects of the dark humor and submit to the infection of *daydreaming*, an alienation in the pathological sense of the term. Another subjugation begins. (Admittedly, Montaigne's confession can, up to a point, be ascribed to flirtatiousness and aristocratic pretension: it was considered improper for a noble to engage in the occupation of writing. To another great lady Montaigne would say, "I am less a maker of books than of anything else."[62] The melancholic humor and the injunction to labor that it imposes serve as temporary alibis for a gentleman who, in taking up the pen, is forgetting what is his due, even if his only purpose is to mock those whose occupation is to confect books.)

The concern with writing is thus a consequence of *strangeness* intruding from outside, strangeness which does violence to the soul's free will and robs it of its first fruits. Or better still: for Montaigne the concern with writing was aimed at regaining a hold on himself that had been threatened by the divagation of his idle mind, by the irresistible daydreams provoked by melancholy gloom. Writing is his last hope of coping with the multifarious passivity into which he lapses after his hope of achieving active possession of himself has failed.

And his passivity does indeed take many forms. We saw in the previous passage that Montaigne's mind not only behaved like a "runaway horse" but even engendered monsters in a process of spontaneous generation: the primary subject is thrust into the passive situation of witness of the swirling spectacle that wells up within. The major difference between the two passages in which Montaigne explains why he chose to begin writing lies in the contrast between the density evoked by the first (*a hundred times* more . . . one upon the other") and the vacuity alleged in the second ("finding myself entirely destitute and *void* of any other matter). But both the surfeit and the lack stem from an excess of the melancholic humor. It is in the nature of this humor to produce extremes, which it causes to alternate with one another or even to coexist in the most surprising manner. Since ancient times philosophers and physicians had made this point repeatedly. And Montaigne, discussing Tasso's madness, shows that he was aware of it:

> Plato says that melancholy minds are the most teachable and excellent: likewise there are none with so much propensity to madness. Countless minds have been ruined by their very power and suppleness. What a leap has just been taken, because of the very restlessness and liveliness of him mind, by one of the most judicious and ingenious of men, a man more closely molded by the pure poetry of antiquity than any other Italian poet has been for a long time! Does he not have reason to be grateful to that murderous vivacity of his mind? to that brilliance that has blinded him? to that exact and intent apprehension of his reason, which has deprived him of reason? to the careful and laborious pursuit of the sciences, which has led him to stupidity? to that rare aptitude for exercises of the mind, which has left him without exercise and without mind?[63]

Admittedly, there is nothing like this in Montaigne, but only awareness of a danger, and the feeling that a reversal is always possible.

Note, moreover, that in assigning melancholy a decisive role in the origin of his book, Montaigne speaks of it as something unusual or exceptional with him, something contrary to his true nature. It is, he insists, "a humor very hostile to my natural disposition."[64] Thus he became a writer in the wake of a sudden change of mood, which rendered him temporarily unlike himself. Yet another instance of otherness! How strange: here is a book that will be declared "consubstantial with its author,"[65] yet that comes into being in connection with a divagation, a momentary deviation from life's customary path. The commencement of writing is presented to us as an aberration that becomes an irrevocable decision, which will not be reversed when a less somber mood returns. When freed from the unusual circumstances that drove him initially to take up his pen, Montaigne will continue to write; he will not renounce the "daydreams" that made him an *author*, even at the risk of destroying the *authority* of the book whose origins he deems so futile.

If, by Montaigne's own admission, melancholy was for him an exceptional state of mind, let us try to measure just how unusual it was by comparing it with what he regards as his "natural disposition." There is no dearth of evidence. Here is a brief self-portrait: "For the rest, I have a strong, thick-set body, a face not fat but full, a temperament between the jovial and the melancholy, moderately sanguine and warm."[66] The description is not content with any one pure type: the *mixed* and the intermediate predominate, in keeping with the concept of *idiosyncrasy*, which allowed the Galenist doctrine to embrace individual peculiarities in a manner presumably acceptable to Montaigne's nominalist preferences. Moreover, this "disposition," situated as it is *"between* the jovial and the melancholy," never settles into any stable equilibrium: it manifests itself, rather, in a series of opposed states. Change, which Montaigne will eventually make the law of the world, normally rules his own body as well as his mind: "Now I am ready to do anything, now to do nothing; what is a pleasure to me at this moment will some time be a trouble. A thousand unconsidered and accidental impulses arise in me. Either the melancholic humor grips me, or the choleric; and at this moment sadness predominates in me by its own private authority, at that moment good cheer."[67] Too changeable to be assigned to any one humor, and as it were fated to be inconsistent for physiological reasons, Montaigne comes into contact with melancholy, or yields to it briefly, only to abandon it in a moment for subjection to yet another inner power.

So far as Montaigne is aware of his own "natural disposition," then, he does not see any pure temperament as predominant. But an individual's "disposition" was thought to determine his own peculiar balance, his own unique mix, which it was advisable (according to the teachings of medicine and the counsels of prudence) to respect, or at any rate to oppose only with the utmost caution. What Montaigne suggests is that he embarked upon his melancholy pursuit of consistency in a moment of *infidelity* to his normal physical makeup: the quest for identity began badly and was destined to be subverted by the ineluctable variability of his temperament. Thus it was not simply in the intellectual sphere that the desire to "stay and settle in itself [i.e., the mind]" gave rise, paradoxically, to agitation; by going against the law of the body, Montaigne subjected himself to extreme changes of "humor." Thus in the very origins of his literary enterprise Montaigne recognizes a desire for stability that runs counter to his natural disposition and is therefore destined to know full well the power of the current that it opposes. Is this an insuperable contradiction? No: it will be resolved, ultimately, by the acceptance of paradox, the coexistence of opposites, and the reconciliation of identity and otherness.

The painter's art

Montaigne did not repudiate identity. He discovered, however, that he could not attain it directly. Instead of unity he encountered fragmentation. Another approach was needed: and this, as was mentioned previously, involved the act of writing, the act of "recording." Melancholy is present every step of the way. It has already inspired Montaigne's refusal of his social *role*, and of the artificial forms that custom imposes upon our actions. And it has also, by putting simple identity out of reach, impelled Montaigne to attempt to fill the "void," to blacken the pages of the "register" in which he will set down his monsters, chimeras, and daydreams—for others to see.

Earlier, we saw how the failure of Montaigne's attempt to govern his own life served to heighten his "curiosity," or interest in pure observation. Against an inexpugnable inner otherness which makes it impossible for the self to feel tranquilly at home and at one with itself, a constantly vigilant gaze will strive to impose the only possible continuity: its uninterrupted presence. This gaze is not without effect on the passions it observes; it is not devoid of power. But it cannot impose the order that it desires. Division cannot be overcome. There will never be perfect coincidence, calm and silent identity, between the observing "I" and the observed "me."

The only recourse remaining to anyone still enamored of unity is to establish it in the discourse that gives voice to change, in the judgment that describes and condemns (or excuses) variability. The project of that discourse is no longer to achieve moral stability but to explain "how" and "why" stability has vanished, to indicate what obstacles have prevented the desired repose from being attained and caused the mirage of a transparent, univocal, and simple wisdom to recede into the distance. The book is a unitary receptacle capable of encompassing diversity. Writing, though it spins itself out in one continuous thread, is not incompatible with the mutability of humors, the clash of contradictory ideas, "passage," movement, travel. And subsequent reading will serve (for Montaigne will be his own first reader) to reinforce the unifying power of the writing, though not without engendering additions, embellishments, and digressions. Duality and otherness are not eliminated but encompassed, with no reduction in magnitude, in the unity of the book. "My book is always one," writes Montaigne, but shortly thereafter he adds, without contradiction, "Myself now and myself a while ago are indeed two."[68]

Here we must pause to assess the implications of this transference, to the book, of the imperative of unity. Montaigne's first hope, as we have seen, was to live up to the moral imperative of constancy; it was to reassert the virtue of his own character by showing it to be in conformity with rules presumed to be known and examples held to be definitive. Books were necessary to this undertaking, but they were the books of others, authoritative books containing precepts to be followed, exemplary histories, models worthy of identification. Access to the truth within, had it been possible, would naturally have involved an inner dialogue, but a dialogue supported by reading of what the masters had already said to perfection. Since virtue prohibits any search for glory or concern for posterity, Montaigne's acquiescence in his own truth, in his virtuous identity, would have remained silent—its radiance would have been wholly internal, invisible to any alien gaze, and "without any desire to prolong life and reputation."[69] The recourse to writing transforms the initial *reader's* experience into an *author's* experience. Simultaneously, it turns the original obedient reading into a *critical* reading, exploiting texts from the past for the benefit of the new work in progress, appropriating their substance for new ends having nothing to do with the original project of identification, the aim of which was merely to reiterate what had already been said. The book, once it becomes the receptacle of "identity," confers an entirely new meaning on the term itself. Identity no longer means that two human beings are bound by unbreakable bonds of loyalty. Nor has it anything to do with the discovery of enduring *essences*, which are grasped from the inside, as it were, prior to contamination by illusory appearances. It is rather a *relation* (involving the external world) which confirms the resemblance between an image and its author, or "original." In other words, identity is no longer a tacit acquiescence of the same in the same, which strengthens and confirms the innermost self; rather, it includes and maintains difference, it accepts the risks of appearing, of becoming, and of language.

Difference and nonidentity cannot be evaded. They remain permanently installed within. There are at least two reasons why this is so: first, the ego, in observing itself, is constantly fluctuating and dissembling, and second, life and the book, no matter how much the writer wishes the one to be a close and accurate portrait of the other, are two distinct levels of reality, and differences between these two disparate levels are constantly threatening to surface.

By way of corollary, it may be added that the ego seeks to manifest itself *doubly*. On the one hand it inhabits the present of the writing, the moment of enunciation, and figures in the exercise of the observer's gaze and judgment; on the other hand it delivers to the reader the various *emotions*, the unstable, changeable *humors*, and the many *daydreams* that it has discerned, objectified, and transcribed. It is a portrait that we will read, but the painter does not want us to forget about him; the act of observing and representing is itself an object that is represented to us. The "register" shows us the painter at work, facing both the mirror and the canvas bearing the self-portrait in progress. The author in his book declares himself distinct from, yet at one with, his work; conversely, the book, with its perpetual imperfection, includes its author as judge of that imperfection.

A maneuver of this kind brings an aesthetic criterion into play. The pictorial metaphors that Montaigne uses so insistently, together with the images he borrows from other arts (to paint, portrait, colors, to mold, to build), are profoundly revealing. Identity is entrusted to the work, to the production of an image. Montaigne's work, begun in the hope of achieving repose for the soul (which goal is never forgotten), ends as a literary masterpiece. The recourse first to writing and then to self-portraiture must not be viewed as stages in a gradual "self-discovery." The self was, as we have seen, a primary object of concern and attention from the beginning. What takes place, rather, is a gradual transfer to the writing, to the book, to the image, of responsibility for establishing identity. What was an immediate moral task becomes instead an artistic task and plays a deferred moral role. The effect of this shift is not merely to incorporate the avowed failure of the moral attempt to achieve stability as one of the themes of the work, one of the *features* of the portrait; nor is it simply to allow alienation, dissembling, and mutability to be confessed without compromising the unity of the work that "records" them. Beyond these effects, it turns out that the requirement of communication, the need to obtain the acquiescence of the witness (the reader or spectator of the portrait), ensures that the work conceived in conformity with the aesthetic imperative will point the way to a new ethic—an ethic that imposes upon the individual a new requirement, not to keep to himself in silent self-sufficiency, but rather to be *honest* in representing himself to others and to seek from them guarantees of his presence to himself. (It is worth noting, incidentally, that whenever a requirement of identity of any nature whatsoever is imposed, an ethic is at work. Even those whose ethic calls for instinctual freedom require that that freedom be permanent.)

Thus the aesthetic imperative of self-resemblance implies the mediation of others. It is true that the previous requirement of virtuous identity, of self-equality, also required extrinsic intervention: namely, by the example and the precept—models invested with sovereign authority, which the individual was responsible for making his own and obeying implicitly. But the differences are striking. The precept and the example emanated from the past. Vanished yet saved from death, they owed their force to the *perfection* of a bygone era. By contrast, the mediation of the living spectator, which is solicited by the veracity of the portrait, belongs to a different temporal dimension; it is the act of consciousness that the text expects from its "receiver." Obviously the aesthetic requirement of resemblance takes the place in Montaigne's work left vacant by the relative decline of the traditional authorities (Christian and Stoic) inscribed in the great books of the past. Henceforth the deciding criterion is the success of the "portrait," feature by feature, as judged by the future spectator, and in the first place by the writer himself as first judge of his own work. The "relation to others" (about which we shall have more to say later) is no longer a peril, a loss of oneself, a superfluity, but an obligatory passage without which identity can never be sure of itself. The notion of *good faith* with which Montaigne begins his introductory note to his readers defines a morality based first and foremost on relations with others. The rest of the note boldly promises a faithful portrait, but this aim is made subordinate to the aim of communication. Good faith and loyalty, categories relative to the reader, precede and accompany the effort to look at oneself.

> This book was written in good faith, reader. It warns you from the outset that in it I have set myself no goal but a domestic and private one. I have had no thought of serving either you or my own glory. My powers are inadequate for such a purpose. I have dedicated it to the private convenience of my relatives and friends, so that when they have lost me (as soon they must), they may recover here some

features of my habits and humors, and by this means keep the knowledge they have had of me more complete and alive.

If I had written to seek the world's favor, I should have bedecked myself better, and should present myself in a studied posture. I want to be seen here in my simple, natural, ordinary fashion, without straining or artifice; for it is myself that I portray. My defects will here be read to the life, and also my natural form, as far as respect for the public has allowed. Had I been placed among those nations which are said to live still in the sweet freedom of nature's first laws, I assure you I should very gladly have portrayed myself here entire and wholly naked.

Thus, reader, I am myself the matter of my book; you would be unreasonable to spend your leisure on so frivolous and vain a subject.

So farewell, Montaigne, this first day of March, fifteen hundred and eighty. [Cited after Frame's translation, p. 3, with slight modifications.—Trans.]

If we examine this brief but important passage in the original French, it is obvious that the *book* is named first and that it is kept present throughout the page by use of the locative pronoun *y*, which represents it and constitutes the (as it were) anaphoric mooring of every sentence. The obstinate repetition of the locative *y* constitutes the foundation of an identity. It is in this stable location that the "I" who wields the pen and addresses the reader can encounter the *me*-object of which "I" claims to be the painter. The multiplicity of the me-spectacle emerges from the use of plural nouns (*traits, conditions, humeurs*) in the phrase "features of my habits and humors." Unity, expressed in the singular, is recovered by the appearance of the intended recipients of the work, "relatives and friends," who are to take an active role in "keeping the knowledge they have had of me more complete and alive" after the writer has died. The plenitude expressed by the word "complete" is in the thought and memory of the others who Montaigne hopes will achieve it. Although Montaigne dismisses the inadequate reader at the end of this invocation, he nevertheless wants to be scrutinized ("I want to be *seen* here") and read ("My defects will here be *read* to the life"). *Form* and *manner*, in which singular identity is inscribed, can manifest themselves only in a style that has taken upon itself the task of representing the writer's "habits," "humors," and "defects" to a (supposedly intimate) group of readers. Whether or not the book finds readers matters little; it is enough that it was conceived "for others": for Montaigne will then receive his identity directly from his book. Paradoxically, then, an activity whose original intention was merely to *record* existence in conformity with the aesthetic requirement of verisimilitude may prove an effective means of achieving order, stability, and self-instruction. The book as "register" takes on the function that Montaigne had originally assigned to "Cato, Phocion, and Aristides," namely, to "make them controllers of all your intentions."[70] Unable to achieve self-discipline directly by allowing normative examples to govern his conduct, Montaigne discovers that he can delegate this responsibility to his book by representing himself in it faithfully, in the manner of the sculptor and the painter.

The project of communication, which is mentioned in this passage, is from the first presented as a desire for an exclusive relationship: it is for the limited circle of "relatives and friends" that the book has been conceived, and it is because the work is "dedicated to their private convenience" that the minuteness of the portrait is excusable, that the likeness can be "more complete and more alive." In an almost paradoxical fashion, the limitation of the audience is the counterpart of the fullness of the portrait; the quantitative *minus* (that is, the smaller number of readers) gives rise to a qualitative *plus* (a greater veracity in the message). What the *private* destination causes the discourse to lose in universality is compensated, in the realm of individual comprehension, by the *completeness* of the knowledge communicated.

Yet the unknown reader is also challenged; no sooner is the title of "reader" conferred upon him than he is turned back and given his farewell. The author's coyness is obvious: nothing arouses a greater desire to read than an injunction to leave off reading. The status that Montaigne initially assigns to his reader is that of an intruder who meddles in what does not concern him and whose "service" is of no interest. But this denial that a relationship exists, this farewell to the reader are in fact the beginning of a relationship. And this relationship is a demanding one: Montaigne requires an "adequate reader." Among the profits that he "draws from writing," moreover, he counts the possibility of attracting new friends. For by giving to everyone—to the "public"—the opportunity to know him as well as or better than his own family, is he not offering them the means to become his true intimates?

> Besides this profit that I derive from writing about myself, I hope for this other advantage, that if my humors happen to please and suit some worthy man before I die, he will try to meet me. I give him a big advantage in ground covered; for all that long acquaintance and familiarity could have

gained for him in several years, he can see in three days in this record, and more surely and exactly. Amusing notion: many things that I would not want to tell anyone, I tell the public; and for my most secret knowledge and thoughts I send my most faithful friends to a bookseller's shop.[71]

This time the book seems to neglect loyal friends to the advantage of the "people" or of some stranger who is invited to join the author. Thus, in one way or another Montaigne likes to establish relationships on the basis of nonrelationship, upon a situation of rupture or estrangement: with his "relatives and friends" the basis of the relationship is his imminent demise; with his reader, it is the farewell offered at the end of the introduction. Distance and fullness mutually determine one another (I shall say more about this later on), and Montaigne makes us aware of this as soon as we open his book.

Furthermore, the aesthetic requirement to paint or draw a good likeness (associated initially with the mimetic fidelity that replaces the ideal of constancy) would bring Montaigne to the point of accepting, under certain conditions, what he previously denounced with such vehemence: appearance, the external. The note to the reader lets it be known that Montaigne has set himself a rule of avoiding show and artifice. But to paint oneself is an art, and no art can do without artifice in one form or another. Elsewhere Montaigne says:

> There is no description equal in difficulty, or certainly in usefulness, to the description of oneself. Even so one must spruce up, even so one must present oneself in an orderly arrangement, if one would go out in public. Now, I am constantly adorning myself, for I am constantly describing myself.[72]

From verisimilitude to fiction runs a slippery path that the act of writing cannot avoid. But the return of appearance and artifice, far from discrediting the book, marks the final phase of Montaigne's experiment and indicates a belated reconcilation with the evils that figured in his original indictment. A source of energy, the original antithesis is resolved, at the end of lengthy labors, in a synthesis of a new type.

In the series of stark contrasts and strong antitheses wherein Montaigne states his preferences, the silence of *doing* was originally favored over the sound and fury of *saying*. But *saying*, a necessary prerequisite of any self-portrait, is not condemned beyond all hope of appeal. For once more, within the sphere of language, Montaigne establishes a new opposition that enables him to proclaim his preference for *lively speech* over clotted *writing*. Yet ultimately writing will win his approval too: this choice is justified by his preference for *spiritual* offspring over children *of the flesh,* the former being more faithful, better likenesses of their parent than the latter:

> What we engender by the soul, the children of our mind, of our heart and our ability, are produced by a nobler part than the body and are more our own. We are father and mother both in this generation. These cost us a lot more and bring us more honor, if they have any good in them. For the worth of our other children is much more theirs than ours; the share we have in it is very slight; but of these all the beauty, all the grace and value, is ours. Thus they represent and report us much more to the life than the others. . . . To this child [i.e., the *Essays*] such as it is, what I give I give purely and irrevocably, as one gives to the children of one's body. The little good I have done for it is no longer at my disposal. It may know a good many things that I no longer know and hold from me what I have not retained and what, just like a stranger, I should have to borrow from it if I came to need it.[73]

In making his own a more modest version of Plato's metaphor of spiritual children blessed with immortality, Montaigne is willing to dispossess himself for the sake of his book; for this "richer" image of himself he agrees to become a stranger. Paradoxically, the book is both an independent being and "more our own" than a child of the body. The book will live in our stead, whereas our lot is oblivion and, soon enough, death.

The conclusion is inescapable: the life of an individual does not become fully determinate until it exhibits itself; but as we come under the scrutiny of others, we pay for the support we derive from them by undergoing, even in our own lifetime, the ordeal of death, or negativity; and it is by way of this ordeal that we acquire our full personal identity. Indeed, by showing ourselves we lose a part of what we are, we expose ourselves to risk, we entrust ourselves to the safekeeping of others, we "mortgage" our lives. For Montaigne, the act of writing is the deliberate accentuation of the relation that delivers us unto ourselves by way of the image that spectators deprive us of only to restore. To write is to behold oneself in a second body created by deliberate alienation of the self; it is to produce a verbal tissue—the text—offered to the comprehension of the virtual reader. The text is that strange object that draws its life from the disappearance of the craftsman who made it. The written work, a vicarious form of life, a likeness destined to survive its original, externalizes life and internalizes death. In a significant passage that at first glance seems to be merely a hyperbolic outburst, Montaigne writes: "I leave nothing about me to be desired or guessed. If people are to talk about me, I want it to be truly and justly. I would willingly come back from the other world to give the lie to any man who portrayed me other than I was, even if it were to honor me."[74] Here Montaigne imagines a sojourn among the dead, while the passion for truth takes the form of an angry return to the world of the living to correct the falsehoods spread by those whom he regards as liars. This metaphorical passage from one world to another makes it abundantly clear how absence alternates with presence and severance of a relationship with its renewal.

The imminence of death

"So that when they have lost me (as soon they must)": it is worth noting that in Montaigne's note to the reader the whole project of writing is seen in the perspective of death; but the reason for this is so that the book may be immediately rescued from death and made into the living, surviving image of a person who will not resign himself to oblivion. A *complete, living* image is to take shape in these pages, in anticipation of an imminent *loss.* To paint himself is Montaigne's life's work, which stands out against a melancholy background of impending doom. The farewell to the world precedes the aesthetic option and conditions the process of literary representation. What is now speech prepares to confront a future in which it will stand as the substitute, the unique trace, of a vanished individual. Like the emperor Charles V, Montaigne is looking forward to his own funeral—not so that he can indulge in the somber luxury of a sumptuous burial but so that he can seize the most striking images of the life that is slipping away. Yet he writes to Mme de Duras at the end of 2:37 that he is not sure that he has managed to preserve what is best in himself: "For this dead and mute portrait, besides what it takes away from my natural being, does not represent me in my best state, but fallen far from my early vigor and cheerfulness, and beginning to grow withered and rancid."[75]

Let us imagine Montaigne drawing support from the thought that, after his death, he will live on in the memory of his friends and as a result savoring more fully the life that remains to him. While still alive he establishes a bridge to the afterlife, and then crosses it in the reverse direction in order to heighten his enjoyment of life here in this world, before death. Had he not feared total annihilation in oblivion, would he ever have put pen to paper? If not, his attitude is hardly

Christian. He is anxious to survive, according to his private notion of truth, in the memory of another generation, because he has lost faith in the immortality of the soul and eternal light that the Church promised to those elected to enter into the heavenly fatherland. "The stupid project he has, to paint himself":[76] Pascal's reproach is aimed, I think, not only at an act of pride but, more profoundly, at the sin of despair that Montaigne commits when he responds to death, not by an act of faith in the divine promise, but by recourse to literature, to art, in order to fashion an image of his life to be bequeathed to posterity. To exist in the pages of a book is better than to vanish into nothingness and oblivion. The *Essays* are to have the value of a *monument*.

Not, however, a monument of the sort that many gentleman had built to glorify their feats of arms and heighten the family renown. The memory that Montaigne hopes to perpetuate is not one of a series of military or political deeds but that of a "humble and inglorious life,"[77] like any other.

Nor did the monument that Montaigne constructed resemble those erected by those poets and artists who, following the example of Horace, triumphantly celebrated the work they had previously done: *Exegi monumentum*. Montaigne had no finished work behind him that he could boast of having cast in incorruptible matter. His work consisted entirely of the memorial whose text he had not yet finished composing. There was no previous masterpiece that he could claim as his own. In fact he followed the opposite course, criticizing the negligence and imperfection of his manner of expression. Thus his fine style acquired its sinew, freed as it was of the need to produce a finished product in keeping with accepted models, in contrast to so many other writers and orators of the time who, ambitious for admiration, shackled themselves with a pompous, Ciceronian language. The posterity that Montaigne imagines, incidentally, is a brief one. The monument that will secure his survival is itself perishable: "I write my book for few men and for few years. If it had been durable matter, it would have had to be committed to a more stable language."[78]

Finally, it is surely unnecessary to point out that Montaigne's account of his life in no way resembles the accounts given by various Christian apologists who, following the example of Augustine's *Confessions*, hold out God's intervention in their lives as a model for others. Montaigne's purpose is merely to leave a record of an ordinary life in the pages of a book: this was what was so outrageous and scandalous. For life in its simplest, most naked form, life in its unredeemed, natural condition, but captured in an art that denied art, was now seen to make claims that had once been made by others on behalf of feats of arms or divine election. What was being set forth was just what was *not* exemplary in a common, ordinary life; hence this life stood out as a counterexample to all the paradigms that had previously served as models of the moral, the martial, or the religious life. Where there are no more examples, moreover, anything may become an example. The tomb that Montaigne erects for himself refers us to trivial aspects of a "common and private" life, which will soon come to an end. The last essay (3:13, "Of experience") minutely details the "bodily habits," the predilections, and the petty acts that fill the daily routine of one "private" individual. It is death that gives necessity to the vibrant style in which the writer attempts to capture on paper his familiar tone of voice: "I speak to my paper as I speak to the first man I meet."[79] The digression encompassing the thought of death leads us not to the hereafter but back to the most intimate and apparently pointless detail of everyday life, as it is caught up in the web of mortality.

The lost friend

In 1569 Montaigne published his translation of the *Natural Theology of Raymond Sebond*, thus fulfilling a request of his father, Pierre de Montaigne. The dedicatory letter was deliberately dated Paris, 18 June 1568: this was the day Pierre de Montaigne died (probably at Montaigne, where he was buried). His son was not present when he died, but atoned for his absence by the gift of this book.

In 1570 Montaigne sponsored the publication of two volumes of "booklets" containing material from manuscripts left to him by Etienne de La Boétie, who had died seven years earlier: included were translations of Plutarch and Xenophon, Latin verse, and French poetry. The dedicatory letters accompanying these booklets date from the period April–September 1570. In the same year Montaigne sold his councilorship in the Bordeaux Parlement.

Several months later, in March of 1571, Montaigne dated the votive inscriptions in his library that mark the beginning of his "retirement" from the date of his own birth. Soon thereafter, he began writing the *Essays*, the 1580 edition of which concluded in a postscript (to 2:37) with a dedicatory letter to Mme de Duras; the book begins with the note to the (anonymous) reader analyzed above, which was no doubt written after the book was complete.

Thus a series is formed by Montaigne's manifestations of devotion to beloved individuals (the father and the friend he had lost), his renunciation of public office, and his undertaking to write a work of his own for the benefit of those friends and relatives who would survive him.

Montaigne began his book because he believed he had only a short time left to live. His reasons for writing are reinforced, however, when he thinks of his late friend, whose literary legacy he had saved in its entirety from oblivion: "He alone enjoyed my true image, and carried it away. That is why I myself decipher myself so painstakingly."[80] Thus the connection between death and the act of writing is twofold, for it involves not only the impending death of the writer himself but also the much earlier death (in 1563) of the friend who has not ceased to haunt Montaigne's thoughts.

It is hardly necessary to recall the many occasions on which Montaigne speaks of the loss of his friend and his subsequent mourning. Among them are the letter of 1563 to his father in which he recounts La Boétie's illness and death; the five dedicatory letters of 1570; and the entire chapter "Of friendship" (1:28) in the 1580 *Essays:* "Since the day I lost him . . . I only drag on in a weary life. And the very pleasures that come my way, instead of consoling me, redouble my grief for his loss."[81] In 1581 he relates, in his *Travel Diary*, how, while taking the waters at the baths of La Villa, a sudden thought plunges him into sadness: "I was overcome by such painful thoughts about M. de La Boétie, and I was in this mood so long, that it did me much harm."[82] Then, in a marginal addition to chapter 2:8 of the *Essays*, which would ultimately be incorporated into the edition of 1595, he wrote: "O my friend. Am I better off for having had the taste of it [friendship], or am I worse off? Certainly I am better off. My regret for him consoles and honors me. Is it not a pious and pleasant duty of life to be forever performing his obsequies? Is there an enjoyment that is worth this privation?"[83] This loyalty, this assiduity in mourning, here turns into "enjoyment," for mourning makes Montaigne feel that he is better off. For this uninterrupted escort, in memory, of his departed friend, these "obsequies" that Montaigne is "forever performing," constitute an element, perhaps the only element, of constancy and continuity in a life that knows itself consigned to inconstancy and discontinuity. Here we find avowal of an egocentric interest ("was I better off?") combined with a confession of voluntary dependence on an external object. The attention that Montaigne bestows upon himself and the sorrow for his lost friend, here so singularly mixed, together reveal the close interdependence between the sentiment of the ego and thought turned toward the privileged *other* ("O my friend!"); this conjunction is reflected in the paradoxical experience of simultaneous mourning and "enjoyment." The memory of one who is never finally laid to rest is accompanied by pleasure, attesting to the omnipotence of thought, to an ability to vanquish oblivion wherein the individual becomes conscious of his own strength.

For Montaigne, his friend's regard performed an essential function of moral instruction and direction. His friend was in possession of one version of the complete truth about Michel de Montaigne, a truth that Montaigne's own conscience was unable to carry to a comparable degree of fullness. Reread what he says: "He *alone* delighted in my true image, and carried it away with him." La Boétie's death robbed Montaigne of his only mirror: the loss of his friend effaced forever the image that La Boétie possessed. The fuller, more truthful *copy (double)* was erased. Inward reflection must belatedly come to the rescue: "That is why I decipher myself so curiously." It is important to pay close attention to what substitutes for what in these two parallel sentences. The "I" takes the place of "he alone" and the verb "decipher myself" replaces "delighted in my true image." It is clear that something has been lost in the exchange, that the truth of the image no longer has a possessor, which means starting all over from the beginning. Rather than the "delight" which was the friend's province, rather than the full, direct intuition of the same order as that exercised (according to Neoplatonist doctrine) by the celestial intelligences, Montaigne must resign himself to the laborious effort and partial revelations of introspective decipherment. Instead of the *immediate* knowledge that La Boétie possessed, the only knowledge of Montaigne now available requires a more tentative approach, and is marked by concern (the word he uses, "curiously," derives from *cura* and in the sixteenth century still connoted "concern"). With decipherment, the best that could be hoped for was a series of approximations to the truth, juxtaposing one word with another and thus constituting a *discursive* knowledge by means of a series of discontinuous strokes. But Montaigne has aged since La Boétie's death: thus he will never be able to reconstruct the image that existed in his friend's mind and that was carried with him to the grave: the portrait of the young Michel de Montaigne by Etienne de La Boétie is lost forever. What must be produced—at the cost of considerable effort— for the inspection of other viewers is a different image, as close as possible to the effigy spontaneously made available to his departed friend and just as spontaneously welcomed by La Boétie. In place of the faithful mirror reflecting the "true image," which enabled Montaigne to live two lives, one in himself and one in his friend's regard, there remains only the white page on which the aging Montaigne must tell about himself (*se dire soi-même*), in words that will remain forever inadequate compared with the reciprocity of life. The perfect symmetry wherein friendship is explained by its individual cause— "because it was he; because it was I"[84]—has become forever impossible. The friend's death has destroyed this tautology which, through mutual encouragment and exhoration, shared projects, and commerce in ideas, culminated in the mute "enjoyment" of brotherly likeness. Henceforth it will be necessary for Montaigne to enter into an asymmetrical relationship with himself and others, to save all that can be saved of this abolished happiness by giving it another body: the written word, the book. To perpetuate what one cannot resign oneself to having lost is to commit oneself to a work of replacement, substitution, translation.

Now we can more readily understand an attitude that Montaigne exhibits in the dedication (to his dying father) of Sebond's *Natural Theology*. Writing is justified primarily as the accomplishment of an assigned mission, a task that one has promised to perform; Montaigne indicates how scrupulously he viewed his role: "Monseigneur, in carrying out the task you set me last year at your home in Montaigne, I have cut out and trimmed with my own hand for Raymond Sebond, that great Spanish theologian and philosopher, a costume in the French style."[85] The translation has dressed the text in a new "fashion." And this transformation offers one great advantage: the book can now "present itself in all good company." Thus it will be able, thanks to the wishes of Pierre de Montaigne and the labor of his son Michel, to do itself credit, now that it has been stripped of its scholastic Latin ("this wild bearing and barbaric demeanor"). The "improvement and correction" go beyond the work's outer dress, however. Pierre de Montaigne (to whom Michel respectfully imputes the paternity of the translation) remains a "debtor": "For in exchange for his excellent and very religious arguments, his lofty and as it were divine conceptions, it will turn out that you for your part have brought him only words and language: a merchandise so vulgar and so vile that the more of it a man has, peradventure, the less he is worth."[86] Pride in having improved the text by translation becomes humility: compared with the "conceptions" of the philosopher, the translation is nothing but idle words, a mere change of costume. The second life of Sebond's book in no way attests to the value of the person who provided it with "words and language." But who is that person? Michel de Montaigne, the translator of the work, is confounded with the *vous* addressed to his father, whose wish was the prime mover of the translation. The fact that the date of the dedication is the very day of the father's death says that the published work is the *continued* and realized wish of the late Seigneur de Montaigne. The survival of his father's wish will be recalled at the beginning of the "Apology for Raymond Sebond" (2:12) and, on the pretext of defending the ideas of the Spanish theologian, Montaigne will be able, in the "Apology," to secure a new lease on life for his father's last wish:

> (A) Now some days before his death, my father, having by chance come across this book under a pile of other abandoned papers, commanded me to put it into French for him. . . . It was a very strange and a new occupation for me; but being by chance at leisure at the time, and being unable to disobey any command of the best father there ever was, I got through it as best I could; at which he was singularly pleased, and ordered it to be printed; and this was done after his death.[87]

Sebond's book, which was recommended to Montaigne's father for the conservative effect it might exert by winning increased respect for "our old belief," thus bore a double responsibility for prolonging lives threatened with destruction: Montaigne's father, when Pierre Bunel gave him the Spanish theologian's work, had not much time to live; and the old religious "customs" had been shaken by the "innovations of Luther," which Montaigne compares to an "incipient malady."[88] In any case the point is to save what is in danger, to treat the symptoms of ruin. But just as the dedicatory letter ironized about that "base and vulgar commodity," words and language, so the "Apology for Raymond Sebond," in its attack on the book's adversaries (who are indirectly the enemies of Montaigne's father as well), develops arguments for skeptical nominalism so well that it jeopardizes the very authority that Montaigne would like to preserve. He had hoped to culminate his argument with a humble confession of personal "inadequacy," while forcing Sebond's adversaries to make a similar confession. Readers were not slow to notice that Sebond's own thought, far from being protected by this defense, itself succumbed to the implied radical critique of human knowledge. The son, eager in his humility to champion his father's cause, nearly undid it by excess of zeal. This was an undesired result, and perhaps a ruse of the unconscious. So far as his conscious desires are concerned, Montaigne tried his best to keep reminders of his father constantly before him. The list of things he wished to *preserve* in honor of his father's memory is a long one: habits of dress, trivial items, public offices, even pieces of masonry from the family residence.

(B) My father loved to build up Montaigne, where he was born; and in all this administration of domestic affairs I love to follow his example and his rules, and shall bind my successors to them as much as I can. If I could do better for him, I would. I glory in the fact that his will still operates and acts through me. God forbid that I should allow to fail in my hands any semblance of life that I could restore to so good a father. Whenever I have taken a hand in completing some old bit of wall and repairing some badly constructed building, it has certainly been out of regard more to his intentions than to my own satisfaction. (C) And I blame my indolence that I have not gone further toward completing the things he began so handsomely in his house; all the more because I have a good chance of being the last of my race to possess it, and the last to put a hand to it.[89]

The will of the father, already prolonged by the publication of the Sebond translation, was further prolonged in the work of finishing off the family residence, carried out under the son's direction. Montaigne did not want to fail in the task of continuing and conserving what had been transmitted to him: this, one might say, was the *private* aspect of his political conservatism, and indeed it may have been the latter's secret cornerstone. Here again, self-accusation on Montaigne's part accompanies his vow to safeguard that which was entrusted to him by a dying man: he has discharged his father's wishes well enough, but he might have done more. He blames "indolence" for his inability to carry through the things that his father had "begun so handsomely" to equally handsome conclusions. But he also furnishes an excuse: he has no male offspring to whom he can bequeath both his house and his name. Thus he is able to build his life, his book, while abandoning any thought of "building up Montaigne" apart from the plans that his father had already made.[90] Now by making his book he would be able to ensure that his father's will would survive, whereas the walls of the castle, fated as they were to pass into the hands of others, could no longer guarantee such survival: the same intention of filial piety, the same desire to preserve an "image of life" have merely changed their locus, found new material in which to cast themselves and a new focal point for their expression.

As for Etienne de La Boétie, Montaigne openly proclaims a like desire to perpetuate his memory after death. He proposes to do this first by publishing his friend's works and second by the gift he makes of them in his dedicatory letters to selected readers: to them is entrusted the *safekeeping* of the *reliquiae* that bear witness to the personality of the departed friend. The witness that they bear, however, Montaigne regards as comporting an imperfect image of what La Boétie was, and even more of what he promised. His qualities and his promise remain unknown. He makes the following argument in the first place to M. de Mesmes:

> I think . . . it is a great consolation to the frailty and brevity of this life to believe that it can be *strengthened and prolonged* by reputation and renown. . . . So that, having loved above all else the late Monsieur de la Boétie, the greatest man of our time, in my opinion, I would think I was grossly failing in my duty if I wittingly let a name as rich as his and a memory so worthy of commendation vanish and be lost, and if I did not try, by those same parts of him, to *revive him and bring him back to life.* I do believe that he has some sense of this, and that these services of mine affect him and give him joy. In truth, he is still lodged in me *so entire and so alive* that I cannot believe that he is so irrevocably buried or so totally removed from our communication. Now, sir, because each new revelation I give of him and of his name is a *multiplication of this second life of his,* and, moreover, because his name is ennobled and honored by the place that receives it, it is up to me not only to spread it as much as I possibly can, but also to *entrust it to the keeping* of honorable and virtuous persons.[91]

Later, Montaigne stated to Michel de L'Hospital his opinion that La Boétie was never granted employment commensurate with his abilities on behalf of the *res publica* and that he wrote only "by way of passing the time." He never won recognition for himself; he was "careless about pushing himself into the public eye."[92] La Boétie's Latin verses must be regarded as the point of departure for a prophetic *induction.* Montaigne therefore begs Chancellor de l'Hospital to "*rise* through this work of his to the knowledge of him, and consequently to love and embrace his name and memory. . . . For there was not a man in the world in whose acquaintance and friendship he would rather have been *lodged* than in yours."[93] Montaigne here feels free to argue from what was visible (and sometimes imperfect) to the admirable whole that lacked the opportunity to make itself manifest: "The very sports of great personages reveal to the clear-sighted some honorable mark of the rank from which they come."[94] In a similar vein, when he speaks in the *Essays* of Alexander playing chess, he remarks: "Each particle, each occupation of a man betrays him and reveals him just as well as any other."[95] La Boétie lacked the time to show what he was worth: "The true juice and marrow of his worth have followed him, and all we have left is the bark and the leaves."[96] While saying that he is incapable of making his friend's qualities "visible," Montaigne nevertheless enumerates what they are: "the disciplined movements of his soul, his piety, his virtue, his justice, the liveliness of his mind, the weight and soundness of his judgment, the loftiness of his conceptions, so far elevated above those of the vulgar, his learning, the graces that were ordinary companions of his actions, the tender love he bore to his wretched country, and his mortal and sworn hatred of every vice, but especially of that ugly traffic that is hatched under the honorable name of justice."[97] La Boétie deserved an important mission; he himself, during his final illness (according to Montaigne's account[98]), regretted that he had not been given one; and Montaigne asks to be taken at his word, for he wishes to secure a "lodging" for this figure in danger of oblivion, this friend whose writings by themselves are not sufficient to guarantee survival: "I am prodigiously eager that at least his memory after him, to which alone from now on I owe the good offices of our friendship, should receive the reward of his merit and *be well lodged* in the good opinion of honorable and virtuous persons."[99] Montaigne can act as guarantor of this value because "no spoken or written statement in the schools of philosophy ever represented the rights and duties of sacred friendship as exactly as did the practice that my friend and I formed together."[100] He repeats this judgment in the dedicatory letter to M. de Lansac, in which he asks Lansac to "continue" his "good opinion and good will" toward the "name" and "memory" of La Boétie, and then adds the following by way of magnifying the image of his lost friend:

> And to speak boldly, sir, do not be afraid to find your good feeling for him somewhat increased; for since your taste of him has been only from the public evidence he gave of himself, it is my duty to assure you that he had so many degrees of ability beyond this that you are very far from having known him whole and entire. When he was alive, he did me the honor, which I count among my greatest good fortunes, of forming with me a bond of friendship so close and tight-knit that there was no slant, impulse, or motive in his soul that I was not able to consider and judge, at least unless my vision at times fell short. Now, without prevarication, taken all in all, he was so nearly a miracle that in order not to fly beyond the limits of plausibility and be completely disbelieved, I am obliged, in

43

speaking of him, to restrain myself and say far less good than I know about him.[101]

Writing to M. de Foix, Montaigne relies even more explicitly on what he has been told in confidence in order to justify his claim that La Boétie's greatness is insufficiently reflected in his public record and written work. The "glory" that he wishes to attach to his friend's "virtue" is, he says, not undeserved. What he, Michel de Montaigne, says, moreover, should be believed just as if he were an apostle or a disciple of Socrates, for he is the first to admit how "pernicious" is the "license to toss . . . to the winds as we wish the praises of one and all"; and he offers the judgment that the "vice of lying" is "most unbecoming to a well-born man":[102]

> And his bad luck will have it that whereas he has provided me, as well as a man can do, with very just and very manifest occasions for praise, I have just as little means and ability to render him his due—I indeed, *to whom alone he communicated himself to the life, and who alone can vouch* for a million graces, perfections, and virtues which molded idle in the midst of so fair a soul owing to the ingratitude of his fortune. For since the nature of things has allowed, I know not how, that however beautiful and acceptable truth may be of itself, yet we embrace it only if it is infused and insinuated into our belief by the instruments of persuasion, I find myself so very destitute both of the credit that might give authority to my simple testimony and of the eloquence to enrich it and set it off well, that I have come very close to giving up this whole effort, for I have not even anything of his left by which I can worthily present to the world so much as his mind and his learning. . . . But finally I decided that it would be much more excusable for him to have buried with himself so many rare favors of heaven than it would be for me to bury also the knowledge he had given me of them.[103]

Montaigne justifies his arbitrary juxtaposition of the various "booklets" written by his friend on the grounds that it is necessary to spread his memory abroad as widely as possible. This literary legacy, so heterogeneous in nature, is incommensurate with the sovereign personality of the departed: Montaigne deliberately published his friend's works piecemeal, in systematically scattered fashion, in order to increase the number of persons to whom he could address portions (within a volume that resembles an edited anthology):

And therefore, having assiduously collected everything complete that I found among his *notebooks* and papers *scattered* here and there, the playthings of the wind and of his studies, I thought best, whatever it was, *to distribute and divide it up into as many parts as I could,* in order thereby to take the occasion to commend his memory to all the more people, choosing the most notable and worthy persons of my acquaintance, and those whose testimony might be the most honorable to him.[104]

The diversity of the recipients will presumably help to spread his friend's posthumous renown. On the other hand, in order to preserve the unique image of this unique man, Montaigne, the privileged confidant, offers his own consciousness as the focal point in which the scattered fragments can converge; he is the sole repository, the unique guarantor of his friend's worth, the only person to whom was revealed "how great was his full worth."[105]

Posterity may believe me if it please, but *I swear to it upon all the conscience I have that I knew and saw him to be such, all things considered, that even in desire and imagination I could hardly reach beyond,* so far am I from assigning him many equals. I very humbly entreat you, sir, to *assume the general protection not only of his name* but also of these ten or twelve French poems, which cast themselves, as if out of necessity, *under the shelter of your favor.*[106]

These lines of French verse are to be read, therefore, as a mere exercise:

This was neither his occupation nor his study, and . . . he hardly put his hand to his pen once a year, witness the little we have left from his whole life. For you see, sir, unseasoned and dry, all of his poetry that has come into my hands, without selection or choice, so that there is even some from his boyhood. In short, it seems as though he put his hand to it only to show that he was capable of doing anything. For as to the rest, thousands and thousands of times, even in his ordinary remarks, we have seen things come from him that were even more worthy of being known, more worthy of being admired.[107]

This superior soul did not, however, have the time or the opportunity to figure on the world's stage. Montaigne, inclined as he is to indict the "vanity of words" (the title of 2:51), feels obliged to note that his own words are the only intermediary between what La Boétie was and the glorious memory of him that he hopes will be sustained, lodged, and taken *in safekeeping* by any number of important personages. Furthermore, when Montaigne addresses his wife in the last of the dedicatory epistles, his purpose is not merely to remind her of the legacy of papers and books that "this dear brother of mine" left her when he died, but even more to recommend that she read, following the death of a daughter "in the second year of her life," La Boétie's translation of a "letter of consolation" that Plutarch wrote to his wife in similar circumstances.[108] What better way to hear the voice of philosophy than to attend to it at a time when "fortune" has subjected us to a similar ordeal? "I am sorry," Montaigne writes, "that fortune has made this present so appropriate for you." In this case it is the mother's suffering that guarantees that his friend's image will be appropriately received or "kept," as he wishes in all his dedications. Once again, La Boétie's voice, which has insinuated itself into Plutarch's thought, cannot fail to be perpetuated. Of the circle of friends whom Montaigne wished to "apprise" of La Boétie's writings (so as not "stingily to enjoy them all alone"), "none is more intimate" than his wife. Once again, Montaigne proposes his own weakness as grounds for effacing himself and allowing La Boétie (who had likewise placed himself at the service of an exemplary ancient text) to speak: "I leave to Plutarch the charge of consoling you and advising you of your duty in this, begging you to believe him for my sake. For he will reveal to you my views, and what can be said in this matter much better than I could myself."[109]

In this latter aspect of his *second life*, La Boétie, the interpreter of Plutarch, is expressly called upon to encourage the work of mourning. Rescued from his first death, the brother resurrected in the form of the book is to help heal the wound caused by the loss of the child, by the continuing lack of offspring.

Here it is worth pausing to reread an important passage in the long letter that Montaigne wrote to his father to inform him of the final hours of La Boétie's life:

> Then, among other things, he began to entreat me again and again with extreme affection to *give him a place;* so that I was afraid that his judgment was shaken. Even when I had remonstrated with him very gently that he was letting the illness carry him away and that these were not the words of a man in his sound mind, he did not give in at first and repeated even more strongly: "My brother, my brother, do you refuse me *a place?*" This until he forced me to convince

him by reason and tell him that since he was breathing and speaking and *had a body*, consequently he had *his place*. "True, true," he answered me then, "I have one, but it is not the one I need; and then when all is said, I have no being left." "God will give you a better one very soon," said I. "Would that I were there already," he replied. "For three days now I have been straining to leave."[110]

The dying man's entreaty, which Montaigne apparently did not comprehend at the time, had since been fully appreciated. La Boétie's place (in French: *place, lieu*) will henceforth be not only the library to which Montaigne had his departed "brother's" books and papers transported but also the memory of the important persons to whom Montaigne publicly offered the "collection of his works" while urging them to take the name of La Boétie under their protection. Those who read these dedicatory letters in 1570 could hardly ignore the honorable home or "shelter" that an unknown author, Michel de Montaigne, was asking for a man struck down before his time, while still neglected by the world at large. The task was not yet complete, for Montaigne set apart the *Discours de la servitude volontaire*, reserving for it a *place* of honor at the center of the first book of the *Essays*. The *Discours* deserved such a place of honor because it was like a "rich, polished picture, formed according to art," around which Montaigne arrayed his own prose in a frame of decorative *crotesques*.[111] Here again, as in the dedicatory letters, Montaigne proclaims his own inferiority and "inadequacy," although his friend's work was nothing more than an adolescent exercise, "tentatively" written (*par manière d'essay*). The essay "Of friendship" (1:28) takes up and freely develops a theme already broached in the dedicatory letters of 1570. Montaigne then recounts the history of his friendship with La Boétie and compares it to other friendships in order to justify his contention that this was unlike any other.

Hence Montaigne can, with justice, consider himself to be the faithful executor of his friend's last wishes. He has preserved La Boétie's image, given him a place, and made himself the jealous guardian and trustee of both: "And if I had not supported with all my strength a friend that I lost, they would have torn him into a thousand contrasting appearances."[112]

Yet, having safeguarded the name of La Boétie and made his writings available to the public, Montaigne still feels that he has not done enough to ensure the survival of one who gave more of himself to the duties of friendship than to the duties of writing or public life (where others failed to use him for the important tasks for which his talents suited him). Was publication of his works enough to give him, in full measure, the "place" for which he asked?

The experience of friendship had been one of a reciprocal "transport" of wills—on both sides, a voluntary alienation. Let us read once more the following celebrated lines:

> (A) It is not one special consideration, nor two, nor three, nor four, nor a thousand: it is I know not what quintessence of all this mixture, which, having seized my whole will, led it to plunge and lose itself in his; (C) which, having seized his whole will, led it to plunge and lose itself in mine, with equal hunger, equal rivalry. (A) I say lose, in truth, for neither of us reserved anything for himself, nor was anything either his or mine.[113]

La Boétie's place was in Montaigne, who in turn "lost" himself in his friend's will. Note, in passing, that this paradigm (of complete reciprocity in total giving) brings to fruition in a pair of friends the same movement that Rousseau, at the beginning of the *Social Contract*, describes as occurring between the individual and the entire community at the moment of foundation: "Each of us makes common property of his person and all his strength. . . ."[114] This "total alienation" then becomes constitutive of a new *body* or will—the general will. It would not be unreasonable to argue that Rousseau applied the model of *philia* and *amicitia* (which he might have taken from Aristotle and Cicero, or from Montaigne) to the *polis*, to the City animated by a "common *self*."[115] Nothing in Montaigne's writing stands out more clearly than the image of two bodies inhabited by a single soul ("their relationship being that of one soul in two bodies, according to Aristotle's very apt definition"[116]) and of a will which, though based on personal conviction, is confounded with the will of another. Nevertheless, for Montaigne the perfect friendship consists of two friends, no more. Only "common friendships" can be "divided up."[117] The superior friendship can only involve two people, who achieve a form of twinship. Montaigne cites the Roman example of Tiberius Gracchus and Caius Blossius: "(C) Having committed themselves absolutely to each other, they held absolutely the reins of each other's inclination."[118] The result, says Montaigne, is "the complete fusion of our wills," so that "I have no doubt at all about my will, and just as little about that of such a friend."[119] Certainty as to the wants of one's "brother" in friendship is no less complete than certainty as to one's own wants: "It is not in the power of all the arguments in the world to dislodge me from the certainty I have of the intentions and judgments of my friend."[120]

Now, this exchange of wills is also a reciprocal exchange of regards, so that each man's mind becomes transparent to the other and free of shadows:

> (A) Not one of his actions could be presented to me, whatever appearance it might have, that I could not immediately find the motive for it. Our souls pulled together in such unison, they *regarded* each other with such ardent affection, and with a like affection *revealed* themselves to each other to the very depths of our hearts, that not only did I know his soul as well as mine, but I should certainly have trusted myself to him more readily than to myself.[121]

Along with the "fusion of wills," then, went this exchange of images, so that each friend stood before the other as a true mirror. In this doubling there was unity: a unity that was felt all the more strongly in that it overcame duality, and a doubling that was all the more valued in that it enabled each man to entrust the whole truth about himself to the other—a truth which neither possessed within himself with the same degree of certainty ("I should certainly have trusted myself to him more readily than to myself"). For the self, *effacement* in the will of the friend is also a form of *aggrandizement:* "The secret I have sworn to reveal to no other man, I can impart without perjury to the one who is not another man: he is myself. It is a great enough miracle to be doubled."[122] To be doubled (*se doubler*): the phrase suggests both *increase,* or redoubling (*redoublement*), of a primary identity and scission, or splitting (*dédoublement*), of a unique substance. My will is redoubled and augmented in the will of my friend; my image is split (*se dédouble*) in the truer image that my friend receives in order to offer it back to me as a gift. Should he die, I am plunged back into my original singularity, as into a *half-life,* as well as shorn of my certainty that the whole truth about me was lodged outside myself, in the severe and fraternal gaze of my friend:

> (A) For in truth, if I compare [all the rest of my life] . . . with the four years which were granted me to enjoy the sweet company and society of that man, it is nothing but smoke, nothing but dark and dreary night. Since the day I lost him . . . I only drag on a weary life. And the very pleasures that come my way, instead of consoling me, *redouble my grief* for his loss. We went *halves in everything; it seems to me that I am robbing him of his share* . . . I was already so formed and accustomed to being a second self everywhere

that only *half of me seems now alive*. . . . There is no action or thought in which I do not miss him, as indeed he would have missed me. For just as he surpassed me infinitely in every other ability and virtue, so he did in the duty of friendship.[123]

The survivor is both guilty (because each time he enjoys a pleasure alone, he is "robbing" his friend of his share) and from now on forced to live a mutilated existence. He feels in himself both a superfluity and a lack. Deprived of his confidant, he must bear unaided life's all too heavy burden. Yet that life is also a mere fragment, nothing but "smoke," now that it has lost the ontological consistency of a doubled existence. It knows only the "redoubling of grief."

To perpetuate the name of La Boétie—"to prolong his existence,"[124] to preserve his "living image"—is therefore not merely to discharge a pious obligation to a lost friend. It is also a way, a forever inadequate way, of allowing Montaigne to continue to see (in the fraternal image he carries in his memory) the light of the gaze that La Boétie directed at him, and the image of himself that La Boétie's gaze offered. The place that his dying friend wanted him to secure lies in Montaigne's own consciousness: in this way Montaigne can return a shadow, as it were, of the pleasures robbed from his friend's share and at the same time (through the "curious" process of self-decipherment) perform the duties that his friend is no longer capable of discharging. And so it is that, tbrough *memory* and *reflection*, in a relationship made asymmetrical by death, the pair of fraternal images can be perpetuated by the efforts of a single mind. Having "supported a friend that (he) lost,"[125] Montaigne was obliged, by the duty inherited from his friend, to keep a close and vigilant watch on himself, as La Boétie had done previously.

Thus after La Boétie's death, Montaigne continued to feel, and indeed felt even more strongly, what he had felt while his friend was still alive: namely, that being close to one another was superfluous, while being separated enhanced both men's "possession" of life:

> (B) We filled and extended our possession of life better by separating: he lived, he enjoyed, he saw for me, and I for him, as fully as if he had been there. One part of us remained idle when we were fused into one. Separation in space made the conjunction of our wills richer.[126]

Separation, when it had been possible to follow it with reunion, bestowed fullness; estrangement made possible a more agile exercise of reciprocity. The friendly dialogue was carried on at a distance. What sort of exercise was this, if not practice for the definitive estrange-

ment? "He *saw* for ME, and I for HIM." The chiasmus, which is a
figure for the crossed glances of two friends, becomes a resource for
the one who is left alone, provided he keeps alive the image of his
departed friend. The reflected gaze or sovereign judgment that Montaigne preserves in his own mind, incorruptible and solid, somehow
replaces the half of himself he is aware of having lost. In this way La
Boetie's friendly, lucid gaze is internalized, or "introjected": it is the
light turned inward, the affectionate vigilance that observes and
"controls" (*contrerolle*) Montaigne's mutable and fantastic existence.
From the abyss of death it continues to watch, in the living eye of self-
consciousness and writing. The inner duality, which divides the act
of introspection into an observing subject ("consciousness") and an
observed object (variable existence), is a product of death: and it is the
observing subject—in which we normally locate our purest and most
independent act—that takes the place of the dead friend, as his second life and heightened absence. Self-consciousness and judgment,
in their continuity, fixity, and incessant desire to establish the truest
possible image, carry within themselves the persistent presence of an
other: the experience and denial of his death. Consciousness escapes
change because it belongs not to life (*la vie*) but to survival (*la survie*).
It is both the most intimate witness and the spectator from beyond
the grave. Thus the writer's solitude is haunted and traversed by the
internalized continuation of a lost "society," just as it is oriented by
the expectation of a future "society," composed of other friends: the
act of writing is intended to link Montaigne and his departed friend
indissolubly in the public mind, in order to put across the living image of an author who himself will soon have no *place* to reside, no
body, no "sponsor,"[127] other than his own book, offered as a gift to
posterity. The period of studious retirement thus takes on meaning as
the interval between two moments of "communication": the exalted
communication with the chosen companion (which precedes the
book) and the posthumous communication (achieved through the
book) with those who will be the intimates of Seigneur de Montaigne.
Whichever way we face in time, the essay works in relation to absence, in memory or anticipation of loss. And all its efforts go toward
preserving proximity. What Montaigne has done for his father and La
Boétie (namely, to preserve their living images), his book must do for
him. His free intercourse with the authors in his library had shown
him how reading might defy space and time: and it is based on this
model of survival through the written word that Montaigne, with
modesty and audacity (for he claims to be nothing and to have nothing to say), entrusts himself to posterity. Solitary subjectivity keeps

itself alive only by means of external society, which it carries over into itself and either protects or foments.

Recall the words that Montaigne used in the dedicatory letter to M. de Mesmes: *"In truth he is still lodged in me so entire and so alive* that I cannot believe he is either so irrevocably buried or so totally removed from communication." And to M. de Foix he wrote: "I indeed, to whom alone *he communicated himself to the life."* The terms are exactly the same as those that he will later use in the introductory note of his book to define, not only for his "relatives and friends" but also for the unknown reader, the intention of the *Essays:* "by this means keep the knowledge they have had of me *more complete and alive. . . .* My defects will here be read *to the life."*[128] The repetition is noteworthy: the book is given the task of securing indirectly ("by this means") the living plenitude that Montaigne's closest friendship had been able to achieve directly, through immediate communication. Now we can more fully understand the place that La Boétie and Montaigne's father occupy in the *Essays:* both are in different ways instigators who justify the act of writing; Montaigne cannot write *about himself* without referring to them, as if he received from *them* both the mandate for his work and the pardon for his imperfections. Though his writing begins with them and with their deaths, however, he does not imitate them or look to them as models: he will never be like them. Unlike his father, he has no male offspring; and he lacks La Boétie's virtue, all of which went to fulfilling the obligations of friendship. To the friend whom fortune had deprived of works Montaigne offered a work whose author, "deprived of the sweetest of friends," admits that it would have been surpassed by the books that his friend might have written: "And if at the more mature age when I knew him, he had adopted a plan such as mine, of putting his ideas in writing, we should see many rare things which would bring us very close to the glory of antiquity."[129] The only thing that La Boétie *built* was a great friendship ("So many coincidences are needed to build up such a friendship that it is a lot if fortune can do it once in three centuries"[130]), and it is left to Montaigne to "furnish and *build"*[131] himself, for, and by, his book.

The solitude in which Montaigne conversed with himself and, as the humanist expression would have it, became his own crowd (*sibi turba*), is therefore not sustained solely by the strength of the ego. It bears within itself the needs of the other, the memory or desire of intimate commerce with an alien consciousness. It is the late fruit of the interrupted dialogue with the person who, as Cicero puts it, "est . . . tanquam alter idem" (*De amicitia* 21). It sets the stage for the presentation to the reader of a posthumous self-portrait. The requirement of communication fills all temporal dimensions in Montaigne. It looks back to the past:

> (A) . . . For, as I know by too certain experience, there is no consolation so sweet in the loss of our friends as that which comes to us from the knowledge of *not having forgotten to tell them anything* and of having had *perfect and entire communication* with them.[132]

And it also turns toward the future: the friend *with whom* one has fully communicated is also the person *of whom* one will speak, to another audience. It is not enough to have told the friend everything: after his death one must outdo him in benevolence, gratuitously and without hoping for anything in return:

> (B) Those who have deserved friendship and gratitude from me have never lost it through being no longer there; I have paid them better and more carefully in their absence and ignorance. I speak more affectionately of my friends when there is no way left for them to know of it.[133]

"At tibi certamen maius"

In populating the entire temporal spectrum—the past, taken up by memories of the friend, as well as the future, filled with plans to talk about him "more affectionately" than is possible now, in the present, which is given over to mourning and loss—the writer's consciousness dedicates itself to a project of self-exploration in time that both alters and enhances the exaltation experienced during the friend's lifetime.

Montaigne had read the *Discours de la servitude volontaire* before meeting La Boétie, and this work had aroused in him a desire to know its author:

> (A) And yet I am particularly obliged to this work, since it served as the medium of our first acquaintance. For it was shown to me long before I had seen him, and gave me my first knowledge of his name, thus starting on its way this friendship which together we fostered, as long as God willed, so entire and so perfect that certainly you will hardly read of the like, and among men of today you see no trace of it in practice.[134]

If Montaigne saw in the *Discours* an invitation to friendship, it was not only because he read in it a denunciation of oppressive monarchs, couched in the form of classical allusions that would have been immediately intelligible to a man of his education, but even more because La Boétie rounded out his definition of tyranny by contrasting it with friendship, which he portrayed as something radically precluded by the omnipotence of the tyrant. Friendship, according to La Boétie (who in this respect adhered to a standard humanist *topos*), is that form of "society" which tyranny makes impossible at every level of collective life:

> It is certain that the tyrant neither loves nor is loved. Friendship is a *sacred name*, a *holy thing*; it arises only between decent people. It is sustained not so much by profits as by the good life. What makes one friend sure of the other is the knowledge he has of his friend's integrity: the signs he has of this are his friend's natural goodness, faith, and constancy. There can be no friendship where there is cruelty, disloyalty, or injustice. And when wicked men assemble, one has a conspiracy, not a company. They do not love but fear one another. They are not friends but accomplices.
>
> Though tyranny may not prevent sure love, it would be difficult to find such in a tyrant, for, by standing above all others and having no companion, he is already beyond the bounds of friendship, which finds its true quarry in equality, which wants never to stand out and so is always equal.[135]

Friendship, a reciprocal, honest, and disinterested exchange of selves, is diametrically opposed to the self-seeking obsequiousness of the person willing to cast himself into voluntary servitude. Great though the privileges of vice may be, the outcome is certain, The *assentator*, at first pampered and heaped with reward, will sooner or later become the victim of the tyrant's devastating whims. After describing at length the imitative mechanism that causes the relationship of servility to be reproduced from the top to the bottom of any society ruled by tyranny, La Boétie fails to offer any specific model of a free society by way of contrast, other than that of brotherhood among a limited circle of friends. Clearly, for him friendship offers the only possibility of resistance or salvation—and it is limited to "decent people." The examples cited—Harmodius and Aristogiton, Brutus and Cassius—raise, on the horizon of legend, the prospect of tyrannicide as the heroic work to which a great friendship may devote itself. It was certainly not a work of this sort that would seal the friendship between Montaigne and La Boétie, however;

rather, at a time when power was dispersed among tyrants great and small (rulers, "parties," anarchic mobs), it was the idea of seeking, outside power and safe from its arbitrary acts, a secure shelter in that "sacred name" and "holy thing," friendship. They would devote themselves to a private commerce and yet be so worthily employed in the worship of virtue as not to suffer the reproach of having abandoned all concern for the general welfare.

In the letter in which Montaigne recounts La Boétie's illness and death, the dying man is described as apostrophizing his "brother" in terms reminiscent of those just cited from the *Discours de la servitude volontaire*:

> And then, turning his words to me, he said: "My brother, whom I love so dearly and whom I chose out of so many men in order to renew with you that virtuous and sincere friendship, the practice of which has for so long been driven from among us by our vices that there remain of it only a few old traces in the memory of antiquity, I entreat you to accept as a legacy my library and my books, which I give you.[136]

Actually, in building up this friendship, La Boétie constantly appealed to those "old traces," to those exemplary images preserved "in the memory of antiquity." Clearly, he is the link between the admirable past and the friend he has chosen for himself. He is living proof that the ancient examples can be brought back to life, just as the two friends revived the Latin tongue for their own private use. La Boétie used Latin only in the poems he wrote for his male friends; French was the language of choice when he addressed himself to ladies. For Latin, as Montaigne would later say, was endowed with an energy, a density, a moral vigor that outstripped the feeble powers of the vulgar tongue, the image of a degenerate age. Latin was the language of virile example, by reason of its higher ontological status. In the three Latin poems addressed to Montaigne, La Boétie assumes the role of guide. His age had put him in the lead (he was three years older than Montaigne). He took the initiative in discharging one of the duties Cicero had ascribed to friendship: *monere et moneri*, to admonish and be admonished, "to alert one another."[137] It was he who, with his eye fixed on virtue's immutable star, scolded the younger man and reproached him when he misbehaved or showed weakness with respect to the temptations of the flesh. It was he (as well as Montaigne's father) who encouraged his young friend to set his course in life by reference to the great men and incorruptible essences. Montaigne was exhorted to follow in the footsteps of his brother, who spoke to him in the language of striving and outdoing. Sometimes the exhortation is to *depart* (along with Belot in a company of three, for another hemisphere, far from the devastation of the civil wars yet without forsaking the melancholy souvenir of the mother country); sometimes it is to *climb* the path of virtue; sometimes it is to shun illusory pleasures, to conquer the *repose* reserved for men of wisdom. At the end of a quest propelled by the energy of refusal and sacrifice awaits legitimate pleasure, tranquil master of all time's horizons:

> Aut nihil est felix usquam, aut praestare beatum
> Sola potest virtus. Sola haec, quo gaudeat, in se
> Semper habet, bene praeteriti sibi conscia, sorti
> Quaecumque est praesenti aequa, et secura futurae.
> Indiga nullius, sibi tota innititur: extra
> Nil cupit aut metuit, nullo violabilis ictu,
> Sublimis, recta, et stabilis, seu pauperiem, seu
> Exilium, mortemve vehit currens rota, rerum
> Insanos spectat, media atque immobilis, aestus.
> Huc atque huc fortuna furens ruit: illa suis se
> Exercet laeta officiis, secum bona vere
> Tuta fruens, ipsoque sui fit ditior usu.
>
> O mihi si liceat tantos decerpere fructus,
> Si liceat, Montane, tibi! Experiamur uterque:
> Quod ni habitis potiemur, at immoriamur habendis![138]

Translated freely, this reads as follows:

> Either there is no such thing as happiness, or virtue alone can make us happy. It alone always possesses within itself the object of its pleasure, fully conscious of the past, capable of coping today with whatever blows fate may bring, confident in its future destiny. It needs nothing, but relies entirely on itself: outside, it neither desires nor fears anything; nothing can cause it harm; reaching for the heights, erect and stable, it scarcely matters if fortune, by a turn of the wheel, subjects it to poverty, exile, or death: it remains immobile, it occupies the center and contemplates the senseless fury of events. Mad fortune runs to and fro: but serene virtue attends to its duties; keeping its own company, it enjoys treasures that can never be taken from it, and grows wealthy on the profit it draws from itself.

> O, that I may reap such handsome fruits! And that thou
> too, Montaigne, may reap them as well! *Let us both try it:*
> and if we do not become the possessors of these fruits, let
> us die in seeking to possess them!

Here we recognize the voice that Montaigne first heeded and that
exhorts him to seek stability, self-possession, self-consistency, and
contemplative serenity in the face of mankind's restlessness. The insistence on what is one's "own," on the exclusive relationship to
oneself, can encompass two lives in a relationship that subsumes a
dual being: "And our free will has no product more properly *its own*
than affection and friendship."[139] Admittedly, these are words taken
from books (and perhaps transcribed verbatim). But La Boétie, with
his affectionate emphasis, proves that it is possible not only to repeat
the words but also to relive and reincarnate the lesson they set forth.
The injunction *experiamur uterque* might also be translated as "let us
both undertake the *essay*," and would thus define one sense of the
word *essay* (a sense that Montaigne quickly abandoned): an attempt
whose object is known in advance, indeed all too well known, since it
involves the sovereign good, sovereign in respect of its superiority,
uniqueness, and universality—namely, virtue. Virtue is the sacra-
ment of the friendly communion. The invocation of the exemplum,
presided over by antique models and formulated *now* in a language of
the past, is an exalted modality of the friendship bond. It implies
emulation as well as sharing, and the devotion of one's life in its entirety to this unique task: *At immoriamur habendis!* What was the purpose of life becomes the purpose of death: to die in the hope of
possessing these marvelous "fruits." This friendship's banner bears
the motto "Virtue or Death!"

As we shall have occasion to note more than once in what follows, to
sacrifice one's life is the capital act of the exemplary destiny. To proclaim the imperative of virtue is nothing if one does not know how to
die for what one has proclaimed. To die according to one's discourse
prevents that discourse from dissipating itself in "vain words," in
futile rhetoric. Death sets upon judgment the seal of authenticity,
which confirms and solidifies what will never achieve a pleasing consistency so long as it is compounded solely of words. The great men of
the past live on in memory because they died according to their word.
To avoid empty grandiloquence, speech must confront death and appropriate it; it must make death over into the supreme rhetorical effect.
Death thus becomes the punctuation that gives meaning, the defining
feature, the superlative oratorical act, which does not accompany dis-

course as a mere gesture but completes it, in the stasis from which there is no return. Only after death has intervened does it become permissible to assert that speech carried within itself a "performative" power, that *doing* began at the same moment as *saying*. An eloquent death retroactively projects its powerful meaning on all the life that precedes it. The exemplum culminates in a monumental death, erected as a column or a trophy, which compels the men of the future to remember, to be amazed, and to strive to imitate the model. Then, nature and fortune permitting, a new exemplum arises in response to the call of the old: thus La Boétie is able, in Montaigne's eyes, to show himself the equal of his ancient models and to die an admirable death, punctuated by a series of maxims. From the first day of his friend's illness, Montaigne collected these maxims with avid fascination. In the minds of contemporaries the *ultima verba* were more than just a spiritual testament; they offered a foretaste of the "direct vision" of the blessed.

> Thus I was as attentive as I could be. . . . For to portray him thus proudly steadfast in his brave demeanor, to make you see that invincible courage in a body struck down and battered by the furious attacks of death and pain, would require, I confess, a far better style than mine. Because although whenever he spoke about weighty and important matters during his life, he spoke about them in such a way that it would have been hard to write them so well, yet at this point it seemed that his mind and tongue were vying in their effort, as if to do him their ultimate service. For without a doubt I never saw him so full of such beautiful ideas or of such eloquence as he was all through this illness.[140]

Throughout his long agony, La Boétie under his friend's watchful eye does an admirable job reciting the role of the dying sage: he dies like a book. Montaigne will remain struck by this for a long time to come. In his memory, his friendship with La Boétie does not merely deserve a place alongside such exemplary friendships as that of Caius Blossius and Tiberius Gracchus ("they were friends more than citizens"[141]), nor is it merely an answer to La Boétie's expectation, as expressed in a letter to Montaigne: "I am not afraid that our nephews will refuse to inscribe our names (provided destiny affords us life) on the list of famous friends."[142] More than this, according to Montaigne, their friendship actually surpassed the examples found in books: "You will hardly *read* of the like."[143] Infused with the hyperbolic enthusiasm to outdo, it surpassed even its models: "Our friendship has no other

58

model than itself, and can be compared only with itself. . . .[144] For
the very *discourses* that antiquity has left us on this subject seem to me
weak compared with the feeling I have. And in this particular the
facts surpass even the precepts of philosophy."[145] La Boétie was possessed of a mind "molded in the pattern of other ages than this,"[146]
but the friendship that he had "built up" with Montaigne had so fully
fused with its ancient models as to have become its own model. Successful imitation had made it unique and inimitable. No longer was it
a mere approximation to the fullness of friendship; it was that fullness, achieved and incarnate. The gap between the living reality and
the model having vanished, it became possible for existence to confound itself with essence. It was not enough that this friendship
should have risen above "*common usage*"[147] and surpassed "other
common friendships,"[148] nor was it enough that it did not "conform to
the pattern of mild and regular friendships":[149] in the surpassing of
every model that Montaigne describes, a modern reader might decipher aesthetic pride at escaping all norms, the overestimation of a
narcissism *à deux* that throws off the initial guidance of the examples
by going farther and farther in the direction they indicate. Idealizing,
Montaigne concludes that his friendship freed itself of all models to
such an extent that its only model was itself: no other could come
close.

La Boétie's death plunged Montaigne into "dark and troubling
night." The feeling of dizzying superiority that he had achieved at his
friend's instigation gave way to self-depreciation, with a melancholic
tinge: Montaigne speaks of a black "smoke." Having heard Montaigne haughtily measure the distance that separated him and his
friend from the "common" mass (their souls "mingled and blended
with each other so completely" as to "efface the seam that joined
them"[150]), we find him now, left alone after the loss of La Boétie,
declaring more than once that he numbers himself among the *common*
crowd: "I consider myself one of the common sort, except in that I
consider myself so."[151] Friendship had enabled him to *rise above*, to
transcend, the empire of exempla; but the loss of his friend casts
Montaigne into "*humble* and inglorious life,"[152] a life whose variety,
polymorphic abundance, and unstable progress refuse in a different
way to conform to the unifying dictates of the models. Montaigne is
faced not with the singleness of virtue but with the multiplicity of a
"fluctuating and various existence."

What a strange reversal death has brought about! Of the two members of this fraternal couple, La Boétie was the one more advanced in

wisdom, better versed in the requirements of virtue, more in control of his passions: the mold that gave shape to his soul subsumed it completely under a single "mark." Fortune (to use the term that Montaigne himself uses indefatigably), having snuffed out La Boétie's life at the age of thirty-two, all at once set upon his immense perfection the sign of incompleteness, of fragmentation. In his sorrow Montaigne sees his friend's incomparable moral grandeur ill served by the acts and works in which that greatness lacked the opportunity to fully objectify itself. La Boétie has left no monument in which the nobility of his soul is fully recognizable. It then becomes clear that the *testimony* of Michel de Montaigne is indispensable as proof that the absence of an important political career and a literary production amounting to no more than a few posthumous pamphlets are at best poor indicators of his friend's true "capacity": mere *sport* that could not possibly reveal to anyone, with the exception of a few keen observers, the true worth of a superior individual. The surviving friend is the only person capable of attesting to the fact of a *disparity* between the limited, heterogeneous nature of the actual work and the great actions and major books of which the author, fortune permitting, would have been capable. By publishing his friend's papers, duplicating his pamphlets, and writing the chapter "Of friendship," Montaigne attempted to demonstrate that the slim legacy actually left by La Boétie was unequal to his miraculous personality. In this connection, the forced imperfection of the work only gives relief to a perfection of spirit that was reduced to remaining almost entirely *internal*. This type of inequality between the outer work and the inner perfection is so closely associated with the assertion of sovereign subjectivity that many "modern" writers (from the Romantics to Valéry and beyond) would later edit themselves as Montaigne edited La Boétie, taking upon themselves the role of the posthumous *sponsor:* the unfinished, the fragmentary, the interrupted text, offered to the reader as a game in which the writer has not fully committed himself or in which he has been unable to lay hold of the infinite object of his desire, all stand as evidence that the writer's unfettered subjectivity surpasses its own products.

But the reversal brought about by La Boétie's death does not end with this aspect of his posthumous fortune. It affects Montaigne as well. After publishing the papers entrusted to him he attempts to continue on his own the work of moral unification in which his friend had tried to enlist him. But this, as we have seen, drags him down into the motley, fragmented world of diversity, to criticize it, to be sure, and yet ultimately to join it, since it is the human condition to live in this world. And whereas La Boétie's admirable unity left as its only external and public record no more than a few brief works, Montaigne's subjective diversity will be collected in a "register" and cast in the form of a book (*livre*) rather than a series of pamphlets (*livrets*), a book incorporating innumberable citations and ornaments in a multifarious whole. The duty of unity, which conscience knows it cannot escape, will be delegated to the book, which will never lack for the *thread* that serves to make of a multitude of "other people's flowers" a single "bunch," a unique bouquet: "Even so someone might say of me that I have here only made a bunch of other people's flowers, having furnished nothing of my own but the thread to tie them. Indeed I have yielded to public opinion in carrying these borrowed ornaments about on me. But I do not intend that they should cover and hide me; that is the opposite of my design, I who wish to make a show only of what is my own, and of what is naturally my own."[153] But what is it to make a show of what is one's own? For Montaigne, it is to incorporate into the very thread of his work an attack on his own propensity to lose the thread: "If in speaking I am emboldened to digress however little from my thread, I never fail to lose it."[154] It is also to declare: "(B) I have little control over myself and my moods. Chance has more power here than I. . . . (C) This also happens to me: that I do not find myself in the place where I look; and I find myself more by chance encounter than by searching and judgment."[155] But just as in the case of the borrowings, or use of "other people's flowers," the text provides the "thread" that enables Montaigne to make a "bunch" of the self's scattered fragments and moments, and even as he says that he has lost the thread of his thought, he never allows the discourse of reflection to be interrupted—indeed, that discourse turns ignorance and forgetfulness to advantage. La Boétie's strength remained bottled up in himself and culminated in a noble death; Montaigne's avowed weakness will transform itself into strength by objectifying itself in his book: a book that moves, that "marches," but with a free and whimsical "step," no longer subject to the injuction to follow the narrow path of virtue.

In the long Latin epistle addressed to Montaigne, La Boétie sees himself as having a mind more limited and stable than that of his friend; Montaigne, whose soul is more complex, seems to him destined to great things but at the same time exposed to the strongest of temptations and the greatest of risks: "But for you there is more to combat, you, our friend, whom we know to be equally suited to impressive vices and impressive virtues." *At tibi certamen maius.*[156] Montaigne, during this time of youth, is subject to contradictory demands and dangerous deviations; he stands in need of "warnings and corrections." Another poem addressed to Montaigne evokes the emblematic situation of Hercules at the crossroads between vice and virtue.[157] Here again, the risk of deviancy and the dangerous attraction of libertinage are the themes of friendly admonition. Indeed, these assertions are true, in a more general and enduring sense, of Montaigne's thought itself. For him there exists no road without a fork, no virtue that does not turn into its opposite, no example that does not call forth a contradictory example.

For Montaigne, the conflict involves more than simply a clash of moral values which, as defined *within* the language of Christianized humanism, are antinomic. Indeed, the conflict challenges the very validity of that language and casts doubt on the obligation to obey its dictates. La Boétie allowed himself to be guided by the precepts of that language to the end of his very brief life, but Montaigne, for his part, puts them to the test, questions them, deviates from them. At first he respects those precepts but eventually he comes to see them as problematic, as one possible set of moral teachings among others. This being the case, it is permissible to choose an independent philosophy, an *"art de vivre"* of one's own.

With the advantage of hindsight, knowing Montaigne's finished work as we do, we may take the liberty of slightly twisting La Boétie's Latin to remark that, for Montaigne, *the greatest combat* lay precisely in his ambiguous relationship—at once attentive and unfaithful—to the lesson he had learned. The *essay*, skeptical and reflective but also full of improvisation, will be obliged to fill the void left by the decision to give up the guidance of exemplary models. La Boétie had been a living example, and his death, before the writing project was even begun, takes on an emblematic meaning: he will never be forgotten, but the virtue that lived in him is now without a representative or a field of action in this world. Whatever he might have done, in which he doubtless would have involved Montaigne, can be done no longer. The only thing left to do, which can and must be done, is to articulate the impossibility of fulfilling the destiny that was La Boétie's; this must be written down and communicated to the reader.

La Boétie left Montaigne with the memory of an exemplary *resolution* in the face of death:

> Because, owing to the unique and brotherly friendship that we had borne each other, I had a very certain knowledge of what he had intended, judged, and willed during his life, no doubt as great as one man can have of another. And

because I knew this to be lofty, virtuous, full of very certain *resolution,* and in short admirable, I readily foresaw that if illness left him the power to express himself, nothing would escape him in such a necessity but what was great and full of good example.[158]

After La Boétie's death, however, Montaigne finds himself without the person who was the very example of resolution. Even as he makes "room" in his own conscience for his friend's image and voice, he does not expect that these will afford him the advice and admonition that formed the sinew of the living friendship. The role of witness, however deeply internalized, will have lost much of its pragmatic urgency and efficacy; it will survive in severe and serene judgment and in self-scrutiny but not in the injuction to act or in the expectation of future glory. It will not have the disciplinary but disastrous effects that modern psychology attributes to a tyrannical superego. It is as if La Boétie's death suddenly revealed to Montaigne his own death, and thus made seem inane any project guided by hope and turned toward the future. "My plan is everywhere divisible; it is not based on great hopes; each day's journey forms an end. And the journey of my life is conducted in the same way."[159] Nothing prevented Montaigne from falling back into that *irresolution* from which La Boétie had hoped to retrieve him; from now on he is willing to let his irresolution show, as a "scar" in his self-portrait—"irresolution [is] a most harmful failing in negotiating worldly affairs. I do not know which side to take in doubtful enterprises. . . . I can easily maintain an opinion, but not choose one."[160] Choice and resolve were possibilities of shared friendship. The cause of melancholy is none other than the veil of "smoke" that now clouds the future and forces consciousness to fall back either on the present or, often enough as well, on the territory inhabited by retrospective memory. All that Montaigne has been able to save from the wreckage and incorporate into himself is the act of vigilant reflection; he will want to secure for that act an ample field of leisure, from which the need for *combat,* which La Boétie had foreseen for his friend, will gradually disappear. Happy relaxation will supplant bellicose ardor.

Once the anticipation of action ceases to create tension and a need for efficiency in the use of time, Montaigne's style is free to become sinuous, to wander endlessly: no urgency hastens his pen. Since the only purpose of the writing is to make itself manifest, no digression can divert it from its goal. Its time is the time of pleasure and not that of active life, which imposes a strict economy on persuasive rhetoric: a prelude or postlude to pragmatic existence, the time of *private* retirement or death. Underlying the *Essays* is an infinite leisure redolent of both the intimacy of life and the emptiness of death. To borrow a term favored by Maurice Blanchot, it is *idleness (désoeuvrement)* that gives rise to the "work" (*ouvrage*), with all its various forms.

La Boétie, himself a model of resolution, celebrated virtue and addressed the injunction "experiamur uterque" to Montaigne. At the same time, as we have seen, he gave a first definition of the essay: an attempt whose goal is known in advance, though it is not known whether that goal can be attained. La Boétie wanted to take the straightest path to the goal. Montaigne, left alone, will not prohibit himself from *divagating*, circumventing, "swerving aside." Montaigne's irresolution radically transforms the meaning of the essay, whose highly original form can be fully understood only by measuring the distance that separates it from La Boétie's *experiamur:* "If my mind could gain a firm footing, *I would not make essays,* I would make decisions; but it is always in apprenticeship and on trial."[161] What will propel the movement of the essay is the avowal of ineffective effort, constantly starting over only to fail all too quickly, despite the fascination of the great models:

> It happens even to us, who are but abortions of men, sometimes to launch our soul, aroused by the ideas or examples of others, very far beyond her ordinary range; but it is a kind of passion that impels and drives her, and which to some extent tears her out of herself. For when this whirlwind is over, we see that without thinking about it she unbends and relaxes of herself, if not down to the lowest key, at least until she is no longer the same; so that then, for any occasion, for a lost bird or a broken glass, we let ourselves be moved just about like one of the vulgar.[162]

The suspicion is carried to the point of supposing that even "in the lives of the heroes of times past" heroism predominated only "by fits and starts," in "miraculous moments": "But they are indeed mere moments."[163]

Even more, the essay will be the realization of a new type of identification: sympathy of a wholly intellectual sort, comprehension of the great souls of the past, reasoned admiration of models of virtue. But at the same time the writer of the essay is acutely aware of belonging to a different "form," of failing to command the strength necessary to move from intuitive identification to active imitation. The ego perceives itself, then, through its distance and its disparity; and it chooses this very difference as the theme of its discourse. It will articulate the reasons why it chooses to venerate the exemplary figure and, at the same time, the reasons why it cannot hope to live up to the model. At this point it may be useful to reread the beginning of chapter 1:37, "Of Cato the Younger" (taking care to distinguish the various layers of the text):

> (A) I do not share that common error of judging another by myself. I easily believe that another man may have qualities different from mine. (C) Because I feel myself tied down to one form, I do not oblige everybody to espouse it, as all others do. I believe in and conceive a thousand contrary ways of life; and in contrast with the common run of men, I more easily admit difference than resemblance between us. I am as ready as you please to acquit another man from sharing my conditions and principles. I consider him simple in himself, without relation to others; I mold him to his own model. I do not fail, just because I am not continent, to acknowledge sincerely the continence of the Feuillants and the Capuchins, and to admire the manner of their life. I can very well insinuate my imagination into their place, and I love and honor them all the more because they are different from me. I have a singular desire that we should each be judged in ourselves apart, and that I may not be measured in conformity with the common patterns.
>
> (A) My weakness in no way alters my necessarily high regard for the strength and vigor of those who deserve it. (C) *There are men who praise nothing except what they are confident they can imitate* [Cicero]. (A) Crawling in the slime of the earth, I do not fail to observe, even in the clouds, the inimitable loftiness of certain heroic souls. It is a great deal for me to have my judgment regulated, if my actions cannot be, and to maintain at least this sovereign part free from corruption. It is something to have my will good when my legs fail me. This century in which we live, at least in our part of the world, is so leaden that not only the practice but even the idea of virtue is wanting; and it seems to be nothing else but a piece of school jargon—
>
> (C) They think that virtue's just a word,
> And a sacred grove mere sticks
>
> —Horace
>
> —*something they should revere even if they cannot understand it* [Cicero]. It is a trinket to hang in a cabinet, or as an ornament on the end of the tongue, like an earring on the tip of the ear.
>
> (A) There are no more virtuous actions to be seen; those that wear virtue's appearance do not for all that have its essence; for profit, glory, fear, habit, and other such extra-

65

neous causes lead us to perform them. The justice, the valor, the good nature that we then exercise may be so called in consideration of others and of the appearance they bear in public, but in the doer this is not virtue at all; there is another end proposed, (C) another motivating cause. (A) Now virtue will avow nothing but what is done by and for itself alone.[164]

To write, to exercise one's judgment, does not merely mean to return, via a circuitous path (and with a detour that encompasses the thought of death), to that which was indicted initially and which, as the foregoing shows, continues to be rejected: appearance. It is also to remain in contact—albeit negatively—with what one had sought behind appearances and which had eluded one's grasp: essence, exemplary virtue. The relationship to essence and virtue is from now on devoid of hope and stamped with humility, but it has become the *subject* of an endless discourse. The *ego* that goes "crawling in the slime of the earth" is the same ego that proclaims itself the "subject of [this] book."

The question raised at the outset was that of the self's identity and reasons for writing in a world given over to illusion and hypocrisy. We have seen Montaigne's answer take shape in stages, marked by encounters with death, aesthetic form, and the problem of relations to others. And we have seen that Montaigne, after a vain attempt to free himself from the prestige of external models, was led to a reflective acceptance of the phenomenal world, as compiled and represented in works of literature. In what follows, I should like to take a closer look at some of the particular issues whose schematic interrelationships have been traced in the preceding chapter: the recourse to being, the "relation to others," the writer's commitment to the work. Will this more detailed examination confirm the itinerary outlined above? If, as we pursue these various lines of inquiry, we were to discover in Montaigne's writing a persistent fundamental direction, then we would not only gain a better grasp of the "controlling form" that he steadfastly maintains governs the composition of the work in all its varied and changing aspects; we would also perceive more clearly what that work, somehow still close to us for all its remoteness, invites us to think about our own presence in the world.

T W O

«This mask torn away»

"The true appearance of things"

Initially the task seems clear. If lying and sham are a mere getup, one has only to tear them away as one might tear away a mask. Not only from ourselves but from all things must we subtract what has been added, get rid of what has been borrowed, and clear away whatever hides the fundamental nudity: we must cure ourselves of the temptation to mingle in what has nothing to do with us, we must reject what comes to us from outside, and we must control those desires that might cause us to turn outward. As soon as the murky "surround" that stands between us and the world is dispelled, we discover both our own real visage and "the true price of each thing."[1] A new world and a new self present themselves simultaneously to our eyes: a world cleansed of the mist cast over it by our desire and our imagination, and a self purified of all alien dross. At this point it becomes possible to reestablish a proper relation between our own life and the world, between the external and the internal. Liberated from the "violent prejudice of custom,"[2] man will finally be able to decipher "the true appearance of things" of which "usage robs us."[3] After his purification has been completed (but when is it finally done?), man regains his footing in reality and lets wisdom guide his steps. Giving in for a moment to what one might call the joy of "unmasking," Montaigne asserts that "when this mask is torn off, and [man] refers things to truth and reason, he will feel his judgment as it were all upset, and nevertheless restored to a much surer status."[4]

If rigorously pursued, where will the attempt to strip away the artificial and uncover the authentic that lies beneath come to an end? How far does one have to penetrate beneath deceptive appearances before coming upon a definitive and stable substance? By what sign does one recognize that the end has been reached, the true self, the pure gold that lay hidden beneath so many misleading layers of crust? When will Montaigne allow himself to act and to speak out, Montaigne who is supposed to have resolved to remain silent and refrain from any enterprise until he should have in hand the truth about himself, about others, and about the world, a truth exempt from all suspicion?

Montaigne's answers to these questions are equivocal. Is it simply a matter of removing masks, or is it one of never putting them back on again? Many passages in the *Essays* claim to guarantee their author's spontaneous veracity: he offers himself to us as he is, at his first impulse, without alteration. This is the privilege that he reserves for the small circle of his "relatives and friends": he has taken up the pen on their behalf in order to preserve the image of his "natural form." He has no ambition other than to be known, hence nothing obliges him to dissimulate. He has no scruples about giving in to his mood. He is at each moment in possession of a truth *in the nascent state*, and the difficulty (as we shall see) is simply not to corrupt that truth in the retelling. And language is presumed to be not incapable of cleaving closely enough to thought and feeling to faithfully record their every variation. Such is Montaigne's first response—what I shall call his "optimistic" response—to the problem of self-knowledge.

By contrast, one can point to innumerable pages in the *Essays* in which inner knowledge is the always elusive goal of an interminable pursuit. Rather than deliver itself up at first blush, the true self evades the introspective gaze. The quest is lured away into remote distances; no matter how far introspection progresses, the inner truth remains impossible to grasp: it can neither be possessed as a thing nor even fixed as a pattern. It refuses to lend itself to any sort of objectification and evades Montaigne's grasp even as he thinks he is drawing near. The truth about himself seems to beckon from afar, from a confused and boundless horizon—an intimate transcendence:

> (C) It is a thorny undertaking, and more so than it seems, to follow a movement so wandering as that of our mind, to penetrate the opaque depths of its innermost folds, to pick out and immobilize the innumerable flutterings that agitate it. . . . There is no description equal in difficulty, or certainly in usefulness, to the description of oneself. . . .[5] The more I frequent myself and know myself, the more my deformity astonishes me, and the less I understand myself.[6]

Should the ego be regarded as intimately in touch with itself or as obscurely absent? Equivocation on this point is one of the fruitful paradoxes of Montaigne's thinking. The essay as practiced by Montaigne is by turns (or simultaneously) an instantaneous revelation of the self and a pursuit that can never be concluded. It quickly becomes apparent that this equivocation is related to another, having to do with the aptitude of language to speak the truth about existence.[7]

If the first impulse is the bearer of truth, as it is in what I have called the optimistic view, then the *nascent state* enjoys ontological primacy and superiority in all respects: at every moment a new sensual experience is born, a new impulse of thought and will, a fresh manner of expression. To the extent that these are original they are infallibly correct. Their truth is guaranteed by the primary character of their emergence. Apparently nothing precedes them: no reflection, no premeditated purpose is able to introduce distortion. We have only to attend as closely as possible to the ever fresh evidence and to refrain from transgressing the boundaries of the present in which the revelation unfolds. The world's sensuous message has to be received at every instant, and along with it the thought that prolongs sensation. We must also take care not to embellish artificially (with preexisting concepts or with eyes fixed on some far-off goal) what is granted to us in the grace of the moment. But who can presume upon such privilege? Can we count on truth to manifest itself intact, even for the most fleeting of instants? Don't the very precautions that we take to protect the truth help to obscure it? Isn't everything distorted in advance? We are hindered, whatever we do, by a mendacious power—custom—that alters our sensations, our thoughts, and our words. By our senses, our bodies, and our finite condition we are imprisoned in a "form" that has no common measure with the "original being" of things. The conventional rules of our language lock us into an arbitrary system where we play with shadows. Treachery is everywhere, even if it is not our fault: it is not that I wear a mask but that reality, within me as well without, eludes me. Thus suspicion may seem to be the beginning of wisdom. To have faith in initial appearances is to be naïve, to allow oneself to be duped.[8] Behind the seductions of the first impulse is an evil, cunning power that amuses itself by making me believe. How am I to outwit it? How am I to master it? Not by lurking about myself in ambush, waiting for the moment when my life and the world will reveal themselves to me, but by destroying the intervening obstacles: I must wrest myself free of a deceptive *here* and plunge myself into pursuit of a *there* that hides behind appearances.

Now, what will be the end result of such a search for being? To what are we committing ourselves when we attempt to grasp, beyond the variable qualities of sensuous experience, a permanent substance, "the very essence of truth, which is uniform and constant"?[9] Are we not likely to transform what we think we have discovered beyond appearances into still other appearances? If error is inseparable from phenomena, will we ever escape error? For at the end of the journey our senses are still what they were at the beginning; our eyes and our hands contaminate any images with which they happen to come into contact, even those where they believe they are encountering pure being: "As if our touch were infectious, we by our handling corrupt things that of themselves are beautiful and good."[10]

Behind illusory discourses Montaigne discovers only other discourses, woven of the same stuff. Behind sensations lie other sensations, equally uncertain and misleading. He knows in advance that he will never escape the dominion of words, and that substituting one word for another does not alter the fact that all words are human words, hence shrouded in darkness and ambiguity. Montaigne therefore makes no attempt to reform language or to lay down rules of conduct. His ambition did not extend in this direction.

Yet he is not unmoved by the heroic aspects of a philosophy that rejects all masks as a matter of principle. If he doubts that the truth of things can ever be known, he continues to be attracted by the hope that the moral truth can be conquered. For men have the power to reveal the truth about themselves, without sham or disguise, through the major decisions that they take and through the brilliance of their premeditated acts. In a world where the truth about things is denied us, there is at least this path to truth about the self. If we cannot know the truth, at least we can live it.

The ultimate: Suicide

Does Montaigne himself embark upon this path? He tries it out vicariously, out of curiosity to know where it leads and to judge the results, and perhaps stimulated by the malicious pleasure of denouncing the ultimate vanity and failure of the enterprise. He attentively examines what happened to others—in the books of the ancients—who took to heart the heroic mission of taking up the challenge posed by appearances. Now, among these sovereign souls, one in particular arouses Montaigne's admiration: Cato vanquished but victorious in spite of his defeat, dying by his own hand and by this supreme act combining acquiescence in fate with refusal of servitude. Montaigne asks himself what image is most apt to perpetuate Cato's exploit: he decides to depict the very instant before death, the moment when the veracity of thought is countersigned by the sacrifice of life:

> (A) And if it had been up to me to portray him in his proudest posture, this would have been all bloody, tearing out his own bowels, rather than sword in hand, as did the

statuaries of his time. For this second murder was much more savage than the first. . . .[11] (A) When I see him dying and tearing out his entrails, I cannot be content to believe simply that he then had his soul totally free from disturbance and fright; I cannot believe that he merely maintained himself in the attitude that the rules of the Stoic sect ordained for him, sedate, without emotion, and impassible; there was it seems to me, in that man's virtue too much lustiness and verdancy to stop there. I believe without any doubt that he felt pleasure and bliss in so noble an action, and that he enjoyed himself more in it than in any other action of his life. (C) He so departed from life, as if he rejoiced in having found a reason for dying [Cicero]. (A) I go so far in that belief that I begin to doubt whether he would have wanted to be deprived of the occasion for so fine an exploit. And if his goodness, which made him embrace the public advantage more than his own, did not hold me in check, I should easily fall into this opinion, that he was grateful to fortune for having put his virtue to so beautiful a test and for having favored that brigand in treading underfoot the ancient liberty of his country. I seem to read in that action I know not what rejoicing of his soul, and an emotion of extraordinary pleasure and manly exultation, when it considered the nobility and sublimity of its enterprise:

(B) Prouder for having chosen death.

—Horace

This enterprise was not spurred by some hope of glory, as the plebeian and effeminate judgments of some men have judged (for that consideration is too base to touch a heart so noble, so lofty, and so unbending), but was undertaken for the beauty of the very thing in itself, which he, who handled the springs of it, saw much more clearly in its perfection than we can see it.[12]

The moment that Montaigne would wish immortalized in sculpture is the moment of final effort, of bare-handed suicide, in which the hero truly *gives* himself death. This is the perfect emblem of that violent philosophy, Stoicism of the Roman and republican variety. Here we see the culmination in bloody glory of the work of subtraction that strips away all that is inessential and imaginary in life, all the involvements that render man a stranger unto himself: life must be subtracted with all the rest. In committing suicide, Cato sets his own limit and gives proof of absolute possession. His entire being is in his hands, within his reach and at his mercy. Nothing more can elude him. The cutting edge of judgment, turned against the hero's own entrails, proves that discourse has definitively acquired the force of action and stands forever beyond all refutation.

The stripping away of masks here reaches its culmination. What had seemed an interminable process—no sooner was one's visage bared than new masks immediately covered it up—finally exposes the individual's true being, *defining* him in his *final* moment, when the conscience, finally its own mistress, joyously destroys all further possibility of evasion and hypocrisy. Inner truth, reduced to its bare essentials and stripped of the tawdry tinsel that had hidden its true character, coalesces and shimmers in the glow of imminent death. Truth takes death for its accomplice, as if only a background of nothingness could make it stand out, in the brief instant when the hero confronts the shadows before disappearing into them. There being no further exit into a living future—i.e., no way to "think elsewhere"— being is established upon the fullness of *here* and *now*. The hero displays as well as beholds his full powers, which can never again be challenged: his powers are *infinite* because no external force can limit them. And there remains the chance of glorious immortality, since the name of the hero courageous enough to prefer death to ignominy may yet be perpetuated by the words of others.

Thus death, and especially voluntary death, initiates a process of laying bare the truth. The hour of death is the truthful mirror in which, for the first and last time, being lays hold of itself. Enduring qualities are finally brought to light, and blemishes uncovered, It becomes clear which were false and which were true: vice or virtue, courage or cowardice—the last hour decides forever and makes possible retrospective judgment of an entire life:

> (A) In everything else there may be sham: the fine reasonings of philosophy may be a mere pose in us; or else our trials, by not testing us to the quick, give us a chance to keep our face always composed. But in the last scene, between death and ourselves, there is no more pretending; we must talk plain French, we must show what there is that is good and clean at the bottom of the pot:
> At last true words surge up from deep within our breast,
> The mask is snatched away, reality is left.
> —Lucretius
> That is why all the other actions of our life must be tried and tested by this last act. It is the master day, the day that is judge of all the others. "It is the day," says one of the ancients [Seneca], "that must judge all my past years." I

> leave it to death to test [*essai*] the fruit of my studies. We shall see then whether my reasonings come from my mouth or from my heart.[13]

The "last act," then, not only possesses the privilege of authenticity but immediately becomes the touchstone by which all our previous actions are judged. The hour of death illuminates and fixes irrevocably the hitherto undecided meaning of our entire past. It is not without significance that Montaigne here uses the word *essay:* the idea of essaying, putting to the test, contained in this passage is the same as the idea set forth in the very title of the *Essays,* and the intention of calling death to the rescue because death is the premier assayer is one of the first moves of Montaigne's mind—wholly in accord, as we have seen, with the lesson of La Boétie.

"To philosophize is to learn to die." Montaigne makes this proposition of Cicero's the subject of an entire essay (1:20).[14] Philosophy ordinarily draws a distinction between the knowledge of the truth and the obligations of morality; it speculates on the one hand about being and on the other hand about virtue. Ethics itself may be subdivided into a theory (knowledge of the sovereign good) and a practice. But to learn to die is to reunite all of philosophy's objectives, to make them converge in a single point. It is to reconcile knowledge and practice and to appropriate impersonal truth so as to make it *my* truth. In the moment that decides my life for all time, there ceases to be a gap between word and act, discourse and conduct. To anticipate that moment is therefore to possess in advance the unity that most men lack. Life is in fact a perpetual evasion, a chaotic recommencement: death is the barrier that shuts off our escape. If we make ourselves at home with the thought of death before the fact, we bestow coherence upon what is otherwise "but patchwork and motley."[15]

Death thus becomes the "sole support of our freedom,"[16] for I am my own master, my sole master, only to the extent that I am master of my death, to the extent that I hold my death in my own hands. For then no tyranny can harm me, no other will can encroach upon my own. Voluntary death raises me almost to the level of a god, for isn't it a divine faculty to be able to define myself and determine my life? If I am capable of ending my life, of "unmaking" myself at my own pleasure, then I gain assurance that I alone have made myself and given myself existence—so long as I choose to prolong my life.

The privilege of authenticity, which, as we saw earlier, Montaigne was tempted to bestow upon the moment of birth, the first impulse, he now bestows (in a tentative way) upon the *moment of death.* If truth does not lie in the first impulse, that is because it lies instead in the last breath. If it is not stated in the first words, that is because it is enveloped in the final silence: the mind is tempted to seek incontestable certainty in the twinned, antithetical moments of life's emergence and disappearance. Eternity surrounds the *ultima verba* uttered on the far shore, bestowing upon the last words of the dying the supreme importance of ultimate truth. Now, judgment, whose density is limned by death, tends to reintroduce the crucial energy of the *ultima verba* into life as it is lived here and now. The Stoic creed is nothing other than a sentence of death deliberately transferred to the center of life.

To this argument Montaigne lends the support of his own voice, at considerable length. Death unmasks. Why fear it, then? Rather than see death as a liberator, most men consider it a dreadful menace. But dread is a product of the imagination: horror is the mask with which the common man disguises death. Let us begin, then, by stripping death of its hideous appearance, so that it can bring us knowledge of our true identity. Death unmasked becomes death the unmasker. It then becomes easy for me to make death a part of my own identity. The unveiling truth of death merges with the unveiled truth of life. By unmasking this menacing *thing*, I discover my own personhood. Montaigne paraphrases Seneca as follows: "Children fear even their friends when they see them masked, and so do we ours. We must strip the mask from things as well as from persons."[17]

"The goal of our career is death. It is the necessary object of our aim."[18] If I anticipate this goal in my mind and act as though every moment of my life were the last, then I will belong to myself immutably. In this way, by premeditation, I take possession of this "day that is judge of all the others"[19] and incorporate it into my present life, thus discovering the whole truth and meaning of my existence. By framing the thought of death in the abstract, I learn to think of *my* own death and to conceive of myself from the standpoint of my demise: to do this is to introduce continuity and consistency into my actions, it is to unify the diverse moments of my life in the light of the final hour. Having a "death of my own" gives me a "form of my own," a form of which I had been deprived by wearing so many different masks.

Critique of death

But Montaigne's argument becomes so carried away with itself that it undermines—by excess of ardor, as it were—what it is trying to prove. The reasoning used to strip away death's mask of horror actually has the effect of depriving the "last day" of its exceptional role. It will cease to be the "master day." The propositions that are intended to tame death, to make it familiar, simultaneously abolish its privileged position. In a "dialectical" reversal death will lose those qualities that had made it the bearer of an unimpeachable revelation.

In order to ward off the fear of death Montaigne makes use of everything at his disposal. Tradition provides a vast arsenal of arguments that can be turned to advantage. I shall cite only two, whose consequences will prove destructive of death's ontological prerogatives and especially of its right to establish the criteria by which the rest of life is judged. To begin with, death is *already* present in us from birth. Without being aware of it we are in fact dying at every moment: the final moment will be like all the rest, about which we would never dream of complaining. "Why do you fear your last day? It contributes no more to your death than each of the others. The last step does not cause the fatigue, but reveals it. All days travel toward death, the last one reaches it."[20] If my death is *diffused* throughout my life, how can I view it as the supreme event, which, by willing, I can transform into a pure act? The heroic demand literally has no further object: death will elude my grasp just as life does. No longer is it a specific task to be carried out in one final, supreme effort. I must endure it, like it or not; I am dying without being aware of it, much as I breathe. Hence I cannot count on death to reveal me to myself. On the contrary, it is death, which subverts the present and which lies lurking in the shadows as my joys and sorrows unfold, that causes me to fail in my efforts to know myself. Death is too intimate, too close, to offer me any support. It has vanished before my very eyes, and I can only make it out vaguely beneath the mutable and familiar fabric of life, which causes me no fear. Henceforth, death is constantly present; it accompanies me so faithfully that I can no longer separate it from life and set it up in splendid isolation as the moment of final glory.

This argument, which dissolves death and refuses to grant it the dignity of an isolable event, is coupled with another, which denies that death has any hold over us and hence also that we have any hold over it. "It does not concern you dead or alive: alive, because you are; dead, because you are no more. . . . Neither what goes before nor what comes after is any appurtenance of death."[21] Here, rather than being internalized and confounded with the instants of our life, death is externalized: it becomes an absolute *exterior*. It is so *different* that it no longer concerns us. My personal consciousness always falls short of death. For objective knowledge death becomes the occasion of a general judgment, which recognizes it as a universal necessity, of the same order as night and day. Thus death, far from defining me as an individual in my singular truth, is actually what makes me similar to all other living things: death "deindividualizes" me and refers me back to the common condition. This is the final consequence of the argument based on death's unmasking: "We must strip the mask from things as well as persons. When it is off, we shall find beneath only *that same death* which a valet or a mere chambermaid passed through not long ago without fear."[22] Death ceases to act as a spur, and rather than pervade all of our sensual experience it becomes simply the limit of sensual experience for each individual.

Death ceases to be the *act* of dying, the taking leave of life, and becomes the *fact* of having ceased to live. It is idle to fear it and idle to want to confront it: it is nothing. Wisdom consists in restoring this nothing to its rightful place, which is outside us, outside our subjectivity; it is what no one can ever encounter. The wise man, ensconced in his inner fortress, will not bestow an imaginary visage upon a faceless nonentity. He knows in advance that the moment of death has no reality, that it is not an event. In any case that moment is too insubstantial to serve as the support of a heroic act. Death is always with us, Montaigne declares, but all of life is a prelude to death. The two statements are contradictory, but neither permits us to view suicide as a way to unveil hidden being. Both make it pointless to concern ourselves with premeditated death, which deserves condemnation as much as any wish dictated by desire or passion. "We trouble our life by concern about death, and death by concern about life."[23]

And there is yet another fact that finally destroys the hope that the final hour of life should be the hour of truth. A careful reading of history reveals that quite often the final scene yields not unity but contradiction. Rather than being a moment of exemplary recovery of order and truth, death merely caps the scandalous falsehood of the rest of life. The ambiguity inherent in all human behavior does not vanish; it deepens. Who can assure us that a beautiful death is not a masterpiece of artifice? "In my time three of the most execrable and infamous persons I have known in every abomination have had deaths that were ordered and in every circumstance composed to perfection."[24] Death brings not an unmasking but the last misdeed of the mask.

Perhaps, then, it is better to give up the idea of judging a life by its end and to proceed instead in the opposite direction. A unique moment cannot constitute the decisive criterion. The whole of life must be looked at: "Every death should correspond with its life. We do not become different for dying. I always interpret the death by the life. And if they tell me of a death strong in appearance, attached to a feeble life, I maintain that it is produced by a feeble cause corresponding with the life."[25] Cato's suicide is only the final expression of a life that is already wholly in conformity with virtue. The privilege of the final hour, its light of truth, comes only from the attention paid to it. It teaches us nothing that we could not learn better from consideration of the life. Hence we should not seek to isolate a soul's essence in an instant that has no reality. Above all, we must take care not to regard as inessential everything that precedes the final act. By isolating the "act of dying" we make it into a contentless abstraction, whereas its real content lies in the life of which it is the culmination. The imminence of death is still part of life, and the virtue that shines forth in the final moment only continues a virtuous habit formed long ago. Commenting on the deaths of Cato and Socrates, Montaigne writes:

> We see in the souls of these two persons . . . so perfect a habituation to virtue that it has passed into their nature. It is no longer a laborious virtue, or one formed by the ordinances of reason and maintained by a deliberate stiffening of the soul; it is the very essence of their soul, its natural and ordinary gait. They have made it so by a long exercise of the precepts of philosophy, coming upon a fine rich nature.[26]

The unmasker believes that he has set aside habit, usage, and custom to disclose a more stable essence. But now, in an unexpected reversal, we find that we must return to these things and question them. They seemed to hide the substantial being, but now we discover that a *habit*, combined with a *fine rich nature*, may indeed constitute "the very essence" of the soul. Appearance is thus not the irreducible enemy of being: on the contrary, it is an obligatory ally, a necessary complement. If the truth of the self cannot be grasped in the realm of sensual experience, it will not be revealed to us at the instant of death, which is only the last sensual experience, in no way distinguished from the series of such experiences that constitute the fabric of our lives. If the inner being is to be unmasked in the final hour, it will also be unmasked at every moment of our existence. Hence we have no further excuse for not attending to life and the appearances it offers.

Of this attitude—even as Montaigne turns away from all examples—there remains an exemplary image: that of Socrates. In Montaigne's last texts Socrates exemplifies willing humility and inflexible vigilance. His knowledge (which the skeptic can accept) is to know that he knows nothing, and he pays close attention to all the actions of everyday life. This ultimate example does not inhabit a place apart from the ordinary world: he is like us, a living man, a mortal man, a conscience "at peace with itself." His lesson, for those who know how to hear it, does not take us outside ourselves but restores us to ourselves: the universal is not alien; it is in us, in our individual lives, provided we know ourselves as individuals, i.e., as unique and limited beings, irrational but called to develop a reason of our own.

The moment of birth, which is preceded by the darkness of night, and the moment of death, which opens onto the darkness of the hereafter, are moments abutting nothingness. They stand out in sharp contrast to their surroundings but are not entitled to any ontological privilege. The fullness of being does not lie in these moments any more—or less—than in the rest of our lives. There is no more *final* truth than there is a *first* truth, Our lives may well be unstable, changeable, pervaded with illusion: life is still a long moment of truth, and the only one granted to us. The moments of birth and death are not the dwelling places of being, the receptacles of essence: they are mutations, made of the same stuff as our temporary existence, accidents of the same nature as all those we encounter in everyday life. It is the idea of *passage* that triumphs, for when we look at matters closely we find that birth lies hidden in death and that death insinuates itself into each moment of life. "The failing of one life is the *passage* to a thousand other lives. . . . I do not portray being: I portray passing."[27] This is not a matter of choice or preference: only passing is available for portrayal.

Here again we encounter the attitude that we found so striking in the introductory note "To the Reader." While the imminence of death incites the Christian to direct his thoughts to the hereafter, Montaigne on the contrary directs his gaze to this world. The threatening absence sends him back to a presence enhanced and made more precious by its very precariousness. In this rediscovered present he is granted the power to conceive his own finiteness and granted freedom as the reward of accepting that finiteness. For Montaigne the *memento mori* is converted into the project of bestowing upon each moment of life the fullest possible justification. In this way he manages to reconsile, and almost to confound, the *expectation* of his life's ultimate commingling with death and with the lives of a thousand unknown others, with *attention* to each detail that touches this present life. Words, with their intrinsic slipperiness, will play an important part in this ephemeral plenitude and perpetuate the memory of a life that, without this futile and yet unquenchable discourse, would have vanished without a trace.

The happiness of feeling: Between wakefulness and dream
Parallel to this, the "Apology for Raymond Sebond" (that dangerous complement of negative theology added to the positive theology of the *Liber Creaturarum*) concludes that the transcendence of being is absolute: the truth of things is out of reach, the world of essences eludes our grasp even if we believe we are making progress toward understanding the phenomena that we witness. Man never touches anything firm, constant, or assured. Truth dwells with God and belongs to Him alone in a beyond that man can only "imagine unimaginable." One of the worst of human defects—presumption—consists in man's imagining himself to be in possession of the true image of things and the true figure of God, when actually we only forge these to suit our purposes. We construct simulacra. Authentic wisdom knows limits that the mind will never transgress. Such "powerful and generous ignorance" establishes the impossibility of knowledge: "No, no, we sense nothing, we see nothing; all things are hidden from us. We cannot establish what any one of them is."[28] Thus reason, at the end of its quest, culminates in a philosophical suicide, and its highest lucidity consists in sacrificing itself: reason is immobilized in the suspension of all judgment, except for that judgment by which it abstains. This is the peak of its courage, just as for Cato suicide was the last resort of virtue.

The only hope left us is that being may come to us and reveal itself to our eyes, under the aspect of Grace. Man rises toward truth only if "God by exception lends him a hand."[29] The initiative of movement no longer belongs to us, then, for at that moment we have already ceased to be ourselves. The last sentence of the *Apology* ends with the evocation of a "divine and miraculous *metamorphosis*."[30] To move toward being, then, is to become *another*. As in the instant of death, the emergence of true being strangely coincides with the final vanishing in a life that is always in the process of disappearing. The alternative is either to live exiled from being or to exile oneself from life; there is no appeal, and in either case one must endure a break: one can either exist here, separated from being, or attain the realm of being by relinquishing one's hold on the self. We cannot count on reconciliation. For Montaigne there is no incarnate *mediator*, nor is there a possibility of ascension through analogy (as traditional theology maintains). Finally, nothing is more foreign to Montaigne's thought than the Platonic notion of *participation* in essences: "We have no communication with being."[31] Permanence, stability, plenitude, and substance stand alongside what is radically *other, alien,* and *not my own.*

> (A) Our faith is not of our own acquiring, it is a pure present of another's liberality. It is not by reasoning or by our understanding that we have received our religion; it is by *external* authority and command. . . .[32] We cannot worthily conceive the grandeur of those sublime and divine promises, if we can conceive them at all; to imagine them worthily, we must imagine them unimaginable, ineffable, and incomprehensible, (C) and completely different from those of our miserable experience.[33]

What remains properly ours is the void. Man is "naked and empty";[34] he is a "blank tablet."[35] What can he find within himself? In coming back to himself, in regaining his self-possession as the ethics of self-control urges him to do, man comes nowhere near achieving fullness: he delivers himself to the void. "The worst position we can take is in ourselves."[36] For the general run of life, then, we are condemned to endure an irrevocable absence, to feel time slip away into an ontological hole, and to know nothing but the superficial and the transitory. Our only knowledge consists in this doubt that "carries itself away."[37] We are carried away ("they carry us away"[38]) in a perpetual flux. "Every human nature is always *midway* between birth and death, offering only a dim semblance and shadow of itself, and an uncertain and feeble opinion."[39] This "middle ground" is the very location of the void, where things and we ourselves are mere appearances. Is it even possible simply to describe them? Our language, "wholly formed of affirmative propositions,"[40] still gives too much being to that which possesses none. Not content to denounce, as so many others have done, the *feebleness* of language in the face of the essential reality, Montaigne reproaches language for its excessive force, its presumption of being, when all it can really do is describe the inessential illusion: "They [the Pyrrhonian philosophers] would need a new language."[41] A language that would *posit* nothing, that would deny itself without formulating its negation: *"What do I know?"*[42] Doubt in its interrogative form is born of the confrontation between an impossible affirmation and an impossible negation. One cannot say either "I know" or "I do not know." Only an unanswered question can indicate the suspension of judgment, the verbal equivalent of the "motto inscribed over a pair of scales."

Montaigne's skepticism, according to his own avowed intention, is aimed at making man into a "blank tablet" upon which the finger of God will write what it pleases Him to write. And since, in order to arrive at this skeptical fideism,[43] Montaigne began from a position quite close to that of the Stoics, it is not unreasonable that we should be reminded of the successive moments in Hegel's *Phenomenology:* stoicism, skepticism, and the unhappy consciousness.[44] In moving from stoicism to skepticism consciousness affirms its absolute freedom with respect to the world: no longer is it free merely relative to its own circumstances and universal necessity; now it is free in its irreducible individuality and its complete independence of phenomena. Neither the idea of necessity nor the idea of an organized external world (the Stoic *system,* or cosmology) survives this development. If the mind is rigorous in its skepticism, no truth value can be attributed to doubt. Everything falls away, and the mind is overcome by vertigo. Should the mind come to imagine, beyond its own limited sphere, an inaccessible region of Being from which it is permanently separated and with respect to which it feels humiliated and inadequate, we then reach the stage that Hegel calls the "unhappy consciousness": man sees himself as isolated and unimportant compared with God's transcendence. Montaigne, however, is resolute in his determination to transform the "unhappy consciousness" into a happy one.

Being is *elsewhere.* Yet so strong is the attraction of the *here,* so vigorous the preference for what is *ours* (against the blandishments of the *alien*), that Montaigne returns to phenomena after having established the infinite remoteness of God and of pure essence. For him the lesson of skepticism is precisely the return to appearances. Appearances cannot be transcended: but this fact, rather than turn us away from appearances, frees us from the need to search for a hidden reality that would justify our contempt for them. We can now abandon ourselves to appearances without afterthought, and without idle ambition to discover an intelligible world beyond sensible phenomena. Man is simply "bound to follow them and to let himself be swayed by appearances."[45] Despite the void that marks man and his condition, the possibility of *fullness* is restored. Montaigne tells us literally that this is the case. The skeptic sage "does not fail to carry on the functions of his life *fully* and comfortably."[46] Compared with the realm of pure essences our life seemed empty, and plenitude remained beyond our reach. But once this realm is considered to be unattainable, we have only to place our confidence in fugitive perception, which offers us the full range of pleasure and maintains its value in spite of the objections of metaphysics. Even when we discover that it does not grant access to "the very essence of truth,"[47] *for us* this experience retains its value of existential plenitude. What does it matter if it is for us alone? If it does not put us into communication with any stable truth, at least it offers us a full measure of self-presence, of contact with our empirical selves.

In an outburst of ontological pessimism, as we noted earlier, Montaigne had cried out: "No, no, we sense nothing, we see nothing."[48] But this does not prevent him from exhibiting in all circumstances a most intense desire to feel; the proof of this is that he chooses his words for the sake of their sensory richness (he is particularly fond of words that give "phonic pleasure," acoustic or muscular, words evocative of actions that place us in a situation of physical contact). The *vouloir sentir* (will to feel), always alive in Montaigne, is a *vouloir être* (will to be) that tends to realize itself in immediate perception, for lack of other substantial support. Incapable of saying anything about the nature of things, phenomenalism (which accepts phenomena as they are and which supplants the skeptical *epoche* that had denied them any ontological legitimacy) falls back on the certainty of the perceptible. Correcting what he found excessive in his praise of indolence, Montaigne writes: "I am glad not to be sick; but if I am, I want to know I am; and if they cauterize or incise me, *I want to feel it*."[49] Thus after proving that a radical separation exists, after relegating God and Being to a position infinitely remote from where we stand, Montaigne urges us to attach ourselves through *feeling* to our vulnerable existence, shorn of all participation in the absolute. This is the positive counterpart of skeptical "negation":

> You see only the order and government of this little cave you dwell in, at least if you do see it. His divinity has infinite jurisdiction beyond. . . . It is a municipal law that you allege; you do not know what the universal law is. *Attach yourself to what you are subject to,* but not him; he is not your colleague, or fellow citizen, or companion.[50]

Thus the remoteness of God brings man into greater intimacy with his condition in the very heart of the world of appearances. What had been reduced to *nothing* in comparison with absolute being recovers the right to presence and existence. The unjustifiable recovers a justification for want of anything better. Montaigne tells us that "there is nothing I treat specifically except nothing, and no knowledge except that of the lack of knowledge."[51] But henceforth it is *nothing* that counts: *lack of knowledge* is the only possible knowledge. Both are worthy of being *treated*. This nothing is at least *our own:* it is our body, traversed by pleasure and joy, attacked by illness and pain. Sundry flavors are constantly offering themselves to us, and we would be fools not to accept and sample them. In the very heart of nothingness each object imposes upon us its clear immediacy, and even though we cannot explain it in terms of its intrinsic nature, it is no less capable of satisfying us to the full. Consenting to the *nothingness* of existence allows us to enjoy each presence that appears to us, thanks to which nothing is gradually transformed into a multitudinous all. What was initially only *vanity* or *wind* regains legitimacy as soon as we recognize it as *our own*. The quite negative image of wind thereupon swells with joyous and positive values: the wind has merely to accept itself and take pleasure in its own fickleness: "And even the wind, more wisely than we, loves to make a noise and move about, and is content with its own functions, without wishing for stability and solidity, qualities that do not belong to it."[52] What does it matter if the *causes* of things elude us? For we remain among the *things* themselves and have "perfectly full use" of them.

Thus we must give up the right to appeal to Being's authority in order to contest the appearances that surround us. Once we cease to be blinded by presumption, we must admit that there is no escaping appearances and that we are always moving from one appearance to another. How can we object to our own condition? The problem of the mask in the realm of knowledge evaporates, just as it did in the realm of ethics. There can be no mask unless there is a possibility of discovering a true visage behind it. But the visage we are looking for has receded into the infinite distance, while we remain in a world where everything is equivalent to everything else, where to say that everything is false leads also to the conclusion that everything is true. In front of us are moving things, the source of whose movement lies both inside us and outside. It is impossible to distinguish between the change that dwells within and the flux of things around us. Having turned our attention back to this world, we are once again plunged into the whole range of phenomena; we are so tightly bound to the world that we are wholly implicated in its "agitation" (*branle*). The solipsism of sensation, in which we might have been held captive, is immediately transcended.

In the essay entitled "Of the inconsistency of our actions" (one of those in which Montaigne is most insistent upon the fluidity and impermanence of the human mind), we find the very idea of the mask explicitly called into question:

Even good authors are wrong to insist on fashioning a con-
sistent and solid fabric out of us. They choose one general
characteristic, and go and arrange and interpret all a man's
actions to fit their picture; and if they cannot twist them
enough, they go and *set them down to dissimulation.*[53]

We are merely a rapid succession of dissimilar instants. And if (argues Montaigne), in the midst of joy our faces suddenly exhibit sadness, that does not mean that we are hiding our joy: it means simply
that we have suddenly changed, and that we have been abandoned
by the joy that we were exhibiting a moment before. We have become
different. Our states succeed and contradict one another, and none of
them is ever stable enough to serve as a basis for the superimposition
of being and appearance. When "we laugh and cry for the same
thing,"[54] that is not hypocrisy but the effect of the "volatility and
pliancy of our soul." A brief essay in book 1 (1:38) also shows in an
admirable manner how incessant change dissipates and dissolves the
antithesis between the mask and truth. The far too rigid antinomy of
being and appearance is subsumed in the intuition of universal
change:

When they presented Caesar with the head of Pompey, the
histories say, he turned his eyes away as from an ugly and
unpleasant sight. There had been such a long understanding and association between them in the management of
public affairs, such great community of fortunes, so many
mutual services and so close an alliance, that we must not
believe that Caesar's countenance was entirely false and
counterfeit. . . . For although most of our actions are indeed only mask and make-up, and it may sometimes be
truth that
  An heir's tears are a laugh behind the mask,
                                      —Publilius Syrus
yet in judging these accidents we must consider how our
soul is often agitated by *diverse* passions. And just as in our
body they say there is an assemblage of diverse humors, of
which that one is master which most ordinarily rules within us, according to our constitution; so in our soul, though
various impulses stir it, there must be one that remains
master of the field. Its advantage is not complete, however;
because of the *volatility and pliancy* of our soul, the weaker
ones on occasion regain the lost ground and make a brief
attack in their turn. . . . (C) No quality embraces up purely
and universally. . . . (B) Whoever supposes, to see me
look sometimes coldly, sometimes lovingly, on my wife,

that either look is feigned, is a fool. . . .(A) They say that
the sun does not give off a continuous light, but that it
incessantly darts new rays so thick on one another that we
cannot perceive the intervals between them . . . just so our
soul diversely and imperceptibly darts its rays.[55]

This, then, is the perfect image of change: change is no longer a continuous and smooth flow but a discontinuous series of instants following one another in rapid succession, each of which inaugurates a
new self to supplant the one that preceded it. In his image of sunlight
Montaigne abandons the "wave" model in favor of a "particle"
model that makes each lived instant more emphemeral and more independent; each instant is granted its brief interval of authenticity
and full legitimacy, only to be denied a moment later. "The turn is so
quick that it escapes us."[56] Montaigne calls this discontinuous sequence a succession (*suite*). But he is careful to add that this succession does not form a *body:* it is shapeless. It is an error to insist on
attributing a form to it. "And for this reason we are wrong to try to
compose a continuous body out of all this succession of feelings."[57]
To compose a continuous body would be to create something artificial, to impose a constant figure on something subject to perpetual
motion. Form, constancy, stability, solidity—all qualities invoked
earlier to define essences—are only illusions, of use only to professional logicians (who teach their *art* to students). It is their job to *presume,* that is, to attribute a unique and stable identity to that which
has a thousand faces. But are they successful at it?

(B) I leave it to artists, and I do not know if they will
achieve it in a matter so complex, minute, and accidental,
to arrange into bands this infinite diversity of aspects, to
check our inconsistency and set it down in order. Not only
do I find it hard to link our actions with one another, but
each one separately I find hard to designate properly by
some principal characteristic, so two-sided and motley do
they seem in different lights.
(C) What is remarked as rare in Perseus, king of Mac-
edonia, that his mind, sticking to no one condition, kept
wandering through every type of life and portraying such
a flighty and erratic character that neither he nor anyone
else knew what kind of a man he was, seems to me to fit
nearly everybody.[58]

This is not a philosophy of evolution or "pure duration." It would be
a mistake to see it as a sort of pre-Bergsonism. Montaigne is setting
forth the idea of a spontaneity which, from moment to moment, re-

gains its nascent state and improvises its actions without ever building on the basis of previous accomplishment. Nothing is conserved (except, with age, certain "forms" that have become habits). The moment we are living now is not the consequence of the preceding moment. We can say of each instant that it is an absolute *beginning*, that it causes us to be reborn both for ourselves and to the world. But it is a beginning without a future. When Montaigne complains about his lack of memory, he is only emphasizing the perpetual *forgetting* that is the counterpart of innovative spontaneity. Every new action gives rise to a new self, upon which no past weighs (except the past to which the book will already have given shape), and which will disappear without a trace if not closely observed.

Thus the mere passage of time does nothing to resolve the problem of identity. If the succession of instants is incapable of constituting a body, the isolated instant is still less so. It is confused, shapeless, and hopelessly feeble, at best no more limpid than a dream. That is why Montaigne is so willing to characterize his thought as a *reverie*, a *dream*, or a *fantasy*. The metaphor evokes an intermediate state between wakefulness and sleep, between the suspect activity of the senses and the impossible activity of reason.

Reverie, once accepted, thus serves as a synthesis or a compromise—a third possibility—that follows the two previous stages: the rejection of seductive illusions and the discovery that a philosophy of pure vision is impossible.

In the mask/reality system of metaphors, as well as in the antonyms appearance/essence, artifice/nature, we have repeatedly encountered a "dialectical" pattern in which the third term of the dialectic involved a return to the first term, now better understood and more fully accepted: Montaigne reconciles himself to the fact that this world is inevitably a world of appearances, and that aesthetic form, and hence artifice and disguise, cannot be avoided in the pursuit of personal identity. In making use of the opposition between sleep and wakefulness—a commonplace, and easily interchangeable with the mask/reality antithesis—Montaigne discovers that sleep and wakefulness are more fluid, more easily combined, than mask and reality. Sleep and wakefulness can be mixed: the result is *reverie*. By contrast, mask and reality are sharply divided, as the true and the false, the "natural" and the "addition." It is harder to say what the middle term between them might be: the mask that sticks to one's face, perhaps, or the discipline that becomes "second nature." The mask/reality opposition is harder to "depolarize." It forces us to make a clear-cut distinction between the open and the hidden, the surface and the depths. Montaigne loves—in writing—the battle of opposites, the energies that are joyfully released in the clash of antagonistic words. There he finds the stimulant that carries him forward and obliges him to reopen all the debates. Nevertheless, he feels the need to come to some conclusion, if only a temporary one, if only a mixture (*mixtion*) that combines contraries without abolishing them. Duality lends itself to exclusion as well as inclusion: witness the following passage, where *reverie* is the resolution of the conflict between wakefulness and dreaming:

> (B) Those who have compared our life to a dream were perhaps more right than they thought. When we dream, our soul lives, acts, exercises all her faculties, neither more nor less than when she is awake; but if more loosely and obscurely, still surely not so much so that the difference is as between night and bright daylight; rather as between night and shade. There she sleeps, here she slumbers: more and less. It is always darkness, and Cimmerian darkness.
>
> (C) Sleeping we are awake, and waking asleep. I do not see so clearly in sleep; but my wakefulness I never find put and cloudless enough. Moreover sleep in its depth sometimes puts dreams to sleep. But our wakefulness is never so awake as to purge and properly dissipate reveries, which are the dreams of the waking, and worse than dreams.[59]

Where the antithesis of mask and reality *divided* the world, the image of the dream gives sensuous experience a sort of *unity* and uniformity that expresses the confusion from which none of our conscious states can deliver us. Here, mixture and interpenetration are realized in a grammatical chiasmus: "Sleeping we are awake, and waking asleep." The unity of time is measured out in an infinity of dissimilar instants, each as opaque and ill-defined as the next. The only limit to the dispersion and diversity of life's moments is that all belong in one way or another to a single dream and a single dreamer and, later on, to a single book, a compendium of its author's "imaginations."

Another comparison—which brings into our lives the sonorous diversity of the cosmos, the great diapason of the music of the spheres—also allows for the possibility of *mixture*, the reconciliation and felicitous fusion of opposites:

> (B) Our life is composed, like the harmony of the world, of contrary things, also of different tones, sweet and harsh, sharp and flat, soft and loud. If a musician liked only one

kind, what would he have to say? He must know how to use them together and blend them. And so must we do with good and evil, which are consubstantial with our life. Our existence is impossible without this mixture, and one element is no less necessary for it than the other.[60]

I mentioned the word "synthesis"; Montaigne, in celebrating mixture, rediscovered the Aristotelian ethic of the middle term, the precise center, but conceived of it harmonically, as a musical *composition*. *Synthesis* and *composition:* the same word in two different languages.

THREE

«The relation to others»

The desire for independence

It is very pitiful and hazardous to be dependent on another. . . . I have conceived a mortal hatred of being obliged either to another or by another than myself. I employ every power to the utmost to do without, before I employ the kindness of another, however slight or weighty the occasion.[1]

Montaigne constantly proclaims his desire for independence and his hatred of obligation—that is to say, of obligation beyond "the ordinary and natural obligations."[2]

Montaigne develops these arguments to justify the travels that took him as far as Rome. Civil unrest had reduced him to a state of dependence upon his neighbors' benevolence: "As things stand, I live more than half by others' favor, which is a harsh obligation."[3] In this situation he cannot escape the feeling of being in debt—and what is worse, in debt for his own safekeeping:

(B) Now I hold that we should live by right and authority, not by (C) reward or (B) favor. How many gallant men have chosen rather to lose their lives than to owe them!

(B) I avoid subjecting myself to any sort of obligation, but especially any that binds me by a debt of honor. I find nothing so expensive as that which is given me and for which my will remains mortgaged by the claim of gratitude, and I more willingly accept services that are for sale. Rightly so, I think: for the latter I give only money, for the others I give myself. . . . (B) Oh, how much I am obliged to God that it was his pleasure that I should receive all I have directly from his grace, and that he has kept all my indebtedness for himself privately! (C) How earnestly I beseech his holy mercy that I may never owe thanks for essential things to anyone![5]

God, invoked by Montaigne with such circumspection, is here thanked for having preserved him from falling into the debt of others. (Rousseau would later be inspired by this argument when, with greater effrontery, he professed his own ingratitude: favors serve to subjugate those who accept them.) The gift of the self is reserved for the unique friend. Every other "commitment" of our will is a capital danger.

The traveler who has escaped from domestic dependency and the "favors" of his neighbors encounters along the way other aspects of the risk of dependency. He cannot evade the looks of others, for example, when he spends his money. And he admits that he is not insensible to their consideration: "If [my expenditure] makes a show and is useful, I let myself go injudiciously; and I tighten up just as injudiciously if it does not shine and does not please me."[6] But this confession is the occasion of a far more general reflection, in which Montaigne denounces the "relation to others" (*relation à autrui*) as an injury we inflict upon ourselves:

> (B) Whatever it is, whether art or nature, that imprints in us this disposition to live with *reference to others* [*par la relation à autrui*], it does us much more harm than good. We defraud ourselves of our own advantages to make appearances conform with public opinion. We do not care so much what we are in ourselves and in reality as what we are in the public mind. Even the joys of the mind, and wisdom, appear fruitless to us, if they are enjoyed by ourselves alone, if they do not shine forth to the sight and approbation of others.[7]

We desert our being; we allow ourselves to be robbed. Who is responsible? *Public opinion* and *the public mind*, to be sure. But the responsibility is ours to the extent that we willingly submit to these judgments. What the more general cause of our behavior is remains unstated: Montaigne leaves unanswered the question whether it is "art" or "nature" that inspires such behavior in us. (Notice, by the way, that in regard to the theft of our being by the gaze of others, Montaigne here sets forth in the traditional language of moral censure a judgment that Sartre would repeat in his phenomenological description of the *pour autrui*, or "for others"—a description that Sartre promptly turned back into a moral lesson when he couched his philosophy in the form of a play [*No Exit*]: "Hell is other people.")

Montaigne does not fail to elaborate the precepts of a "for itself" diametrically opposed to the evils of the "relation to others." It is enough to know oneself to know one's vices and virtues. In "Of repentance" (3:2) Montaigne does not hesitate (as he did earlier between "art and nature") to ascribe to *art* the part of ourselves accessi-

ble to the gaze of others, *art* being the deliberate work that we inter-
pose between ourselves and the outside world:

> (B) There is no one but yourself who knows whether you
> are cowardly and cruel, or loyal and devout. Others do not
> see you, they guess at you by uncertain conjectures; they
> see *not so much your nature as your art*. Therefore do not
> cling to their judgment; cling to your own.[8]

These others, who do not see us, nevertheless take it upon themselves to look at us and to promulgate their "judgments." We must
seek refuge in our intimate knowledge of ourselves. Note, however,
that the vices (*cowardly and cruel*) and virtues (*loyal and devout*) of
which we are the sole witnesses define attitudes toward others: they
are character traits affecting our social behavior. What is rejected,
then, is our subjection to the judgment of others, and not the system
of ethical values that governs and characterizes our conduct toward
them.

Independence breaks the bonds of obligation and opens up a gap.
How is this gap experienced? One way, of which there is no dearth of
examples, is to leave the world—to die to the world—and live in
silent loyalty to oneself. But what if one remains among men? Even
more, what if one accepts public office? Independence can then easily
take on the aspect of scornful superiority. A person bent on preserving his precious inner truth, his untainted virtue, cannot avoid exas-
perating the "common" run of men. His indifference to public
opinion makes him stand out, whether he wished to or not, and can
earn him the hostility of those from whom he shows himself to be so
different. Is he willing to accept these risks and, if the community
casts him out, to confront death? Here again, examples of such disdainful consistency are not lacking. But what if a person wants to
escape this fate? The answer is to maintain the integrity of one's relation to oneself while setting between oneself and others the ap-
perances required by circumstance: externally one projects an untrue
image, not so much to dupe others as to protect oneself.

> (C) He who walks in the crowd must step aside, keep his
> elbows in, step back or advance, even leave the straight
> way, according to what he encounters. He must live not so
> much according to himself as according to others, not ac-
> cording to what he proposes to himself but according to
> what others propose to him, according to the time, accord-
> ing to the men, according to the business.[9]

If necessity obliges him, he will turn against others the mechanism of prestige that had initially worked to his detriment. The desire for autonomy, reinforced by the counsels of prudence, fixes the conditions under which, at court and confronted with hidden enemies, one may wear a mask without dishonor or at least separate "inner" feelings from "outer" conduct by making the latter conform to a *common model* that will disclose nothing untoward to any ill-disposed observer. If the world is too foolish to accept our wisdom, let the respect that we show to vulgar laws and customs be entirely external. In a period of unrest it is no disadvantage to pass unperceived, indeed to pass even for someone else. Montaigne thus formulated the rules of what the Italians would in the next century call "honest dissimulation": "The wise man should withdraw his soul within, out of the crowd, and keep it in freedom and power to judge things freely; but as for externals he should wholly follow the accepted fashions and forms. Society in general can do without our thoughts."[10] The precepts of independence can lead to a superficial conformism, closer to complacency than to a deliberate act. Still, this is a lesson in duplicity. Montaigne is here subscribing to an opinion expressed many times before: men are so made that it is necessary to deceive them for their own good—an aristocratic or "Machiavellian" conviction that authorizes the courtier, the magistrate, or the legislator to use deceit when the end justifies the means:

> (B) Not the thing but the appearance pays them. If they hear no noise, it seems to them that we are asleep. . . . I could easily check a disturbance without being disturbed, and punish a disorder without losing my temper. Do I need anger and inflammation? I borrow it and wear it as a mask. . . .
>
> (A) Since men, because of their inadequacy, cannot be suficiently paid with good money, let false be employed too. This means has been practiced by all lawgivers.[11]

This is an acknowledgment that, even if one has abandoned the public realm oneself, it is still important to take account of the ineluctable presence of public opinion in human affairs. The responsible man, once put on his guard against seductive appearances, will use those appearances in an expert manner in order to preserve the social order and public peace. Concern for opinion cost us a large share of our true reserves; the judgment of others caught us in the trap of consideration, and we allowed ourselves to be exploited and manipulated. Now it is the turn of others: we will lead them without their knowing it in a direction dictated by wisdom and concern for public stability (at a time when "everything is in collapse"). At first sight this does no harm and causes no change in the inner truth that we are thereby protecting: we do not expose ourselves, for a dummy acts in our place.

But if we simply conceal our "true" feelings, we overcome our dependence upon public esteem only by duping the public. We alter the equilibrium of our relationship to the world by turning the tables to the detriment of others. We aggravate the evil of the social bond, we exacerbate the malady, while securing for ourselves a sort of immunity. The infection will not harm us, but the price of the surgery that cuts away everything not strictly *our own* is to subject others to the illusions from which we have freed ourselves. We believe that, by breaking away and completely isolating ourselves, we are curing ourselves of an illness caused by a distorted relationship to others. From our remote refuge we doubtless do a better job of running the world's affairs, but we are no longer in the world, "among the living."

Hence the following question immediately arises: can such a break be sustained indefinitely? Does it result in true deliverance? Won't it turn out ultimately to be intolerable? Let us look in particular at whether or not Montaigne is able to maintain his position. And let us look first at what becomes of the "inner" life of the self after the break with the world. Once the polemical duality between the inner and the outer, *mine* and *theirs*, is abolished, can the ego establish itself upon a simple and massive truth? Recall the advice not to "cling to their judgment; cling to your own."[12] Now, in order to pronounce this "judgment" that will be my own, and in order that I may cling to it, I must, paradoxically, perpetuate within myself the division that earlier separated the internal from the external, "mine" from "theirs." The dualistic schema, maintained by the persistent structures of syntax (which distinguish between the subject and the object on either side of the verb of action, even when the action in question is reflexive), perpetuates the gap between the judicatory consciousness and its object, in this case my being. Expressions such as "to preoccupy oneself" and "to converse with oneself" project inward one's relationship to other people. The massive intimacy that Montaigne wished to recreate within himself and the plenitude that he hoped to substitute for the dispersion of the outside world cannot be established. There is, in a manner of speaking, too much "inner space" to prevent plurality and otherness from insinuating themselves. As soon as Montaigne attempts to regain control of himself by an act of judgment, he is forced to establish a distance that makes him a stranger to himself, or to endure the effects of such a distance. Remember the "chimeras and fantastic monsters" that burst in upon his retirement and solitude.

Something in him becomes a *fact* for a gaze that is not a fact but a pure and free demand. The act by which he perceives himself causes him to exist as a thing analogous to all the things that make up the external world. He eventually comes to judge himself, deliberately, as he would "a neighbor or a tree."[13] Objectification of his inner feelings causes them to cease to be truly "inner." The outer world carries over into the inner.

So it is also with changeability and instability, which at first seemed the exclusive vices of the outside world. The rhetoric of mutability has by definition neither end nor limit. If an individual attempts to break free of the world, does he cease to be part of it and subject to its laws? The more he attempts to regain his self-possession, the more composite and contradictory his own nature will seem to him, subject as it is to changes that are constantly carrying him away and preventing him from ever finding repose. We cannot remain true to our beginnings, for we inevitably drift a long way from wherever we start. What if inner being were subject only to changes in nature itself? Then even its diversity would always be natural. But everything is spoiled by the introduction of a source of discontinuity and heterogeneity: for wasn't the natural law that propels and governs us perverted once we became aware of the possibility of artifice? And when I turn my affection upon myself, eager as I may be to possess the truth about myself, isn't artifice incorporated into each of my acts and each of my perceptions? Hasn't appearance—that cause of all great change—insinuated its evil effects between me and myself? Even worse, hasn't it cast its spell over me as both subject and object? In the end, the very process of change, or what Montaigne calls the "passage," is unrepresentable. The *topos* of perpetual change prevents any realization of the moral *topos* of self-appropriation. Montaigne tries to "assent to nature," to allow himself to be "gently" carried along, to give nature free sway: "My plan in speaking is to display extreme carelessness and unstudied and unpremeditated gestures."[14] No doubt this was intended as a warning against all the possible affectations of language, but to speak at all subjects us to the common conventions of intelligibility. "Natural speaking," no matter how faithful it may be to its inner source, has to have some outlet and must therefore submit to external criteria, to learned rules. In the end, consciousness, unable to free itself entirely from social obligations, discovers that it is artificial and cunning in its very depths (which leads to the question whether man does not define himself precisely by his aptitude for putting nature's impetus to use in the creation of a *work*). Man's habits become his nature; as he discovers and describes himself, he is forced to recognize that this second nature cannot help *intervening* between the "fortuitous" data of immediate experience and the act whereby consciousness attempts to "represent" what it feels. To speak is always a social act. Montaigne refrains, moreover, from contradicting the traditional view that man is naturally sociable: "There is nothing to which nature seems to have inclined us more than to society."[15] Thus the evil of appearances, an evil that we are bound to endure because of the necessity of "living with reference to others," is an inescapable part of our natural condition. To oppose art and nature is naïvely to misunderstand the evidence: that man's aptitude for artifice is part of his nature, or at any rate derives from it. Man is by nature a being with the power to denature what he naturally is. The man who wishes to "cling to his own judgment" is in no less danger than the man involved in "relations with others." Pride, vanity, and desire insinuate their flattery and their lies. Otherness finds ample opportunity without the assistance of others. Montaigne, in defining presumption, provided Pascal and the moralists of Port-Royal with the arguments of their critique: "It is an unreasoning affection, by which we cherish ourselves, which represents us to ourselves as other than we are."[16]

Reestablishing relations

At the end of the "Apology," as we have seen, Montaigne leaves man at the center of an unknowable universe, confronting an inaccessible divinity about which nothing at all can be asserted. Nevertheless, he was not overcome by despair. Having proved that appearances cut us off from access to being, skepticism granted new legitimacy to those appearances: while they may not reveal the essence of objects, appearances are nonetheless delightful and rich. Since appearances prevent us from making contact with a higher ontological order, we must learn to accommodate ourselves to them, to attend to them earnestly and intelligently. Nothing better is available: we must "ignorantly and negligently let ourselves be guided by the general law of the world."[17] Man can never escape from phenomena but he can taste the pleasure in them. The phenomenal world, even though it falls short of certain truth, opens up an infinite field for our sensuous experience and perceptual pleasures. Vertigo and lassitude may lie in wait for the consciousness that would attempt to follow the rhythm of perpetually changing images; but the sameness of those images, their equal ontological shortcomings, and the equal probability of all opinions provide a paradoxical reason for keeping our peace and leaving our fellows in peace.

The same can be said about the truth of the self. Stable and permanent being cannot be grasped; it eludes every attempts. It is like nonbeing. We have seen that neither the *nascent* nor the *dying* state can be counted upon. The man who fails to accommodate himself either to his reflection in the consciousness of others or to the fiction that is constantly being invented in his own consciousness gains nothing in return. Consciousness then has to reconsider its refusals: it has found no secure shelter and has not improved its chances by withdrawing from the "outer" world. On the contrary, it has witnessed the invasion and paradoxical hollowing out of its subjective core by the external world, which creates an analogue of itself within the mind, an inner world marked by distances and depths, subject to change, affected by the universal "movement." By rejecting the "relation to others" a person succeeds only in transferring otherness within himself, so that one can frequent oneself only as one would relate to others. And we are forced to acknowledge that *opinion* dogs us as our own shadow.

Must we be suspicious of other minds? Yes, but only to the extent that we cannot locate in others a necessary and tentative point of reference, a tenuous yet useful guide for our own thinking. Thus from the beginning of his work as a writer, Montaigne relies on the stabilizing power of external judgment. This external intervention contributes to the definition of a *form:* the presence of a witness incites us to set to work, to begin our effort of construction. The notion of form, which Montaigne still uses in the traditional scholastic sense ("each man bears the entire *form* of man's estate"[18]), can be applied, with equal pertinence, to what Nature creates when it produces an individual and to the result of an "operative" *act,* governed by the will of the individual himself.

Here it is important to note, once again, Montaigne's hesitation to choose between two philosophies of form. Was a "form of our own" imparted to us from without, once and for all, by Nature or God? In that case, any action deriving from our culpable liberty, any action incited by our "relation to others," will to say the least be suspected of betraying our primary form, of *"counter*feiting" and deforming us. Or are we, on the contrary, legitimately entitled to participate in the constitution of our form? Are we allowed to "perfect" ourselves? In that case, it is by giving form to a work in the external world that we gain the opportunity to give form to ourselves. This calls to mind a well-known passage: "I have no more made my book than my book has made me—a book consubstantial with its author, concerned with my own self, an integral part of my life." To which Montaigne adds: "Not concerned with some third-hand, extraneous purpose, like all other books."[19] In saying this, he is merely denying that the book has any practical purpose, any utilitarian intention—and thereby declaring that he is a "gentleman," contemptuous of engaging in any common activity. He is not in any way denying the judgment of others, which can be of crucial *assistance* in describing oneself. The lines just cited are immediately preceded by the following:

> (C) In modeling this figure upon myself, I have had to fashion and compose myself so often to bring myself out, that the model itself has to some extent grown firm and taken shape. *Painting myself for others*, I have painted my inward self with colors clearer than my original ones.[20]

Admittedly, the consideration of others here leads to a heightening of the image. The painter *exaggerates*. Is there betrayal? In one sense, yes, if the "original" colors are held to be the only true ones. But if the model changes, if he comes to resemble the clearer portrait he has made, then he will match his image, he will "incorporate" the colors of the portrait, he will have "painted his inward self." He will not have lied.

If, moreover, the presence of a witness at times leads to exaggeration, there are other circumstances in which the interlocutor intervenes to repress and beat down the verbal excess that Montaigne allows to get the better of him:

> (B) I myself, who am singularly scrupulous about lying and who scarcely concern myself with giving credence and authority to what I say, perceive nevertheless that when I am excited over a matter I have in hand, (C) either *by another man's resistance* or by the intrinsic heat of the narration, (B) I magnify and inflate my subject by voice, movements, vigor, and power of words, and further by extension and amplification, not without prejudice to the simple truth. But I do so, however, on this condition, that *for the first man who catches me up* and asks me for the naked and unvarnished truth, I promptly abandon my straining and give it to him without exaggeration, without overemphasis or padding. (C) A lively and noisy way of speaking, such as mine ordinarily is, is apt to be carried away into hyperbole.[21]

The danger of lying and hyperbole is inseparable from the spiritedness of the voice, even in a man of good faith. Enthusiasm is not carried to the point of giddiness, however. "Exaggeration" has its limits, and return to the "naked and unvarnished truth" is possible. What is significant here is that the distorting enthusiasm is first stimulated by external "resistance" and then checked and limited, also from outside. Naked truth is recovered by way of dialogue and the objections of the interlocutor: *the first man who catches me up*. Montaigne immediately recovers the truth he was in danger of losing when he abandoned himself to the intoxicating effects of his "lively and noisy way of speaking." The deviation is due to the "relation to others," without which there would have been no *lively way of speaking*. But so is the return to veracity. The relationship to others first compromises and then reestablishes truth. It is up to us to *regulate* our relationships.

In fact, nothing guarantees that we can actually achieve communication with others; nothing assures that we will find words adequate to the purpose. Nevertheless, Montaigne feels protected by his natural aversion to lying. Having discovered that his self-image depends on others, he finds that veracity is a vital need. (Anyone who would absolutely sever relations with the "outside world" would be obliged to relinquish his own image and thus to accept silence and death.) If I cannot conceive of my own existence or individual form except through my relations with others, then lying is not merely a matter of culpable disloyalty to my neighbor; it is an ontological catastrophe for myself: I lose my true self, because it is impossible for me to preserve its form intact within my own mind, and because, deprived of all outside relations, my mind is nothing but uncertainty. To lie to others is to deceive myself, to make a fool of myself in order to avoid being made a fool by others. Deceit cannot guarantee the loyalty we owe ourselves. Truth is necessarily all of a piece. In the world of *phenomena* (in which the "Apology for Raymond Sebond" tells us our destiny is played out) man is cut off from any relation with external essences: we are left with only our temporal relation to the world and living beings. We are no longer bound to establish a stable relationship with transcendence (God is unknowable), but it is our duty to establish equitable relations in the immanent world. An individual's ties are exclusively to perishable beings and things; he has no contact with any eternal cause or truth. There exists, however, a form of *evidence* that is revealed to us in the sensible universe and in the course of our daily existence: truth is sustained through our fragile relationships with others, other living beings whose condition is as precarious as our own. Sincerity, though unstable as a form of relationship to another person, is especially indispensable to us, since without it we would be reduced finally to nothing: we cannot depend on either transcendence or intimacy, for both lie beyond our grasp. We would be lost between the inaccessible remoteness of God and the inconsistency of our own inner life. Our only chance to *be* is in the society of our fellows, i,e., in the world of common appearance. That is why truthful speech is the mortar of both public life and private identity:

> (A) Since mutual understanding is brought about solely by way of words, he who breaks his word betrays human society. It is the only instrument by means of which our wills and thoughts communicate, it is the interpreter of our soul. If it fails us, we have no more hold on each other, no more knowledge of each other. If it deceives us, it breaks up all our relations and dissolves all the bonds of our society.[22]

That men may cease to have knowledge of each other is of no small consequence for an author *hungry* to *make himself known* and who has *a mortal fear of being taken to be other than I am by those who come to know my name.*[23] Why this fear? Why a "mortal" fear? Because for Montaigne, if there is no one to oppose him, no one to whom he can show himself, then he loses his grip on himself. Of course he can change the distance between himself and others: if he distances himself as much as he possibly can, then he can feel independent. He will feel that he has rediscovered himself, and in fact he will have freed himself from the world's bustle and distraction. But as soon as he undertakes to know himself and, in order to know himself better, to describe himself, then others again come into the picture, albeit in an obscure and surreptitious manner. By ourselves we are capable only of sketching our outlines. As soon as a form is required (even an imaginary form), a witness becomes indispensable. To know oneself and to be known are inextricably associated. The failure of one would be the ruin of the other. "Those who have a false opinion of themselves can feed on false approbations; not I, who see myself and search myself to my very entrails, who know well what belongs to me. I am pleased to be less praised, provided I am better known."[24] Dissimulation toward others leads inevitably to a false opinion of oneself. Hiding from others robs us of our self image: "A man must see his vice and study it to tell about it. Those who hide it from others ordinarily hide it from themselves. And they do not consider it covered up enough if they themselves see it; they withdraw and disguise it from their own conscience."[25] We see nothing about ourselves except what we tell to others, and we tell nothing except to enhance our image in the other person's eyes. At this point appearance is no longer an enemy power: it is no longer an illusory reflection in the eyes of others, by means of which our true substance escapes and is dispersed; on the contrary, it is an outside agent that helps us to solidify our being, that causes it to "take" in the sense that a plaster "takes" when it hardens: "I feel this unexpected profit from the publication of my behavior, that to some extent it serves me as a rule. Sometimes there comes to me a feeling that I should not betray the story of my life. This public declaration obliges me to keep on my path, and not to give the lie to the picture of my qualities."[26] Thus we see Montaigne, opposed as he is to obligation, and tempted as he is by the desire to rave, to equivocate, to escape, nevertheless bound to live up to the portrait he has painted. Once his variability has been set down on paper, it becomes a rule to live by. Admittedly, this fidelity to the portrait that he has begun (and that he will never finish) is not alleged to be a constant concern: if Montaigne is to be believed, it is a consideration whose force he feels only intermittently, *at times*. And since he has taken the precaution of depicting himself as subject to change at times and at other times confirmed in his habits, it will not cost him too much to live up to the representation he has given of his "customs," which he frequently avers to be of a "uniformity and simplicity." The ethics of loyalty, which obliges us to keep our word, implies both concern for others and desire to protect the *form* of our individuality. How could it be otherwise, when to keep one's word is to maintain over a period of time the "content" of one's discourse with respect to a particular individual. Now, the content of Montaigne's discourse is Michel de Montaigne. The moral choice is here fundamental: Montaigne refuses to betray, he refuses to deny the image he has created, which bears not only the mark of a completed present but also an implicit promise. When it is a question of keeping to *his own* path, he accepts the obligation.

Yet this is the same man who wrote: "It seems that to be known is to have one's life and duration somehow in the keeping of others. As for me, I hold that I exist only in myself; and as for that other life of mine that lies in the knowledge of my friends, considering it naked and simply in itself, I know very well that I feel no fruit or employment from it except by the vanity of a fanciful opinion."[27] Is it possible that Montaigne simply could not choose between the thesis and the antithesis, between the affirmation of independence and the avowal of obligation, between the rejection and the need of others? It is a simple fact that he does waver, that neither attitude absolutely wins out over the other, and that this wavering can be interpreted not as a conflict between two logically incompatible positions but as the result of experiencing first one and then the other of two exigencies, each of which implies the other. Montaigne first asserts his right to freedom; he wants to "disalienate" himself. To that end, he is obliged to denounce the "commitments" with which he had "encumbered" himself and to break the many bonds—of custom, opinion, established authority, etc.—that held his consciousness captive before reflection began. But in the course of his efforts to regain possession of himself, to define himself, to identify his "true nature," Montaigne, at his most candid, accepts new bonds, appealing to alien minds which now assume the role of interlocutors, readers, the public. This brings him to recognize the relative legitimacy of his original dependence—man is inconceivable outside civil society—so that he can now do justice to those "artificial bonds," those "customs," that he had initially cast off as bonds of servitude. Now he can freely go back to them, borrowing what suits him: the vigorous inflections of colloquial language originate in this region. The break with the world, the withdrawal into individual existence, can only be an intermediary phase between two styles of "relating to others": the first, a consequence of one's social roots and customary attachments, is experienced in an almost unconscious manner, connected with the specious need for prestige, and directly determined by the surrounding environment; the second, much more far-reaching, implies that one is fully in possession of oneself and virtually open to the universal, which is acknowledged and accepted with full clarity of mind. Thus one's relations to others run the gamut from blind dependence to self-mastery. The example of Socrates is pivotal: it portrays a man who, by throwing off local obligations and asserting his individuality as a free and reasonable human being, actually enhances his ability to submit to the bonds of the universal and accept the verdict of his city's magistrates. Recall these famous lines:

> (A) We are all huddled and concentrated in ourselves, and our vision is reduced to the length of our nose. Socrates was asked where he was from. He replied not "Athens," but "The world." He, whose imagination was fuller and more extensive, embraced the universe as his city, and distributed his knowledge, his company, and his affections to all mankind, unlike us who look only at what is underfoot.[28]

The lesson of Montaigne's travels is of the same order and is the object of an admirable meditation in "Of vanity" (3:9). Starting out on a journey sets us free, temporarily severing our ties to home and family; but this break makes us more fit to enter into an association of a human, general, and universal kind. We gain in the exchange by substituting a bond of solidarity for a bond of necessity, a broader for a narrower community. A few lines later Montaigne argues both for and against our attachments, depending on whether they are universal or particular. Similarly, he uses the word *common* and its derivatives (*communicate, communication, community*) first in a pejorative, then in a laudatory manner. What he is prepared to reject is immediate and unreasoning community, the "community of climate and blood" that is imposed upon us without our consent. On the other hand, nothing is more legitimate than a relationship approved by reason and based on conscience (rather than blood), whose extension to all of humanity nothing prevents. Such a bond is no longer a fetter but a guarantee of liberty.

Montaigne writes: "(B) Nature has put us into the world free and *unfettered;* we imprison ourselves in certain narrow districts."[29] At the moment of departure we leave our prison and recover our original freedom: freedom we know we share in common with all men, as our birthright; hence our liberation immediately brings us membership in a broader society. A natural right and a universal moral philosophy can then be stated: "(B) I consider all men my compatriots, and embrace a Pole as I do a Frenchman, *setting this national bond after the universal and common one.*"[30] The benefits of travel do not end there. Having led Montaigne from the particular to the general, his trip then allows him to return to the particular and to see it in a new light. Separation is preparation for a return, which a certain lapse of time makes desirable: to return to one's native country and familiar territory, to one's family home, after registering one's preference for the wider world, is not to subject oneself to the same immediate bondage as before. The traveler who returns from abroad with renewed zest for his homeland can no longer look at his private estate in the same way as before: he discovers in his home a new aspect, a fresh value, revealed to him by the distance he has traveled. He is more fully aware that he is dealing with the particular and can love it as such. If the effect of knowledge of the universal is to relativize the instinctive love that we formerly felt for our neighbors, still knowledge does not abolish that love but gives it a fuller justification. The desire that calls us back from far off places to the security of home is no longer the unreasoning and sullen attachment that once kept us aloof from the wider world. The familiar place to which we return is no longer the prison that once confined us. With the perspective afforded by travel

Montaigne is able to see how he might achieve a fully harmonious existence at home, where at first, tired of his early commitments, he saw only hindrance. In a striking passage he even goes so far as to see the *interruption* as a source of plenitude, as if estrangement must precede true presence:

> (B) And every man feels by experience that seeing one another continually cannot match the pleasure of parting and being together again at intervals. (C) *These interruptions fill me* with a fresh love for my family and give me back a sweeter enjoyment of my home. Alternation warms my appetite now for the one choice, now for the other.[31]

In a striking oxymoron, the hindrance takes on a positive value: as soon as it ceases to hamper our freedom, the obstacle does us the signal service of *defining* our being by delineating a space subject to our will and by denying us access to an area so vast that it would soon exhaust our strength. Man "must ask you for *hindrance and resistance, as an alms; his being and his welfare are in indigence.*"[32] Our greatest treasure lies in assenting to our finite condition, in confronting the obstacle. Montaigne returns to his point of departure, where he had once felt constricted and devoid of true community; but now he discovers there the possibility of realizing his true "being."

Such is the pulse of Montaigne's thought. The passion for remote places is first approved, then condemned. Now it is foolishness to shut yourself up, now it is madness to set out for uncertain frontiers. After declaring that our mind "is defective only when it reaches out,"[33] Montaigne writes a fine eulogy of reaching out and defines the life of the mind as a hunt in wide open spaces:

> (C)A spirited mind never stops within itself; it is always aspiring and going beyond its strength; it has impulses beyond its powers of achievement. If it does not advance and press forward and stand at bay and clash, it is only half alive. (B) Its pursuits are boundless and without form; its food is (C) wonder, the chase, (B) ambiguity.[34]

In a single essay, "Of three kinds of associations" (3:3), Montaigne first declares himself to be ill suited to human contact and then describes himself as a consciousness destined by nature to communicate. "I have a dreamy way of *withdrawing* into myself,"[35] he asserts, only to add a short while later that "there are private, *retiring,* and inward natures. My essential pattern is *suited to communication* and revelation. I am all in the open and in full view, born for company and friendship. . . ."[36] No pleasure has any savor for me without com-

103

munication. Not even a merry thought comes to my mind without my being vexed at having produced it alone without anyone to offer it to."[37] These declarations do not so much contradict as complement and condition one another. The apparent contradiction is explained by the relations between the mind and the space that is open to it: that space is wide open for the person who meditates in solitude, but for the person who mingles with the crowd the only free space is within:

> (B) Solitude of place, to tell the truth, rather makes me stretch and expand outward; I throw myself into affairs of state and into the world more readily when I am alone. At the Louvre and in the crowd I withdraw and contract into my skin; the crowd drives me back to myself, and I never entertain myself so madly, licentiously, and privately as in places full of respect and ceremonious prudence.[38]

Montaigne's thought is determined in a negative sense by its relation to the environment: *distraction* (in the strongest sense of the word) is his rule. "Our thoughts are always elsewhere."[39] Is it surprising, then, that the interplay of opposites should give rise to expansion in solitude and to inner monologue in the midst of the crowd?

This explains Montaigne's alternating interest in and indifference to public life. In his political activities Montaigne claimed to be incapable of fully devoting himself to pressing tasks: he shuns them on principle, he "tempers his will,"[40] he protects himself by establishing a "zone of indifference" between "the world of affairs" and his own life. But once settled down with himself, again withdrawn into tranquil privacy, Montaigne quickly discovers the historical and moral meaning of his abstention and idleness. Faced with the misfortunes of the age, he finds his solitude hard to justify. He casts his mind upon "affairs of state" and accuses himself of being partly responsible (admittedly to a very limited degree) for France's miseries. The free life, the *otium cum litteris*, the dreams in the tower, and the scholarly researches whose program he had inscribed in the beams of the library—all of these things, now that he has savored them, awaken in him a feeling that he is guilty of desertion. Considering the corruption of the age, he feels some remorse:

> (B) Everyone goes about the duties of his office laxly. The corruption of the age is produced by the individual contribution of each one of us; some contribute treachery, others injustice, irreligion, tyranny, avarice, cruelty, in accor-

dance with their greater power; the weaker ones bring stupidity, vanity, idleness, and I am one of them.[41]

Here we see Montaigne more involved (but in the evils of the age)
than when he was taking an active part in public affairs. And whereas
some inner reserve held him in check when he mingled with the
crowd, the scruple inspired in him by his idleness corrects his inactivity and turns his thoughts back to the misfortunes of the age. The
lines just cited immediately follow a harsh judgment (from which
Montaigne does not exempt himself) as to the vanity of writing in an
age of corruption: "Scribbling seems to be a sort of symptom of an
unruly age."[42] Having sought refuge in his tower, the writer is seized
by bad conscience in regard to his country's desperate situation. But
in order to reach this stage of reflection, he had first to separate himself from that situation.

Montaigne returns to his country, his home, and his family after
becoming aware of the "universal bond." But this universal bond had
first served him as grounds for asserting his liberty, his independence, by severing his bonds to family and nation. The original dependence, immediate and unreasoned, was transcended; but in turn
the resulting estrangement was itself transcended, leading to a deliberate and self-possessed reconciliation with the old attachments. This
is the pattern of Montaigne's movement through three stages of relationship—a pattern that will repeat itself in other kinds of relationship. The first stage is dependence. The second is characterized
by the desire to regain possession of oneself and by the liberating
separation. In a third phase a full legitimacy is restored to the bond,
woven of concrete obligations and duties, that unites us to our surroundings. The particular is rediscovered in its relation to the universal.

Montaigne can therefore approve of our making subtle adjustments
in our relationships to accommodate the demands of the moment and
the qualities of our partners. Each set of circumstances will correspond to a particular type of relationship: it is up to us to evaluate the
consequences, the risks, and the rewards. In short, our relationships
must be delicately modulated, partly for the sake of their own beauty,
partly to protect our repose, and always with respect for the lives and
independence of others. There is "a certain respect, and a general
duty of humanity, that attaches us not only to animals, who have life
and feeling, but even to trees and plants. We owe justice to men, and
mercy and kindness to other creatures that may be capable of receiving it. There is some relationship between them and us, and some

mutual obligation."[43] Obligation, at first suspect, becomes the general
rule of all our relationships.

The rejection of books, borrowings, and appropriation

Reading, writing: Montaigne feels the attraction of great books, of
admirable works. He browses, he assures us, more than he reads.
That is enough to feel the power of the masters: Seneca and Plutarch.
He recognizes himself in them, but they are able to say what he
would like to say so much better than he can do himself. How can he
write without putting himself in their debt? Was he not similarly indebted to the advice and the example of Etienne de La Boétie? Above
all, compared with such predecessors, how can he help but feel his
own "inadequacy"?

> (A) Seeing myself so weak and puny, so heavy and slug-
> gish, in comparison with those men, I hold myself in pity
> and disdain. Still I am pleased at this, that my opinions
> have the honor of often coinciding with theirs, (C) and that
> at least I go the same way, though far behind them, saying
> "How true!" (A) Also that I have this, which not everyone
> has, that I know the vast difference between them and
> me.[44]

But even as he admits his inferiority, Montaigne falls back on one
advantage that no one can challenge: his independence. Possessing
neither knowledge nor memory, he draws what he has to say from
within, "without using any but my own natural resources." And
even when he feels that the ancients surpass him, he is determined to
let his "thoughts run on, weak and lowly as they are, as I have produced them, without plastering and sewing up the flaws that this
comparison has revealed to me."[45] What he wants to offer to his readers is his own "cogitations," his personal "humors and opinions."[46]
Admittedly, his opinions may concern events or other opinions reported by books. But Montaigne claims the right, and the capability,
to speak of them on his own, in his own name, and on his own responsibility—in which respect he differs from those who, "having
nothing of their own worth bringing out, . . . try to present themselves under false colors."[47] In order to realize this program of independence, to speak "absolutely all alone,"[48] it is necessary "to do
without the company and remembrance of books,"[49] in order to prevent the intrusion of other texts in one's personal work, to keep the
voices of others from mingling with that of Michel de Montaigne,
with the attendant danger that those other voices would cover up or

distort his own. The note "To the reader" makes this clear: there will be no embellishment, no "studied posture" in the *Essays*. The author is not far from exposing himself to us, immodestly, naïvely, in his full nakedness.

Now, as part of his claimed independence, Montaigne grants himself the right to scrutinize whatever comes within his reach: his personal life and consciousness in the first instance, but also the wisdom and folly of the world, memorable actions and judgments, laws, customs, and abuses drawn from all over. Why should he not discuss odors (1:55), the post (2:22), or thumbs (2:26)? All things bear signs and serve to communicate. In order to affirm the singularity of the self, its "humors and opinions," is it not indispensable to contrast these with the infinite variety that is not the self—that the self neither can be nor wants to be? Thus it is necessary to engage in dialogue with books, if only because they provide *material* for our judgment in the examples and opinions they contain.

Thus independence is imperiled by what it needed to develop in the first place. Even though Montaigne continues to dismiss or reject examples and opinions one after another, these still provide him with his theme: his judgment will focus on a controversial *topic*, drawn from or at least based on tradition. An opinion cannot be fairly set forth unless its supporters are allowed to have their say: they must be cited, the evidence must be "adduced," before proceeding to criticism or to citing adverse judgments. Thus the texts of others, used as evidence, insinuate themselves into Montaigne's "own" text, which he intends as a response. Still, there is a clear dividing line between Montaigne's judgments and the opinions he opposes. But there is a still greater danger, Montaigne notices, owing to the "coincidence" between his own ideas and those expressed earlier—and more vigorously—by certain ancient poets and philosophers. How can he resist citing writers such as these, who offer such welcome "support?" Several options are available. First of all, he can give prominence to the cited material (and even the action of citing itself) by quoting in the original language and placing the quotation prominently on the page. The quotation then takes on the value of an embellishment, a gloss, an emblem:[50] the reader who understands Latin will encounter not only judgments that forcefully reiterate or complement Montaigne's arguments but also poetic fragments which as a general rule bring nuggets of metaphor or allegory to a discourse already rich in metaphor. The reader can hardly fail to notice that these "flowers" have been deliberately gathered and arranged. Montaigne can also support his argument with French translations as well as quotations from the original. And translation can shade into paraphrase. Mentioning the author's name helps to "authorize" the opinion, but if Montaigne wants to unify his thought he can omit the name, even if he doesn't feel capable of "providing on his own" a style as vigorous as that of his Latin or Greek predecessor. When this happens, the text is no longer a citation but a "borrowing" or "theft" (*larrecin*). Another person speaks in Montaigne's stead; with his permission, of course, but still it is the other author who dictates what Montaigne is to say.

How can Montaigne justify the invasion of his text by the words of others after so vehemently declaring his independence? He comes up with more than one explanation. For the autonomy of his work is at stake (at least in part), and he acknowledges having sacrificed this autonomy in the past. Some of the early essays, he admits, "smell a bit foreign."[51] This is a disavowal of "foreign" authors and as such a way of taking back the initiative that elsewhere has been ceded to them. If the text of the essays is borrowed, the metatext, which indicts the borrowing, restores Montaigne to the position of sovereign judge: the very act of borrowing, described for its own sake, becomes a novel feature of the self-portrait. In describing that act, Montaigne speaks as no one before him ever did: "I have an aping and imitative nature."[52] By adopting this strategy, Montaigne recoups all that he had given up. He ceases to be dependent upon Seneca and Plutarch the moment he turns his penetrating powers of reflection upon the subject of his dependence. He regains the upper hand in the very moment that he informs the reader of the feelings of inferiority that led him to pillage the works of certain ancient writers:

> (B) But it is harder for me to do without Plutarch. He is so universal and so full that on all occasions, and however eccentric the subject you have taken up, he makes his way into your work and offers you a liberal hand, inexhaustible in riches and embellishments. It vexes me that I am so greatly exposed to pillage by those who frequent him. (C) I cannot be with him even a little without taking out a drumstick or a wing.[53]

The more freely dependency is avowed, the more fully the new *author* comes into the world via critical reflection, beyond those "subjects" on which his views happened to coincide with those of others and which he sometimes treats with their aid. Submission to others thus helps to establish a reflective relationship with oneself.

Then, too, it is not only the authority of admired books and authors that explains the use Montaigne makes of them within his own book:

the "relation to others" also plays a role of a different kind. Montaigne has followed fashion; he has loaded himself with "borrowed ornaments . . . more and more heavily every day beyond my intention and my original form, following the fancy of the age and the *exhortation of others*."[54] The borrowing of alien material was itself suggested by alien intervention—a double dose of "alienation." But once such admissions have been made, the most precious personal confidences are recorded and thereby saved. The elimination of the "plumes" and "flowers" with which he has bedecked himself does not frighten Montaigne:

> (C) I will love anyone that can unplume me, I mean by clearness of judgment and by the sole distinction of the force and beauty of the remarks. For I who, for lack of memory, fall short at every turn in picking them out by knowledge of their origin, can very well realize, by measuring my capacity, that my soil is not at all capable of producing certain too rich flowers that I find sown there, and that all the fruits of my own growing could not match them.[55]

Montaigne is not content with this strategy, which assures him, *in extremis*, of a new independence by way of dependence openly avowed and reflectively overcome. For we also find him making a series of arguments to justify the coexistence in the *Essays* of what is his with what is alien. In this way he regains possession of himself not *a posteriori*, on the basis of retrospective observation, but rather by insisting upon the *primary* novelty of his project, or by justifying his borrowing, his "marquetry," as a procedure perfectly compatible with personal *invention*. These justifications are of various kinds, and their diversity shows clearly the importance that Montaigne attaches to the thesis he is trying to defend: the compatibility of borrowing with a genuinely autonomous discourse, the possibility that a personal view can coexist with an outside view without damage. As we shall see, some of these arguments cut both ways.

One of the justificatory images that Montaigne uses (and that he borrows, incidentally, from an ancient tradition) is that of assimilation. The alert reader retains and makes his own nourishment that can help to invigorate him. His reading serves him not merely as ornament or decoration but as an integral part of a wisdom that grows deeper and deeper; Montaigne puts this in a prescriptive form in the 1580 text, "The Education of Children," where he discusses the conduct expected of a young disciple:

(A) If he embraces Xenophon's and Plato's opinions by his own reasoning, they will no longer be theirs, they will be his. . . . He must imbibe their ways of thinking, not learn their precepts. And let him boldly forget, if he wants, where he got them, but let him know how to *make them his own*. Truth and reason are common to everyone, and no more belong to the man who first spoke them than to the man who says them later. . . . The bees plunder the flowers here and there, but afterward they make of them honey, which is all theirs; it is no longer thyme or marjoram. Even so with the pieces borrowed from others; he will transform and blend them to make a work that is all his own, to wit, his judgment. His education, work, and study aim only at forming this.[56]

The labor of appropriation is the work of the "discourse," which "transforms" what comes from without. Although the individual possesses the rational faculty from the first, borrowing still begins at the *beginning*, even if judgment is not *formed* until the assimilative *transformation* is complete. Montaigne here sets forth one of the major theses of the humanist tradition, for which all language is necessarily borrowed language, and all form (as well as all style) is necessarily appropriated from elsewhere.

Consistently, Montaigne makes use of comparisons inspired by the ideas of borrowing and pillage (as in "the bees plunder"). Appropriation may lend an air of legitimacy to borrowing, but the fact remains that it is tantamount to theft. Hence assimilation must be go hand in hand with *dissimulation*, to conceal the alien source of what has been assimilated. In a curious passage, this dissimulation is compared to an expenditure—i.e., to an economic transaction:

(C) Let him hide all the help he has had, and show only what he has made of it. The pillagers, the borrowers, parade their buildings, their purchases, not what they get from others. You do not see the gratuities of a member of a Parlement, you see the alliances he has gained and honors for his children. No one makes public his receipts; everyone makes public his acquisitions.[57]

Is education (and, *a fortiori*, literary production) therefore comparable to fraudulent gain? The comparison with pillagers and borrowers may seem troubling. But it is really just an image that emphasizes the difference between what is *taken* and what is subsequently *displayed*. And Montaigne immediately reassures us by adding: "The gain from our study is to have become better and wiser by it."[58]

In fact, Montaigne often inserts alien texts in his own without indicating their source. He "hides" his borrowings. (We have already encountered one instance of this, in the passage from Plutarch introduced at the end of the "Apology for Raymond Sebond".) He admits this practice, moreover, but in general terms and without indicating where he has hidden his "thefts." If we are to take him at his word, this is both a defensive maneuver and a way to enjoy the wicked pleasure of seeing imprudent critics insult Seneca or Plutarch in attacking Michel de Montaigne:

> (C) In the reasonings and inventions that I transplant into my soil and confound with my own, I have sometimes deliberately not indicated the author, in order to hold in check the temerity of those hasty condemnations that are tossed at all sorts of writings, notably recent writings of men still living, and in the vulgar tongue, which invites everyone to talk about them and seems to convict the conception and design of being likewise vulgar. I want them to give Plutarch a fillip on my nose and get burned insulting Seneca in me. I have to hide my weakness under these great authorities.[59]

One possible objection to this strategy is that, rather than protect Montaigne, it actually *exposes* the great authors whose works he transcribes without acknowledgment. But their authority is held to be so secure that any attack would discredit the critic foolhardy enough to make it. Montaigne therefore warns his detractors: he has laid traps for them. What they are criticizing might well be an idea or argument sanctioned by much higher *authority* than they imagine. Thinking that they were correcting a young author, they might actually be taking on someone stronger than themselves.

"To hide one's thefts": in the chapter "On some verses of Virgil" (3:5) Montaigne will again use the same terms, but in speaking of the strategy of love and the representation of love in poetry: "Both the action and the picture of it should smack of theft."[60] A few lines earlier, Montaigne states that the purpose of hiding something is to stimulate desire, to call attention to it by a *withheld* exhibition or a demonstrative withholding:

> (B) An Egyptian made a wise answer to the man who asked him: "What are you carrying there hidden under your cloak?" "It is hidden under my cloak so that you won't know what it is." But there are certain other things that people hide only to show them.[61]

The use of the same metaphorical vocabulary is here the sign of an eroticization of the theft (or borrowing) and of the ambivalent behavior of sometimes hiding, sometimes showing it.

Not only does Montaigne not hesitate to show his borrowings, but he considers that his judgment intervenes in an active way in *choosing* what to borrow and that the reader can therefore appreciate it:

> (C) Let people see in what I borrow whether I have known how to choose what would enhance my theme. For I make others say what I cannot say so well, now through the weakness of my language, now through the weakness of my understanding. I do not count my borrowings, I weigh them. And if I had wanted to have them valued by their number, I should have loaded myself with twice as many.[62]

The admission of weakness (by comparison with the strength of the "ancients") is coupled with the mention of a quality that Montaigne calls to the reader's attention: his *weighing*, or judgment of the appropriateness of what he borrows. This, as Montaigne frequently reiterates, is not given to everyone. Hence one can show one's worth in this way. To find the citation most *appropriate* to what one wishes to say is in a way to regain ownership of the text that one is writing with the help of others. In the first version of the passage just cited, Montaigne says that this is a way of holding on to the initiative in *invention*, while selecting the most effective support for one's style: "Let people see in what I borrow whether I have known how to choose what would enhance or fundamentally assist *invention*, which always comes from me."

But it is not merely the *choice* of citation that serves as a mark of appropriation. A further stage in the reconquest of alien material is achieved when the borrowing is not merely opportunely chosen but also modified by the borrower so that it says something other than what it said in its original context. *Manipulating* his citations gives Montaigne a sense of mastery that compensates in part for the "weakness" that made the citations necessary in the first place:

> (C) Among so many borrowings of mine I am very glad to be able to hide one now and then, disguising and *altering* it for a new service. At the risk of letting it be said that I do so through failure to understand its original use, I give it some particular application *with my own hand*, so that it may be less purely someone else's.[63]

This procedure goes beyond assimilation: it involves varying the alien theme, by setting one's own *hand* to it and giving it a personal "twist." While others "put their thefts on parade and into account," Montaigne tries to put the stamp of his own authority on the authors he cites, once again reserving to himself the prerogative of invention: "(C) We naturalists judge that the honor of *invention* is greatly and incomparably preferable to the honor of quotation."[64]

Is borrowing the primary act? Or does it come later, to fill in a gap in the argument? In various places Montaigne affirms the truth first of one, then of the other of these two propositions. They are contradictory, to be sure. But both envision some form of compromise between one's own activity and the insertion of alien material. A mixture is formed, in which both personal dynamics and the borrowed texts have their part to play.

When an antecedent presence is attributed to the borrowed material, Montaigne is motivated by the desire to emulate. He does not hesistate to match the greatness of his models, if only by fits and starts:

> (C) Still, I well know how audaciously I always attempt to *match the level of my pilferings, to keep pace* with them, not without a rash hope that I may deceive the eyes of the judges who try to discover them. But this is as much by virtue of my use of them as by virtue of my inventiveness or my power. And then, I do not wrestle with those old champions wholesale and body against body; I do so by snatches, by little light attacks. I don't go at them stubbornly; I only feel them out; and I don't go nearly as much as I think about going.[65]

The relationship to the cited author becomes one of struggle and rivalry. And even though Montaigne admits to some hesitation, and depreciates (as he does in the lines just cited) his personal powers of "invention," the energy that he puts forth is considerable. He recognizes his inferiority but does not resign himself to it. The metaphor of "body against body" (close combat in which he refuses to engage), like that of the race, establishes a combative but fairly close relationship between the adversaries/partners.

By contrast, Montaigne attributes the initiative to himself. Everything that he has written, he tells us, draws upon his own resources: the authors cited serve merely to consolidate a thought that was formed previously, in a spontaneous and independent manner:

(A) This capacity for sifting truth, whatever it may amount to in me, and this free will not to enslave my belief easily, I owe principally to myself. For the firmest and most general ideas I have are those which, in a manner of speaking, were *born with me*. They are natural and *all mine*. I produced them crude and simple, with a conception bold and strong, but a little confused and imperfect. Since then I have *established and fortified them by the authority of others* and the sound arguments of the ancients, with whom I found my judgment in agreement. These men *have given me a firmer grip on my ideas and a more complete enjoyment and possession of them.*[66]

In this passage, pride of place is undeniably attributed to the native (and naïve) "production." The authority of the ancients comes in only at a later stage, in order to secure for Montaigne a firmer "grip" on his own "imaginings." These ideas are thus the mediators in the process by which Montaigne regains his self-possession. The help that he receives is in interpreting his own thoughts, in learning to enjoy more fully a boon that originates in his own mind. In this instance *other people* enable Montaigne to "fortify" his self-sufficiency.

The perspective is the same in the essay "Of giving the lie" (2:18). Montaigne affirms that the writing of his book preceded the study of ancient authors: the "form" of the work owes to no one but himself. His borrowing and his study were certainly a help, a fortification, but by then his thought had already been elaborated; the essential part of the job had already been done:

(C) I have not studied one bit to make a book; but I have studied a bit because I had made it, if it is studying a bit to skim over and pinch, by his head or his feet, now one author, now another; not at all to form my opinions, but certainly to assist, second, and serve those which I formed long ago.[67]

The borrowed material thus plays an ornamental, superfluous role. It is an optional addition. In the end it matters little how much is "mine" and how much "others." Although "someone might say of me that I have here only made a bunch of other people's flowers," at least, Montaigne says, "I have furnished . . . the thread to tie them together,"[68] and he has seen to it that these "borrowed ornaments" accompany his work without covering or hiding it. In this way his book may, over the course of several editions, become weighted down by additional material (about which Montaigne neglects to say whether it comes from other people or is of his own making):

(C) My book is always one. Except that at each new edition, so the buyer may not come off completely empty-
handed, I allow myself to add, since it is only an ill-fitted
patchwork, some *extra* ornament. These are only *over-
weights*, which do not condemn the original form, but give
some special value to each of the subsequent ones, by a bit
of ambitious subtlety.[69]

Additions composed by Montaigne himself (in the form of an inserted
"anecdote") as well as citations or borrowings from others are both
included in the metaphor of an "extra ornament." The additions are
immediately absorbed into a book that seems capable of absorbing
anything. Whether the text grows by addition of "ornaments" or by
inclusion of new "personal" material, it is always a single, growing
organism, even though "some transposition of chronology" may slip
in.

Whether embellishment of an autonomous discourse or support for
an author too feeble to express his own ideas properly, the borrowed
material invariably fits together with the independent parts of the
text. The independent text flows into the rest, at times mixing with it
so indiscriminately as to compromise its independence, at times only
to branch off with increased force at some later stage in the argument.
Montaigne takes the opportunity to measure his own resources, the
value of which he assesses differently depending on his mood. He
offers the reader a picture of his own experience of reading, though
without any intention to show off his memory or learning. At the
very moment when he might claim admiration for what he has re-
tained of his familiarity with the "learned Muses," he declares himself to be ignorant, forgetful, and certain that in saying so he is
revealing an authentic feature of his "being" (whereas a pedant, by
showing off his learning, might attract attention to his name—so
much idle wind—while hiding behind the ornament culled from his
sources).

After aspiring to independence of expression and being forced to
recognize his actual dependence, Montaigne manages to make the
one coexist with the other, while using both to talk about himself.
Independence thwarted and dependence overcome both serve the
ego, despite the inevitable interpolation of other people and their
words. In responding to the demand of the reading public, with its
taste for superfluous ornament, Montaigne is obliged to scatter about
citations *for the sake* of other people. He is also obliged to write *by
means* of others, when a text written by someone else (an ancient author, for example) expresses Montaigne's thoughts better than he

115

himself is able to do. But for Montaigne to employ immortal texts amounts to forgetting about himself, whereas for him, as a mortal individual, to state the limited truth about his circumscribed existence restores his own presence and with it the chance to endure. He therefore strikes a compromise between thought that invents itself, that imposes its "allure," and words that his pen copies from other sources. When, for example, Montaigne speaks of his borrowings, the metaphors that he uses are largely traditional in origin, but the use he makes of them, the way he collects and mixes them together, gives him sovereign power over material subject to a preexisting code. Among the types of metaphors he uses are the following: agrarian (seeding, transplanting); artistic (enameling, marquetry, ornamentation); digestive (assimilation, imbibing, transforming into honey, etc.); economic (borrowing, plundering, buying); vestimentary (in the form of a contrast between the *body* and the gown, the armor, the official garb); conjugal (he contrasts "boarding" knowledge with "wedding" it); and visual metaphors of ostentation (to be "on display" or "on parade"). The list could be extended still further. The point, however, is to notice how Montaigne uses these different metaphorical registers either to acknowledge his debts or to declare himself free of them, as well as the way in which he is able, unlike so many scholarly writers, to conduct the chorus of other people's voices and make them resound as *he* wishes.

The "mine/alien" antithesis takes on a singular importance when we remember what Montaigne has to say about his own linguistic apprenticeship. Latin was his "mother tongue."[70] His father, convinced that ignorance of ancient languages "was the only reason we could not match the greatness [of the Greeks and Romans] in soul and in knowledge," sent him, "after the first loosening of [his] tongue," to study with three teachers who "spoke to [him] in no other language than Latin."[71] This was indeed a curious "mother tongue" that Montaigne learned in obedience to his father's wishes, not from his mother's lips but from a German Latinist assisted by two others "less learned" than himself. If we can take Montaigne at his word, it was Latin grammar that shaped his acquisition of language and the Latin tongue that first introduced him to the symbolic order. Acts and objects received their first names in Latin: the world acquired meaning by means of a language of whose foreignness the child was completely unaware:

> (A) It was an inviolable rule that neither my father himself, nor my mother, nor any valet or housemaid, should speak

anything in my presence but such Latin words as each had learned in order to jabber with me. It is wonderful how everyone profited from this. My father and mother learned enough Latin in this way to understand it, and acquired sufficient skill to use it when necessary, as did also the servants who were most attached to my service. Altogether, we Latinized ourselves so much that it overflowed all the way to our villages on every side, where there still remain several Latin names for artisans and tools that have taken root by usage. As for me, I was over six before I understood any more French or Perigordian than Arabic. And without artificial means, without a book, without grammar or precept, without the whip and without tears, I had learned a Latin quite as pure as what my schoolmaster knew, for I could not have contaminated or altered it. If as a test they wanted to give me a theme in the school fashion, where they give it to others in French, they had to give it to me in bad Latin, to turn it into good.[72]

These famous (and controversial) lines tell us that the language in which the future "ornaments" of the *Essays* would be couched actually had priority in Montaigne's life: Latin was the idiom in which his child's tongue first loosened—thanks to a costly artifice that enabled him to acquire the language "without artificial means" (*sans art*). To master this language was to gratify his father's desire and to furnish proof of the productivity of an investment that sacrificed sumptuary considerations to pedagogical and moral ones (a relatively unusual priority for members of the nobility). But this *instruction*, apparently so omnipotent, was opposed (according to Montaigne) by a rebel *nature*, characterized by an almost physical inertia. If the success of the enterprise did not quite come up to his father's expectations, Montaigne explains that this was due, in the first place, to his "sluggish, lax, and drowsy" nature.[73] In addition, he blames the interruption of his private primary education and his father's decision to accede to the pressure of custom and to send his son, at the age of "about six," to the Collège de Guyenne. There, Latin soon ceased to be a spoken language for the child: "My Latin promptly degenerated, and since then, for lack of practice, I have lost all use of it."[74] But it was to remain a reading language, and indeed to preserve in the realm of reading the priority it had lost in that of oral expression:

(A) The *first* taste I had for books came to me from my pleasure in the fables of the *Metamorphoses* of Ovid. For at about seven or eight years of age I would steal away from

any other pleasure to read them, inasmuch as this language was my mother tongue, and it was the easiest book I
knew and the best suited by its content to my tender age.[75]

The first book, Ovid's, with its playful ease and varied subject matter,
enabled Montaigne to recover the "passive" use of a language whose
"active" practice he had lost. One component of his pleasure no
doubt had to do with the fact that Ovid's "easy" Latin brought back
to its young reader the earlier years in which he had taken possession
of the language and its forms. As he reads Ovid's tale Montaigne is
led back to what he calls "my own language," knowing that, even if it
is his "mother tongue," he owes it to the solicitude of his father, for
Latin was a substitute for the vulgar tongue that he would have
learned had his mother been his sole guardian.

What is more, in the choice of books that exerted their fascination
upon Montaigne's imagination, another substitution occurred, exactly
analogous to the first [i.e., to the substitution of Latin for the vulgar
tongue—Trans.]: ancient pagan mythology replaced the native Ro-
manesque adventure stories (Huon of *Bordeaux!*) that would normally
have furnished the memory of a young Frenchman with legendary
material rather less alien to his region and religion. But Latin humanism obliterated the last vestiges of knightly legend. (The education in
the *collèges* tended to produce the same result, moreover.)

> (A) For as regards the Lancelots of the Lake, (B) the
> Amadises, (A) the Huons of Bordeaux, and such books of
> rubbish on which children waste their time, I did not know
> even their names, and I still do not know their substance,
> so strict was my discipline.[76]

Nothing here, except for the private means and the precocity of the
experience, is unusual in a humanist education, based largely on ancient fables to which superior educational virtues were ascribed. With
Montaigne the substitution was more complete and more successful
than with most; but the only difference between his education and
the normal school program was that the latter took a relatively gradual approach. Montaigne's early pleasure in study was thus already a
kind of "theft." But he merely stole texts whose pleasures were not
forbidden but only abetted by a conniving tutor, he was able to strike
a compromise between the (apparent) prohibition and the (actual)
permission to read what he wanted. The placement of a simulated
obstacle that was in fact easily overcome actually increased Montaigne's pleasure (as Montaigne admits would often be the case later
on with the pleasure of love):

(A) At that point, I happened by remarkable good fortune to come in contact with a tutor who was an understanding man, who knew enough to connive cleverly at this frivolity [*debausche*] of mine and others like it. For by this means I went right through Virgil's *Aeneid*, and then Terence, and then Plautus, and some Italian comedies, always lured on by the pleasantness of the subject. If he had been foolish enough to break this habit, I think I should have got nothing out of school but a hatred of books, as do nearly all our noblemen. He went about it cleverly. Pretending to see nothing, he whetted my appetite [*faim*], letting me *gorge myself with these books only in secret*, and gently keeping me at my work on the regular studies.[77]

The pleasure is safe and retains the savor of forbidden fruit: the implied comparison with more physical gratifications (*debausche, faim*) attests to the libidinal nature of Montaigne's discoveries in the "mother tongue," a language developed and put to use in comic or epic tales. The object of desire thus partially coincides with a lost personal aptitude. An amusing opportunity to resurrect that lost aptitude does present itself, however, in the use of Latin in the theater. Montaigne is eager to tell us that he excelled in the roles given him in the plays staged by his *collège*:

(B) Shall I include in my account this faculty of my boyhood, assurance in expression and flexibility in voice and gesture, in adapting myself to the parts I undertook to act? For before the usual age,

> Scarce had my twelfth year snatched me
> from the year before,

—Virgil

I played the leading parts in the Latin tragedies of Buchanan, Guerente, and Muret, which were performed with dignity in our Collège de Guyenne.[78]

Here we can make out not only Montaigne's aptitude for playing stage heroes as well as his obvious pleasure in sham and the wearing of masks but also, even as he makes himself over into someone else, his happiness at finding himself *in his element*: abandoning himself and finding himself all at once. He plays a role and rediscovers his Latin. It then becomes clear how, at a later date, his retreat into "the bosom of the learned Muses" (consecrated by a *Latin* inscription) and his quest for his self could have coincided. It is also clear that, in citing Latin authors in their own language, Montaigne could have felt that even in using this alien material he was not abandoning a domain, a zone of intimate experience, that he may well have considered *his own*—though surely he knew full well how much this feeling owed to his father's capricious, if benevolent, interest. Montaigne's conviction is rooted in the very substance of the language when, earlier in the same essay, he declares: "I do not speak the minds of others except to speak my own mind better."[79] At almost the same time, however, he has the opportunity again to adopt an external stance, from which he is able to reassert his independence vis-à-vis what once had "lured" him; his denunciation is vigorous: "I have not had regular dealings with any solid book, except Plutarch and Seneca, from whom I draw like the Danaids, incessantly filling up and pouring out. *Some of this sticks to this paper; to myself, little or nothing.*"[80] Or again: "I go about cadging from books here and there the sayings that please me, not to keep them, for I have no storehouses, but to transport them into this one, in which, to tell the truth, *they are no more mine than in their original place.*"[81]

From appropriation to repudiation of the foreign material; from the priority of Latin (learned not by "artificial means" but by means of the perfect artifice) to its relegation to a secondary rank: Montaigne gains the independence he desires only at the cost of recognizing his obligatory dependence, of attending to the ancient idiom that presided over the "loosening" of his tongue, and of subjection to Seneca and Plutarch, whose hold over him he cannot easily "undo." He became free only by accepting the fact that he had not always been so and that his freedom remained imperfect. Is this, then, what it means to be master of one's own words? Surely it comes closer than anything else.

The economy of the relationship

We have now encountered three successive stages in the "relationship to others." For convenience, let me simplify matters by naming these: (1) unreasoned dependence; (2) autarchic refusal; (3) disciplined relationship. To avoid any misunderstanding, let me make clear that I do not, in naming these stages, mean to suggest that they necessarily correspond to distinct phases of Montaigne's life. The names refer to a logical, not a chronological, sequence. If we examined them more closely, we would find that this "dialectic" governs many aspects of Montaigne's experience. Here I shall call attention only to one noteworthy analogy: Montaigne's experiences involving monetary transactions with others follow the same pattern as his experiences having to do with his self-image. Indeed, when it comes to money, the three phases or stages stand out even more clearly and explicitly. In the following passage Montaigne himself identifies three periods of his life—a division far more instructive, in my view, than the one that various commentators have attempted to establish, purely hypothetically, between the Stoic, Skeptical, and Epicurean "phases" of Montaigne's thought:

> (B) I have lived in *three kinds of situation* since I came out of childhood. The first period, which lasted nearly twenty years, I spent with none but casual means and dependent on the authority and help of others, without rule or fixed revenue.[82]

At first everything comes—to this young nobleman whose family does not lack for resources—from others: it is by the grace of others—primarily his father—that he is able to maintain himself and satisfy his fancy. The fear of want must never have assailed him in this period. But he was not his own master: lacking exclusive control of the means necessary to his existence, he remained dependent on the will of another and his "spending," as he tells us, was "all at the hazard of fortune."[83]

The second stage was that of self-sufficiency as the head of his own household. After coming into lawful possession of his fortune, Montaigne made it his business to keep a close watch on its use. Suspicious of others, he maintained close control of his property in order to safeguard and increase what he possessed. In this realm he allows no alien gaze to intervene. He is in full possession of himself. Here, a lengthy citation is in order, for everything that Montaigne says is revealing:

> (B) My second situation was to have money. Having taken to this, I soon laid by considerable reserves, for my circumstances; thinking that a man owns only as much as he has beyond his ordinary expenses, and that he cannot rely on what as yet he merely hopes to receive, however clear his hope. For what, I would say, if I were surprised by such or such an accident? And in the wake of these vain and pernicious imaginings I would go and exercise my ingenuity to provide by this superfluous reserve for all emergencies; and still could reply to him who pointed out that the number of emergenices was too infinite, that if I could not provide for all, I could for some, and many. This did not go on without painful worry. (C) I made a secret of it; and I, who dare say so much about myself, spoke of my money only to lie, as do the others who, rich, make out to be poor, or poor, make out to be rich, and dispense their conscience

from ever testifying sincerely to what they have: a ridiculous and shameful prudence. (B) Was I going on a journey, I never thought I was sufficiently provided. And the bigger my load of money, the bigger my load of fear: now about the safety of the roads, now about the fidelity of those who had charge of my baggage, of which, like some others I know, I was never sure enough unless I had it before my eyes. Did I leave my strongbox at home, how many suspicious, how many thorny and, what is worse, incommunicable thoughts! My mind was always turned in that direction.[84]

Accumulation, concentration, vigilance: Montaigne speaks in much the same way (in the first period of the *Essays*) when he urges the wise man to gather his forces in order to "bind" them against outside encroachments and the fear of death. His concern with parsimony (let us not go so far as to call it avarice) parallels his efforts to depend on no one other than himself and to be in no one's debt: the same defenses are erected, and there is the same reliance on secrecy and even masks. But, paradoxically, the refusal to depend on others invites renewed assault from the outside world. Anticipation of ruin, like that of death, forces Montaigne's mind to abandon the stable present in which it would prefer to remain ensconced. Eager to dominate time, the mind is assailed by thoughts of the *time to dominate*. Worried about evading the onslaughts of others, it tries to remain aloof, but a suspicious mind spins fantasies of aggression out of its fears. Montaigne's *strongbox* represents security, leisure, comfortable retirement among his books, independent thought, and the work that will come into being if only his autonomy can be protected. But the need to safeguard the precious box forces the mind to dwell anxiously on the outside world: it must remain on its guard in order to ward off ambushes and escape injury. Rather than escape others, the mind falls victim to their anticipated malevolence; it remains constantly on alert for whatever plots might be hatched outside. The best course is to give up trying to carry such a heavy burden all alone and to spare oneself the high cost of achieving domination, the effects of which are the opposite of what one had hoped freedom would bring. Beginning with the journey to Italy, Montaigne accepts the need to "spend": he is prepared to rely on others, as well as on the favor of the moment. For he is now strong enough not to allow himself to be fettered. He has learned that solitary worry is a harder servitude than clear-sighted confidence. Risk is inevitable, and the confident man will more fully savor the fullness of the present moment and the temporary relationship, without asking of them more than they can give. Thus Montaigne is able to promise a form of independence that goes almost to the point of voluntary renunciation of his possessions. He has found the secret of communal autonomy, of a self-mastery that includes relations with others, not to say abandonment to them:

> (B) This way I fell into a third kind of life (I say what I feel about it) certainly much more pleasant and more regulated, which is that I make my expense run abreast with my receipts; now one is ahead, now the other, but they are never far apart. I live from day to day, and content myself with having enough to meet my present and ordinary needs; for the extraordinary, all the provision in the world could not suffice. . . .
> (B) If I amass money, it is only in the hope of using it soon; not to buy lands (C) that I have no use for, (B) but to buy pleasure. . . . (C) And I highly praise the fortune of an old prelate, whom I know to have given up so completely his purse, his revenue, and his expenses now to one chosen servant, now to another, that he has let many years flow by, ignorant as a stranger of his own household affairs. Confidence in the goodness of others is no slight testimony to one's own goodness and so God gladly favors it.[85]

Montaigne imagines a superior kind of autonomy, which satisfies the claims of others, because an individual's true interest lies not in watching greedily over his private advantage but rather in "buying pleasure." Montaigne is willing to spend a *portion* of his "provision": this is his calculated improvidence, which turns into intensity of feeling, pleasure in existence. The mind, now freed, returns to the realm of immediacy and heteronomy in the knowledge that an equitable relationship must be established between the inside and the outside, between the "self" and "others," between the integrity of a unique existence and acceptance of physical risk.

The "heaving of the stomach" and the "burning braziers"
In the most polished pages of the *Essays*, openness to the world goes hand in hand with attention to the self. Self-denial is not, as facile opinion would have it, the indispensable precondition of compassion. The unusual chapter entitled "Of coaches"[86] is particularly enlightening on this point: its composition has been a subject of controversy, but its progress—from the subject of Montaigne's own body to that of torture endured by others—is exemplary in its clarity.

Montaigne begins with a confidence concerning his susceptibility to motion sickness; in him, he assures us, this is not an effect of fear, even though the physicians hold that seasickness is due to fear. The self—a free, subjective agency—thus affirms itself in two ways: first, in the exercise of critical judgment with respect to a theory contradicted by personal experience, and second, through confidence in the kinesthetic experience of nausea and "the heaving of the stomach." (This kind of confession, involving bodily sensation, is rare in the prose of the time.) Montaigne's interest in antiquity and in American Indian civilizations then guides his thoughts, under the influence of identifiable readings, toward more remote places in space and time. How does this broadening of the horizon come to pass? The impetus comes from critical thinking: the critique of medical theory, initially limited to that one subject, is generalized to cover more serious deficiencies in our knowledge. Distance in space and time licenses Montaigne to exercise a more sweeping judgment. Broadening his vision provides the pretext for attempting a critique of knowledge in general: the sum total of all that is known is but an infinitesimal part of what is and has been and about which we know nothing. Montaigne then moves from this to a critique of culture: the "pomp and magnificence" of the ancients, particularly in games and circuses, surpassed our own; and the ostentation of the American Indians in many respects leaves nothing to envy in the splendors of antiquity. In these areas, the advantage belongs to others, not to us. Montaigne's criticism does not end here, however: he uses a discussion of the Roman emperors as the basis for a more general criticism of the prodigality of princes who draw upon the resources of their people to cut a brilliant figure through public gifts. And he is particularly critical of the brutality of America's conquerors. Only now does the critique take on an *ethical and political* dimension. Montaigne's very personal commitment thus stands out in contrast to the reality he is describing, which seems to lie at an opposite extreme from his own existence. Events about which he learns from their *relation* in books, from the testimony of the printed page, provoke in this attentive and vulnerable reader a passionate response: in turn he establishes a *relation* to those events of a quite different order, and one that is not limited to the exercise of a distant and neutral judgment. I cannot help thinking that it is Montaigne's initial attention to his own bodily discomfort that prepares and makes possible the lively sympathy he feels with the suffering endured by other men, inhabitants of a remote corner of the earth. Near the beginning of the essay, in speaking of the unpleasantness of "interrupted motion," he tells us that he is "accustomed to wrestle with the weaknesses that are in me and overcome them by myself."[87] His "bodily condition" has taught him, through experience, of discomfort, pain, and the difficulty of resistance. To suffer from stones is to become familiar with torture. How can Montaigne remain indifferent to the torments of the Indian princes whom the Spaniards "put to the torture":

> (B) This lord, finding himself overcome with the pain, surrounded with burning braziers, in the end turned his gaze piteously toward his master, as if to ask his pardon because he could hold out no longer. The king, fixing his eyes proudly and severely on him in reproach for his cowardice and pusillanimity, said to him only these words, in a stern, firm voice: "And I, am I in a bath? Am I more comfortable than you?" The other immediately after succumbed to the pain and died on the spot.[88]

Montaigne's humanist ethic here shows itself without even having to state its principles: the cruel anecdote has a demonstrative value. The example is not put forward simply as a proof of the soul's firmness. It invites us to imagine the suffering endured. And if the beginning of the essay had not shown us Montaigne himself so attentive to physical discomfort and so determined to combat it, the *relation* between Montaigne's personal experience of physical torment and his outrage at the torture endured by the Indians would not be so clear to us. It might even be argued—in praise of a morality of perseverance and endurance no longer as popular today as it once was—that the way in which Montaigne refused to allow himself to be overcome by nausea, and his desire to "tame" his inner weakness, lead directly to his understanding of the tortured king, and to his protest against the inhuman treatment inflicted upon the captured Indians. This is the bond that links the beginning of the essay to its conclusion. It is necessary to attach the greatest value to self-possession in order to feel indignant at the violence whose purpose is to dispossess a human being of his will. In the present instance, the ideal of self-mastery is developed and inverted into an imperative of respect for one's fellow man: the one is the externalized version of the other. Montaigne's individualism, while it satisfies the need for withdrawal into subjectivity, is more than just that: for Montaigne claims the same right for every man, without in any way turning his back (as he has often been accused of doing) on the social and political conditions likely to guarantee that right. Individualism is thus closely associated with a universalist postulate; knowing, through his own body, the weakness and precariousness of individual existence, Montaigne spontaneously takes the side of the weak when violence, injustice, or fanaticism threatens their thought, their customs, or their very lives (since tyrannical power cannot abide the scandal and the challenge of "dissidence," which the expression of individuality always represents). The ideology of which this minor noble of bourgeois extraction is the *exponent* is not so much that of a specific "class" (which class? the provincial nobility? the bourgeoisie?) as of the social *mobility* of which his family was an exemplary specimen. Montaigne's *mobilism* has to do with more than just his view of the world as a place of constant flux; it is connected also with his intuition of the inevitability of change—as the wheel of fortune turns—change in which the poor take the place of the rich, the vanquished of the vanquishers. Every human experience, the highest as well as the lowest, is potentially my own. With such a vision of the world and such an intuition, one can see the profound similarity that is the basis of the "universal bond" linking individuals of all nations and all conditions. A universe of vicissitude, inhabited by conscience, can become a universe of *reciprocity*. The "universal bond" can be safeguarded only by safeguarding each participant: for Montaigne, the ego claims such high privileges for itself only in order to make the point that no human being should be dispossessed. Montaigne too often describes the movement of falling (the fall from the heights of an overly ambitious mind, the fall from a horse, the fall inflicted by old age) for us not to perceive the sympathy concealed in the seemingly impassive story of the fall of the "last king of Peru." The essay ends with these words:

> Let us *fall back* to our coaches. . . . That last king of Peru, the day that he was taken, was thus carried on shafts of gold, seated in a chair of gold, in the midst of his army. As many of these carriers as they killed to make him fall—for they wanted to take him alive—so many others vied to take the place of the dead ones, so that they never could bring him down, however great a slaughter they made of those poeple, until a horseman seized him around the body and *pulled* him to the ground.

Desire and the wider world

As opposites, plentitude and lack are profoundly related. Montaigne has to enter into close relationships before he can either know himself or feel the need to be different; and he has to gain some distance before he can understand the meaning of intimacy. This is the law of desire: an ageless wisdom accuses man of desiring what is not within his power—his neighbor's wife, vanished health, the pleasures of the great. "Every strange woman seems to us an attractive woman."[89] Lack impels us to gaze into the distance, and conversely, distance makes us aware of our indigence. Glory and knowledge are desirable because they are absent, or absent because they are desired. Montaigne, as much as anyone else, felt the attraction of those things that beckon to us even as they elude our grasp. He repeated to himself the teachings of classical morality: what seems precious to us and makes us regret our poverty because it is inaccessible will dissappoint us as soon as we possess it; no sooner do we have it then we turn our attention to other absent things and open our ears to other sirens. There is no end to our thinking ourselves poor. But our penury is wholly imaginary, and it is our sick imaginations that bear primary responsibility for this evil. If we simply resist the seduction of the unreal we will rediscover our true, and inalienable, goods, which always lie within our reach. But Montaigne, in a paradox that goes the wisdom of the ages one better, is prepared to satisfy the folly of desire. He is willing to confess the destitution implicit in his lack. Let the sirens sing![90] Let the temptations of the imagination shimmer! He likes to *feel* his separation and his indigence, but without wishing to fill the void through possession. Space widens and deepens as desire unfolds. And Montaigne keeps his desire alive by leaving it indefinitely in suspense: satiety is not his aim. There is pleasure in knowing desire as desire—the "chase." Want of pleasure creates a realm of transparency in which the powers of intelligence and judgment enjoy free play. Desire demands presence but seeks it only in forbidden or "strange" objects. Carrying on the work of desire, the reflective consciousness maintains its separation from the object and draws pleasure from it. The mind that possesses nothing can view everything with an equal passion and detachment.

Desire, which makes us feel that, though our lives are lacking, nothing is to be done about it, populates the world with objects, none of which is indifferent to our gaze. Tempted, the mind, fleeing itself, seeks objects of every sort but at the same time seeks to regain control of itself, to make the judgments that will restore its autonomy. Desire, projected onto objects remote from us (but never remote enough), creates distance. But the meaning of that distance is subject to reinterpretation: the mind detaches itself from the objects of its desire, it withdraws into intimacy (though again, never far enough), and the distance between consciouness and its objects becomes the distance of detachment. For the mind knows objects only to the extent that it sees itself distinct from them as it retreats into inwardness (i.e., its essential difference from the world) in order to savor the forms and flavors of the alien. Our experience of space ends in vertigo at both extremes. Farthest from us is inaccessible Being, the supremely desirable Good (God, who, as the "Apology for Raymond Sebond" gives us to understand, is not our *peer*). Closest to us is the sensible world. And the absence of God will become the necessary correlative of our precarious and precious self-presence. Mind discovers that it is separate from God to such a degree that its only option is to accept the fullness of sensuous experience and of the "worldly" life: it must recognize this necessity as the expression of God's will, which has laid it down that man shall "be only what he is."[91] This is the fullness of human existence—a fullness without metaphysical guarantees but sustained by the truth of separation.

We can achieve intimacy and the good feeling of completeness, which are the rewards of wisdom, only by accepting distance and the weakness of our grasp. Separation is the secret road to presence, even though the appeal of far-off places is never-ending: we transport ourselves in spirit to places where we are not and should not be, and we concern ourselves only slightly with our present. This is called "gliding" or "sliding" over the surface of the world.[92] And it is good that it is so. Thus *to think elsewhere [penser ailleurs]* is—by turns or simultaneously—both a sign of impatience to abandon the self and a prerequisite of self-discovery. *Here*, the place of our imprisonment, becomes the field in which we flourish. Distance is ambiguous, immediacy no less so. I alienate myself through desire, but I have no identity unless I am willing to accept this alienation. My task is both to separate from and to reunite with myself. This alternation never ends, and Montaigne does not wish that it should end in some final reconciliation. If there is resignation in Montaigne, it is not because some definitive wisdom ultimately wins out: it is rather resignation to imperfection. I am always imperfectly *here* and imperfectly *elsewhere*. To wish to overcome imperfection would be futile, for imperfection is part of the very definition of life: life is "an action which by its very essence is imperfect and irregular; I apply myself to serving it in its own way."[93]

The complicity that Montaigne requires of his readers culminates in *felicitous* solidarity fostered by our awareness of common destitution. Deprived of all knowledge and of any privileged role in the universe, men are extremely limited yet somehow capable of a "meeting of the minds," of conferring and *conversing*. In this ability lies a new source of authority, and we should therefore be glad to give up the quest to grasp essences and causes that are destined to remain forever out of reach. The ego thus discovers its subjective and intersubjective dimension, ending a critical scrutiny that tended initially to discredit the human condition. To be nothing but a mind limited to the *relative* and hence to the network of its own *relationships* is to possess all that a mind linked to other minds can possess. By limiting myself I become aware that I am not—indeed, that I am forbidden to be—infinite, though the thought of infinity is one that I shall always have to bear.

> (C) My conscience is content with itself—not as the conscience of an angel or a horse, but as the conscience of a man; (B) always adding this refrain, not perfunctorily but in sincere and complete submission: that I speak as an ignorant inquirer.[94]

The nothingness of *ignorance* and the inexhaustible possibility inherent in *inquiry* are linked to one another in the *I speak.* If the mind were empty and devoid of knowledge, it could hardly be the unending puzzle that it is for us, nor could it be the agency that calls everything else into question. Therein lies its treasure, which makes the idea of the *world* a far richer one than it would otherwise be. The "Apology for Raymond Sebond" would be of scant interest if it were merely an attack on knowledge and on the infirmity of reason. But by reducing man to the little that he is and confining him within the boundaries of his finite individuality, Montaigne's text does not simply oppose man to the incomprehensible omnipotence of God; it also opposes him to the infinite richness of the world and of nature. Thus even as man is stripped to his naked consciousness, the boundaries of the finite universe of traditional cosmology are dissolved. The world becomes a limitless place, whose contents can never be inventoried. Space expands, living forms proliferate, and nature's fecundity is both revealed as a boundless spectacle and hidden from our gaze. The whole truth about the world is just what will never be revealed to us. Facing the world, man knows that he is a finite creature in a physical infinity. The knowledge he possesses is nothing, but the horizon of possibility that stretches before him is vaster than it has ever been before. Man is not comforted by seeing himself included and comprehended within the abundance of a nature he does not understand, nor by the hope that "he will rise . . . [by] letting himself be raised and uplifted by purely celestial means."[95] His comfort comes, rather, from feeling that, in the face of the immensity of the universe, his mind possesses one invaluable resource, its fragile yet invincible liberty. Able to see "only with his own eyes, and [to] seize only with his own grasp,"[96] man still has plenty of objects to look at and to lay hold of! For the free mind the infinity of the universe is matched by the infinities open to initiative: the inexhaustible possibility of regaining one's self-possession, of shaping the self, by following the road that opens up when we begin to speak: *"Who does not see that I have taken a road along which I shall go, without stopping and without effort, as long as there is ink and paper in the world?"*[97] This infinite road is not a solitary road, however: to write is "to speak to the paper," and Montaigne, as we saw earlier, speaks to his paper as he speaks "to the first man" he meets.[98] And he is perfectly familiar with the law that governs verbal communication, which in its sharpest formulation is as follows: "Speech belongs half to the speaker, half to the listener."[99]

A note on three-part structure

Montaigne loves triads. His book, which originally had just two parts, ended up with three, and it was published in three main editions.[100] Ternary organization is proclaimed in the titles of certain chapters: "Of three good women" (2:35), "Of three kinds of association" (3:3). And we find a similar structure in other chapters, despite titles that make no mention of it. Thus, "Of the most outstanding men" (2:36), which follows "Of three good women," is actually a carefully composed pendant to it: for this chapter too treats *three* illustrious figures, namely Homer, Alexander, and Epaminondas. The triadic arrangement is not used merely to group static examples: we see it at work in the movement of a dialectical argument, in accordance with the model inherited from the medieval *disputatio:* (1) *quod sic,* (2) *quod non,* (3) *sed contra.* Commentators have noticed such tripartite structures in various places, including the chapter "Of names" (1:46).[101] In more than one chapter the attentive reader will notice a three-part form beneath the apparent disorder of Montaigne's exuberant prose. I shall examine just a few examples,[102] to show how Montaigne frequently uses the ternary device to decide where he stands, what position he will take, in opposition to two contraries that he rejects,

After drawing a contrast between two attitudes that constitute a dilemma, Montaigne will quite often introduce a *third* possibility, to which he then subscribes. This is the procedure he uses in the survey of philosophy that occupies much of the "Apology for Raymond Sebond." Montaigne contrasts the affirmative, dogmatic philosophy, which believes itself to exercise sovereign power over knowledge, with the "nonknowledge" professed by the "Academics." But the latter still articulate their ignorance with too much assurance for Montaigne, who introduces a third possibility in the form of Pyrrhonism with its interrogative suspense:

> (A) Whoever seeks anything comes to this point: he says either that he has found it, or that it cannot be found, or that he is still in quest of it. All philosophy is divided *into these three types.* Its purpose is to seek out truth, knowledge, and certainty. The Peripatetics, Epicureans, Stoics, and others thought they had found it. These established the sciences that we have, and treated them as certain knowledge. Clitomachus, Carneades, and the Academics despaired of their quest, and judged that truth could not be conceived by our powers. The conclusion of these men was man's weakness and ignorance. This school had the greatest following and the noblest adherents.
>
> Pyrrho and other Skeptics or Epechists . . . say that they are still in search of the truth. These men judge that those who think they have found it are infinitely mistaken; and that there is also an overbold vanity in that second class that *assures* us that human powers are not capable of attaining it.[103]

The Pyrrhonists are those who allow themselves to be guided and "led without inquisitiveness in the order of the world."[104] This, Montaigne tells us, is the way that offers the greatest "verisimilitude and usefulness."[105]

Furthermore, in the architecture of the "Apology" as a whole, it is easy to recognize a tripartite structure, which corresponds to the stages of a gradually mounting polemic. First, Montaigne responds to the objections of faith against Sebond's rational method. Second, he attacks those who attack the scientific validity of the arguments put forward by the author of the *Natural Theology.* Here, he takes the opportunity to denounce the vanity of science in all its forms. Finally, these two replies are joined by a third, the "final fencer's trick,"[106] in which Montaigne develops to the full the consequences of Pyrrhonism—to the point of rejoining the arguments of faith that he initially opposed.[107] He Christianizes, *in extremis,* skeptical doubt: ultimately it is not "the order of the world" but God that man should allow to lead and guide, to "raise and uplift" him.[108] This is a solution that gives up any claim to rational mastery as well as any certainty of nonknowledge: Montaigne's middle ground is here as elsewhere a compromise between activity ("he will raise himself up") and passive docility with respect to external intervention—God's intervention—

that "by exception lends a hand" to man. The third and final part of this very lengthy chapter thus concludes with an image of *composite* motion: "He *will rise [s'élevera:* literally, he will raise himself—Trans.] by abandoning and renouncing his own means, and *letting himself be raised [se laissant hausser]* and uplifted by purely celestial means."[109]

In the previous chapter, "Of cruelty" (2:11), Montaigne found it to his purpose to classify three types of virtue according to merit and beauty. The highest type presupposes a habituation to virtue that has "passed into . . . nature" so thoroughly that the soul experiences no inner strife; reason's mastery is so complete that no inner sedition can arise.[110] The next highest type does involve inner conflict and the tensing [*roidissement*] of battle: this is militant virtue, which "can shine only by clashing with opposing appetites."[111] The lowest form of virtue stems from incapacity to do wrong:

> (A) Now I do not think there is any doubt that it is finer to prevent the birth of temptations by a lofty and divine resolution, and to have so formed oneself to virtue that the very seeds of the vices are rooted out, than to prevent their progress by main force, and, having let oneself be surprised by the first commotions of the passions, to arm and tense oneself to stop their course and conquer them; and that this *second* action still is finer than to be simply provided with a nature easy and affable and having an inborn distaste for debauchery and vice. For it certainly seems that *this third and last type* makes a man innocent, but not virtuous; exempt from doing ill, but not apt enough to do good. Besides, this condition is so close to imperfection and weakness that I do not very well know how to separate their confines and distinguish them.[112]

Montaigne, in defining his own position, recognizes that he cannot place himself in either the first or the second category: he is incapable of the "resolution" that would attest to the "divine" superiority of his soul over every vicious emotion; nor does he possess the haughty "ease" or sovereign "cheerfulness" of Cato or Socrates. Neither is he well suited to wage battle against the tumult of temptations; he could not withstand the stress of combat. Only the third kind of virtue remains open to him, namely, the feeble merit of a "good natural disposition":[113]

> (A) I am so far from having arrived at that first and most perfect degree of excellence where virtue becomes a habit, that even of the second degree I have hardly given any proof. I have not put myself to great effort to curb the de-

sires by which I have found myself pressed. My virtue is a virtue, or I should say an innocence, that is accidental and fortuitous. If I had been born with a more unruly disposition, I fear it would have gone pitifully with me. For I have not experienced much firmness in my soul to withstand passions, if they are even the least bit vehement. I do not know how to foster quarrels and conflict within me.[114]

The key term that Montaigne chooses is *innocence:* a word marked by the prefix of negation, which means simply inaptitude for evil. Compared with those entitled to claim the title of virtue, Montaigne differs (or so he claims) by having an entirely passive disposition, a consequence of chance and accident. This is the result of the interaction between Montaigne's "complexion," that is, the more or less stable mixture of his humors, and Fortune (evoked in the passage cited above by the word "fortuitous"), that source of variability and unpredictability which, along with Nature, governs the world. In order to "hold most vices in horror,"[115] he has only to accept the most varied influences, e.g., "domestic examples" and the "good education of his childhood," as they come to him:

> (A) What good I *have* in me I have, on the contrary, by the *chance of my birth.* I have gotten it neither from law, nor from precept, nor from any other apprenticeship. (B) The innocence that is in me is a childish innocence: little vigor and no art.[116]

Without strength and devoid of that "art" which La Boétie had hoped to inculcate, Montaigne can boast only of the inborn moderation of his passions. For this he is indebted only to his birth.

Is this to say that he himself plays no part? To be sure, from the way in which he uses the concept, it is clear that *birth* is not without ambiguity. It is, on the one hand, a contingent fact, determined by the accident of procreation, while on the other hand it is what best defines an individual's *natural* constitution, the source of a necessity stronger than anything that learning and study can add. To invoke birth is to have recourse to a third possibility, between what one might derive from others and what autarchic presumption would owe only to oneself.[117]

A fundamental opposition remains, however. The first two categories are characterized by the *possession* of an outstanding quality: the habit of virtue or strength in combat.[118] The category in which Montaigne places himself is characterized only by the wholly involuntary *absence* of certain defects. Thanks to the "instinct and impression" that Montaigne says he has "brought away from [his] nurse,"[119] he is "exempt from a number of vices." But he has others and cannot prevent himself from giving in to his natural predilection, which fortunately is not too violent. He "became involved" in certain "excesses": he did not struggle against them. At most he was able to prevent his "judgment" from "being infected" by them:

> (A) On the contrary, it accuses them [i.e., the vices] more vigorously in myself than in another. But that is all, for otherwise I bring to them too little resistance and let myself lean too easily toward the other side of the balance; except to regulate them and keep them from mixing with other vices.[120]

By taking the precaution of isolating each of his vices, by keeping them from "holding together and intertwining,"[121] Montaigne was able to escape from the gravest perils at scarcely any cost in effort.

This "third" condition is not dishonorable, for evil has no part in it; but neither does it share in the glory that is associated with moral strength. Still, even though Montaigne relegates himself to an inferior rank, he can point to a nonnegligible compensation: he hates cruelty, he is compassionate. Montaigne is not afraid to admit openly to these feelings, which in the classical tradition are not associated with strength of character. For the purpose of such feelings is to help protect the lives of others, whereas the two superior types of virtue aim only at ensuring that the individual does not flinch or waver in the face of death. Thus the three types of virtue are distinguished not only by their force but also by their object. Socrates and Cato, emblematic figures of the highest virtue, exemplify the sovereign confrontation with death. The second type of virtue, that which struggles with the ever-menacing enemy within, also has as its object "unpleasantness and difficulty": it does battle with "shame, fevers, poverty, death, and tortures."[122] Here again, in active battle, it is the evil that we must overcome in our own bodies that is the focus of attention. Come what may, we must strive to keep our composure in the face of "pain," "colic," etc. Strength and self-possession are virtues that counter dangers to our very being. But these two superior types of virtue contemplate only one role for others: that of aggressor. By contrast, the third category, in which Montaigne places himself, is illustrated by examples of a very different kind: the "relation to others" here assumes a form that it did not have in the more exalting (as well as prouder, more disdainful) forms of virtue. Here it may be useful to continue citing from a passage, part of which was quoted above:

> (B) The innocence that is in me is a childish innocence: little vigor and no art. (A) Among other vices, I cruelly hate cruelty, both by nature and by judgment, as the extreme of all vices. But this is to such a point of softness that I do not see a chicken's neck wrung without distress, and I cannot bear to hear the scream of a hare in the teeth of my dogs, although the chase is a violent pleasure. . . . I sympathize very tenderly with the afflictions of others, and would readily weep to keep others company, if I could weep for any occasion whatever. (C) There is nothing that tempts my tears but tears, not only real ones, but all sorts, even the feigned or the painted. (A) The dead I hardly pity, and I should rather envy them; but I very greatly pity the dying. Savages do not shock me as much by roasting and eating the bodies of the dead as do those who torment them and persecute them living. Even the executions of the law, however reasonable they may be, I cannot witness with a steady gaze.[123]

Obviously, then, Montaigne's willingness to place himself in the third and last category amounts both to giving up any claim to egocentric moral excellence and to shifting to the external world, to the fate of others, whether men or animals, the burden of the "goodness" that he is unwilling to claim as a personal merit. Rather than claim for himself the ability to endure violence triumphantly or to withstand the torture of a sick body, Montaigne declares himself to be incapable of watching others endure these torments. The sublime tension of Cato and the marvelous "joy" of Socrates rise to the height of "pleasure" in the mortal scene; but this "enjoyment" (which we would call masochistic) stops at hermetic perfection; it closes in on itself and includes others only as admirers. This virtue isolates the individual by raising him above all others or by involving him in endless struggle against himself. By contrast, Montaigne's "innocence" counterbalances, by the extensiveness of its compassion, what was first presented as a lack of moral energy. The weakness that Montaigne holds against himself is compensated by his powers of sympathy, which extend to all suffering. By opening himself up to the fate of others, the passivity of suffering (which, in Montaigne, is not exempt from the desire to overcome physical disorder as much as he possibly can) develops into "hatred of cruelty." Unable to follow a

model of egocentric perfection in which masochistic pleasure dominates, Montaigne is led to exactly the opposite position: he admits to
having a nature that is imperfect, that can be overwhelmed by the
kind of sadistic behavior that was so widespread during the period of
religious war and colonial conquest in which he lived. Once again,
the "relation to others" brings most generous compensation for the
lack of being and strength that Montaigne claims to find at the center
of his own existence.

We find the same system of compensation, but in the opposite direction and in the sphere of literature, in the essay "Of presumption"
(2:17). Once again, Montaigne introduces a three-part structure. This
time, however, he does not place himself in the weakest category, but
in the category of strength:

> (C) And then, for whom do you write? The learned men to
> whom it falls to pass judgment on books know no other
> value than that of learning, and admit no other procedure
> for our minds than that of erudition and art. If you have
> mistaken one of the Scipios for the other, what is there left
> for you to say that can be worth while? Anyone who does
> not know Aristotle, according to them, by the same token
> does not know himself. Common, ordinary minds do not
> see the grace and the weight of a lofty and subtle speech.
> Now, these two types fill the world. The *third* class into
> whose hands you come, that of *minds regulated and strong in
> themselves,* is so rare that for this very reason it has neither
> name nor rank among us; it is time half wasted to aspire
> and strive to please this group.[124]

As the practitioner of a "lofty" (but not "erudite") and "subtle"
(but not "common and ordinary") speech, Montaigne places himself
in a "third" category that outstrips the other two, which "fill the
world." The compensation will be of the opposite sign: the "minds
regulated and *strong* in themselves" are numerically *weak.* Nevertheless, this tiny minority of *honnêtes gens* (whose moment would
come in the next century, though even then they did not cease to
boast of their rarity) is the only possible group among whom truly
human relations can be formed. Strength of mind is recognized only
within a narrow world: it is there that the finest friendships can come
into being.

Here is one final example of a three-part structure, which is not
wholly unrelated to the preceding one:

> (B) In my youth I studied for ostentation; later, a little to
> gain wisdom; now for recreation. . . . As for the vain and

spendthrift fancy I had for that sort of furniture, (C) not just to supply my needs, but to go *three steps* beyond, (B) for the purpose of lining and decorating my walls, I have given it up long ago.[125]

The tripartition here involves life's three stages and Montaigne's relationship to books in each of them. The successive stages that we have noted throughout this chapter here recur in their sharpest, most concise form. Three styles follow one another. Montaigne is first ruled by the opinion of others (ostentation); this attitude fades as he seeks to regain his self-possession, according to the rules of wisdom; finally, his mind begins to flourish as it learns to think freely, on its own, without compulsion or constraint and, like friendship, without external purpose. (Montaigne disavows his eagerness to go "three steps beyond" his true needs in acquiring books.) Now that La Boétie is no longer alive, Montaigne can "live from day to day"[126] with books and the Muses as mediators in his reflective relationship with himself, in "pleasure, play, and pastime."[127] This is the third condition, ruled by relaxation and self-mastery. Thibaudet, who points out (in connection with the passage just cited) that Montaigne's tower had three stories,[128] might have added that the third story, the library, offered "rich and free views in *three directions.*"[129]

FOUR

The body's moment

Immodesty

More than once, as we saw in the last chapter, Montaigne recognizes the need for "relations with others," even as he expresses, almost simultaneously, his contempt for outside opinion. His verdict is contradictory: relations are necessary, but they are also worthless. Necessary because Montaigne shows himself in order to be seen; worthless because even as he seeks the opinions of others he shows nothing but contempt for their judgments of him. Provided he is seen for what he is, blame and praise are matters of indifference to him. "I take such great pleasure in being judged and known that it is virtually indifferent to me in which of the two forms I am so."[1] Others are free to condemn him if they choose. Reproof does not trouble him. To be sure, his respect for "honesty" is a valid reason for refraining from certain actions or statements. But he is not afraid of causing a scandal by exposing his naked image. As for his own worth, he declares himself to be the sole qualified judge: "I admit that a touch of pride and stubbornness may *enter into keeping me sincere and outspoken without consideration for others.*"[2] Thus he asserts himself by being *outspoken* toward others, while denying them all *consideration*. He appeals to others even as he breaks away from them. The *pride* of which Montaigne accuses himself is indeed not out of place in a declaration of the rights of immodesty. Immodesty both attracts and disqualifies the spectator, it solicits and rejects: it captures the gaze and dismisses the judgment. Montaigne's attitude has an exhibitionistic component: for purposes of simplification, we may say that it is a form of narcissism that uses the gaze of the witness as a mirror. Immodesty forces the attention, and the bared subject, having compelled others to look at a provocative image, finds in that attention that strength it needs to reinforce its uncertain ("confused") sense of its own existence: life acquires a consistency that had been lacking. Forced intimacy goes hand in hand with distancing; the need for communication is coupled with the (temporary) refusal of reciprocity. The relationship between writer and reader is based on a single image, and the reader is reduced to little more than an imaginary and virtual prop to the writer's self-consciousness. In the present case, the value that the ego ascribes to itself is highly ambiguous: on the one hand, it explicitly asserts its special importance, its independence; on the other hand, it implicitly alleges its own radical insufficiency, which is why it must seek external confirmation of its uniqueness, the indispensable reinforcement of its precarious self-image. It is indeed a peculiar form of self-sufficiency that cannot do without exhibition. A mistake by others or their indifference might endanger the image on which Montaigne stakes his all: its outlines would waver, its colors would grow pale, its individual features would lose their definition. In order to avoid having such harm befall him in his second existence, Montaigne decides to "reveal" himself down to his "scars" and deformities.

The intention to show himself "entire and wholly naked" is first stated in the note "To the Reader." And it is frequently and vigorously restated throughout the book: "We must tuck up this stupid rag that covers our conduct."[3] The justification for this is twofold, however. On the one hand, it is a matter of doing justice to our physical nature. We owe "our being" to the "sexual act" [*l'action génitale*].[4] Man's physical functions, which establish his kinship with all living things, must be recognized for what they are. On the other hand, no matter how much we may wish to protect our shameful secrets, God has no difficulty penetrating the shroud of mystery with which we surround the realities of sex and the body. In an addition to the text, the image of the tucked-up "rag" is again used to give concreteness to God's omniscience:

> (C) These are shadows with which we comfort ourselves and pay one another off; but we do not really pay, we rather add to our debt to that great Judge who tucks up our rags and tatters from around our shameful parts and does not merely pretend to see us throughout, even to our inmost and most secret filth.[5]

On the one hand, then, immodesty involves exposing those parts of man that link him to nature, that put him "on the same level" as the "beasts."[6] But on the other hand it is connected to divine knowledge. Man has both the duty to confess his animality and the power to know himself *sub specie divinitatis*. Montaigne's immodesty in *writing* is therefore justified in two ways: what it shows belongs to the realm of nature, and the scrutiny of its regard is akin to the scrutiny of God. That this is a matter of literary strategy and not actual behavior is confirmed by the following statement (first pointed out by Albert Thibaudet[7]), which places a considerable distance between "the man of the book and the man in reality":

> (B) I, who am so bold-mouthed, am nevertheless by nature affected by this shame. Except under great stress of necessity or voluptuousness, I hardly communicate to the sight of anyone the members and acts that our custom orders us to cover up. I suffer from more constraint in this than I consider becoming to a man, and especially to a man of my profession.[8]

This passage acknowledges the legitimate authority, in the realm of *action*, that "custom" has over our lives; but in the realm of *words*, that authority is nullified: in the territory of the book a different kind of liberty is in force.

In fact, when Montaigne comes to speak of modesty, he shows, as clearly as for immodesty, the effects of a dual movement. Modesty, by turning back desire, only irritates it. Whether sincere or cunning, it creates a distance whose effect is to seduce all the more infallibly. Montaigne learned this lesson from Ovid and Virgil, who believed that modesty was the most effective stratagem of the coquette. Also in his mind is the memory of Sabina Poppaea, who according to Tacitus never went abroad without a veil:

> Why did Poppaea think of masking the beauties of her face, except to enhance them to her lovers? Why have they veiled, even down to the heels, those beauties that every woman wants to show, that every man wants to see? Why do they cover with so many impediments, one on top of the other, the parts in which our desire and theirs principally dwells? And what is the use of those great bastions with which our women have just taken to arming their flanks, except to allure our appetite and to attract us to them by keeping us at a distance?[9]

To allure by keeping at a distance: the phrase is striking; it provides a marvelous illustration of the title of chapter 2:15, "That our desire is increased by difficulty." Dissimulation and masks, euphemism nad chaste circumlocution, increase the pleasure of contact by placing obstacles in its way:

> (A) To keep love in breath, Lycurgus ordained that the married people of Lacedaemon could have sexual relations only by stealth, and that it should be as great a shame to find them in bed together as with others. The difficulty of

assignations, the danger of surprises, the shame of the next day . . . that is what gives a tang to the sauce. (C) How many very lasciviously pleasant sports spring from the modest and shamefaced way of speaking about the works of love! . . . (A) Our appetite scorns and passes over what is at hand, to run after what it has not.[10]

In this way the original meaning of the mask and confession becomes complicated: for now we must recognize that the mask hides *and* attracts and that confession brings together *and* separates, at least insofar as confession involves both that *pride* and that *indifference* (of which Montaigne speaks), pride and indifference that refuse to respect (to "consider") the signs of our immodesty. A temperate relationship is possible only between individuals who accept their mutual estrangement without relinquiching the benefits of sustained communication. Thus Montaigne imagines the possibility of taking his distance and then playing with that distance to raise communication to its most exquisite pitch.

The body's rebellion

Immodesty wants nothing about the body to go unnoticed. For man is both mind and body. A man does not adequately portray himself who reports only on his mind's "imaginings." A complete portrait requires a no less exhaustive representation of "corporeal conditions." Montaigne does not fail to give one: he tells us about his size, his constitution, his illnesses, and his appetites. This aspect of his self-portrait has provoked now irritation, now condescending amusement, in his readers over the centuries. The reasons for it have not been clearly understood.

Where the life of the body was concerned, Montaigne was forced to confront the pretensions of medicine—that discipline whose competence extends precisely to the body. The most dramatic form of that confrontation was naturally occasioned by illness. The matter was of sufficient importance for Montaigne to give it a place of particular prominence: in the *last* essay of the second book (2:37, "Of the resemblance of children to fathers"), and then, as though in echo, in the *last* essay of the third book (3:13, "Of experience"). The location at the end of each book is significant in more than one respect.

At first sight, the only reason for it is to serve as the pretext for a general critique of the presumption of knowledge, using as an example the most conjectural, self-important, and, in many respects, dangerous of the traditional disciplines. Montaigne's target is not merely the tenuous nature of this alleged form of knowledge; a more serious objection is that it trespasses on precious ground: it claims to lay down the laws of the body, of *my* body.

One's initial expectation is that Montaigne would show a certain indulgence toward medicine: of all the sciences inherited from antiquity, medicine is the one that attends most closely to individual qualities. The doctrine of "complexions" (of the "crasis" of the humors and of individual *idiosyncrasy*) opens the way to an infinity of possible combinations. From the beginning, classical Greek medicine combined theory with experience, tempering one by the other.[11] It appreciated the importance of unique occurrences. It practiced doubting observation (*skepsis*) even before a skeptical school of philosophy existed. It was receptive to diversity and singularity. Montaigne borrows its language on occasion to describe his "humors." Indeed, he may have been indebted to medicine for a good deal more than this, as we shall see presently.

Yet Montaigne's complaints against the "vast and troubled sea of medical errors"[12] are not unfounded. Medicine, in its literal fidelity to Galen's authority, did not resist the temptation to erect itself into a system; it petrified and became dogma. Even when it claimed to respect the individual temperament of the patient, it introduced imaginary entities. Physicians relied upon a physics and a physiology that hypostatized the data of sense perception and never raised doubts about their validity. They pointed to experience only to confirm what they already knew, not to open the way to discovery. Even medicine's failures taught them nothing: they found in the language of medicine what they needed to interpret and explain away every shortcoming. And, as they never doubted the substantial qualities that they found in all the bodies of the universe—heat, cold, dryness, humidity, bitterness, sweetness, saltiness, etc.—so they boasted of knowing the exact nature of every disease and the specific effects of every drug. Physicians arrogated to themselves the authority to intervene at every opportunity, as if they held the key to the phenomena they observed or provoked. But the remedies they concocted and administered to the patient had little to do with the experience on which medical authority was presumably based. Doctors worked in the dark, and far from drawing authority from knowledge proven and certain, they engaged in risky experiments that brought suffering to patients to whom they had promised the world.

As for the concept of *experience*, Montaigne points out that it can be used in two radically different ways. There is, first of all, the physicians' usage: based on observations that in many cases are woefully inadequate, they cite the *cases* they have dealt with, adduce tenuous causes, and draw misleading conclusions by making questionable analogies and comparisons and invoking infallible powers and salutary effects.[13] Then there is the more modest attitude, Montaigne's own, which sticks to the sensible phenomenon and limits itself to recording without conceptualizing; experience in this sense remains closer to what actually happens, and it would be pointless to look to it for the *means* to a wider knowledge along with insight into antecedent causes and ulterior consequences. We stand on the semantic dividing line that will subsequently develop into an ever-widening chasm between the "objective" experiment [*expérience* in French—Trans.] of modern science, with its insistence upon sophisticated methodology, and "personal" (or "inner") experience, wherein each individual feels the unique quality of his own existence. For the present a semblance of unity still joins the two senses of the word *experience*: the experience adduced by the physicians has the value of an example, which justifies its repetition, whereas the experience that Montaigne claims, which carries its evidence within itself, is also an example, but of another kind, whose direct authority can be used to contest the exempla (generally older) on which the professionals pride themselves: when Montaigne evokes the hereditary malady of kidney stones that runs in his family (along with an equally hereditary aversion of medicine) and yet is not incompatible with a remarkable longevity, he is in fact appealing to both experience and example in order to oppose the pretensions of the physicians with weapons drawn from medicine's own arsenal:

> (A) The antipathy I have for their [i.e., the physicians'] art is hereditary with me. My father lived seventy-four years, my grandfather sixty-nine, my great-grandfather nearly eighty, without having tasted any sort of medicine. . . . Medicine *is based on examples and experience*; so is my opinion. Isn't that a very clear-cut and *very advantageous experience?* I wonder if the doctors can find me three men in their records, born, bred, and dying at the same hearth, under the same roof, who lived as long under their rules. . . . Besides, to tell the truth, I have gained enough advantage over them by my family *examples*, even though they should go no further.[14]

Experience against experience; (external) trial against (internal) trial; example against example: Montaigne places in evidence the authentic records of an iatrophobic family. His personally verified *essay* is worth more than the presumptuous science of the doctors—even though

Montaigne was soon to die of the disease of which he had begun to feel the first effects:

> (A) Human affairs do not have so much constancy. It is only eighteen years short of two hundred years that *this test* of ours has lasted, for the first of them was born in the year 1402. It is truly quite normal that *this experience* should begin to fail us. Let them not reproach me with the infirmities that have me by the throat at this moment. Is it not enough for my part to have lived healthy for forty-seven years? Even if this is the end of my career, it is one of the longer ones.[15]

The words tell the story: a note of personal suffering has crept into the essay; it is something that is experienced and articulated—experienced in order to be articulated. And because he has felt, "savored" the experience himself, Montaigne is able to claim an authority superior to that of medicine. Listen to him as he tells us of his experience of the illness and of his surprise (in its first attacks) not to have found it as frightening as he had feared:

> (A) The really essential and bodily sufferings I feel very keenly. And yet for all that, foreseeing them in other days with a feeble, delicate vision that was softened by the enjoyment of that long and happy health and repose that God lent me for the better part of my life, I had conceived of them in imagination so unendurable that in truth I had more fear of them than I have found pain in them. Wherefore I continue to confirm this belief, that most of the faculties of our soul, (C) as we employ them, (A) trouble the repose of life more than they serve it.
> I am at grips with the worst of all maladies, the most sudden, the most painful, the most mortal, and the most irremediable. I have already experienced five or six very long and painful bouts of it. However, either I flatter myself or else there is even in this condition enough to bear up a man whose soul is unburdened of the fear of death and unburdened of the threats, sentences, and *consequences* which medicine dins into our ears. But the very impact of the pain has not such sharp and piercing bitterness as to drive a well-poised man to madness or despair. I have at least this *profit* from the stone, that it will complete what I have still not been able to accomplish in myself and reconcile and familiarize me completely with death: for the more my illness oppresses and bothers me, the less will death be something for me to fear.[16]

144

This passage clearly points up the contrast between intimate experience and the experience adduced by a dogmatic knowledge that undertakes to forecast the *consequences* of physical phenomena—remote effects of either the illness itself or of the remedies administered to the patient. Intimate experience does not serve as the basis for causal induction of a general order, which first interprets the causes of the observed facts in order to predict their future effects. On the contrary, it remains bound to what it "savors" in the present, to the unique and individual quality of the feeling, from which it derives no law or rule of action in the physical world. Its "profit" does not lie in mastery of the world; it is rather of an ethical and ontological order: it consists in becoming familiar with death. Death, which is situated at the end, beyond the temporal unfolding of phenomena, is at the same time the reality that must be apprehended here and now, within the fabric of the sensuous present. The lesson of the stone reinforces the "excitement" caused by the fall from the horse (2:6). The natural fact of suffering, limited to the suffering consciousness, does not augment our capacity to act upon nature in any way. Its only result is a form of wisdom, the gist of which is to "commit oneself to nature," to allow it to do its work. The key formulation of this attitude occurs on a well-known page of the essay "Of experience" (3:13): "In the experience I have of myself I find enough *to make me wise*, if I were a good scholar."[17] Thus there is a radical opposition between medical experience, which, having made nature the object of its observation, seeks to control or thwart nature's operations, and contemplative personal experience, which resigns itself to ignorance of nature's operations and submits to taking nature for a guide, solely in the hope of leading a wiser life and suffering a less contorted death. Montaigne's preference for intimate experience is not unrelated to the opposition of *being* and *appearance*. For the "promises" of medicine are illusory, they are pure appearance and vain presumption and hence require excessive confidence on the part of the patient: "It was a good rule in their art, and one that accompanies all fantastic, vain, and supernatural arts, that the patient's faith should by good hope and assurance anticipate their effective operation."[18] If medicine's results were *solid* and *certain*, medicine would possess the qualities of being; but since those results depend upon the *credence* given to the art, it cannot claim to be more than mere appearance—whence the qualifications "fantastic, vain, and supernatural."

Inner experience is also the touchstone for judging another "science"—philosophy—to see whether the behavior it prescribes falls under the head of being or appearance. For anyone who, like Montaigne, has been tried by physical pain, it is obvious that the serenity prescribed by the philosophers is merely a false front and a mask:

> (A) I have always considered that precept formalistic which so rigorously and precisely orders us to maintain a good countenance and a disdainful and composed bearing in the endurance of pain. Why does philosophy, which has regard only for real substance and actions, go playing around with these *external appearances?* (C) Let her leave this care to the actors and teachers of rhetoric who set so much store by our gestures. Let her boldly grant to pain this cowardice in the voice, provided it is neither in the heart nor in the stomach, and let her assign these voluntary complaints to the category of the sighs, sobs, palpitations, and pallors that nature has put *out of our control.* Provided the heart is without fear, the words without despair, let her be content! What matter if we twist our arms, provided we do not twist our thoughts? Philosophy trains us for ourselves, not for others; for *being,* not for *seeming.*[19]

Although philosophy can still shore up our "courage," it exceeds its rights if it claims to govern the physical movements of the patient—whose voluntary acts, "cries," are so hard to distinguish from involuntary reactions. Then let philosophy "prevent Socrates from blushing for affection or for shame, from blinking his eyes at the threat of a blow, from trembling and sweating in the fits of fever."[20] By marking the limits of a philosophy of absolute self-control, bodily experience—brought home to Montaigne through pain—results in a humble wisdom, which does not bridle up at the sight of our involuntary acts or our vanquished will, signs of which we read in our sighs and our moans. It is of course worthwhile saving all that can be saved of our faculties of reflection and judgment: much, but not all. The overwhelming power of suffering sets a limit and establishes a criterion for distinguishing what is possible from what is impossible:

> (C) I test myself in the thickest of the pain, and have always found that I was capable of speaking, thinking, and answering as sanely as at any other time, but not as steadily, being troubled and distracted by the pain. When I am thought to be the most stricken and those present are sparing me, I often test my powers, and myself broach subjects as remote as possible from my condition. *I can do anything by a sudden effort;* but don't make it last long.
> Oh, why have I not the faculty of that dreamer in Cicero

who, dreaming he was embracing a wench, found that he
had discharged his stone in the sheets! Mine extraordinarly
diswench me![21]

Awareness of the body, heightened by illness, defines the boundaries
of a territory in which the subject is under the jurisdiction of no other
authority than nature, whose sentence is to endure the fate of the
body. It is a tenuous and threatened territory, notwithstanding the
protection that man is entitled to expect from nature. It is the domain
of *mine*, of *possession*, of the inalienable. It is also the domain where
time works its ravages, plunging the body into old age and death.
Nature, an ambivalent power, both protects and alters us. What is the
good of medical intervention that claims to modify the body in accordance with a coded system of entities and qualities randomly attributed to nature (a system whose all too schematic conceptual
model includes an aspect of conjectural reasoning that does not escape Montaigne's notice)? The suffering body rejects the intervention
of philosophy, which wants to impose upon it a "countenance," an
"external decency," when it is beyond the body's power to submit to
such rules. Just as the library at the top of Montaigne's tower served
him as a refuge from the world, so his body served him as a refuge
from the "arts"—so long as he was able to maintain the independence of judgment that enabled him to test himself "in the thickest of
the pain." What the individual feels in his body has to do only with
his immediate relationship to nature, i.e., to an authority capable of
spontaneously mainifesting itself inside him without the intermediary of an interpretive technical discourse. (Among mystics in this
same period, especially Theresa of Avila, the body superseded nature
as the theater wherein God manifests his grace and his wrath, directly
and unmistakably in the flesh; this development did not fail to cause
alarm among those claiming to possess knowledge, namely, the-
ologians and confessors.)

"Medical errors"

Montaigne knew the medical system of his day sufficiently well to be
able to give a detailed and accurate summary. But he does so only to
show how the tangle of factors taken into account can lead to errors.
Exactly what weight should be attached to each factor? How can one
consider them all? The slightest error takes its toll:

> (A) If *the doctor's error* is dangerous, we are in a
> very bad way, for it is most unlikely that he will
> not fall into it again often. He needs too many de-

147

Physiology

tails, considerations, and circumstances to adjust his plan correctly: he must know *his patient's constitution*, his temperament, his humors, his inclinations, his actions, his very thoughts and fancies. He must be responsible for the external circum-

Hygiene

stances, the nature of the place, the *condition of the air and weather*, the position of the planets and their

Pathology

influences. He must know *in the disease* the causes, the symptoms, the effects, the critical days; *in the*

Therapeutics

drug the weight, the power, the country it comes from, the appearance, the age, the way of dispensing it; and he must know how to proportion all these factors and relate them to one another in order to create *a perfect symmetry*. Wherein if he makes ever so slight an error, if among so many springs there is even a single one that pulls askew, that is enough to destroy us.

    God knows how difficult is the knowledge of most of these details; for how, for example, shall

Semiology

he find the *proper symptom of the disease, each disease being capable of an infinite number of symptoms?* How many controversies and doubts they have among themselves over the interpretation of urines! Otherwise whence would come this continual altercation that we see among them over the diagnosis of the malady? How should we excuse this mistake into which they fall so often, of taking marten for fox? In the illnesses I have had, however little difficulty there was, *I have never found three of them in agreement*. I more readily note *the examples that concern me*.[22]

In enumerating the list of items that the physician must take into account, Montaigne adheres strictly to the methodical order set forth in the medical treatises of his day. Most books recommended first examining the patient's *physiology,* or "natural causes": his humors and his constitution (or "crasis" or "temperament"), which determines the mixing of the humors according to age, season, and individual idiosyncrasy. The second item of examination was *hygiene,* which involves the use the individual makes of the "six nonnatural" or "indifferent" causes, air being the principal of these, along with food and drink, work and rest, sleep and wakefulness, excretion and retention, and the soul's passions.

    Knowledge of the illness (or "antinatural causes") came under the head of *pathology,* which the principal works treated in terms of the categories that Montaigne enumerates: causes, symptoms (or signs), effects, and critical days. Finally, Montaigne, following the lead of medical writers, takes up the subject of *therapeutics*, or the art of choosing the drugs appropriate to each set of circumstances. Medications were to be administered so that, through the interaction of opposites (evacuation as the antidote to congestion, heat as the antidote to chill, moisture as the antidote to dryness, "tonic" substances as the antidote to relaxation, etc.), the patient's equilibrium or "symmetry" might be restored, and with it, his compromised health. For health was defined as an exact balance of internal functions and elements under the favorable effect of external influences on bodily life—in accordance with the principle of *isonomy* accepted by Greek science ever since the writings of Alcmeon of Crotona.[23]

Montaigne, in a few succinct lines, brings together the whole conceptual apparatus used by contemporary physicians when they discussed—under the technical name of *indications*—the decisions that observation of the situation imposed on the man of art. In the writings of Ambroise Paré, for example, we can read the following:

> Surgeons and Physicians use the word Indication, which is peculiar to them and not in common use. . . . In Surgery we call indication that which the Surgeon sets before his eyes, as a sign, to advise him as to what remedy he should use to cure or save the person. . . . Now, there are three general kinds of Indications, each of which is further divided into several specific kinds: the first is that of natural causes, the second that of nonnatural causes, and the third that of antinatural causes. The natural causes indicate and signify what must be preserved by their like: and under this head are included all the Indications that we take from the body and subject placed in our hands, which are the indications taken of the patient's strength, temperature, age, sex, habits, custom and manner of living.[24]

As for the "nonnatural causes," Paré goes on, the quality of the *air* above all must be taken into account (this was also singled out by Montaigne):

> For it is necessary, whether we like or it not, to bear and endure the present condition of the *air*. The air therefore gives us some indication, or, rather, coindication: for if it is similar to the malady, it symbolizes in indication with the malady, and therefore the indication is to correct; if it is contrary to the malady, it indicates and shows that it must be conserved.[25]

Finally, "the antinatural causes indicate to us that they must be removed and prohibited, or corrected by their contrary. Therefore, in order to *deduce* the whole from the small, the kinds of indications, or signs taken of the natural causes, which we call conservative, are *several.*"[26]

The medical doctrine of Paré (as well as Fernell and Escale, the authors mentioned by Montaigne[27]) treats a variety of signs (or symptoms) of disease and explains that variety in terms of a multiplicity of causes or "etiologies." Because each cause can produce several effects and can be linked to various stages in the patient's past, Montaigne sees error as inevitable. His argument is relentless. Suppose a physician observes a sign (in the urine, for example) from which he derives an indication for the use of *one* therapeutic remedy to relieve or cure the suffering of a *particular* individual. How can he make the *deductions* necessary to go from general rules (purely verbal as they are) to the specific case (given the prevalence of rather careless observation)? In the specific case the argument becomes so convoluted that the physician, unable to make out the "proper sign of the disease," misses the mark: he "mistakes a marten for a fox," as the popular proverb has it—in other words, he gets the species wrong. The unfortunate thing is that the error not only aggravates the malady, i.e., the specific form of a general disease type, but also causes the individual patient to suffer. And if the life at stake is my own, error is intolerable.

If deductive reasoning in medicine is liable to so many pitfalls, the same is true of *inductive* reasoning, which claims to establish general rules or laws on the basis of observational data. Registering his concern as a patient, Montaigne levels his criticism at what physicians have to say about the efficacy of various drugs. They state laws on the basis of haphazardly selected "examples" and establish *simple* cause-and-effect relations that again fail to take account of the actual variety of disease and hence of the innumerable ways in which a simple causal argument can go wrong. Beyond his critique of the theory of indications, Montaigne (in this a precursor of Descartes) is taking aim at the substantial qualities and occult virtues attributed to natural objects. He is thus striking at the very foundation of therapeutic medicine. And indeed, the vulnerability of therapeutics can hardly be denied. Physicians almost always based their case on a *unique* experience, ignoring the fact that it is illegitimate to reason by induction from a single instance to a general law and then to argue that that law is applicable to a whole set of special cases.

As he reaches the end of his polemic against the doctors in 2:28, Montaigne notices that he has not yet concluded the discussion of experience that his argument has raised. As early as the 1580 edition there is a closing section (prior to the letter to Mme de Duras) that may have been added as an afterthought:

> (A) I cannot tear myself away from this paper without saying this one word more about their giving us *their experience* as a warrant of the infallibility of their drugs. The greatest part, and, I believe, more than two-thirds of the medicinal virtues, consists in the quintessence or occult property of simples, concerning which we can have no other instruction than *use;* for quintessence is nothing else than a *quality of which we cannot by reason find out the cause.*[28]

On what experience do physicians base their claims? Montaigne envisions *three* possibilities. First, there is "inspired" experience, which is often referred to by Paracelsus and his disciples. This is a mode of immediate knowledge, or intuitive vision, from which Montaigne respectfully dissociates himself as soon as it is a question not of knowledge of the self but of the truth of the world; his attitude is tantamount to dismissal, and the irony in his words is unmistakable: "(A) Among such proofs, I am content to accept those that they say they acquired by the inspiration of some demon (for as for miracles, I never touch upon them)."[29] Second, there is a kind of experience of which "the proofs . . . are drawn from things that often fall into our use . . . for example, if in the wool which we are accustomed to wear there is found by accident some occult desiccative property that cures chilblains on our heels."[30] The common man has as much knowledge of such things through "custom" as the physician through learning. Montaigne is again ironic. A banal observation that is part of common experience has been translated into medical jargon by adducing some "occult desiccative property." Being what we are, we all remedy our ills in customary ways. Adding jargon changes nothing.

The third and final possibility is that the physician will by chance discover some property of a natural object. He may then hypothesize that the object always produces the same effect and wait for an occasion to verify this hypothesis. Such is the working principle of "blind" empiricism but not of true "experimental science," of whose methodology Montaigne had no more inkling than his contemporaries. Not only was it impossible to multiply the number of observers at will (and a consensus of a large number of observers would have seemed to Montaigne more worthy of credence than a single observation); but to have done so would not have helped to *organize* experience in any way (Lanson's opinion to the contrary notwithstanding[31]). Montaigne therefore criticizes traditional empiricism without proposing anything to take its place:

> (A) But in most of the other experiments [*expériences*] to which they say they were led by fortune and had no other guide but chance, I find the progress of their investigation impossible to believe. I imagine a man looking around him at the infinite number of things: plants, animals, metals. I do not know where to have him begin his experiment; and even if his fancy lights first upon an elk's horn, which requires a very pliant and easy faith, he still finds himself just as perplexed about the next thing to do. He is faced with so many maladies and so many circumstances that before he has attained certainty about the point that the successful completion of his experiment should reach, human wit is wasting its ingenuity.[32]

Innumerable logical paths lead from the agent, chosen at random and supposed to possess some medicinal virtue, to the illness of which that agent might be the specific remedy. This is tantamount to saying that there is no logical path at all, for the sufficient condition remains unknown:

> (A) And for him to find, among that infinite number of things, that the right one is this horn; among this infinite number of diseases, epilepsy; among so many constitutions, the melancholic; so many seasons, in winter; so many nations, the French; so many times of life, old age; so many celestial mutations, at the conjunction of Venus and Saturn; so many parts of the body, the finger—since he is guided in all this neither by theory, nor by conjecture, nor by example, nor by divine inspiration, but by the sole movement of fortune—he would have to be guided by a perfectly workmanlike, regular, and methodical fortune. And then, even if the cure should be performed, how can he be sure that this was not because the illness had reached its term, or a result of chance, or the effect of something else he had eaten or drunk or touched that day, or the merit of his grandmother's prayers? Moreover, even if this proof had been perfect, how many times was the experiment repeated? How many times was that long string of chances and coincidences strung again *for a rule to be derived from it*.[33]

This is where the 1580 text ends. In 1588, Montaigne added a final paragraph to make a more impressive conclusion, still focusing on the conditions under which an experiment might be said to yield valid results; and a brief final phrase, added at a still later date, shows that the problem had not ceased to preoccupy him in the interim:

> (B) When the rule is derived, then by whom? Out of so many millions there are only three men who have undertaken to record their experiences. Will chance have lighted precisely on one of these? What if another man, and a hundred others, have had contrary experiences? Perhaps we would see some light if all the judgments and reasonings of men were known to us. But that three witnesses, and three physicians, should lay down the law to mankind is not reasonable, unless human nature had deputed and chosen them and declared them to be our arbiters (C) by express power of attorney.[34]

The search for a universal "rule" can only be vague and vagabond. When an assertion intended to be general is based on the observations of at most *three* men (the same "three" that Montaigne has found to be "never in agreement"), then no necessity can be ascribed to the causal prediction. (As we saw earlier, Montaigne, for his part, can cite *three* antimedical examples in his own family—his father, his grandfather, and his great-grandfather: "Isn't that a very clear cut and very advantageous experience? I wonder if the doctors can find me *three* men in their records."[35]) The relationship of these three cases is in all probability accidental, dependent on "chance." General knowledge is not only *inapplicable* in practice owing to the diversity of "indications"; it is also, given its ambition of certainty, *unconstitutable* owing to the inadequacy and doubtful validity of the causal sequences it considers to be regular.

There is no doubt that Montaigne, after finishing the essay "Of the resemblance of children to fathers" [from which the passages cited above are taken—Trans.], felt that he had not yet exhausted the subject of experience: he had dealt with it only in a polemical manner, directed against those who claim experience in order to inspire confidence and to lend respectability to their theory and their practice, their knowledge and their art. Moreover, as significant as his revelations about his own disease are in this essay, he has still not set forth all the reasons that for him legitimate the other type of experience, direct and intimate, in its singularity and uniqueness.

Comparison of the end of 2:37, which we have just been discussing, with the beginning of 3:13 reveals passages that continue, in more general terms, the arguments examined above. It would not be unreasonable to maintain that the essay "Of experience" is a lengthy gloss on the earlier "Of the resemblance of children to fathers."

> (B) There is no desire more natural than the desire for knowledge. We try all the ways that can lead us to it. When reason fails us, we use experience—
> (C) Experience, by example led,
> By varied trials art has bred
>
> —Manilus
>
> (B) which is a weaker and less dignified means. But truth is so great a thing that we must not disdain any medium that will lead us to it.[36]

Once again Montaigne admits that he cannot "tear himself away," this time not just from his "paper" but from his entire book, without considering afresh the question of knowledge and experience. In his opening lines he then makes clear his belief that experience is a "mediate" form of knowledge and that, within the category of mediate forms, it occupies a lesser rank because, being based on example, it is necessarily contaminated by sense data. Empirical knowledge is thus distinguished from pure rational knowledge, which relies exclusively on logical chains of concepts.

Thus the essay "Of experience" provides us with the opportunity to reconsider an idea whose importance has already been stressed: namely, that it is pointless for man to train his eyes on a few exceptional examples and focus his attention exclusively on them. Ordinary lives are no less exemplary than illustrious ones for the person who knows how to take advantage of them. Ultimately, our own lives are an abundant source of examples, if only we are willing to make negative examples of our errors. The following passage is worth singling out for special attention, since it echoes the passage cited above in which Montaigne enumerated the reasons why physicians must inevitably make mistakes:

> (B) He who remembers the evils he has undergone, and those that have threatened him, and the slight causes that have changed him from one state to another, prepares himself in that way for future changes and for recognizing his condition. The life of Caesar has no more to show us than our own; an emperor's or an ordinary man's, it is still a life subject to all human accidents. Let us only listen: we tell ourselves all we most need. He who remembers having been mistaken so many, many times in his own judgment, is he not a fool if he does not distrust it forever after?[37]

Montaigne has told us previously that "the physician's mistake is dangerous" for his patient. Here we take another step in the progress of consciousness: for now experience consists in remembering that we ourselves have often been "mistaken." The failure of the experience whose self-proclaimed goal was objective knowledge here turns into knowledge of failure. This knowledge, which returns from experience empty-handed, as it were, makes us "distrustful forever after"—a healthy thing. Here is experience of quite another kind—earlier I called it ethical and ontological—in which one's relation to oneself is primordial. Reflection upon failure constitutes an example that I can call *my own*. In the felt evidence of the present moment, when what is at issue is my own life, my emptiness paradoxically comes to possess the authority that no longer inheres in the authors of the past.

For Montaigne, this living authority is not limited solely to the testimony of man's fallible consciousness. He is willing to grant authority also to what we hear directly from our intimate friends. If we must trust in someone, why not give preference to our friends over what we read in print, notwithstanding the "popular" reverence for the printed book:

> (B) What shall we do with this people that admits none but printed evidence, that does not believe men unless they are in a book, or truth unless it is of competent age? . . . It carries very different weight with this people if you say "I have read it" than if you say "I have heard it." But I, who do not disbelieve men's mouths any more than their hands, and who know that people write just as injudiciously as they speak, and who esteem this age just as if it were another that is past, I quote a friend of mine as readily as Aulus Gellius or Macrobius, and what I have seen as what they have written.[38]

Examples collected from our own intimate surroundings, from what we see, hear, and feel, gain in validity. Montaigne continues:

> (B) I often say that it is pure stupidity that makes us run after *foreign and scholarly examples*. There is as great an abundance of them in this age as in that of Homer and Plato. But is it not true that we seek rather the honor of quoting than the truth of the statement? As if it were greater to borrow our proofs from the shop of Vascosan or Plantin [two well-known printers of the time—Trans.] than from what may be seen in our own village. Or rather, indeed, that we have not the wit to pick out and put to use

what happens before our eyes, and to judge it keenly enough *to make it an example?* For if we say we lack authority to gain credence for our testimony, we say so without reason. By the same token, in my opinion, from the most ordinary, commonplace, familiar things, if we could put them in their proper light, can be formed the greatest miracles of nature and the most wondrous *examples*, especially on the subject of human actions.

Against the foreign examples and experience cited by "scholars" (and especially physicians), Montaigne feels *authorized* to raise objections based on examples and experiences of which he is the sole witness. The paradox is obvious: what was not believable when its source was *"three* men who have undertaken to *record their experiences"*[39] (gleaned from the world of external objects and couched in the form of general rules) suddenly becomes worthy of attention when its source is *a single man*—but whose full attention is devoted to keeping "a record of the essays of [his] life."[40] Montaigne's is the experience of a single subject who limits his record to the particularity of what he himself has tried, tasted, and felt—leaving his reader free to decide whether *his* experience is or is not similar and thus to take the first step toward a possible generalization ("Each man bears the entire form of man's estate."[41]).

Because of the nature of the attention he pays to himself, Montaigne believes he has the right to offer his experience to others, so that they may derive the benefit. To be sure, his bodily experience is limited to himself alone, but he is not afraid to throw down a challenge to those "artists" who claim to possess a general knowledge from which no patient ever benefits. Had he accomplished nothing more than to demonstrate the possibility of one individual setting his private knowledge against that of the schools, the undertaking would have seemed to him worthwhile.

Studied confessions

Although Montaigne has no desire to emulate those scholars and erudites who pass their time making systematic classifications according to genus and species,[42] the long concluding essay "Of experience" is clearly structured in a manner both rigorous and supple. After a lengthy introduction devoted to the notion of experience and the difficulties of interpretation in legal and religious matters, he lays down the *principle* that guides his study of himself, his substitute for the accepted disciplines, and then adds a word of explanation to prepare the reader for the conclusion to come:

(B) I study myself more than any other subject. That is my metaphysics, that is my physics. . . . (C) In this universe of things I ignorantly and negligently let myself be guided by the general law of the world. I shall *know* it well enough when I *feel* it.[43]

It is to *feeling*, then, that Montaigne shifts the burden of *knowing:* the role of the body stands out from the first. To be sure, it is also a proper function of the mind to feel, intuitively, by means of one of the faculties attributed to the "spiritual sense." *Sensation*, in the broad sense, refers to the perception of thoughts as well as of modifications of the body. But to know oneself "through sensation" is to do so without the aid of discursive reason: "I *judge* myself only by *actual sensation*, not by reasoning."[44] Feeling is a necessary condition of judgment—this is Montaigne's first topic: not only does he never finish observing himself,[45] but observation of himself enables him to know and advise others.[46] In practical life this capacity would have made him a fit adviser for a prince, whom he would have protected against the perfidy of "his flatterers."[47] Self-description must not end with the faculties of mind, however; to be complete, it should also record bodily aptitudes and habits. Montaigne is clear about the distinction:

(B) In fine, all this fricassee that I am scribbling here is nothing but a record of the essays of my life, which, for *spiritual health*, is exemplary enough if you take its instruction in reverse. But as for bodily health, no one can furnish more useful experience than I, who present it pure, not at all corrupted or altered by art or theorizing.[48]

Admittedly, the two subjects that Montaigne here distinguishes for the sake of clarity, namely, spiritual health and bodily health, he will later try to combine, drawing out the intimate connections between the two, the "mutual services" that each performs for the other.[49] But he will do this only after he has fully described the bodily "condition." The conclusion of the essay, conciliatory and calm, will be given over to tranquil affirmation of the reciprocal obligations of mind and body, whose "conjugal" harmony makes the enjoyment of life possible. To put the point in a striking fashion, he makes use of one his most expressive chiasmi: "But I . . . am unable to cling so completely to this single and simple object as to keep myself from grossly pursuing the present pleasures of the general human law—*intellectually sensual, sensually intellectual*."[50]

157

But before this point is reached, the body must first be *articulated;* its leading characteristics must be exhibited without false modesty, if only to set in relief what Montaigne has just said about his "spiritual" faculties (judgment, sincerity, ignorance, and feebleness).

Now, it is true that this is not the first time that Montaigne sets out to give a full portrait of himself according to the traditional division between mind and body. In a lengthy section of 2:17, "Of presumption," he undertakes the same task but in reverse order, beginning with what will be the conclusion to "Of experience," i.e., with the assertion that there is an intimate connection between our "two principal parts."[51] Montaigne then develops his theme by considering the question of beauty,[52] giving a rather cursory description of his body (his small stature, his features, his complexion, his health, his age, and his aptitude for various forms of exercise). He then goes on to talk about his mind and its faculties and passions, which he treats in a quite leisurely fashion,[53] particularly emphasizing his lack of memory. The mind/body dichotomy and the transition from physical to spiritual qualities are clearly indicated by the contrast between the first sentences of two successive paragraphs: "My *bodily* qualities, in short, are very well matched with those of my soul. . . . *I have a soul all its own,* accustomed to conducting itself in its own way."[54]

In "Of experience," not only is the order of discussion reversed, but the descriptions of mind and body receive inversely proportional amounts of space: in this later essay there is much more discussion of Michel de Montaigne's body than there is of his mind (the faculties of which he sums up briefly by saying what he "would have thought himself good for," had he applied them: "For nothing. . . . But I would have told my master home truths, and watched over his conduct, if he had been willing."[55]

Plainly, then, telling the truth about his body was nothing new for Montaigne; he did not defer it until the final essay of 1588. Never before did he devote so many consecutive pages to this subject, however. What is more, these pages occupy the central portion of the essay. The important posthumous emendation (included in the 1595 edition) to chapter 2:6 ("Of practice") contains the justification of Montaigne's total candor. To paint one's own portrait is "mainly" to portray one's "cogitations." But it is not enough to stop there.

> (C) I expose myself entire: my portrait is a cadaver on which the veins, the muscles, and the tendons appear at a glance, each part in its place. . . . It is not my deeds that I write down; it is myself, it is my essence.[56]

And then there is this further addition to the "Art of discussion" (3:8): "(C) I present myself standing and lying down, front and rear, on the right and the left, and in all my natural postures."[57]

The eloquent cupbearer

In the two realms that constitute man—body and soul—Montaigne is determined to heed the lesson of intimate and direct experience in preference to what the specialized *arts* have to say (and promise): for the soul, theology and philosophy; and for the body, medicine. Let us resume our reading of the essay "Of experience":

> (B) The arts that promise *to keep our body in health and our soul in health* promise us much, but at the same time there are none that keep their promise less. And in our time those who profess these arts among us show the results of them less than any other men. The most you can say for them is that they sell medicinal drugs; but that they are doctors you cannot say.[58]

Montaigne will attempt to reverse these roles. In place of the arts, which transform life into their *object* and claim to govern it, he substitutes life itself, as he directly experiences it: life raised to the level of art. "My trade and my art is living."[59] The individual subject, declaring that he will not be bound by general reasoning of others on his behalf, claims for himself alone the *authority* of a radically different kind of knowledge, in some respects almost identified with feeling or sensation (as we saw in the previous section).

Montaigne claims to be convinced that, so far as the body is concerned, this new knowledge, derived from his own experience, makes all external supervision unnecessary. The competition with medical science does not frighten him. He can even call upon ancient authorities for support: to begin with, there is the emperor Tiberius and then, more honorably, the Socrates of the *Memorabilia* and the Plato of the *Republic*, who state that, in order to maintain one's health, personal experience of illness, diet, and therapeutics is necessary and sufficient. To be fully independent, an individual must accept his "regimen" from no one other than himself and must, in all circumstances, be his own healer:

> (B) Experience is really on its own dunghill in the subject of medicine, where reason yields it the whole field. Tiberius used to say that whoever had lived twenty years should be responsible to himself for the things that were harmful or beneficial to him, and know how to take care of himself

without medical aid. (C) And he might have learned this from Socrates, who, advising his disciples, carefully and as a principal study, the study of their health, used to add that it was difficult for an intelligent man who was careful about his exercise, his drinking, and his eating not to know better than any doctor what was good or bad for him.

(B) And indeed, medicine professes always to have experience as the touchstone for its workings. So Plato was right in saying that to become a true doctor, the candidate must have passed through all the accidents and circumstances that he is to diagnose. It is reasonable that he should catch the pox if he wants to know how to treat it.[60]

The ancient authorities invoked by Montaigne were concerned with a medicine whose methods involved mainly dietetics, understood broadly to mean not just discipline in eating but "hygienic" regulation of all of an individual's activities. He takes as his allies men who fought against the professionalization of dietary knowledge; Hippocrates' early writings, which argue in favor of the legitimacy of a specialized practice of medicine, show that not everyone found scientific specialization justified on its face.

Montaigne backs up his three authorities with further support derived from what I shall call the tradition of "primitivism" in ancient literature: the earliest men (so this tradition holds), ignorant as they were, led a life more innocent, happier, and above all healthier than our own. In this respect, Montaigne was an important link between the primitivsm of the ancients and the antimedical ideas that Rousseau would later express in the *Discourse on Inequality* and *Emile*, and whose influence may still be detected in contemporary debates. Projecting mythical images of the golden age onto the world of the "cannibals," Montaigne does not fail to celebrate the man-eaters' good health: "For the rest, they live in a country with a very pleasant and temperate climate, so that according to my witnesses it is rare to see a sick man there; and they have assured me that they never saw one palsied, bleary-eyed, toothless, or bent with age."[61] In the "Apology for Raymond Sebond" Montaigne attributes our maladies both to *the agitation of our minds* and to our hasty recourse to the services of medicine:

> Compare the life of a man enslaved to such imaginings with that of a plowman letting himself follow his natural appetites, measuring things only by the present sensations, without knowledge and without prognostication, who has pain only when he has it; whereas the other often

has the stone in his soul before he has it in his loins. As if he were not in time to suffer the pain when he is in it, he anticipates it in imagination and runs to meet it. . . . What they tell us of the Brazilians, that they died only of old age, which is attributed to the serenity and tranquillity of their air, I attribute rather to the tranquillity and serenity of their souls, unburdened with any tense or unpleasant passion or thought or occupation, as people who spent their life in admirable simplicity and ignorance, without letters, without law, without king, without religion of any kind.[62]

Montaigne establishes a perfect analogy between the savage and the common man (which again Rousseau would take up years later). All of these ideas are formulated in chapter 2:37, apparently indisputable in their generality:

(A) There is no nation that has not been without medicine for many centuries, and those the first centuries, that is to say the best and happiest; and one-tenth of the world does not use it to this day. . . . And among us the common people get along happily without it. . . . Everything that is found to be salubrious for our life may be called medicine.[63]

In order to discredit the medicine of the universities and the learned language of the "scholars," Montaigne simply repeats classical objections to technology. He refers to arguments commonplace in his cultural milieu—apologizing for "apathy" as a preventive of disease and praising instinctive self-medication—in order to cast doubt on the illusory benefits of culture. When, for example, Montaigne attributes the health of the Brazilians to the "tranquillity and serenity of their *soul*," he is not abandoning the language of medicine; rather, he is making a choice between two causal categories established by medicine itself (as we shall have occasion to recall) among the "six nonnatural causes" subsumed under the head of hygiene.

Montaigne is speaking as a layman, however, a mere private individual, and he is at some pains to make this clear. He does not try to establish his authority with any degree or title before stating his objections to the diplomaed practitioners of medicine. This shows (if proof is necessary) that Montaigne's time was not that of the early "renaissance of letters" with its respect for all ancient sources. He was far more a man of that later age when the critical spirit, first developed for the purpose of restoring the ancients texts in all their philological purity, finally turned against the doctrines contained in those texts. Montaigne sees himself as a man free of the prejudices of a science that others persist in venerating (thought it is contested from within by certain dissidents, some of whom Montaigne mentions: "Paracelsus, Fioravanti, and Argenterius"[64]). He prefers to heed the lesson not of medical science but of the object of which it speaks—our bodies—which can speak for itself, and more directly than medicine. Montaigne proposes, at first for his own use but with an eye to winning us over to his cause, an antimedicine based on what he has learned about his own body rather than on the teachings of the dubious "art" that has appointed itself to deal with bodily matters. The "science of the body" can and must be understood as a science that the body possesses and not as a science that is applied, without proof of efficacy, to the task of describing and manipulating the human machine. With discreet assistance from the faculty of judgment, the body must become a subject of personal knowledge.

To appeal in this way to the "wisdom of the body," to place one's confidence not in dogmatic obscurantism but in the obscure workings of the indwelling forces of nature, runs counter to a powerful current in Renaissance science: the drive to correct and outstrip the ancient masters, particularly in describing the human body. Montaigne urges his readers to abandon medicine at the very moment when others are busily, and successfully, seeking to perfect it. Through dissection, emphasis on visual examination, and concern for detailed graphical representation, Renaissance physicians refined and enriched our knowledge of the human organism as a natural object—a thing (however admirable) among other things. The progress made in anatomy from the time of Leonardo and Vesalius transformed the human body into an open-air spectacle: an anonymous cadaver exposed to the view of observers ranged in ranks on the steps of an "anatomical theater." The complexity of the nervous system (of which the ancients knew nothing) was revealed by the fine, cold tip of the scalpel for all to see, and then preserved by the burin of the engraver upon the pages of a printed book. Over the long run such careful inventories of the human organism would augment the powers of a science whose promises Montaigne held to be illusory. All signs suggest that Montaigne remained indifferent to the corrections that a rejuvenated science of anatomy was making to ancient medieval ideas (insofar as he even knew what those corrections were). While anatomists busied themselves with the refutation of Galen and with bettering Galen's observations, Montaigne was looking back to a stage in the history of medicine well before Galen, to the Socratic idea that each individual is competent to govern all aspects of his own life, the diet of the body as well as the diet of the soul. But by thus neglecting medicine's ambitions to establish an objective medical science Montaigne became (unwittingly to be sure) a precursor of the protest that would develop once the new medical science, based on systematic description of the human body viewed as an "extended substance," had been established. At each stage in the evolution of an objectified, impersonal, "mechanical" model of the body, there was a "subjectivist" reaction that invoked inner experience to deny that man is a thing like other things. Marcel Raymond, writing about how up-to-date Rousseau's thought is even today, says the following: "The same fundamental needs and requirements remain. We are still obsessed by the thought of immediate knowledge, by the idea of thoughts that have weight, by the prospect of obtaining *knowledge through the body*, through sensation and through the soul."[65] Hence Montaigne, Rousseau's most direct precursor in this respect as in so many others, is also up-to-date. His retreat to prescientific knowledge prefigures a kind of intellectural reaction that is relatively common in what I shall call our postscientific culture. Montaigne's nostalgic wish for the ability to maintain one's health without art (in the technical sense of the word) is undoubtedly related to the need we feel today for an art (this time in the aesthetic sense) that would bring home to us physically the purely pragmatic powers with which science and technology have endowed us.

At various times in history, the development of rational, objective science has provoked disorganized rebellion on the part of those whose judgment it was that scientific knowledge, with its "abstract" generalizations, imposes its rigor in opposition to the "concrete" essence and unique individuality of its object. As a defensive maneuver, opponents attempted to restore to the objects of science (whether nature or man) the dignity and prerogatives of *subjects* capable of apprehending themselves directly by means of inarticulate inner knowledge—and also capable of allowing themselves to be *comprehended* by a different kind of science, a science predicated on respectful attentiveness rather than reductive *explanation*. Such a reaction, which can be a most fruitful stimulus to philosophical reflection (witness the recent development of phenomenology) and to the finest in poetry, has often given rise to the most dubious sorts of "science," i.e., to "heterodox" forms of knowledge that aspire to retain the status and prestige of science without submitting to the methodological requirements that any science worthy of the name must satisfy: viz., that a true science must limit itself to stating verifiable propositions about a deliberately restricted domain, the objects of which are defined in terms of measurable parameters. In Montaigne's century, Paracelsus held that nature confides her secrets to the few privileged individuals capable of reading her "signatures" and lending an ear to her mysteries.[66] In the eighteenth century, the hypothesis that inanimate objects possess sensibility and even powers of thought came as an eloquent riposte to the sometimes outsized ambitions of "geometrized" physics.[67] Similar conflicts are not lacking in our own century, most notably in the psychological sciences. As a counter to certain naïvely objectivist forms of psychology and psychoanalysis, which took as their task the mapping and measuring our psychic energies, another form of psychoanalysis was developed, which, by asserting that truth can be expressed only in the language of the unconscious, forfeited all claims to scientific status. By trying to avoid the dangers involved in modeling the language of psychology too closely on that of natural science, this psychoanalysis fell into a worse trap by claiming to possess knowledge while shunning all experimental control.

Clearly, this kind of opposition to science always leads to renewed emphasis on individual experience, which is sometimes made the starting point of a general theory of some sort. In Montaigne's thought, the importance accorded to the ego and the attention of which it was the object required that epistemological primacy be granted to "sensation," spiritual as well as bodily. The main point bears repeating: the corporeal subject, insofar as it has the *sensation* of existing, claims to have a greater right to govern the body than any scientific discourse. Nothing could be farther from Montaigne's mind, however, than the thought of creating a new school by professing a heterodox science: his rebellion is in essence aimed at restoring poetry to what science inevitably articulates without it. For Montaigne, the end result of the effort to articulate a science of the body is to allow the body to express itself through its own voice, acts, movements, etc. He also uses the body as a source of metaphors for representing thought and emotion in his book. To articulate the body is truly to go back to the source, because it is possible, through it, to give voice to so many objects—and possibly to say whatever can be said.

In telling us about his own health, therefore, Montaigne is speaking as an opponent of medicine, whose opposition is justified by the fact that he has a greater right than the physicians to speak from experience, which medicine, as we saw earlier, has made the "touchstone of its workings."[68] "Antimedical" knowledge is transmitted from author to reader in the context of an uninhibited conversation on the pleasures of living. Trust in the experience of a single individual,

Montaigne urges us, and allow him to pass his knowledge on, not to the scientific community but to another individual: "(B) I have lived long enough to give an account of the practice that has guided me so far. For anyone who wants to try it I have *tasted* it [*j'en ay faict l'essay*] like his cupbearer."[69] In this sentence the word *essay* takes on a new meaning: through a metaphor (which might also be considered a metonymy) the sensuous experience of tasting stands for bodily experience in general. The tasting metaphor has a further, "convivial" connotation: before inviting the reader to join him, to celebrate life as he does, Montaigne has sampled the food and drink at life's banquet. Montaigne's antimedicine substitutes pleasure for knowledge, just as it substitutes intimate experience for empirical reasoning. It also states its preference for one meaning of *art* over another: art in the sense of the production of pleasure is said to be preferable to art as technical knowhow. The physician's *technē* or *savoir-faire* is replaced by the patient's *savoir-vivre*. It is important, in other words, to grasp fully the paradoxical thrust of Montaigne's statement: "My trade and my art is living."

For a good example of Montaigne's ability to articulate the singular uniqueness of physical experience, the reader would do well to consult the account of his fall from a horse and subsequent fainting (in 2:6). He was later able to interpret this event as an anticipation of a more permanent privation: death. The narrative imposes an ineluctable order of its own, notwithstanding the digressions with which the narrator surrounds it.

But how can we write about life's habits, about our bodily rituals? Narrative does not lend itself to the task. Each habit must be described in detail. And if we are determined to adopt an offhand style, a certain descriptive frame of reference is indispensable. What could be more suitable than the common descriptive vocabulary of the time, strongly influenced as it was by medical terminology? For Montaigne's attention was focused on a set of facts whose nature and importance had for generations been discussed and developed by physicians. He says that he wants to inform us about some of the "items" of "the practice that has guided me thus far . . . as remembrance [*souvenance*] supplies me with them."[70] But remembrance does not contain all of the past, and still less does it yield up all that it contains: it selects the material it deems worthy of surrendering. And remembrance is guided, in its choice and even its perception, by a language in which the role played by medical terminology is greater than it suspects. To articulate the body better then medicine does, an adequate and intelligible terminology is essential: ordinary language is ready for service, but the problem is that ordinary language is heavily influenced by medical terminology. Therein lies the difficulty of speaking against medicine: medical language is inescapable.

Even a cursory glance at the medical books of the time reveals that Montaigne cannot tell about himself without borrowing the language of the physicians, without making use of their categories for his own purposes, following the same rule as for all his other borrowings.

An excellent example of this surreptitious use of medical concepts and Montaigne's modification of them may be found in the conclusion to "Of repentance" (3:2). Montaigne might have read the following passage in Ambroise Paré: "Old age, however vigorous, is by its very nature *like a species of malady*."[71] Paré therefore concludes that it "seems better to nourish it [i.e., the disease of old age] with food of opposing temperament, which is to say, food that is warm and moist, in order to retard the causes of death, namely, cold and desiccation, which follow closely on its heels." In the final paragraph of the essay *Of repentance*, Montaigne echoes this thought in his own style, lending a poetic cast to a moral observation:

> (B) It seems to me that in old age our souls are subject to more troublesome ailments and imperfections than in our youth. . . . *It is a powerful malady*, and it creeps up on us naturally and imperceptibly. We need a great provision of study, and great precaution, to avoid the imperfections it loads upon us, or at least to slow up their progress. I feel that, notwithstanding all my retrenchments, it gains on me foot by foot. I stand fast as well as I can. But I do not know where it will lead even me in the end. In any event, I am glad to have people know whence I shall have fallen.[72]

Nor does Montaigne neglect the therapeutic value of *heat* (as a remedy for the "coldness and desiccation" of old age). But as we shall see, it is in the chapter "On some verses of Virgil" (3:5) that he mentions heat in discussing not "food" but love, a cause of heat that medical science might do well to accept as a specific remedy. The chapter on the force of the imagination (1:21) includes ideas and examples heavily influenced by the writings of the physician-philosopher Marsilio Ficino and widely reported in the medical literature (Johannes Wier, Ambroise Paré, Levinus Lemnius, Fienus, Huarte, etc.).

Montaigne's lengthy discussion of his "bodily health" in "Of experience" falls almost entirely under the head of what physicians called "nonnatural" or neutral causes: as the term indicates, these are factors not directly related to an individual's nature (i.e., his humors and temperament) but rather to the manner in which he arranges (or endures) his living conditions. Nonnatural factors are in themselves neutral, but the *use* an individual makes of them can influence his health. In this area—hygiene—the physician takes into account the way the patient lives and questions him about his habits. Paré gives an excellent account of prevailing opinion on the subject, and it is worth citing what he has to say at length:

> Such things [i.e., nonnatural causes] . . . are included in the second part of medicine, called Hygiene, or rules for the preservation of health, not because any of these things are such that are always salubrious, and others such that they are always insalubrious by nature, but simply because they are made and rendered so by proper or improper *use*.
>
> Four conditions determine whether the use is proper or improper: these are quantity, quality, occasion, and manner of use. If you respect these conditions, you can ensure that these things, which are in themselves neutral, are always salubrious. For all the rules and precepts of this part of Medicine, which has to do with the preservation of health, depend upon these four conditions. As Galen says in the first book of *De sanitate tuenda*, the nonnatural causes belong to four universal classes or categories, which are called *sumenda, admovenda, educenda*, and *facienda*. The *sumenda*, or things that are taken in through the mouth or elsewhere, are air, drink, and food. The *admovenda*, or things applied externally, include all medications or other substances applied to the body or any of its parts. The *educenda*, or things drawn off from the body, are excrements that are expelled from the body, all the strange things that can be drawn out of it. The *facienda*, or things that one must do, include work, rest, sleep, and waking, among other things. Commonly, however, these things are divided into six categories, as follows:
> Air.
> Food and drink.
> Work, or exercise and rest.
> Sleeping and Waking.
> Excretion and retention, or repletion and inanition.
> The perturbations of the soul.[73]

Paré is careful to add that in all these areas, especially those having to do with nutrition, it is important to pay the utmost attention to custom, which contributes to forming the individual's specific temperament (idiosyncrasy):

It is not enough simply to know the quantity and quality of foods; one must also understand the *custom* and manner of taking them, if it is correct, as the leading Physicians say, that *custom [i.e., the manner of living] is a second nature.* For custom sometimes changes the natural temperament and leaves another, acquired one. Accordingly, custom should be maintained not only in the healthy but also in the ill. For by suddenly replacing bad habits with better ones, you will certainly do more harm than good.[74]

Is it surprising that we find Montaigne, as he begins his discussion of "bodily health" in "Of experience," emphasizing the power of custom? On the part of a man whose wish it is to free himself from the tutleage of medicine, does this show undue willingness to accept the very language of the doctors?

(B) My way of life is the same in sickness as in health; the same bed, the same hours, the same food serve me, and the same drink. I make no adjustments at all, save for moderating the amount according to my strength and appetite. Health for me is maintaining my accustomed state without disturbance.

It is for habit to give form to our life, just as it pleases; it is all-powerful in that; it is Circe's drink, which varies our nature as it sees fit. How many nations . . . regard as ridiculous the fear of the night dew, which appears so hurtful to us; and our boatmen and peasants laugh at it.[75]

To be sure, Montaigne had no desire to become a slave of habit: "The best of my bodily qualities is that I am flexible and very stubborn. I have *inclinations* that are more personal and customary, and more agreeable to me, than others, but with very little effort I turn away from them, and easily slip into the opposite habit." But custom has become more imperious with age, and we are given a long list of habits that Montaigne is unable to break:

(B) Habit, imperceptibly, has already so imprinted its character upon me in certain things that I call it excess to depart from it.[76] And I cannot without an effort, sleep by day, or eat between meals, or breakfast, or go to bed without a long interval, (C) of about three full hours, (B) after supper, or make a child except before going to sleep, or make one standing up, or endure my sweat, or quench my thirst with pure water or pure wine, or remain bareheaded for long, or have my hair cut after dinner; and I would feel as uncomfortable without my gloves as without my shirt, or without washing when I leave the table or get up in the morning, or without canopy and curtains for my bed, as I would be without really necessary things. . . . (B) I owe many such weaknesses to habit."[77]

Here it is clear that Montaigne is not drawing on the example of his own life in order to contradict the teachings of medicine, for he actually confirms those teachings by furnishing so many details about unusual aspects of his life. When he generalizes, moreover, he reminds us of the generality of medical discourse, though his style is more finely wrought. The following comparison will make this clear. Paré writes:

> According to Hippocrates . . . sudden and rapid changes are dangerous. For this reason, if we wish to change a customary way of living that is harmful or that engenders or maintains illness, this *change* must be made slowly so as not to anger nature, and so that she can accommodate herself to new habits without too much disturbance. For although a food may be good nourishment in itself, it will be warmed and digested either less, or later, than another that is less good but habitual. That this is so is apparent from the fact that we see country people cooking lard or beef for their ordinary use rather than partridge or capon or other succulent meats.[78]

Montaigne puts the same point more pithily:

> I have no idea where sick men can better place themselves in safety than in keeping quietly to the way of life in which they have been brought up and trained. *Change* of any sort is disturbing and hurtful. Go ahead and believe that chestnuts hurt a native of Perigord or of Lucca, or milk and cheese the mountaineers.[79]

Montaigne draws upon his personal experience in order to "fill in the blanks" in the general questionnaire compiled by the physicians, the main points of which he himself enumerates in the last essay of book 2 (where he lists the various considerations that physicians must take into account in order to avoid "mistakes"): "the patient's constitution, his temperament, his humors, his inclinations, his actions, his very thoughts and fancies . . . external circumstances . . . the nature of the place, the conditions of the air and weather."[80] Of course he cannot answer all the questions that concern the physicians: "the position of the planets and their influences"—so remote and conjectural—leaves him indifferent. As for the "causes, symp-

toms, effects, and critical days" of his illness, he has duly informed
the reader of all these matters in the essay "Of the resemblance of
children to fathers," where he treats heredity as an almost miraculous
phenomenon:

> There are in the works of nature certain qualities and con-
> ditions that are imperceptible to us and whose means and
> causes our capacity cannot discover. . . . What a prodigy it
> is that the drop of seed from which we are produced bears
> in itself the impressions not only of the bodily form but of
> the thoughts and inclinations of our fathers! Where does
> that drop of fluid lodge this infinite number of forms?"[81]

By pointing to his father's drop of semen as the *necessary cause* of his
ailment, Montaigne is careful to underscore the limits of our understanding, which cannot grasp, beyond the necessary cause, the truly
sufficient causes. In pathology the *patient* knows full well that knowledge of causes is not open to him (but he doubts, with good reason,
that the professional knows any more than he does). What he can say
from having experienced illness is that diseases are like "animals"[82]
in that their life span is limited. Montaigne took this *ontological* concept of disease from the philosophers and physicians, but he credits it
to his own experience: "(B) Experience has further taught me this,
that we ruin ourselves by impatience. Troubles have their life and
their limits, (C) their illnesses and their health."[83] As for his "constitution, temperament, and humors," Montaigne informs his readers about these matters, in the language of medicine itself, in chapter
2:17, "Of presumption": his constitution is "(B) between the jovial
and the melancholy, moderately (A) sanguine and warm." What he
still has left to say in the very last chapter of the *Essays* concerns his
"inclinations, actions, thoughts, and fancies," especially the various
forms of behavior and experience that fall under the head of the "six
nonnatural causes."

Montaigne's confidences on these subjects may have seemed pointless or indecent to readers unfamiliar with the content of systematic
medical research. When we look closely at what Montaigne discloses,
it becomes clear that, despite his apparent total lack of system, nothing that he says cannot be fitted into the accepted categories of medical classification, none of which is omitted from his account. For
example, the plan of his essay follows the order of the "six nonnatural causes" established by Ambroise Paré.

First comes the "air" or "atmosphere." Montaigne almost con-
vinces himself that "dew" is more dangerous before sunset.[84] "I fear

a stuffy *atmosphere* and avoid smoke like the plague. . . . My breathing is free and easy. . . . The rigor of summer is more of an enemy
to me than that of winter.[85]

Then comes food and drink. Montaigne discusses this subject in
several places, following his custom of proceeding "by leaps and
gambols":[86] "Both in health and in sickness I have readily let myself
follow my urgent appetites."[87] But here he is still speaking of the
whole range of passions (or bodily appetites) and treating the pleasures of eating on a par with the pleasures of sex.[88] His discussion of
the more specific topic of eating and drinking, which is interrupted by
several digressions, begins with the declaration: "(B) I make little
choice at table."[89] Montaigne then continues: "(B) Long sessions at
table (C) annoy me and (B) disagree with me."[90] The loss of a tooth
serves as the pretext for a digression about death and the way it steals
over us imperceptibly, following which Montaigne returns to his major theme: "(B) I am not excessively fond of either salads or fruits,
except melons."[91] The subject of fasting, of the amount of food to be
eaten, and of the frequency of dining occupies the next few paragraphs: "(B) Ever since my youth I have occasionally skipped a
meal. . . . I think it is healthier to eat more slowly and less, and to eat
more often."[92]

Next is *drinking*, which, as a matter of correct method, ought to
have been treated together with *eating*. Montaigne's discussion of the
subject is delayed by the interpolation of a brief paragraph on the
subject of *clothing* (which was also a traditional part of medical
hygiene, classed under the head of *admovenda* or *applicata*): "(B) I do
not keep my legs and thighs more covered in winter than in summer:
silk hose, nothing else."[93] Montaigne then returns momentarily to
the question of the hour of the last meal of the day and then, finally,
turns to the subject of drink: "(B) I am not much subject to thirst,
either in health or in sickness."[94] Once again, Montaigne praises
custom: "The most usual and common way of living is the best; all
particularities seem to me things to be avoided; and I should hate as
much to see a German putting water in his wine as a Frenchman
drinking it pure. Public usage lays down the law in such things."[95]

On the subject of *sleeping and waking*, as well as *work, exercise, and
rest*, Montaigne has much to tell us: it is not insignificant that the first
of the actions he mentions is that of "talking":

> I have noticed that when I am wounded or sick, talking
> excites me and hurts me as much as any irregularity I may
> commit. It is costly and tiring for me to use my voice, for it
> is loud and strained. . . . The tone and movement of my

voice express and signify my meaning; it is for me to guide
it to make myself understood. There is a voice for instructing, a voice for flattering, a voice for scolding. I want my
voice not only to reach my listener, but perhaps to strike
him and pierce him.[96]

Much later in the text, the subject of *exercise* is reconsidered, and this
time Montaigne begins with a discussion of sleep and waking:

(B) There is nothing that should be recommended so much
to youth as *activity* and *vigilance*. Our life is nothing but
movement. I have trouble getting under way, and am late
in everything: *getting up, going to bed*, at meals. Seven
o'clock is early for me.[97]

Since the subject of sleep and waking is traditionally associated with
that of exercise, it is not surprising to find Montaigne, after admitting
his "lazy propensity,"[98] going to the opposite extreme by pointing to
his aptitude for sustained effort, when necessary even sacrificing the
eight or nine hours he normally devotes to sleep. And he is at pains to
point out that he has manfully discharged his military obligations:

(B) I am weaning myself profitably from this lazy propensity, and am obviously the better for it. I feel the impact of
the change a little, but in three days it is done. And I hardly know anyone who can live with less sleep when necessary, or who stands up better under exercise, or who is
bothered less by military duties. My body is capable of
steady but not of vehement or sudden exertion. These
days I shun violent exercises which put me into a sweat;
my limbs grow tired before they grow warm. I can stay on
my feet a whole day, and I do not weary of walking . . .
and I have always liked to rest, whether lying or sitting,
with my legs as high as my seat or higher.[99]

There is still more to say about exercise. A few pages later, after discussing food, drink, the atmosphere, and mild eye fatigue, Montaigne adds a new detail: "My walk is quick and firm."[100] But this
leads straightaway to the more special problem of the relation of mind
to body: "(A) And I know not which of the two, my mind or my
body, I have had more difficulty in keeping in one place."[101] Montaigne admits that he finds it difficult to remain calm and keep his
attention from wandering: "I have never succeeded in keeping some
part of me from always wandering." This is followed immediately by
a confession of his gluttonous habits at table, and though this again
falls under the head of eating and drinking, he uses it to introduce a

new subject, that of the competition between *eating* and *speaking*.[102]
Once again, we discover rivalry between the activities of the spirit
and those of the body: "There is jealousy and envy between our pleasures."[103] Though still discussing "nonnatural causes," Montaigne is
already setting the stage for the theme of the final pages of the essay,
his acceptance of the interdependence between soul and body. There
are so many sudden shifts from one subject to another that it is difficult to recognize the underlying structure, though its broad outlines
are in fact clearly marked out. Accordingly, what Montaigne says
about the expressiveness of his features clearly falls under the head-
ing of exercise: "(B) My face immediately betrays me."[104] Here the
subject is medical symptomatology; the question of moral symptomatology, that is to say, of the relation between physiognomic
signs and character, was treated earlier, in the closing pages of the
chapter "Of physiognomy" (3:12). But now the face is considered as a
mirror of health and sickness: "(B) [All] my changes begin there, and
seem a little worse than they really are. I often move my friends to
pity before I feel the reason for it." Is it possible, then, to read the
state of Montaigne's health on his face, as though he were an open
book? Not in the least. The physicians, puzzled whenever Montaigne's face varied from its natural color and unable to discover an
organic or humoral cause, invoked the sixth of the "nonnatural
causes," the "passions of the soul," thereby shedding no additional
light on the matter:

> (B) My mirror does not alarm me, for even in my youth I
> have more then once found myself thus wearing a muddy
> complexion and an ill-omened look, without any serious
> consequences; so that the doctors, finding inside me no
> cause responsible for this outward change, attributed it to
> the spirit and to some secret passion gnawing me within.
> They were wrong. If my body obeyed my orders as well as
> my soul, we should get along a little more comfortably.[105]

Thus the signs bearing on one's physical condition are dealt with in
the same way as the signs of moral character discussed in the essay
on physiognomy and, more generally, in the same way as any presumed causal relation:

> The cast and formation of the face and those lineaments
> from which people infer certain inward dispositions and
> our fortunes to come, are things that do not fall very di-
> rectly and simply under the heading of beauty and ug-
> liness; any more than every good odor and clear air

promises health, or every closeness and stench promises
infection, in time of pestilence. Those who accuse the
ladies of belying their beauty by their character do not always hit the mark. For in a not too well formed face there
may dwell an air of probity and trustworthiness; as, on the
contrary, I have sometimes read between two beautiful
eyes threats of a malignant and dangerous nature. . . . The
face is a weak guarantee; yet it deserves some consideration.[106]

Before the passions of the soul, however, Paré's list mentions *excretion* and *retention*. On this point Montaigne is scrupulous about filling
in the questionnaire. He has no reason to avoid the issue: "(B) Both
kings and philosophers defecate, and ladies too. . . . Wherefore I will
say this about that action."[107] Here, too, custom must be our guide:
defecation should be postponed until "certain prescribed nocturnal
hours," and we must "force and subject ourselves to them by habit."[108] Is Montaigne here being indiscreet or immodest? Of course.
But since his purpose is to reply point by point to the physicians, how
can he leave out a subject to which they attach so much importance?
Also included under the head of excretions is the subject of Montaigne's kidney stones, which comes in for lengthy discussion. Of all
his "bodily conditions" this is the only one to be classed as a disease.
In all other respects custom has established a salutary equilibrium.
Here, however, the internal menace rears its head. Now, it is on just
this point that Montaigne is determined to declare his hostility (as he
did earlier in 2:37) to medical procedures and practice. The best
course, he says, is to adopt an attitude of resignation: "It is unjust to
complain that what may happen to anyone has happened to someone. . . . The gout, the stone, indigestions, are symptoms of length of
years, as are heat, rains, and winds of long journeys. . . . We must
learn to endure what we cannot avoid."[109] Granting this principle,
what need is there to call upon the services of doctors, especially
when the only therapy they have to offer is the form of alarming
prognoses:

(B) I do little consulting about the ailments I feel, for these
doctors are domineering when they have you at their mercy. They scold at your ears with their forebodings. And
once, catching me weakened by illness, they treated me
insultingly with their dogmas and magisterial frowns,
threatening me now with great pains, now with approach-
ing death. I was not floored by them or dislodged from my

position, but I was bumped and jostled. If my judgment
was neither changed nor confused by them, it was at least
bothered. It is still agitation and struggle.[110]

"Agitation and struggle": these are passions of the soul. Thus the
sixth and last of the "nonnatural causes" turns out to be closely related, in Montaigne's case, to the illness stemming from his urinary
problems. That this is so is hardly surprising: according to the generally accepted medical doctrine, the passions of the soul are now
causes of disease, now consequences. Montaigne tells us how he is
holding up against the difficulty caused by his stones in two ways: he
continues to keep track of his excretions and he tells us about the
passions aroused in him by the "stony disease" [*maladie pierreuse*],
wherein he senses the lurking presence of death.

Clearly, then, this is such an important subject that it deserves to be
treated in a special manner of its own. How does Montaigne go about
it? In the first place, he sets his discussion of this topic in a central
position, exactly in the middle of an essay devoted to his bodily habits. He also dramatizes it, devoting much more space to this topic
than to the others that he considers. Thus immediately after evoking
the "magisterial frowns" and unsparing judgments of the physicians,
he resorts to a long prosopopoeia to make a number of points directed
against the professionals. The device he uses is to *quote* (or, rather, to
pretend to quote) the words that his *mind* is in the habit of using to aid
and comfort his *imagination:*

> (B) Now I treat *my imagination* as gently as I can, and would
> relieve it, if I could, of all trouble and conflict. We must
> help it and flatter it, and fool it if we can. *My mind* is suited
> to this service; it has no lack of plausible reasons for all
> things. If it could persuade as well as it preaches, it would
> help me out very happily.
>   *Would you like an example?* It tells me that it is for my own
> good that I have the stone; that buildings of my age must
> naturally suffer some leakage. . . . That the company
> should console me.[111]

Here, then, the exposition takes the form of a speech within a speech.
A short while earlier, when he began describing his "habits," Montaigne appealed to the reader: "For anyone who wants to try it [i.e.,
life], I have tasted it like his cupbearer." Here the reader is addressed
even more directly: "Would you like an example?" Montaigne inter-
rupts his discussion of the many "items" furnished by his "remembrance" in order to give the floor to another speaker—his

mind—who takes his place at the podium and insists that the reader pay closer attention. The mind's apostrophe to the imagination is an internal debate, told to us in allegorical form. It is a debate between two of the faculties that, according to traditional doctrine, constitute the *sensus internus*. There are three such faculties in all: the mind or reason; the imagination or fancy; and memory. Memory, the third faculty, is not left out of Montaigne's account: at the very beginning of his description of bodily experience, he sounded the call to gather his memories so that he might record all their pertinent details.

The self has split into two agencies. The mind (which Montaigne designates using the third-person masculine pronoun *il*) speaks (using the second person familiar *tu*) to the imagination, i.e., the being that is in danger of going mad, of being overcome by trouble and suffering. In the functional hierarchy of the *sensus internus* the mind holds the superior rank. Montaigne thus presents to us the speech of the most authoritative of the faculties:

> (B) Fear of this disease, says my *mind*, used to terrify *you*, when it was unknown to *you*; the cries and despair of those who make it worse by their lack of fortitude engendered in you a horror of it. It is an affliction that punishes those of *your* members by which you have most sinned. *You are* a man of conscience:
> Punishment undeserved gives pain.
> —Ovid
> Consider this chastisement; it is very gentle in comparison with others, and paternally tender. Consider its lateness; it bothers and occupies only the season of your life which in any case is henceforth wasted and barren, having given way, as if by agreement, to the licentiousness and pleasures of your youth.
> The fear and pity that people feel for this illness is a subject of vainglory for you; a quality of which, even if you have purged your judgment and cured your reason of it, your friends still recognize some tincture in your makeup. There is pleasure in hearing people say about you: There indeed is strength, there indeed is fortitude! They see you sweat in agony, turn pale, turn red, tremble, vomit your very blood, suffer strange contractions and convulsions, sometimes shed great tears from your eyes, discharge thick, black, and frightful urine, or have it stopped up by some sharp rough stone that cruelly pricks and flays the neck of your penis; meanwhile keeping up conversation with your company with a normal countenance, jesting in

the intervals with your servants, holding up your end in a sustained discussion, making excuses for pain and minimizing your suffering.[112]

Even though this apostrophe makes use of all the devices of rhetoric (interrogation, injunction, maxims, dialogisms, hypotyposis, etc.), it does not exhaust the arguments that the mind addresses to the imagination. Much remains to be said. But at this point Montaigne's tone changes. The apostrophe is followed by remarks in the first person, in which it is again Montaigne who seems to be speaking: "I am obliged to Fortune for assailing me so often with the same kind of weapons. She fashions and trains me against them by use, hardens and accustoms me."[113] The reader might easily think that Montaigne is again speaking to him directly, as he does for the most part throughout the *Essays*. But three pages later it turns out that this, too, is a case where Montaigne is citing himself, a continuation of the speech within a speech:

(B) By such *arguments*, both strong and weak, I try to lull and beguile my *imagination* and salve its wounds, as Cicero did his disease of old age. If they get worse tomorrow, *tomorrow we shall provide other ways of escape.*[114]

This, then, is the sort of conclusion to be drawn from the exemplary discussion of Montaigne's kidney stones in the central portion of his physical summary. Earlier, in an addition to the text, Montaigne tells us that he has kept a diary of his illness, that he has made himself a "memory of paper,"[115] and that by leafing through "these little notes" he can find "grounds for comfort in some prognostic from past experience."[116] The nature of the argument changes: whereas the mind had berated the imagination in moral terms, now the text is quick to mimic the language of medicine in offering an encouraging prognosis. Despite himself, Montaigne makes arguments astonishingly similar to those a physician might have made, even though his purpose is to contradict doctors: he lulls his fears with plausible promises that are worth about as much as the warnings with which the physicians had tried to bludgeon him:

(B) Age weakens the heat of my stomach; its digestion being thereby less perfect, it sends on this crude matter to my kidneys. Why cannot the heat of my kidneys be likewise weakened, at some other turn, so that they can no longer petrify my phlegm, and nature may take steps to find some other way of purgation? The years have evi-

dently made some of my rheums dry up. Why not these
excrements that provide material for the gravel?[117]

But what need is there to speculate on the favorable outcome of the
illness? Why not simply reflect upon the pleasure that comes when
the crisis passes and the pain subsides?

(B) But is there anything so sweet as that sudden change,
when from extreme pain, by the voiding of my stone, I
come to recover as if by lightning the beautiful light of
health, so free and so full as happens in our sudden and
sharpest attacks of colic? Is there anything in this pain we
suffer that can be said to counterbalance the pleasure of
such sudden improvement? How much more beautiful
health seems to me after the illness, when they are so near
and contiguous that I can recognize them in each other's
presence in their proudest array, when they vie with each
other, as if to oppose each other squarely! Just as the Stoics
say that vices are brought into the world usefully to give
value to virtue and assist it, we can say, with better reason
and less bold conjecture, that nature has lent us pain for
the honor and service of pleasure and painlessness. When
Socrates, after being relieved of his irons, felt the relish of
the itching that their weight had caused in his legs, he rejoiced to consider the close alliance between pain and pleasure, how they are associated by a necessary link, so that
they follow and engender each in turn.[118]

The mind's prosopopoeia showed us lithiasis in its most acute phase,
whereas this later stage of the argument focuses on the calm that
follows the attack. The relief that Montaigne describes is no doubt an
authentic record of his experience: the "beautiful light" metaphor is
not only a rhetorical figure but also a way of indicating a deeply felt
synesthetic experience. Nevertheless, Montaigne goes to some
lengths to invoke the authority of Socrates and the Stoics in support
of his account. (Even as he dismisses all impersonal knowledge, he
cannot overlook such important confirmation of what he himself has
felt, namely, "the close alliance between pain and pleasure." After
all, he has to anticipate possible resistance or ill will on the part of the
reader toward the individual experience of one Michel de Montaigne:
"Those who will not conclude their own ignorance from so vain an
example as mine, or as theirs, let them recognize it through Socrates,
(C) the master of masters."[119]

Even these remarks do not conclude Montaigne's case. He has still other arguments up his sleeve:

> I argue that the extreme and frequent vomitings that I endure purge me. . . . Here is another benefit of my illness, peculiar to it: that it almost plays its game by itself and lets me play mine . . . I notice also this particular convenience, that it is a disease in which we have little to guess about. We are freed from the worry into which other diseases cast us by the uncertainty of their causes and conditions and progress—an infinitely painful worry. We have no concern with doctoral consultations and interpretations; the senses reveal to us what it is, and where it is.[120]

In other words, he can live with his gravel in the present, in feeling, without speculating about the past or trying to divine the future.

Kidney stones, then, are distinguished by being a malady with which one can live without taking "troublesome precautions." Montaigne attempts to prove that this is the case by letting his argument range over the whole temporal spectrum: past, present, and future. Looking to the past, he recalls old attacks and his subsequent recovery. In the passage where he cites himself at length, the first portion (the mind's prosopopoeia) is cast in the present indicative, but to no avail: the *representation* of the mind's speech makes it seem to refer to a time that has elapsed, that is recalled in memory. The second portion, in which Montaigne returns to using the first-person singular and speaks in his own name, is more clearly expressed in the present (but in a present that requires help from a "paper memory"). Finally, Montaigne alerts us to the fact that his argument is still incomplete. If need be he will exhort himself in the same way in the future. Earlier, we saw another example of such hypothetical anticipation of what the future may bring: "If [my wounds] get worse tomorrow, tomorrow we shall provide other means of escape." Since the *Essays* were in fact composed in stages, Montaigne—in one of the rare passages where he himself calls attention to an insertion—keeps his promise by adding a postscript or update to his original text:

> (C) Here is proof. Now it has happened again that the slightest movements force the pure blood out of my kidneys. What of it? I do not, just for that, give up moving about as before and pricking after my hounds with youthful and insolent ardor. And I think I come off well from such an important accident when it costs me nothing but a

dull heaviness and uneasiness in that region. It is some big stone that is crushing and consuming the substance of my kidneys, and my life that I am letting out little by little, not without some natural pleasure, as an *excrement* that is henceforth superfluous and a nuisance.[121]

The malady has reappeared. And what if the relapse is a harbinger of death itself? If death were to take this form, it would not be so fearsome, its toll would not be too high.

Even as Montaigne regales us with the spectacle of his disease and consoles himself for his suffering, he continues to compile information about his urinary excretions (and related vomiting) as required by standard medical procedure. The passions of the soul are also revealed as the mind attempts to exert its power over them. Indeed, it is precisely here, in regard to the physical functions, that the mind most clearly evinces the fraternal assistance it lends to the body. Thought is lavishly expended in every way, from the interpretation of disease as a penitential "punishment" (though it is "very mild in comparison with other punishments") to the dispensing of reassuring prognostic speculation. Montaigne hopes that his illness will be cured by a gradual general *cooling* of his body: the heat of the kidneys, which "petrifies the phlegm," may abate as the heat of the stomach has done already. As the vital flame wanes, healing may come from advancing age itself. No matter how sharp the pain may have been at times, the draining of the kidneys, in the aftermath of which only a "dull heaviness" lingers, is in fact the draining away of life, and "not without some natural pleasure." This astonishing sentence bears rereading: "It is some big stone that is crushing and consuming the substance of my kidneys, and my life that I am letting out little by little, not without some natural *pleasure,* as an *excrement that is henceforth superfluous and a nuisance.*"[122] It is impossible to read these words without being reminded of other passages in the *Essays* where the text is likened to excrement: "Here you have . . . some excrements of an aged mind, now hard, now loose, and always undigested."[123] Or again, at the end of "On some verses of Virgil," where Montaigne speaks in a condescending manner about the pages he has just written: this "notable commentary has escaped from me in a *flow of babble,* a flow sometimes impetuous and harmful." The bodily metaphor establishes an equivalence between the flow of life and the flow of text. It is the individual's own body that is dissipated and dispersed as it eliminates the substances it had "digested" or "cooked." (Remember, too, that Montaigne also uses digestive metaphors, but involving the idea of absorption, when he likens learning to the assimilation of foreign nutrients; and also remember that he refers frequently to thought as *rumination.*)

The "natural *pleasure*" that Montaigne feels as he "lets out his life little by little" calls to mind the story of his fall from the horse, where he emphasizes the "pleasure" that accompanied his stupefaction as he felt himself slipping into a state that seems, upon reflection, to have been virtually identical with death. He describes this as being like "the sweet feeling that people have who let themselves slide into sleep."[124] In discussing his surprise brush with death, Montaigne does not forget that for the physicians, breath, too, is an excremental element: "It seemed to me that my life was hanging only by the tip of my lips; I closed by eyes in order, it seemed to me, to help *push it out.*"[125] The final breath, it seems, is both evacuation and deliverance. And Montaigne does not tire of repeating how pleasant the experience was: "Meanwhile my condition was, in truth, *very pleasant* and peaceful. . . . When they had put me to bed, I felt *infinite sweetness* in this repose. . . . I was letting myself slip away *so pleasantly*, in such an easy and *pleasant* way, that I hardly did anything with less of a feeling of effort."[126]

From extreme pain [*douleur*] to extreme pleasure [*douceur*]: the range of experience in illness and disease is measured by a pun.[127] Montaigne experiences sickness not simply in contrast to health and pleasure but in relation to them as well. Our physical experience, which brings home to us "the close alliance between pain and pleasure," prepares us to accept another, equally close alliance: that of body and soul. Time and again we have seen the two terms of an antithesis linked; opposites must coexist, Montaigne tells us, or they must join together. The final pages of the essay "Of experience" set forth in unforgettable terms the "mutual services" of soul and body and the need for cultivating both at the same time.

Now if the *theme* (or argument) of the essay is the joining of opposites, it is important to point out that its formal structure (and more particularly, its mode of argument) exemplifies in a striking manner the overcoming of contradiction. There is homology between the intricacies of the thought and the style that Montaigne invents. The experience of a lifetime is made to culminate in discreetly lyrical praise for the mutual assistance that soul and body must provide one another. And this all takes place within the confines of an essay in which spontaneity, associated with the life of the body, is seen to be necessarily, if forcibly, allied with the artifices of learning.

To any reader of the essay "Of experience," nothing at first seems more clear-cut than the distinction between the discursive systems elaborated by reason in the sciences and the arts (law, theology, philosophy, and medicine—where everything is subject to the "conflict of interpretations") and the truth that lets itself be known in us, and especially in our bodies, by way of feeling, through direct experience and all that makes our own experience unique and different and for that very reason suitable for generalization. If taken seriously, this theoretical distinction is not without implications for the manner of exposition: an essayist bent on communicating his own experience in opposition to science and the arts ought to repudiate the language of those disciplines in order to remain true to an inner nature for which such high claims are made. But just as custom and habit "insinuate themselves" into nature to such an extent that they actually create a second nature, so, too, is the mind called upon to comfort the suffering body: Montaigne, despite the *ordo neglectus* that he indulges in his writing, is unable to describe the "form" of his life without making use of categories established by the medical art. The very idea of a "form of life" comes from medicine: since the time of the Greeks the term had referred to the sphere defined by the concepts of diet and hygiene, subsumed, in the Galenic tradition, under the head of the "six nonnatural causes." Even though Montaigne's intention is to attack medicine, and even though his ambition is to articulate the body's irreducible singularity, he cannot dispense with such medical notions as the *faculties* of the soul (including both the internal senses, i.e., reason, imagination, and memory, and the external senses), the *constitution* or complexion determined by the mixture of the humors, and the various physiological functions sanctioned by medical texts; indeed, these form the central thread of his essay.

Forced to use the codified language of the medical art to say what he would have liked to express directly, without art, Montaigne embellishes his language to cover his tracks. He gives us commentary, digressions, exhortations, details, generalities, examples, and memorable maxims: no one could accuse him of dropping his uneven and "extravagant" tone even for so mundane a matter as filling out the physicians' questionnaire. He has not gotten rid of medical language but he has destroyed its coherence and unity, only to scatter the *disjecta membra* in a "marquetry," as he calls it, concocted of a hodgepodge of different styles. His art consists in the denial of art. More than that, his most remarkable extravagance—the mind's long apostrophe to the imagination—takes him away from the language of medicine only by heightening that language: this enemy of eloquence here produces a fine specimen of eloquent rhetoric. Is it not surprising that, when the time comes to express his body's deepest hurt, Montaigne pretends to allow someone else to speak? And in this eloquent apostrophe to himself, we find a rhetorical reference to the very mainsprings of classical drama: "*The fear and pity* that people feel for this illness is a subject of vainglory for you."[128] *Phobos kai eleinos!* The artifice becomes more and more apparent—we are at the theater. We hear the admiring exclamations of the audience: "There indeed is strength, there indeed is fortitude."[129] We are shown the body's worst sufferings from without, as it is *seen* by everyone, an actor in a play "for one character [130] "They *see* you sweat in agony, turn pale, turn red, tremble."[131] At the climax of his suffering, as though no further language could issue from his body directly, Montaigne lists in a detached, historical manner the external *signs* visible to his relatives and friends, gathered around the body of one whom they think is dying but who in fact admirably holds up his "end in a sustained discussion."[132] Everything is made dramatic and dialectical: the scene of the mind addressing his imagination recalls the deathbed scene where Montaigne, in order to make sure that life remains a dialogue right up to the very end, engages in conversation with the "company" and jokes with his "servants." This is the height of art. The actual experience, with all its literal poignancy, is depicted to us as a scene of pathos—a successful rendition of the *ars moriendi* as set forth by the true philosophy—inserted into a speech of commiseration, itself inserted into a discussion of *custom* and the practices that have governed Montaigne's physical life, and all intended for his reader/dinner companion.

Was it then impossible to articulate the body in any way other than indirectly, through the faculties of an allegorical "mind," which in turn evokes a scene of martyrdom observed by still other spectators? In any case, let us acknowledge that the appeal to inner truth rendered inevitable the recourse to an external witness. Articulating the experience of the body demands a "close alliance" between language and art, even when the object is to surrender to nature. Even as the individual suffers in the depths of his flesh, meaning can be articulated only where the experience of suffering makes contact with others: for us, Montaigne's readers, sweating, turning pale, flushing, and trembling are *events* that we experience by identifying ourselves first with the man racked by his stone and then with the spectators that his text gathers around him to *watch* his suffering. It is because he shows himself as he looked from the outside that we have the sense of participating in what he feels within.

So it is with the suffering body. Similarly, the body in love, no matter how much it desires to dispense with artifice and dissimulation, can express what it feels only by way of the utmost artifice and dissimulation: poetry. This will be the subject of the next chapter.

FIVE

Speaking love

"On some verses of Virgil" (3:5) is the place where Montaigne most fully develops his thinking on the subject of the "relation to others," since love, which is the central theme of this essay, is (along with friendship though "far beneath it"[1]) the quintessential such relation. It will repay us, therefore, to look closely at the way in which Montaigne unfolds his argument as the essay proceeds.

Forbidden books, desired books

His starting point is his relation to himself. Movement is introduced by way of a series of inversions: old age brings a surfeit of such qualities as fullness, gravity, weightiness, temperance, dryness, cold, etc., and each of these calls to mind its opposite. The suffering body is an inescapable inconvenience that must be counterbalanced by "moderation" and self-control:

> (B) It does not leave me a single hour, sleeping or waking, unoccupied with instruction about death, patience, and penitence. I defend myself against temperance as I once did against sensual pleasure; for it pulls me too far back, even to the point of insensibility. *Now I want to be master of myself in every direction.* Wisdom has its excesses, and has no less need of moderation than does folly.[2]

Montaigne's motives are plainly of two kinds. He is guided, first of all, by the medical (and moral) principle according to which an excess of one quality can be counteracted by administering a dose of its opposite: cold is compensated by heat, severity by gaiety, and "wisdom" itself by "folly," in order to arrive at a proper "temperament." In addition, he is concerned lest he fall under the sway of one of his "parts" (in this case the body), which has come to exercise undue dominance over the rest. To be truly and freely in possession of oneself, one must take care to indulge nothing in excess, not even "wisdom," paradoxical as that may seem. This is why Montaigne says that I "deliberately let myself go a bit to license."[3] By this he means simply that he occasionally lets his mind dwell on "youthful

wanton thoughts"[4] and "remembrance of my past youth."[5] Faced
with the "stormy and cloudy sky"[6]—i.e., with death—Montaigne indulges his memory for the sake of diversion: "As long as my eyes can
discern that lovely season now expired, I turn them in that direction
at intervals. If youth is escaping from my blood and my veins, at least
I want not to uproot the picture of it from my memory."[7] Yet another
example of the diversion recommended in the previous chapter (3:4),
this return to the past is a "ruse," a remedy taken "in a dream": "a
feeble struggle, that of art against nature"[8] All the movement on this
page has its source within Montaigne: he calls upon his own
thoughts, images, and memories for aid. Only an addition made in
1595 invokes the authority of Plato in support of another method,
which calls for turning one's attention to the outside world: "Plato
orders men to attend the exercises, dances, and games of youth, *in
order to rejoice in others* at the suppleness and beauty of body that is no
longer in themselves."[9] But this is advice gleaned from reading, not a
remedy envisioned by Montaigne himself.

The compensations of the imagination, in which awakened images
of the past enable the mind to "feed on its own substance" (to borrow
the words of Rousseau, who resigned himself to this kind of pleasure), may be seductive but can never mask the absence of real pleasures. The caprices of "fancy" are never more than a pale substitute.
Nothing surpasses genuine pleasure. "Even the slightest occasions of
pleasure that I can come upon, I seize. . . .[10] My philosophy is in
action, in natural and present practice, little in fancy. Would I might
take pleasure in playing at cobnut or with top."[11] Montaigne would
like to find in the present moment the antidote to the "grave subjects
[that] grieve us."[12] He would like to banish weighty concerns in favor
of light amusements, games concerned with slight and unimportant
matters. Now the very thought of face-to-face confrontation in a
game, the desire for carefree amusement, awakens the hope of a
meeting, the wish for a relationship with another person:

> (B) I, who have no other aim but to live and be merry,
> would run from one end of the world to the other to seek
> out one good year of pleasant and cheerful tranquillity. A
> somber, dull tranquillity is easy enough to find for me, but
> it puts me to sleep and stupefies me; I am not content with
> it. If there are any persons, any good company, in country
> or city, in France or elsewhere, residing or traveling, who
> like my humors and whose humors I like, they have only
> to whistle in their palm and I will go furnish them with
> essays in flesh and bone.[13]

Thus it is association with others in friendship and conversation (a subject treated a short while before in the essay "Of three kinds of association with others" (3:3)) to which Montaigne turns first. Though this may be a desire destined to remain unrequited, it is clear why the thought of another *person* or *company* (so much more effective as remedies than anything the lonely imagination has to offer) brings to an aging and sick old man the hope of amusement that he needs. For what has he to hope from a private conversation with himself? Very little, to judge by the following sentence: "Though I tickle myself, I can scarcely wring a poor laugh out of this wretched body any more."[14] Given the tight "bond" between mind and body, it is impossible for the mind "to rescue itself from old age"[15] when the body's health is failing. The beautiful image of the mistletoe growing green and flourishing "on a dead tree"[16] expresses a wish that cannot be fulfilled. The mind "has such a tight brotherly bond with the body that it abandons me at every turn to follow the body in its need. I take it aside and flatter it, I work on it, all for nothing."[17] The mind is not an independent partner in conversation. The participation of others is therefore indispensable to anyone who wants to escape the lugubriousness of old age and disease. "I love a *gay and sociable* wisdom":[18] gaiety and sociability go together, and they require "communication."

Rather than "furnish essays in flesh and bone" to "persons or good company" that would somehow have to be found, Montaigne settles for the association with his contemporaries established through his book. No sooner does he mention this relationship, however, than he describes it in terms of opposition: his attitude, which is to "dare to say all that I dare to do,"[19] is the exception that proves the rule. Other people, obedient to the "laws of ceremony," are unwilling to go so far toward establishing complete and tranquil equality between *saying* and *doing*. In a time of insincerity Montaigne is alone in confessing himself with total candor.

> God grant that this excessive license of mine may encourage our men to attain freedom, rising above these cowardly and hypocritical virtues born of our imperfections. . . . The diseases of the soul grow more obscure as they grow stronger; the sickest man is least sensible of them. That is why they must be handled often in the light of day, with a pitiless hand, be opened up and torn from the hollow of our breast.[20]

This is one of many places where Montaigne is concerned to show how different he is from his contemporaries (to whom he refers as *ils*, *on, les autres*), whose paths are opposite to his own. But even as he directs this scolding polemic against his contemporaries, he is fixing and specifying his own project as a writer, his desire to make himself known for what he is (unlike "those who have a false opinion of themselves" and "can feed on false approbations"[21]). We have seen him, on many occasions, resign himself to take his distance, to stand aloof in this way, but only in order to show himself as he really is, to *represent* his true being in the most exact manner possible. "A man must see his vice and study it to tell about it. . . . *It is only for a waking man to tell his dream* [Seneca]."[22] At this point Montaigne narrows the focus of his remarks in a most singular manner: he addresses himself to "the ladies" and expresses the hope that (because of the nature of the theme he is about to take up) he will be read in a place more intimate than the "parlor":

> (B) I am annoyed that my essays serve the ladies only as a public article of furniture, an article for the parlor. This chapter will put me in the boudoir. I like their society when it is somewhat private; when public it is without favor or savor.[23]

Having turned his attention to his own youth, Montaigne found that he was not satisfied to dwell in memory alone. He imagined a "company" that suited him, that he would gladly "run" to join were he invited to do so. Yet his only real resource is his book of essays; with this he will entice his female reader into the intimacy of the boudoir. The offer of something to read is a symbolic seduction: it is the form of association that comes closest to love. With the statement of his theme—"the sexual act" [*l'action génitale*][24]—and the statement that he himself is consubstantial with his work, Montaigne crosses into forbidden territory. As soon as his book crosses the threshold of the boudoir, where his reader is in the habit of being alone with her most intimate secrets, he begins to caress the body of another. There is nothing illicit about such intimacy, since it coincides with *separation* of the most radical kind: the preparation for death. At no other time, perhaps, does Montaigne establish such a close relationship between opposites as when he pens the following lines, which immediately follow those cited above: "(B) In farewells we exaggerate the warmth of our affection toward the things we are leaving. I am taking my last leave of the world's pastimes; here are our last embraces. But let us come to my theme."[25]

It is Thanatos that liberates Eros and gives him voice. Thus this chapter of the *Essays* presents itself as the harbinger of death as well as love. Because he is bidding life farewell, Montaigne feels he has the right to speak of what used to fuel life's fires (already he shifts to the imperfect tense). It is a final flame that will catch fire in this chapter, nearly every paragraph of which has its image of heat, intended to ward off the cold that threatens to break in at any moment. Embraces remembered (or still vaguely hoped for) are "our final accolades." Thus there is no frivolity in this portrait set against a background of death. It is possible to discuss the most intimate bonds of the flesh when all bonds are about to come undone. Here the workings of Montaigne's dialectic are plain to see: imminent loss confers an infinite value upon that which can still be articulated and possessed; at the same time death makes it legitimate to take every liberty with language so as to uncover even the secretest of thoughts.

Language itself is the first item of concern. Once again, the problem is the disparity between *saying* and *doing*. The first thing that Montaigne has to say about sexuality is that we are not allowed to talk about it. Hence there is, at first sight, a very close connection between love and words. But this connection is a paradoxical one, because the less one talks about sexual matters, the more one thinks about them: "Does this mean that the less we breathe of it [i.e., sex] in words, the more we have the right to swell our thoughts with it."[26] Montaigne elaborates upon this idea as follows:

> (C) For it is a good one that the words least in use, least written and most hushed up, are the best known and most generally familiar. No age, no type of character, is ignorant of them, any more than of the word "bread." They impress themselves on everyone without being expressed, without voice and without form. It is also a good one that this is an action that we have placed in the sanctuary of silence, from which it is a crime to drag it out even to accuse and judge it. Nor do we dare to chastise it except roundaboutly and figuratively. . . . Is it not the same as in the matter of books, which become all the more marketable and public by being suppressed."[27]

Sexuality is omnipresent, hedged about with proprieties that demand we say nothing about it. And yet, according to Montaigne's text, sexuality is itself attached to the words that people suppress; it is written within us, *impressed* upon our bodies but not expressed by our tongues—without "voice" and "form." Montaigne is quick to compare this "criminal" whom no one dares chastise "except roundaboutly and figuratively" to a proscribed *book* (which immediately calls forth the desire to acquire and possess its forbidden text).

In the case of sexuality, the mask we wear consists in our not saying anything about it, in our not giving it a name. But what is the
essence of this hidden reality, which in any case is no secret from
anyone? The reader will soon see that Montaigne suggests at least
two answers to this question: first, sexuality is repressed speech, and
second, its heat burns only briefly. Let us start by considering the first
of these two answers: love is a hidden language whose words are
imprinted "in each and every one of us." It is given to the Muses and
to the most sublime poetry to express its full force. Only literature can
give body to the imagination and represent the fictional component
that is an essential part of love's value. This explains why Montaigne
invokes the name of Virgil in the very title of his essay—an allusive
title but in fact related to a central theme of the piece:

> (B) Whoever takes away from the Muses their amorous
> fancies will rob them of the best subject they have and the
> noblest matter of their work. And whoever makes Love
> lose the communication and service of poetry will disarm
> him of his best weapons. . . . Dried out and weighed
> down as I am, I still feel some tepid remains of that past
> ardor. . . . But from what I understand of it, the powers
> and worth of this god are more alive and animated in the
> painting of poetry than in their own reality,
>> And verses have their fingers to excite.
>>   —Juvenal
> Poetry reproduces an indefinable mood that is more amo-
> rous than love itself. Venus is not so beautiful all naked
> alive and panting, as she is here in Virgil:
>> The goddess ceased to speak, and snowy arms outflung
>> Around him flattering, soft fondling as she clung.[28]

This admirable erotic passage from Virgil is not only literature, it is
also a conversation of husband and wife ("the goddess ceased to
speak . . . he spoke"). The body's burning heat and ensuing languor
are mixed in with a *conversation*. The images of ardor are interpolated
between the poetic representation of an exchange of words between
husband and wife and an evocation of the thunderbolt that rends and
illuminates as it descends from heaven. The flame of love that passes
through the body of the goddess is portrayed as both the consequence of a linguistic act and as something resembling a natural phenomenon. If, as Juvenal says in a line cited earlier by Montaigne,
verses have fingers, the reason is that words made flesh can penetrate
the body, and this "painting" of love can surpass "love itself." Earlier

Montaigne seemed critical of the prohibitions that prevent us from "chastising" the "sexual act" except "roundaboutly and figuratively." Now, however, he expresses his preference for what the "painting of poetry" has to tell us about love. What is more, after adding to the passage from Virgil (which depicts the loves of Venus and Vulcan) a fine passage from Lucretius concerning the loves of Venus and Mars, he praises both authors for not saying all that might be said about the act of love. This painting that he ranks higher than the reality of love itself owes its superiority to what remains hidden, to what entices the imagination without violating the disguise that love cannot do without. The ellipsis *shows* more than it conceals:

> (B) The verses of these two poets, treating of lasciviousness as reservedly and discreetly as they do, seem to me to reveal it and illuminate it more closely. The ladies cover their bosoms with a veil, the priests many sacred things; painters put shadows in their work to bring out the light more; and it is said that the sun and wind strike harder by reflection than direct. . . . But there are certain other things that people hide only to show them. Listen to this man, who is more open:
>
> And pressed her naked body unto mine.
>
> —Ovid
>
> I feel that he is caponizing me. Let Martial turn up Venus' skirts as high as he pleases, he will not succeed in revealing her so completely. He who says everything satiates and disgusts us; he who is afraid to express himself leads us on to think more than there is. There is treachery in this sort of modesty, and especially in half opening to us, as these do, so fair a road to the imagination. Both the action and the picture of it should smack of theft.[29]

The power of love poetry to surpass love itself and to produce, as does the verse of Lucretius and Virgil, "an indefinable mood more amorous than love itself," is linked to the *reserve* that contrives to give us a fuller image of Venus by keeping her veiled, by not saying all that might be said about her. The language of love, which Montaigne accuses his contemporaries of concealing beneath a facade of hypocritical prudishness, turns out to derive its power from the fact that it is itself a language that *conceals* and that uses the heightening power of chiaroscuro to capture the imagination. In love our feelings are so full that they need an object whose final secret seems to elude our grasp. Montaigne sees this language, which arouses love by feigning reticence, as having the virtue of "presence." He discovers in it not only the presence of thought but also the presence of the body: the words in true poetry are not mere "conceits" or "verbal tricks." When he "ruminates" upon the syllables of Lucretius or Virgil, he feels that "their language is *all full and copious with a natural and constant vigor. They are all epigram*, not only the tail but the head, stomach, and feet. . . . This painting is the result not so much of manual dexterity as of having *the object more vividly imprinted in the soul*."[30] This is also the case with Horace, who "sees more clearly and deeply into the *thing*."[31] In the amorous scenes of Virgil and Lucretius, even though these deal with mythical subjects, "the sense illuminates and brings out the words, which are no longer wind, but flesh and bone. The words mean more than they say."[32] If Montaigne is right, the power of *incarnation* and sexualization that language has is indistinguishable from the *excess* of meaning that surrounds each word like an aura and thus bridges the gap that Montaigne believes generally separates the word (mere "wind" that it is) from the thing. ("Of glory" [2:16] begins: "There is the name and the thing.")

Montaigne, whose work is in so many ways comparable to mannerist art, is critical of poetry that cultivates "mannerism," in its primary sense of "manual dexterity"; of such poetry only the wind remains. Against poets who rely on "conceits" and epigrammatic "tails" he protests: "If I were of the profession, I would naturalize art as much as they artify nature." But so much art is needed to give life to amorous conversation! The poetry that best expresses love is that whose words are invested with meaning ("the sense that illuminates and brings out the words"), that which makes itself "flesh and bone" by *meaning* more than it actually *says*, that which adds to physical love something more, the veil that transfigures the reality. The same transformation that enables words to mean more than they say also enables love that is attended by the Muses to transcend the very "essence" of love. Now, as we saw a moment ago, this addition is, paradoxically, the result of an impediment (the veil or mask or detour) that *culture* places between our desire and the *natural* satisfaction that is its goal. This accounts for the praise—rather surprising in any enemy of deception—that Montaigne here bestows on fraud and illusion, which he sees as strategems of modesty or coquetry that keep hope in a state of breathlessness: "Let us teach the ladies to make the most of themselves, to respect themselves, to beguile and fool us."[33] The duration of desire (and the pleasure associated with it) is increased by delay of the final conquest, which is represented as part of an allegorical itinerary:

(B) He who has no enjoyment except in enjoyment, who must win all or nothing, who loves the chase only in the capture, has no business mixing with our school. The more steps and degrees there are, the more height and honor there is in the topmost seat. We should take pleasure in being led there, as is done in magnificent palaces, by divers porticoes and passages, long and pleasant galleries, and many windings. This arrangement would redound to our advantage; we would stay there longer and love there longer. Without hope and without desire we no longer go at any worth-while gait.[34]

We must proceed in love as in a labyrinth. Love must be enhanced if it is to transcend the disappointing brevity of physical pleasure: therein lies the need for poetic *discourse*, for a tour through the galleries of the metaphorical palace.

Montaigne prefers his love with a dash of fiction because he knows all too well what the "act" is worth when reduced to its simple physical reality. All that survives is the temporary, but constantly renewed, heat of passion. In a passage of the "Apology for Raymond Sebond" (2:12) Montaigne seems to foreshadow the theory proposed by Freud in *Beyond the Pleasure Principle*, that desire seeks only to quell some "pain," to be "assuaged" and "set at rest":

(A) For that very tickling and sting that is found in certain pleasures and seems to raise us above simple health and absence of pain, that active, stirring, and somehow or other burning and biting voluptuousness, even that itself points only to freedom from pain as its goal. The appetite that sweeps us away into intercourse with women seeks only to drive out the pain that ardent and furious desire brings us, and asks only to assuage it and to be set at rest and exempted from this fever.[35]

But the pursuit of rest is ever restless. "There is no passion more pressing than this."[36] Through a sequence that Montaigne's sentence seeks to imitate, love can never settle permanently for one object: "It is contrary to the nature of love if it is not violent and contrary to the nature of violence if it is constant."[37] Even in its physical aspect it is a "frantic desire for what flees from us."[38] Unlike the beasts, however, man is not concerned solely with physical satisfaction; a component of imagination always enters into his pleasure: "It is not simply a bodily passion. . . . It still lives after satiety; no constant satisfaction or end can be prescribed to it, for it always goes beyond its possession."[39] Of course, knowledge of love's excesses requires no familiarity with books and poets. If Montaigne attributes insatiable sexual appetites to women, it is not so much out of misogyny as out of desire to emphasize the contrast between the chastity imposed upon women and the reality of the desire that torments them just as much as it torments men: "There is not a word, not an example, not a trick that they do not know better than our books: it is a teaching that is born in their veins. . . . The whole movement of the world resolves itself into and leads to this coupling. It is a matter infused throughout, it is a center to which all things look."[40] Ubiquitous and irresistible, sexuality, as soon as one takes away the share of "fancy" and the value attached by culture, can be seen to be nothing more than a natural function, an "insipid pleasure."[41] The exaltation of love in Neoplatonic thought (known to Montaigne through Marsilio Ficino, Bembo, Leon Ebreo, and Equicola) requires the corrective of medical knowledge, which ever since antiquity had held, as in the writings of Hippocrates and Galen, that love is simply one form of "evacuation" among others: "Now then, *leaving books aside* and speaking more materially and simply, I find after all that love is nothing else but the thirst for sexual enjoyment in a desired object, and Venus nothing else but the pleasure of discharging our vessels—a pleasure which becomes vicious either by immoderation or by indiscretion."[42] What a gap between love reduced to its material expression and the exalted image of it presented in books! What are we to think of that gap? To begin with, we must agree with Plato, who held that physical pleasure is a humiliating affliction that reduces us to the level of the beasts:

> (B) I believe that (C) what Plato says is true, that (B) man is the plaything of the gods . . . and that it was in mockery that nature left us the most confused of our actions to be the most common, in order thereby to make us all equal and to put on the same level the fools and the wise, and us and the beasts. . . . Truly it is a mark not only of our original corruption but also of our inanity and deformity.[43]

But this reference to Plato and to the Christian dogma of the Fall makes only a brief appearance, in the midst of a denigrating commentary. What can be reduced to nature soon finds full justification in nature itself. The reader of the "Apology for Raymond Sebond" knows full well that the behavior of animals sometimes reveals a wisdom deeper than man's: what puts us on the same level as the beasts therefore does not degrade us. Montaigne's text continues, particularly in its later additions, in the form of a plea on behalf of the physical aspects of love:

> (B) On the one hand Nature pushes us on to it, having attached to this desire the most noble, useful, and pleasant of all her operations; and on the other hand she lets us accuse and shun it as shameless and indecent, blush at it, and recommend abstinence. (C) Are we not brutes to call brutish the operation that makes us? . . . We regard our being as vice.[44]

Since Montaigne has previously located what is best in love in the words of the poets—in the *verses* of Virgil and Lucretius—his assent here to the physicality of sexual life might lead us to believe that he has now accommodated himself to the coexistence of opposites, to the persistence of antinomy. But as we continue our reading, we find that it is the acceptance of physical pleasure in its materiality and universality that brings Montaigne back to the "verses of these two poets"[45] and that leads him on to develop his praise of imagination, reserve, and the seduction ritual, the importance of which we have already seen. For physical pleasure, reduced simply to what the body experiences, is brief and fleeting. In making this point, Montaigne slips in a personal confidence:

> (B) I don't know who it was in ancient times who wanted his throat as long as a crane's neck so as to relish longer what he swallowed. That wish is more appropriate in this quick and precipitate pleasure, especially for such natures as mine, for I have the failing of being too sudden. In order to arrest its *flight* and prolong it in preambles, everything among them serves as a favor and a recompense: a glance, a bow, a word, a sign. . . . This is a passion that with *very little solid essence* mixes in much more vanity and feverish dreams: it should be satisfied and act accordingly.[46]

This is the route that leads to rehabilitation of appearances. The reader will recall that this chapter, like so many others, begins with a critique of dissimulation: silence surrounds matters of love, which no one dares to name. Still, in the hands of those who use it most effectively, the language of love preserves some shadows and slips a gossamer veil back over things. Shall we snatch away this veil and accept love as nature has made it? Certainly. But desire, with its "very little solid essence," is fugitive and hard to seize; and if its essence eludes us, our faulty grasp is this time not to blame, for insubstantiality is indeed the reality of physical pleasure. Whoever wants to "halt its flight" must call upon vanity, "deception," "gradation," and that "languor in dispensation" with which the ladies grant their "favors." Accordingly, Montaigne, even though he is an enemy of appearances, does not hesitate to advise women to use duplicity, to accept their lovers even as they play out the comedy of chastity: "So I counsel them abstinence, as I do to us; but if this generation is too hostile to it, at least discretion and modesty. . . . If she will not keep her conscience clear, let her keep her name clear; if the substance is not worth much, let *the appearance be preserved.*"[47] To be sure, the appearance that Montaigne here approves is deliberate appearance, shorn of naïvete, appearance that dupes no one: a lady's name, worthless though it is, is nevertheless worthy of protection.

In the digression on the art of writing that follows the citation from Lucretius, Montaigne speaks of the mind's flights of fancy in almost the same terms as he speaks about the flight of desire. He leads the argument to this point by stages. To begin with, he declares his wish to be independent of books and all other prior authorities. This being the case, he must make the best of the fact that French is inferior to the languages of the ancients: "(B) When I write, I prefer to do without the company and remembrance of books, for fear they may interfere with my style. Also because, in truth, the good authors humble me and dishearten me too much."[48]

Montaigne's ambition, as we know, is to write a book that possesses him as much as he possesses it: "(B) I would have done it better elsewhere, but the work would have been less my own; and its principal end and perfection is *to be precisely my own.*"[49]

Now, this intention is thwarted by the admiration that Montaigne feels for certain authors, whose ideas take hold of his mind. Their alienating influence is too powerful:

> (B) But it is harder for me to do without Plutarch. He is so universal and so full that on all occasions, and however eccentric the subject you have taken up, he makes his way into your work and offers you a liberal hand, inexhaustible in riches and embellishments.[50]

More generally, Montaigne admits that he has "an aping and imitative nature,"[51] which causes him to adopt the manner of speaking of those with whom he has been most recently. When this happens it is impossible for him to render himself as he truly is, which he claims is his sole desire. How can this constant loss of self-possession be reconciled with the desire to write a book that is, as Montaigne says, "precisely my own"? One way, of course, is to admit his inevitable dependence, his receptiveness to the words of others. Another is to avoid "well-worn topics, for fear I may treat them at someone else's expense."[52] It is better to speak about unimportant matters that have never caught anyone's attention:

> (B) Any topic is equally fertile for me. *A fly* will serve my purpose; and God grant that this topic I have in hand now was not taken up at the command of so *flighty* a will! Let me begin with whatever subject I please, for all subjects are linked with one another.[53]

The remedy for loss of self-possession thus consists in making oneself extremely available, so that a fortuitous event (the passage of a "fly" or a "flighty" caprice) may set in train a chain of associations culminating in the universal matters that concern the mind.

Is this the full and final revenge of self-sufficiency? No. For even after the mind has regained possession of itself, there remains a constant danger of interruption; the flight of fancy never ends. The best thoughts will not allow themselves to be seized or articulated. Ultimately, it is in the innermost recesses of the mind that illumination and obscurity, possession and dispossession, acquisition and loss are experienced, all mixed up together:

> (B) But I am displeased with my mind for ordinarily producing its most profound and maddest fancies, and those I like the best, unexpectedly and when I am least looking for them; which suddenly vanish, having nothing to attach themselves to on the spot: on horseback, at table, in bed, but mostly on horseback, where my thoughts range most widely. . . . It turns out as with my dreams. While dreaming I recommend them to my memory (for I am apt to dream that I am dreaming); but the next day I may well call to mind their coloring just as it was, whether gay, or sad, or strange; but as to what they were besides, the more I strain to find out, the more I plunge it into oblivion. So of these chance thoughts that drop into my mind there remains in my memory only a vain notion, only as much as I need to make me rack my brains and fret in quest of them to no purpose.[54]

The dream offers itself but remains elusive, hard to grasp. Memory preserves no trace of it. Love (as sung by Virgil), the Latin tongue, and Montaigne's dream visions are the multifarious representatives of an already vanished presence that it is hopeless to try to recapture

197

or pin down. It inhabits a lost past. What remains as a possibility is the articulation of the failure, so that *oblivion* itself becomes the chance "fly," the shapeless, flighty trifle to which the essayist can attach his argument without imitating anyone, at once revealing himself and giving shape to his book.

Mutual services

Montaigne, as a man of his time, distinguishes between marriage and amorous relations. "We do not marry for ourselves, whatever we say; we marry just as much or more for our posterity, for our family."[55] He will therefore confide to us, in a manner explicit yet vague, how he behaved in both situations. It is not difficult to see in both accounts a three-part pattern: first, he feels a sudden need for autonomy; then his autonomy is lost, and he is carried along involuntarily; finally, he accepts the *obligation* to enter into relationships with others and consequently gives up trying to protect the precious substance of the self, which initially he wanted to defend against all alienation.

Montaigne's definition of a "good marriage" comes straight to the point: "(B) A good marriage . . . is a sweet association in life, full of constancy, trust, and an infinite number of useful and solid services and *mutual obligations*."[56]

Speaking about his own life, however, Montaigne stresses first of all his unfitness for marriage: "(B) Men with unruly humors like me, who *hate any sort of bond or obligation*, are not so fit for it."[57]

He had to be led to it, a passive victim (as his very grammar indicates):

> (B) Of my own choice, I would have avoided marrying Wisdom herself, if she had wanted me. But say what we will, the custom and practice of ordinary life *bears us along*. Most of my actions are conducted by example, not by choice. At all events, I did not really bid myself to it, I *was led* to it, and *borne* by extraneous circumstances. . . . And I *was borne to it* certainly more ill-prepared and contrary than I am now after having tried it.[58]

It never occurred to him, as to others whom he reproaches, to despise the "laws of marriage" and take back his liberty:

> (B) And, licentious as I am thought to be, I have in truth observed the laws of marriage more strictly than I had either promised or expected. It is no longer time to kick when we have let ourselves be hobbled. A man must hus-

band his freedom prudently; but he has submitted to an obligation, he must keep to it under the laws of common duty, at least make an effort to. Those who make this bargain only to behave with hatred and contempt act unjustly and harmfully. . . . (C) It is treachery to get married without getting wedded.[59]

The final situation confirms that two kinds of transcendence have occurred. Transcending his unruly humor, Montaigne has accepted the "bond and obligation" of matrimony. But that bond, having expressed itself in the reflexive and reciprocal relationship implicit in the notion of "getting wedded" [*s'épouser*: the verb is reflexive in French—Trans.], also transcends the passivity implicit in being "borne along" and "led," a passivity that revealed an inability to resist "extraneous circumstances." Knowing what Montaigne thinks of friendship (whose pleasures, he tells us, referring to his own friendship with La Bóetie, can surpass the pleasures of love), we cannot say that he is speaking condescendingly of marriage when he contrasts it to love and compares it with friendship: "(B) A good marriage, if such there be, rejects the company and conditions of love. It tries to reproduce those of friendship."[60]

When he comes to discuss love, Montaigne will only slightly alter the terms of the three-part pattern just described: his writing becomes richer, subtler, bolder. Again we find the wish for autonomy: "For the rest, in this business I did not let myself go entirely; I took pleasure in it, but I did not forget myself; I preserved entire the little sense and discretion that nature has given me, for their service [i.e., the service of women] and mine."[61] Now, the reader has a short while earlier been told, in the essay "Of three kinds of association" (3:3), that Montaigne in his younger days fell prey to amorous excesses. His passivity and self-indulgence came first. The painful lesson this taught him brought him both his reserve and his desire for independence:

> (B) But it is an association in which we must keep a bit on guard, especially those in whom the body has much power, as in my case. I burned myself at it in my youth, and *suffered* all the furies that the poets say come upon all those who *let themselves go* after women without restraint and without judgment. It is true that this whiplash has since been a lesson to me.[62]

In the time between his youthful period of self-indulgence and the wisdom of old age (now that he can no longer "forget himself"),

Montaigne felt the need to regain control of himself, as he mentions explicitly in another essay:

> (B) When I was young *I opposed* the progress of love, which I felt advancing too far upon me, and *took care* that it should not be so pleasing to me as in the end to overpower me and hold me completely at its mercy.[63]

But careful and calculated self-control is more in keeping with philosophical models of self-sufficiency than with the experience of love, of which it is not the final term. We discover what that final term is in the essay we have been interpreting ("On some verses of Virgil," 3:5), where Montaigne gives one of his most beautiful examples of a tempered relationship.

Between passive excitement, which delivers us to a "frenzy" that is not our own, and reflective self-control, in which the individual retreats behind the inviolable walls of his own identity, there is a middle term, a difficult balance, to which Montaigne subscribes and which he claims few men of his day achieved. In one sense, this balance is a matter of internal regulation, which steers a middle course between an excess of tension and an excess of liberty:

> (B) I hate almost equally a stagnant and sleepy idleness and a thorny and painful busyness. The one pinches me, the other puts me to sleep. I like wounds as much as bruises, and cutting blows as much as dry ones. I found in this business, when I was more fit for it, *a just moderation between these two extremes.* Love is a sprightly, lively, and gay agitation; I was neither troubled nor afflicted by it, but I was heated and moreover made thirsty by it. A man should stop there; it is hurtful only to fools.[64]

Wounds and bruises: in this same essay Montaigne recommends the use of "our jargon of hunting and war"[65] to give more "fashioning" and energy to the French language. Later, he draws on the language of commercial exchange (this was an age when the word "commerce" had a more extensive meaning than it does now) for metaphors with which to represent love's equity: bargain, payment, commodity, change, etc. He uses these metaphors to indicate the reciprocity of the erotic transaction, not its reification or transformation into a "commodity value." It is, says Montaigne, a "free compact" that does not entitle the lover to any "usurpation of sovereign authority."[66] He cannot imagine love in its physical form as a unilateral possession; to possess a body without its consent and affection seems to him scarcely different from fetishism or necrophilia:

> (B) It is the will that must be courted and solicited. I abhor the idea of a body void of affection being mine. And it seems to me that such frenzy is close to that of the boy who went and defiled out of love the beautiful statue of Venus that Praxiteles had made, or that of the frantic Egyptian hot after the carcass of a dead woman he was embalming and shrouding. . . . I say likewise that we love a body without soul or sentiment, when we love a body without its consent and desire.[67]

To be sure, we find at least one occasion when Montaigne displays an attitude toward love in which the woman serves him only as a pretext to pursue a very personal purpose of his own, which has nothing to do with her. After La Boétie's death, he turned to "amorous associations" in search of the "violent diversion" he needed and "by art and study," he says, "I made myself fall in love."[68] Discreet yet specific, this confidence suggests an affair consciously dominated by the desire to substitute a tangible object for a painful memory, a (heterosexual) affair of the flesh for a (homosexual) association of the spirit. His efforts to conquer a woman were part of the "work of mourning" for his lost friend. This voluntary distraction may not have gone without secret self-reproach on Montaigne's part. For subsequently he hit upon a far more satisfactory compromise, turning his "art and study" to his book, that image of himself accessible to his inward gaze in which his friend survived. In seeking oblivion in a love affair he was acting a part in order to cure himself of another pain. And he does not tell us (as he does on other occasions) that his feigned sentiments gradually turned into true ones.

Yet he states his dislike for deception in no uncertain manner. If he is afraid of excessive commitment and of becoming a slave of love, Montaigne shows himself even more severe toward those who are content to feign passion:

> (B) It is madness to fasten all our thoughts upon it and to become involved in a furious and reckless passion. But on the other hand, to go into it without love and without binding our will, like actors, to play the standard role of our age and customs and put into it nothing of our own but the words, that is indeed providing for our safety, but in cowardly fashion, like a man who would abandon his honor, his profit, or his pleasure for fear of danger. For it is

certain that from such a relationship those who form it can
hope for no fruit that will please or satisfy a noble soul.[69]

In the end, deception is harmful to the deceiver himself. If men are
not loyal, they must expect their wives to betray them and to flirt with
others. Even before there was a myth of Don Juan, Montaigne knows
that the *burlador* is ultimately no less a dupe than his victims:

> (B) Now the necessary outcome of this common and ordi-
> nary treachery of the men of today is what experience is
> already showing us, that they [the women] rally and fall
> back upon themselves or each other to escape us; or else
> that they too, for their part, fall in line with this example
> that we give them, play their part in the farce, and lend
> themselves to this negotiation, without passion, without
> interest, and without love. . . . Thus this cheating recoils
> on the man who does it. It does not cost him much, but he
> gets nothing worth while out of it either.[70]

The loss of the relationship is defined in economic terms as a worthless bargain.

Now the love "bargain" is an exchange of desire. This implies open
recognition of female desire (at a time when hypocrites denied its
existence) as well as rejection of whatever hinders reciprocity in sexual exchange. Men, by arrogating to themselves the right to establish
the rules of this game, have driven women to ruse and suspicion. The
distance between *us* and *them* therefore seems to separate the adversaries in a contest. Montaigne, for his part, refuses to let his conscience become involved "to the point of ingratitude, treachery,
malignity, and cruelty."[71] For himself he adopted a rule of veracity:

> (B) These days love calls for more temerity, which our
> young men excuse on the pretext of ardor; but if the wom-
> en considered the matter closely, they would find that te-
> merity comes rather from contempt. I used to be scrupu-
> lously afraid of giving offense, and I am inclined to respect
> what I love. Besides, in these negotiations, if you take
> away respect you rub out the glamor.[72]

> (B) In my time I have handled this business, as far as the
> nature of it would permit, as conscientiously as any other
> business and with some air of justice; and . . . I swore to
> them only what I felt about my affection, and represented
> to them candidly its decadence, its vigor, and its birth, its
> fits and its lapses. One does not always go about it at the
> same pace. I have been so sparing in promising that *I think*

I have carried out more than I promised or owed. . . . If I have left them with any reason to complain of me, it is rather for having found in me a love which, compared with modern usage was stupidly conscientious. *I have kept my word* in things in which I might easily have been excused.[73]

If marriage and love have anything in common for Montaigne, it is that he kept his word in both kinds of relationship. Recall his previously cited remark about marriage: "I have in truth more strictly observed the laws of marriage than I either *promised* or hoped." Montaigne prides himself on never having allowed his words to outstrip his behavior or feelings in his relations with women. Hence he is not guilty in this "business" of any fraud: he always portrayed himself as he was, without sham or verbal excess. His deeds (or as he likes to say, his "effect") even delivered more than he promised: generosity here is equated with a kind of overpayment. This is what he likes about poets when their words "mean more than they say." It would be too much to see tenderness where Montaigne speaks only of benevolence or to think him concerned not to cause suffering, when his reluctance to break off an affair stems from consideration for himself alone:

(B) I have never broken with them as long as I held to them even by a bit of thread; and whatever occasions for it they have given me, I have never broken with them to the point of scorn or hatred. For such intimacies, even when acquired on the most shameful terms, still oblige me to some good will.[74]

Montaigne is quite open about the fact that for him, the essence of the amorous bargain is the exchange of pleasure. His whole argument is aimed at establishing this avowal and, concomitantly, at disarming those who might find it shocking: "Each one of my parts makes me myself just as much as every other one. And no other makes me more properly a man than this one."[75] The part in question is his penis. And it is through physical exchange, through reciprocity in pleasure, that love, by reaching its goal, becomes a tempered relationship—a gift that does not alienate, a self-presence that is also presence to the other:

(B) Now this is a relationship that needs mutuality and reciprocity. The other pleasures that we receive may be acknowledged by recompenses of a different nature; but this one can be paid for only in the same kind of coin. (C) In truth, in this delight the pleasure I give tickles my imagination more sweetly than that which I feel. (B) Now there is no nobility in a man who can receive pleasure where he gives none.[76]

Probably nowhere more than in this essay does Montaigne dilate so broadly upon the theme of "mutual services." He makes this theme, to one degree or another, a central part of his discussion of the "good marriage" and of love. Further extending the theme of reciprocity, he also maintains that for the person who experiences love, body and soul serve each other mutually:

> May we not say that there is nothing in us during this earthly imprisonment that is purely either corporeal or spiritual, and that we do wrong to tear apart a living man, and that it seems somewhat reasonable that we should behave as favorably at least toward the use of pleasure as we do toward pain.[77]

In the 1588 text Montaigne had, rather oddly, cited the example of the saints and the way in which they subject their bodies to penitential exercises:

> (B) Pain, for example, was vehement even to perfection in the souls of the saints, through penitence; the body naturally had a share in it by virtue of their union, and yet could have little share in the cause. Yet they were not content that it should simply follow and assist the afflicted soul; they afflicted the body itself with atrocious and appropriate torments, in order that, vying with each other, the soul and the body should plunge man into pain, the more salutary for its harshness.[78]

An important emendation in the 1595 edition reverses this masochistic relationship. Whereas in the saints the body's suffering assists the penitent soul, the experience of pleasure should provide an opportunity for the soul to assist the body. Reciprocity is expressed by the very words of the text, in a perfectly balanced chiasmus:

> (C) In a similar case, that of bodily pleasures, is it not unjust to cool the soul toward them and say that she should be dragged to them as to some constrained and servile obligation and necessity? It is rather for her to hatch them and foment them, to offer and invite herself to them, since the authority of ruling belongs to her; as it is also for her, in my opinion, in the pleasures that are her own, to inspire and infuse into the body all the feeling their nature allows, and

to strive to make them sweet and salutary to it. For it is indeed reasonable, as they say, *that the body should not follow its appetites to the disadvantage of the mind; but why is it not also reasonable that the mind should not pursue its appetites to the disadvantage of the body?*[79]

In the "mutual services" between lovers or between body and soul, Montaigne makes us see a bond similar to that which, in the highest forms of poetry, unites word and thing, sound and sense, idea and expression. For instance, the examples that he chooses from Lucretius and Virgil are not merely emblems (at the level of the "referent") of marriage (between Venus and Vulcan in Virgil) or adultery (between Venus and Mars in Lucretius). They also furnish Montaigne with a secular (literary) model of a felicitious interpenetration of word and flesh. Poetry by its very essence makes metaphor of love and of the substantial union of body and soul.

This is the model of reciprocity that Montaigne would like to see dominate the linguistic and erotic order and that he likes to think Nature itself has prescribed. He is obliged to admit, however, at the very beginning of the essay, that his age forbids him to hope for any easy fulfillment of his amorous dreams: they are destined to remain reverie and fantasy. Unlike La Boétie, Montaigne was never a poet; he tried his hand at poetry, "played the child." But his only real experience of poetry is as a *reader*. At the end of the essay he comes to the point: true love (under the sign of Venus) can have as its object only someone blessed with all the graces of youth. What can an old man like him (Montaigne was fifty-three at the time of writing!) hope for? For all his praise of reciprocity, will he be permitted to enjoy it?

> (B) We demand more when we bring less; we most want to choose when we least deserve to be accepted. Knowing ourselves for what we are, we are less bold and more distrustful; nothing can assure us of being loved, knowing our condition and theirs. I am ashamed to find myself amid this green and ardent youth,
> Whose member firmer stands, in its undaunted pride,
> Than a young tree upon a mountainside.
> —Horace[80]

(As the reader will no doubt have noticed, Montaigne often refers to specific sexual matters—in this case, erection—by incorporating a citation from a Latin poet into his text.)

No symmetry in erotic relations is possible for an "old man," especially since Montaigne rejects the only possibility of reestablishing equality: to those who would urge him to seek out women of his own age, he responds without illusions:

> (C) I find more sensual pleasure in merely seeing the just and sweet union of two young beauties, or in merely considering it in imagination, than in *myself making the second in a sad and ill formed union.*[81]

In a bargain where exchange takes place at close range, from body to body, anything that impairs the body's integrity compromises the anticipated pleasure:

> (B) But is it not a great impudence to bring our imperfections and weaknesses where we desire to please and leave a good opinion and recommendation of ourselves? For the little that I need nowadays,
> > Even for one
> > Encounter, limp,
> > > —Horace
> I would not want to trouble a person whom I have to reverence and fear.[82]

On the related subject of his lack of success in his former career as a lover, Montaigne (though he has no qualms about saying "I have no other passion to keep me in breath"[83]) is prepared to lay the blame upon his physical construction, and specifically upon the all too scanty size of his *mentula*, as the Latin verses that he cites, and incorporates into his personal confession, make quite clear—he uses ancient poetry as a prosthesis to make up for a deficit in the French language, and for its taboos:

> (B) When I have seen one of them grow weary of me, I have not promptly blamed her fickleness; I have wondered whether I did not have reason rather to blame Nature. Certainly she has treated me unfairly and unkindly—
> > But if the penis be not long or stout enough . . .
> > Even the matrons—all too well they know—
> > Look dimly on a man whose member's small.
> > > —Priapea
> —(C) and done me the most enormous damage.[84]

The "most enormous damage" that Montaigne has suffered is compounded by the fact that women have been misled (prior to experience) by graffiti that lead them to expect quite the contrary, that is to say, enormous organs: "(B) What mischief is not done by those enormous pictures that boys spread about the passages and staircases of palaces! From these, women acquire a cruel contempt for our natural capacity."[85]

Montaigne complains of having been treated cruelly by nature. Thus he blames, and links to a humiliating phallic deficiency, that very nature that he so often states should be taken for guide and norm. Previously, it was *art*, institutions, and custom that Montaigne most readily blamed for disorder and lack of reciprocity in the performance of "mutual services." Now we discover that nature, so *just* in all her operations and so generous and maternal in her gifts, is also capable of deprivation, castration, and "unfair" treatment; she is capable of upsetting the equilibrium and pleasing symmetry that she seems always to seek. Therein lies a wicked mystery.

Physically impaired and diminished by age, Montaigne also believes himself handicapped by the "common" language in which he writes. Alongside the confidences we have just examined may be set another, concerning the verbal organ wielded by the French writer. The parallelism in the two confessions of weakness is striking:

> (B) In our language I find plenty of stuff but a little lack of fashioning. . . . I find it sufficiently abundant, but not sufficiently (C) pliable and (B) vigorous. It ordinarily succumbs under a powerful conception. If your pace is tense, you often feel it growing limp and giving way under you, and that when it fails you Latin comes to your aid, and Greek to others.[86]

Wherever Montaigne insists upon harmonious relations and "mutual services" he encounters some lack or limitation, some want of material resources or energy. Inferiority is here articulated in a language pervaded by sexual metaphor, the same language that Montaigne used earlier to praise the virtues of the ancient poets. The contrast is one between power and impotence: "(B) This is not a soft and merely inoffensive eloquence; it is sinewy and solid, and does not so much please as fill and ravish. . . . It is the sprightliness of the imagination that elevates and swells the words."[87]

Unfortunately, by Montaigne's time this eroticized language is no longer current. His contemporaries do not speak amorously or love eloquently.

Montaigne is not content merely to remark upon this fact. He feels the need to find a remedy, to repair the defect. There is more than one answer to the language problem. Latin citations may add useful vigor to a French style that "goes limp" and "gives way" (and Montaigne of course uses Latin to articulate his own sexual strengths and weaknesses). But the recourse to citations is ambiguous: it is not only an *ostentatious* display of knowledge but also a display of *borrowed* knowledge and hence of one's own inadequacy. Another possibility is to employ in a figurative sense "phrases" that "are used in the streets of France":[88] "(B) For there is nothing that might not be done with our jargon of hunting and war, which is a generous soil to borrow from. And forms of speech, like plants, improve and grow stronger by being transplanted."[89]

The image of transplantation is itself a metaphor to express metaphoric *translation*. Art here justifies itself by drawing an analogy with crops and agriculture, i.e., with a quasi-natural world.

But the transformation that Montaigne will carry out successfully is that which will establish between himself and his book a bond of mutual service. Though he regards himself as being far from achieving the "sinewy and solid" perfection of the ancients and sees the linguistic implement that he wields as hopelessly "soft," it is enough that he can say that in any case his book is *his own*. At the level of *representation*, and through the acceptance of *defect* and irregularity, the principle of expressive regularity is reestablished; the chiasmus links the book and the self: "(B) Isn't this the way I speak everywhere? Don't I represent myself to the life? Enough, then. I have done what I wanted. Everyone recognizes me in my book, and my book in me."[90]

In plain view of all, the language of love is drawn back and transplanted in the soil of subjectivity. The representation of the self in the book and of the book in the self—a mirror image—is presented as the narcissistic substitute for all the relations of reciprocity never realized or now unrealizable. The very imperfections of the language can be turned to advantage provided they mirror the imperfections of the writer and hence allow the accommodation of *verba* to *res* that it is the function of good writing to achieve.

Does this imply that, for Montaigne, the essay "On some verses of Virgil" is meant as a substitute for amorous exchange at a time in his life when the bodily *heat* so essential to the erotic act has all but disappeared? And therefore that he is resigned to replacing the pleasure of the flesh by the pleasure of writing, and, more precisely, by the pleasure of *writing about himself* in such a way as to give free rein to his narcissistic tendencies? Why indeed does he write this chapter and express in it his wish to enter by its good graces into the boudoir of the ladies, if not to say how difficult it is for him to resign himself to the change in his life and how justified he feels, since nature has failed him, in having recourse to antinature, i.e., to *art*—which on so many other occasions (when the contrast with triumphant nature was still possible) he has lambasted?

Recall that, at the beginning of the essay, he gave no sign of anticipating the victory of *art*, if what is expected from art is anything more than gratification in fantasy: "(B) I am merry only in fancy and in dreams, to divert by trickery the gloom of old age. But indeed it would require another remedy than a dream: a feeble struggle, that of art against nature."[91]

Now, the fanciful hypothesis of a therapy (i.e., an art) by and for love reappears at the end of the essay. Montaigne approves (for once) of one of the fundamental tenets of Galenic medicine: chilly "dyscrasia" must be countered with heat. The proper remedy must be dispensed by a young body:

> (B) It is a vain occupation, it is true, unbecoming, shameful, and illegitimate; but carried on in this fashion, I consider it healthy, proper to enliven a heavy body and soul; and as a physician, I would prescribe it to a man of my temperament and condition as readily as any other recipe to rouse him and keep him in vigor till he is well on in years, and to keep him from the clutches of old age. While we are only in its outskirts and the pulse still beats . . . we need to be stimulated and tickled by some biting agitation such as this. See how much youth, vigor, and gaiety it gave back to the wise Anacreon. And Socrates, when older than I am, speaking of an object of his love, said: "When I had leaned my shoulder against his and brought my head close to his, as we were looking into a book together, I suddenly felt, without prevarication, a stinging in my shoulder like some animal's bite, and I was more than five days with it prickling, and a continual itching flowed into my heart." A touch, and an accidental one, and by a shoulder, to inflame and alter a soul cooled and enervated by age, and the first of all human souls in reformation![92]

A *bookish* memory—of a statement by Socrates (who is himself *reading* alongside a companion) cited by Xenophon—provides an example of *living* medication. And the example is that of a fortuitous touch

209

of the skin, a chance, superficial encounter: that touch, transmitted to the very center of being (the "heart"), produces a *heating* that revives both body and soul ("a soul cooled and enervated by age"). From the merest caress! In speaking of the serenity of a dying man's farewell to life, Montaigne expresses the fear that in his case "the touch of a well-known hand" might upset him.[93] But elsewhere he hopes that a dying man might have "a gentle *hand*, suited to his feelings, to scratch him just where he itches."[94]

Socrates's authority is invoked in this instance to justify what so many others would have condemned in the name of philosophy itself: "Indeed, why not? Socrates was a man, and wanted neither to be nor to seem anything else."[95] And Montaigne, who strove so often to discredit the efforts of the physicians, introduces yet another comparison borrowed from the healing art to reinforce his wish that he might regain his bodily heat: "(B) For a run-down body, as for a broken-down stomach, it is excusable to warm it up and support it by art, and by the mediation of fancy to restore appetite and blitheness to it, since by itself it has lost them."[96]

Here again we find the imagination (or "fancy") hoping to achieve palingenesis. Why not abandon oneself, for a moment at any rate, to the dream of rejuvenation, of starting over?

> (B) [Love] would restore me to vigilance, sobriety, grace, care for my person; would secure my countenance, so that the grimaces of old age, those deformed and pitiable grimaces, should not come to disfigure it; (C) would take me back to sane and wise studies, whereby I might make myself more esteemed and more loved, ridding my mind of despair of itself and its employment, and reacquainting it with itself; (B) would divert me from a thousand and troublesome thoughts, (C) a thousand melancholy moods, (B) that idleness (C) and the bad state of our health (B) loads us with at such an age; would warm up again, at least in dreams, this blood that nature is abandoning; would hold up the chin and stretch out a little the muscles (C) and the soul's vigor and blitheness (B) for this poor man who is going full speed toward his ruin.[97]

The fantasy of rekindling the extinguished flame does not have as its object the image of an unknown woman (Mlle de Gournay was apparently unable to fill the bill); it unfolds, rather, in a list of personal benefits that Montaigne might hope to obtain from a last love affair. But he is no fool. At the end of the essay he recognizes how hopelessly far he is from love: "(B) Shall I say it, provided no one takes me by the throat for it? Love does not seem to be properly and naturally in its season except in the age next to childhood. . . . (C) Nor beauty either."[98]

We must at the same time relinquish any hopes we have in *art* and resign ourselves to contemplating love's ways from afar, now that we are no longer permitted to follow in her train: "(B) See how he goes reeling, tripping, and wantonly playing; you put him in the stocks when you guide him by *art* and wisdom, and you constrain his divine freedom when you subject him to those hairy and callous hands."[99]

There remains one final dream, borrowed, or rather derived from, Plato's utopia: that the sexual privileges that Plato awards to worthy warriors should also be granted to those who have proved their merit in other ways. This is the fantasy of fleshly reward for the right-speaking, for those who, like Virgil, are poets or, if no poets are to be found, for those capable of perceiving the exquisite heat of great love poetry:

> (C) What he finds so just in recommendation of military worth, may it not also be so in recommendation of some other kind of worth? And why is not one of them seized with desire (B) to gain before her sisters the glory of this chaste love? And I do mean chaste,
> For if it comes to love's encounter,
> Like fire in straw, mighty in size, with little power,
> They spend their rage in vain.
> —Virgil
>
> The vices that are stifled in thought are the worst.[100]

This straw fire is all that remains of the fantasy of rekindling the waning flame of love.

To end his essay, Montaigne affirms the equality of the sexes. But he does so at the end of a sentence in which he speaks in derogatory terms of what he has just written and into which he incorporates six lines from Catullus:

> (B) To conclude this notable commentary, which has escaped from me in a flow of babble, a flow sometimes impetuous and harmful—
> And as an apple, secret present from her love,
> Falls out from the chaste bosom of the maid,
> Where she has quite forgot it, hid beneath her robe,
> When at her mother's step she starts, afraid;

As she rises it falls, rolls off at a swift pace;
A guilty blush spreads o'er her downcast face
—Catullus

—I say that males and females are cast in the same mold;
except for education and custom, the difference is not
great.[101]

"Flow of babble": after insisting for an entire page on what an old
man he is, Montaigne again invokes a defect of age (dominated by
"rheums" and "flows") as the reason for the long essay that we have
been analyzing throughout this chapter. And before making his final
assertion, that the sexes are equal, he takes all the distance that he
needs: "cast in the same mold," both sexes are considered as *objects*
from the standpoint of the smelter or demiurge. The chill of old age is
reflected in the chill of objectivity, which scarcely need attend to so
minor a difference.

But the lines of Latin poetry shift the meaning of the sentence no-
ticeably; the effect is similar to that which Montaigne ascribes in the
course of his essay to Virgil and Lucretius: that is, the cited poem
verbally compensates for what is missing in life. At first glance, the
lines cited here contribute nothing more than an ingenious simile
based on the image of an object that *escapes*. The "flow of babble" that
escapes from Montaigne is like the apple that escapes from the young
girl's accommodating garment. The analogy has to do with making
visible what is hidden. Now, the passage from Catullus not only
brings to life images of extreme youth[102] but also casts Montaigne in
the role of a young maiden whose love is revealed by the token she is
incapable of hiding. Is this not in a way a confirmation of what Montaigne intends to say, namely, that there is little difference between
the sexes? But this confirmation has a converse. The power of poetry
manifests itself one last time: it is rejuvenating, feminizing, it evokes
the contact between the ripe fruit and the young breast, it restores life
in all its red heat. It is love regained, even though Montaigne declares
himself in his own essay to be finished with all that. In this respect,
the citation, by stretching out the sentence, achieves the restorative
effect of art; it is "more amorous than love itself." In the same stroke
it redeems the "flow of babble" of the prose essay by ascribing to it,
by analogy (and contradiction), the value of a token of love.

The final sentences, short and mocking, end with a proverb that
evokes the familiar implements of the hearth: "(B) It is much easier to
accuse one sex than to excuse the other. It is the old saying: the pot
calls the kettle black."[103] In French this proverb reads: *Le fourgon se*

moque de la poêle [literally: the poker makes fun of the frying pan]. Another version is: *La pelle se moque du fourgon* [literally: the shovel makes fun of the poker]. Both implements serve the same fire. One is as black as the other, and away from the fire both are made of the same *cold* metal. The poker *[le fourgon,* masculine] is quite foolish to make fun of the shovel *[la pelle,* feminine]. The idea that reciprocity is essential is still on Montaigne's mind: the trivial popular saying serves to heap ridicule on those who refuse to accept its truth. The ironic use of the familiar proverb is intended to shame a world in which men refuse to meet women on terms of equality.

SIX

«Each man in some sort exists in his work»

Nature and the work

"We have no communication with being,"[1] says Montaigne. But elsewhere he writes: "Man can be only what he is."[2] As far as he may be from essential truth, man has his place amid what is; and "inadequate" as his condition may be, it somehow represents a particular mode of being, in consequence of which man *is* what he is. Even though Montaigne, in developing his argument in favor of skepticism, is at pains to describe and to multiply the number of obstacles that stand between our minds and true Being (defined as that which remains eternally one and unchanging), he elsewhere proposes a quite different definition of that concept: "Being consists in movement and action."[3] Thus the idea of an immutable being that transcends us gives way to the idea of being as something dynamic, which is not only a source of change and a creator of unstable forms but is itself carried along by its mobile power.

If we need an authority, should we not turn to Nature? Isn't Nature precisely "movement and action?" She rules the world; why shouldn't she also be present in the turbulent, dream-laden flow of time? In what we are, which seems so insignificant compared with the fanciful idea of a fixed Being, we must recognize the will of this admirable Mother who gives birth to both the inexhaustible diversity of the world and its perennial reflection in us. To live in harmony with Nature (as we are urged to do by the Stoics and so many others), we must shed our ontological illusions and give in to the demands of our inner spontaneity, which all too often we work against. Therein we find, despite the eclipse of the absolute, a new norm that rescues us from our worries about remote being. If Nature cannot be understood from the standpoint of her causes, she can be *accepted* from the standpoint of her effects. No longer is the problem to grasp Nature's secret; now it is to let her carry us along.

We might have thought that our separation from transcendent Truth would leave us blind and vulnerable to arbitrary authority. But now a new law emerges, not from outside our existence but within its boundaries. Nature includes us within herself. She is active in us. Let us heed her and allow her to do her work. "We cannot go wrong by following Nature. . . .[4] I let myself go as I have come."[5] As changeable as Nature's impulse may be, to obey it is to establish wisdom on a solid and, what is more, a universal basis, apt to bring men together. "In every man who is not *denatured*," Montaigne tells us, "the seed of *universal* reason" has been planted.[6] Without engaging in philosophical speculation, without requiring that reason raise itself to the level of conceptual clarity, every man (even the simplest rustic) carries within himself the infallible rule that enables him to live well, to die peacefully, and to be everything that nature intends him to be. For our duty coincides with the dictates of natural necessity. Unquestioning obedience and tranquil passivity suffice; it is as if this "naturalistic" quietism restored (in a somewhat altered form) our "communication with being," which philosophy, abandoning its early hopes, had resigned itself never to achieve.

No sooner is this belonging to Nature discovered, however, than it is called into question. For isn't man alone among the animals to have the power to deny Nature, to go against her will? There is left "in us no apparent trace of Nature. And men have done with Nature as perfumers do with oil: they have sophisticated her with so many arguments and farfetched reasonings that she has become variable and *particular* for each man, and has lost her own constant and universal countenance."[7] Furthermore, "it is credible that there are natural laws, as may be seen in other creatures; but in us they are lost; that fine human reason butts in everywhere, domineering and commanding, muddling and *confusing the face of things* in accordance with its vanity and inconsistency."[8] Here again it is confirmed that, paradoxical as it may seem, it is man's "nature" to use his rational faculties to contradict and disfigure what is *given* in Nature, that is, to particularize the universal. We shall probably be no happier when we are willing to let nature have her way than we were when we hoped to apprehend her true visage. An ethics in harmony with Nature is no less difficult to achieve than a science of Nature. Nature's power is not unlimited: there exists a realm "outside nature" to which man has access—but it only brings him woe.

Is it then necessary to launch yet another attack on human reason? Must it be found guilty of crimes against nature even after "presumption" has been laid aside? Montaigne argues in this way on more than one occasion. But on other occasions he makes the opposite argument, giving his approval to those of our powers (liberty, judgment, reason, custom) that oppose Nature and resist its claims. What is "outside nature" then becomes, as for so many humanists, the expression of *dignitas hominis:*

> (A) Since it has pleased God to give us some capacity for reason, so that we should not be, like the animals, slavishly subjected to the common laws, but should apply ourselves to them by judgment and voluntary liberty, we must indeed yield a little to the simple authority of Nature, but not let ourselves be carried away tyrannically by her: reason alone must guide our inclinations. I, for my part, have a taste strangely blunted to these propensities that are produced in us without the command and mediation of our judgment.[9]

What then must we choose (if the choice be ours to make)? To give in to the "authority of Nature" or to take back some authority for ourselves? Montaigne adopts first one, then the other of these two possibilities, declaring each one in turn to be preferable and the only practicable choice. Sometimes he says that, like it or not, man must obey Nature's requirements (indeed, it is Nature herself who says this in the prosopopoeia that concludes 1:20); other times he sees man as the only creature that makes use, from birth, of his freedom in order to escape the common law: "(B) The young of bears and dogs show their natural inclination, but men, plunging headlong into certain habits, opinions, and laws, easily change or disguise themselves."[10] Herein lies the source of Montaigne's ambiguous attitude toward education. Is education a matter of encouraging the development of inborn faculties? Or is it a matter of ensuring that, by means of agreeable exercises and habits imperceptibly instilled, the child acquires a *second nature* and a "temperament" that becomes his own through practice and ceaseless effort? Through the authority of example and the effect of practice virtue is supposed to be incorporated into the soul, impregnating it and coloring it through and through. For isn't it true that by "counterfeiting being sick" (the title of 2:25) a person really becomes sick? The mask becomes the true visage. As Mignon sings in Goethe, *"Lass mich scheinen bis ich werde"* (Let me seem until I become). Or, as Alain says, "Seeming is a path to being." Only a human act can impose a form on a natural substance, which left to itself would remain indeterminate. Is that good or bad? Neither—it is a fact that cannot be changed. As we saw in the previous chapter, the life of the body is a tissue of habits that it is dangerous to alter. To stay close to Nature is usually to accept *shapelessness*. To sub-

216

mit to custom is to take on a form,[11] and hence to run the risk of *deformity* or distortion. How can Nature and form be reconciled? How, without betraying Nature, can man fulfill his rational vocation?

Reconciliation is not impossible, however. Here again the semantic opposition between internal and external, "mine" and "alien," governs the process of appropriation, with positive value being attached to what is "mine," "internal," "intrinsic." Classed as "external," custom is judged negatively: it is harmful, like any external constraint, and Montaigne exhorts us to obey that nature which exerts its control from within and obliges us simply to abide by its law. On the other hand, as soon as custom and the other external forces that shape us can be considered as attributes or effects of the subject himself, as soon as they can be called "my own," they are exonerated of all charges and made legitimate. Alienation ceases when the external model and constraint are freely assimilated and duly appropriated. For form is then imposed from within; it is the result of individual effort and labor. However docile the individual may be in accepting social custom, he will be obliged to no one but himself for what constitutes him *qua* individual. At the same time, he will have internalized that which was initially alien or hostile. This description applies, for instance, to the practice that enables us to bear up under illness or to prepare for death: familiarity turns the tables on the adverse forces that Nature and destiny hurl against us. "By long usage this form of mine has turned into substance, and fortune into nature."[12] At this moment custom has ceased to be external and become entirely *my own*. It belongs me; it is a *human accomplishment*. Far from altering my true nature, it makes me what I am.

"Being consists in movement and action": earlier, I suggested that this statement raises the possibility of discovering being in the movement of natural forces. But in fact it is to human actions and movements that it pertains. The assertion that follows leaves no doubt that this is the case: "*Wherefore each man in some sort exists in his work.*"[13]

The idea of a work, which here finds its definitive justification, refers to an activity that is not simply distinct from spontaneous natural acts but actually intended to shape and modify them. "I have put all my efforts into forming my life."[14] The work is an intentional act that lends its form to the workman. This is the only worthwhile kind of activity for Montaigne, who ordinarily feels only contempt (owing in part, perhaps, to a nobleman's prejudice) for "transitive actions" whose goal lies in some remunerative object or result. *Making* interests him only when it is a question of *making himself*: he claims to have little aptitude for activities whose only purpose is to produce or

shape objects for utility or profit. Montaigne wants no praise for having been a good magistrate or even for knowing how to write:[15] he
doesn't wish to be a specialist in any discipline, not even that of fine
writing. A well-bred man has no occupation, the men of the seventeenth century would insist. Is it not the case that "all authority, like
all art, has its end outside of itself?"[16] The public welfare requires it,
and Montaigne cannot help approving the principle. But for his part,
Montaigne sees his principal end within himself.

Now, to locate one's end within oneself is once again to see the self
in spatial terms. It is to make the self the field upon which one's
action unfolds. It means that there is initially a subject, which undertakes to act and which, erecting itself as the privileged object of that
act, makes itself into a *thing* (the "self") in order to posit itself as an
end. I thereby invent a semipassive self, which becomes the theme (or
myth) upon which I may base my work. A pseudo-externality comes
between the self and the subject via the metaphor of work. By forming in my mind an image of the distance between me and my work, I
discover my existence: it is (I am) the work to be done, the focus of my
labor. I am, to be sure, the master of this distance, but I was able to
create it only by exploiting a weakness, a possibility of schism that
haunted my life from the beginning. "We are, I know not how, double within ourselves."[17] We do not fully subscribe to what we do or
say we believe. Our natural spontaneity, so bold in its first impulse, is
always vitiated by a fragility that leaves us free to withdraw from, to
disapprove of, our own actions. "We do not believe what we believe,
and we cannot rid ourselves of what we condemn."[18] Even before we
take our distance, the distance exists within us; duplicity undermines
us, our identities are flawed. We have no choice but to accommodate
ourselves to these facts.

Because this split within us is exploitable, the self can become the
subject of its own *work*. It can shape its life as a sculptor fashions a
statue by seeking to awaken a dormant figure within the stone. The
reflexive act whereby Montaigne looks at and accepts himself has a
plastic virtue: in him, self-consciousness is an accomplishment. Has
he not resolved to "consider himself" and to "search *curiously*"? The
effort (*cura*) of perception involves both an "internal effect" and a
desire to "erect an image," fugitive though it may be. The pleasure of
looking is coupled with the pleasure of shaping.

In Montaigne the formative will claims to make no more change
than is absolutely necessary in what is unstable and variable in spontaneous existence. The form "essayed" tends to remain as close as
possible to formlessness. The will is forbidden to do violence to the

fluid and indeterminate nature that it wants to subdue and yet aspires to imitate. Montaigne cannot approve of intentional action except where it comes closest to voluntary perception: the economy of the formative act demands that that act be all but indistinguishable from a mere *discovery* made without prior preparation. Thus the self's action upon itself will be not so much an innovating transformation as a portrait of that which, within us and despite our will, is already subject to change, already linked to the "general agitation" and universal drift of the world. To describe change is both to accept it and to incorporate it into a work, and to represent it is inevitably to modify it.

The formative act is practically identical with acceptance of oneself (*consentement à soi*). Some minimum objectification is in fact necessary to provide a pretext for this self-acceptance. The very etymology of the word (from the Latin *consentire*: to feel together, to agree) shows us what self-acceptance is: it is a question of detaching ourselves from our feelings long enough to approve and subscribe to them. We must suspend, if only for an instant, our usual vague self-involvement. We have already encountered the metaphor that expresses this separation: "I do not love myself so indiscriminately, nor am I so attached and *wedded* to myself, that I cannot distinguish and consider myself apart, as I do a *neighbor* or a *tree*."[19] The neighbor and the tree are indeed "other," but they are also close to me, as close as can be. Judgment dissociates itself from the motives of "ordinary" life, but only in order to see those motives more clearly and to let them emerge with greater freedom. I confront them with receptive attention. When being divides, we discover in ourselves a distinct spectator and spectacle. Montaigne experiences no inner conflict as a result of this division and therefore stops trying to restored perfect unity. If gap there is, it is a gap just wide enough to give consistency to the composite work. Montaigne accepts the spectacle as it appears and lets judgment play "its game apart."[20] The establishing of inner distance and the internal split encourage not conflict but judgment. "Judgment holds in me a magisterial seat, at least it carefully tries to. It lets my feelings go their way, both hatred and friendship, even the friendship I bear myself, without being changed and corrupted by them."[21]

Judgment, having gained its autonomy, wants to survey everything that goes on without being required to intervene. Its aim is to reconcile distance and proximity while leaving the spectacle unchanged. But like it or not, its presence introduces a radical change. Because it is so close to its object, judgment cannot avoid exerting an influence on what it observes. The judgmental gaze, just by objectifying feelings modifies them in the process. This is a good thing as long as the effect is to *slow* the involuntary instability of emotional life: "If each man watched *closely* the effects and circumstances of the passions that dominate him, as I have done with the ones I have fallen prey to, he *would see them coming* and *would check* their impetuosity and course a bit."[22] Yet this is also what makes all sincerity equivocal. How can anyone who wants to express himself with good faith and offer himself naked to the eyes of the world avoid *checking* himself, how can he avoid the distortion (due to giving shape to that which is naturally shapeless) that inevitably comes from the self-conscious use of language? To look at oneself and communicate what one sees is not only to create oneself but also to change oneself in the act of describing. As soon as we define ourselves, we become our own work, and any work is artifice: "What I chiefly portray is my cogitations, a *shapeless subject* that does not lend itself to *expression in actions*. It is all I can do to couch my thoughts in this airy medium of words."[23] It is hard work giving body to airy "cogitations," even if that body is almost immaterial: words, the most tenuous matter there is. But such is the necessary nature of our being, assuming that "each man is in some sort in his work."[24] Our being is complete only at the moment it becomes ambiguous, that is, at the moment when, having been given *form* in language and rendered communicable, it becomes suspect of betraying its true identity. It compromises itself and is altered in the very attempt to display a faithful likeness. The work must disappear to make room for the reality of the subject. But the subject is a workman and cannot appear except in and through the work: a work that will always be ashamed of the artifice required to make it and whose ambition is to rival nature's supple spontaneity, to adopt its rhythm, "to play the fool and follow [its] fancies"[25] as nature does. The work then seems to turn back with nostalgic longing to inconstancy and inadequacy, to the original weakness it was designed to overcome. In this it does not succeed—much as Orpheus and Narcissus are condemned never to grasp the image from which they are separated— and from this impossibility arises the interminable character of the book. The *Essays* "represent" Montaigne's natural inconsistency by giving it an excess of consistency; they are the "verification" of that inconsistency, i.e., the exact yet radically altered image that judgment takes into account.

Therein lies the paradox. The initial dissatisfaction with masks, opinion, and inner instability had sought and found refuge in the unity of the book (or "ledger"); the hunger for being, the ontological hope, had for want of anything better withdrawn into the book once it became clear that the metaphysical quest for essence was doomed to failure. The book was the only means of transcending deceptive appearances. But when the mind discovers that it has been cast back into the world of phenomena and upon itself, as "part" of that world; when it discovers (having rejected all metaphysics and ontology) that it is wisdom to allow itself to be borne along by the universal movement; then it perceives that the book, the work, is itself guilty of a sin, the sin of excessive unity. What little stability and permanence the book possesses is still too much compared with the evanescence that it is the author's sole aim to capture, with the flux to which we are allowed to yield. Being proved to be inaccessible. Will appearances turn out to be any less so? At each attempt an adversary force bars the way. In the long run, however, we must come to some accommodation with these adversary forces: without ceasing to struggle against them we must enlist them as allies, we must use them to gauge our own strength by testing our limits. Whence the various additions to the *Essays;* the effort can only be made in the unifying milieu of language, and yet it lays bare and accentuates multiplicity and change (which Montaigne must represent faithfully if he wants to give a truthful portrait of himself). He moves away from change only to discover that his task is to recreate it and plunge himself back into it, at each new attempt with heightened awareness of the futility of both change and the hope of escaping it. Montaigne is critical of any work that would assume a definitive form once and for all: "We dignify our stupidities when we put them in print."[26] The work should be only a temporary stopping place, a moment when change is *seized* on the fly and then let go to continue on its course. The natural flow is not interrupted, but the heightened attention of the observer will seem to slow its pace and to accentuate the value of each passing moment. The mind then grasps the fullness of the interval between evanescent moments, the rich content of that dreamlike lapse:

> (B) Others feel the sweetness of some satisfaction and of prosperity; I feel it as they do, but it is not in passing and slipping by. Instead we must study it, *savor* it, and *ruminate* it, to give proper thanks for it to him who grants it to us. They enjoy the other pleasures as they do that of sleep, without being conscious of them. To the end that sleep itself should not escape me thus stupidly, at one time I saw fit to have mine disturbed, so that I might gain a *glimpse* of it.[27]

The judgment that perceives and dominates the individual's lethargy is not a pure and abstract intellectual faculty. It barely emerges from sleep just to "glimpse" and "savor" the sleeping state. This is not an impassive gaze, not a limpid, indifferent intellectual mirror unimplicated in the spectacle it reflects. On the contrary, all the senses collaborate with it. Judgment, as Montaigne sees it, is a sensory vigilance: it grasps by touching, tasting, weighing. Its aim is to couple pleasure with knowledge. In the act of judgment the spectator subject participates with all his body in the unstable spectacle that he is for himself. Thus his body is fully involved in attending to his own life, distinct from yet reaching out toward him. We have only to pay attention to Montaigne's style to see that, if the *work* tends to acquire form and body, it is above all the work of a living being who is trying to take "full and entire" possession of his bodily consciousness. Montaigne's style shows us that the operation of judgment is always contaminated, as it were, by the confusion inherent in the body's natural experience. Judgment *glimpses* more frequently than it sees. Its vision is clouded, its grip tentative. For the act of grasping is as ephemeral, as quick to vanish as the unstable object that it attempts to seize. Let us consider this question more closely.

Aspects of movement

"Every movement reveals us."[28] Anyone who wants to discover the true Montaigne should follow his advice and consider his movement. When we read a page of the *Essays*, we perform, under the influence of a marvelously active style, a whole series of mental acts, which convey to our bodies an impression of suppleness and energy. Montaigne at his most intimate emerges through this powerfully communicative, physical vitality.

An adequate description of Montaigne's movement requires close textual analysis. The immodesty of the writing requires an immodest criticism applied directly to its object. Consider the following:

> (A) Now I find my opinions infinitely bold and constant in condemning my inadequacy. In truth, this too is a subject on which I exercise my judgment as much as on any other. The world always looks straight ahead; as for me, I turn my gaze inward, I fix it there and keep it busy. Everyone looks in front of him; as for me, I look inside of me; I have no business but with myself; I continually observe myself, I take stock of myself, I taste myself. Others always go elsewhere, if they stop to think about it; they always go forward;
>
> No man tries to descend into himself;
>
> —Persius
>
> as for me, I roll about in myself.[29]

222

The first sentence [which in French reads, "Or mes opinions, je les trouve infiniement hardies et constantes à condamner mon insuffisance"] has a remarkable aspect: the self is present, in cascade, at every level of the syntax. The French sentence begins with an inversion that highlights the direct object, *mes opinions* [my opinions]. These opinions are then represented by the pronoun *les*, the direct object of the main verb, which candidly expresses a first-person judgment: *je les trouve* [I find them]. Thus "my opinions" (in which various thinking activities are concentrated) are the object of the verb "to find," which is again an act of thought. The *self*, which is the agent of discovery, is also the object discovered, thanks to the possessive pronoun *my* (my opinions). Now, in what follows, those *opinions* are themselves characterized as a form of personal activity (they are "*bold . . . to condemn*"), again focusing on an aspect of the self ("*my inadequacy*"). And the second sentence [which in French reads, "De vrai, c'est aussi un subject auquel j'exerce mon jugement autant qu'à nul autre"] in fact exhibits the same "content structure." For the self here occurs, in the first place, as the subject of the verb in the relative clause ("on which *I exercise*") as well as in the object of that verb (*my judgment*) and finally in the paradigm that refers to "my inadequacy" ("this too is *a subject* on which"), which is placed at the beginning of the sentence by the demonstrative construction ("*this . . . is a subject*"). Clearly, "opinions" and "judgments" are hypostases of the initial *I* (*je, moi*). They represent the instrument and the operation that intervene between an agent (he who says, *I find, I exercise*) and a point of application (named: *my inadequacy, a subject*). The self is distributed over all these various levels of syntax: it enters the scene as an agent, an implement, and a point of application.

Montaigne condemns his inadequacy. Now, in judging and condemning it, his opinions are "bold and constant." This is a rather remarkable sort of constancy, for it sits in judgment upon an inconstancy, a lack, which is the primary object of its attention. What in fact is the inadequacy [*insuffisance*] of which Montaigne speaks? To understand this, we must look to the root of the French word *insuffisance*: the Latin verb *sufficere*, which in its most concrete sense means to give support, to prop up. What Montaigne criticizes under the name "inadequacy" is the absence of inner support. Yet the lack of support will become the theme and the pretext of a pleasurable activity: a kind of vigor derives from the judgment of weakness. The profound infirmity, the want of support, gives rise to a compensatory strength, a redoubled vigilance. With its acuity unimpaired, uncompromised by the weakness within, judgment tirelessly plumbs and interrogates the inner depths. Montaigne will show us, in a series of metaphors, the acts of a mind ensconced in the seat of judgment, a mind that never tires of putting itself to the test. Montaigne lacks an inner foundation or support; he has only his enthusiasm, which renews itself constantly.

"The world always looks straight ahead": it is not simply in opposition to the inner void but also in opposition to the world that Montaigne's words set themselves in motion. He refuses to move in the same direction as other people. The world (here a synthesis of the *vulgus* of the Latin moralists and the *mundus* of the theology of the Fall) has chosen exteriority, escape. Three sentences in the cited passage are constructed as antitheses. These begin by mentioning what *the world* does, what *everyone* does, what *others* do, only to draw a contrast with what *I* do: as for *me*. In each case the "as for me" is followed by a verb of action that reverses the direction of the action verb in the first half of the antithesis, by means of strong adverbial contrasts: straight ahead/inward, in front/inside, forward/about in myself. The ego defines and affirms itself by the energy of its negation. In its inner depths it has discovered inadequacy; outside it sees the most futile agitation. Disappointing figures surround it on all sides. But it does not succumb to vertigo: by a sovereign decision it proclaims its difference and discovers in that act a plethora of free energy. Having failed to find support either within itself or in the outside world, the judgment is reduced to supporting itself by its own decree, and to drawing its energy from within.

"As for me, I turn my gaze inward." Turned inward, his energy will not drain away: the subject, placed ahead of the main clause's forward outposts, guards the territory within. To turn outward, like the world (which looks "straight ahead"), would be to surrender to what is alien, to come under the domination of another, to waste what is most precious in oneself. By reflecting his gaze toward the realm within, Montaigne is choosing to make his stand on a field that others have deserted. Even if there turns out to be *nothing* at the heart of this place, even if the inner depths turn out to be vacant, he will have lost nothing of his own substance, he will have submitted to the domination of no other.

This self-examination, this reflection of the act back upon the actor are expressed in the most clear-cut fashion. Consider the expressive verbs in the following series: *I fix it, I keep it busy, I look inside of me, I have no business but with myself, I continually observe myself, I take stock of myself, I taste myself, I roll about in myself*. The playful spirit is awakened. This is not a simple list of synonyms. The action described is

not a single action designated in a variety of ways, nor is it a continuous and progressive action: with each verb Montaigne begins a new
self-examination, inaugurates a new experiment. Each look, each
movement within himself is followed by a brief period of disengagement, a breathing spell. A reprise, a fresh start, follows the repetition
of Montaigne's condemnation of the customary behavior of the
"world" and of "other people." A comma suffices to represent this
disengagement and gives Montaigne all the time he needs to gather
his forces for a new assault. Even as the verbs pile up, each carries the
force of a new act, now in a serious vein ("I take stock of myself"),
now on a more playful note ("I keep it busy"—*je l'amuse là*). And we
pass through several realms of the senses: after sight, taste ("I taste
myself") and kinesthesia ("I roll about in myself"). Additions, which
elsewhere Montaigne interpolates as he expands his work, often
come in the middle of sentences so supple that they can stretch to
accept every addendum: each comma is like a dormant bud on the
stalk of the sentence, that can suddenly blossom forth with new life.
An unexpected thought or an additional variation can spring to life or
branch off the main shoot long after the first writing. Here, the line of
Persius ("No man tries to descend into himself"), the negative corollary of "they always go forward," has been incorporated right into
the sentence itself—a good example of Montaigne's essential style,
which is to let each sentence ramify as it grows. By introducing the
Latin citation, an alien material tacked on as "marquetry," Montaigne
hoped to add something richer and more substantial than his own
words: the Latin maxim is a flying buttress that temporarily obviates
the inner quest for "support." Far from being a superfluous ornament, it allows a saving of energy: it is a solidifying brace, a sturdy
joint, a remedy for the inadequacy of which Montaigne accuses the
French in which he writes.

The verbs Montaigne uses to describe his activity are almost all reflexive verbs. The last sentence of the cited passage—"I roll about in
myself"—goes still further. In French this reads: "Je me roulle en
moy mesme." As though propelled by all the movement that precedes it, this sentence evokes an act that is doubly reflexive, as indicated by the reflexive pronoun and the adverbial complement of the
verb: *se* rouler *en soi-même*. "We have a soul that can be turned upon
itself"[*Nous avons une âme contournable en soy mesme*], Montaigne says
elsewhere.[30] Visual metaphors ("I continually observe myself," etc.)
here give way to a purely physical movement. The "ego" was at first
a horizon surveyed by a remote gaze; now it is a region of space susceptible to the actions of a body. But the ego is itself that body, the

agent of the motion that region calls to mind. Hence it is both the being in motion and the free space that that motion requires in order to take place: the two are inextricably associated. What is more, the movement is not a limited act but an all-encompassing energy that involves the whole body. "To roll about in oneself" has a positive value: it is a centered movement. In other passages where Montaigne speaks of turning, he has in mind a wild and pointless gyration in the outside world. But for the person who "rolls about in himself" the motor force involves both the propulsive spirit and the fullest possible self-reflection: the result is increased intimacy. On the one hand reflexive figuration of the self multiplies the dimensions of being and produces a "spatialized" image of the self, so fabulously altered in size as to risk losing sight of its boundaries altogether. On the other hand, however, the inner search proceeds with a confident touch, which tends to negate all distance and to reunite, in a compact amalgam of space, body, and movement, all that the reflexive split had seemed to put asunder. The movement so described is thus a "rolling up" [*enroulement*], which opens up the possibility of a future unfolding [*déroulement*], the metaphor for which is the "ledger" [or *rolle*].

To roll about in himself is for Montaigne the most intense and complete form of action that exists: not only is it directed inward but the body as a whole is at once the agent, instrument, theater, and purpose of the action. An examination of various types of actions and, even more importantly, of the values that Montaigne ascribes to them would show that he has little to say about actions involving tools and directed toward objects in the outside world. As we saw earlier in our discussion of the idea of a "work," technical activity, activity that requires an implement in order to "make" something, is a "mechanical" labor and as such of little value. (In this respect Montaigne shares the prejudices of the minor nobility. Not only does he find the liberal arts to be superior to the mechanical arts, but free conversation and disinterested communication are worth more, in his eyes, than any lucrative occupation, even a literary one. Accordingly, Montaigne begs pardon for taking up his pen. He does not make a profession of writing. Writing is for him a last resort, a way of carrying on a conversation at a distance and of prolonging his voice beyond the grave.) In Montaigne's view, work done bare-handed, without the aid of implements, and applied directly to its objects yields products of greater value than work done with the help of tools. To take, to touch, to seize, to fashion, to manipulate: these are acts at once more basic and more noble, that result not in the transformation of material objects but in enrichment of personal experience. *Manipulation* interests Montaigne not because he wants to change things but because the hand [*main*] learns by paying attention to its own *manner* and thereby comes to know itself better. What matters in the *making* of something is the awareness the body develops of the way it *fashions* its own movement; this is style as felt within, as if energy were expended in action only in order to be perceived, to become familiar with itself, retrieving exactly what is paid out. In this intransitive action the self is the source of its own animating energy; it never abandons itself. The initiative is no longer with sight but with the body as a whole; through action the body comes to know itself intimately. It gains knowledge as it experiences pleasure.

Where does this lead? One point bears emphasizing: what we discover is not the geography of the space explored but the energy of the exploring ego. Montaigne does not tell us what he discovers when he turns his curiosity inward to focus on his inner self. From the first he uses a negative term to describe that inner space: inadequacy. He characterizes himself as a void and a lack. We shall learn nothing more about what lies within. Its treasures come exclusively from the movement that has penetrated it. For what Montaigne describes so lavishly, by stages, is the way in which intentional action, directed inward, becomes aware of the tension and rhythm that drives it forward. If the space explored remains an undefined nullity, the exploring body becomes aware of itself in the very act of searching; it takes shape as it develops sensitivity to its own action. What stands out, then, is not a map or portrait of the "deeper" self, finally deciphered, but rather the tireless subject who, knowing nothing, is engaged in a never-ending investigation of himself. However far the ego's self-investigation proceeds, it never acquires anything other than a muscular awareness of its own progress. What Montaigne conveys to us is not ever more minute detail about the vague reality that his mind seeks to grasp, but ever more ample views of a mind and a body preparing themselves for the act of understanding. Here it may not be out of place to recall the notion of "muscular sense," or "proprioceptive sensibility" (Sherrington), terms used by physiologists to designate the way in which the body judges its posture by way of information about the state of contraction of various muscles. Once again we are "on the wheel." Self-knowledge, for Montaigne, is the "exquisite" proprioceptive sensation of the movement whereby he sets out in search of self-knowledge. It is the internal pleasure of the attempt.

Perhaps we have nothing more important to discover: our true self is not the obscure and inconsistent reality that we strive to know yet never do, but rather our very striving and repeated failure. Hence it is not something that remains hidden, that we discover only after much groping in the dark. There it lies, (almost) intact, (almost) here, (almost) now, not in front of the groping hand but in the groping itself, in the void that grows within us, a void without which there would be no groping but only an undefinable stability, ponderous and impenetrable. "I aspire to no other fruit in acting than to act."[31]

"Life is a material and corporeal movement."[32] A carnal movement, which constantly involves and manifests the presence of the body. Elsewhere, however, Montaigne describes another movement, destructive of all material consistency and coherence, an extreme instability, which manifests itself in a discontinuous series of instants that never manages to "compose a continuous body."[33] The body never consolidates itself, never gathers its energies. We allow ourselves to be carried away by an "insubstantial day dream." Man loses his footing in the fluid, indefinite space that he becomes for himself.

This twofold intuition of movement, sustained by the experience of the senses, leads to a proliferation of dynamic images representing the opposing figures of passivity and active tension in a region of space magnificently carved out and populated by language. Movement-as-flow (in which all solid forms gradually dissolve) alternates with movement-as-action (in which the individual deliberately takes on the form of his act, keeps his shape, and easily becomes identified with is motor experience). Some images of motion grant the body the power to produce and freely govern its initiatives, while others leave it disarmed and at the mercy of universal change, wherein it loses itself with resignation. For so great are both the strength and the weakness of our "bodily condition" that Montaigne's thought seems to contradict itself on the subject. On the one hand, he knows his body as a focal point of various energies, which he is at pains to preserve and careful not to squander. The active individual enjoys his exertions only when he overcomes the world's resistance: if he finds no "object" to "aim at,"[34] then there is no point in his sharpening his attention and "stopping in himself" to improve his self-perception. Thus the active body, by constantly taking itself in hand, and with the support it gets from outside resistance, will find its reward in the almost erotic perception of energy carefully husbanded, stretched, and tightly "bound." On the other hand, Montaigne describes this same body as a piece of flotsam, a fragile amalgam, that can be "undone" by the least fillip from outside, as well as by its own vanity, "ineptitude," "inadequacy," and incapacity to keep from drifting internally, "like floating objects, now gently, now violently, according as the water is angry or calm."[35] We can never maintain harmony among all the different tendencies that war within us. The unstable alloy is always disintegrating: "Each bit, each moment, plays its own game."[36] "And we, and our judgment, and all mortal things go on flowing and rolling unceasingly. Thus nothing certain can be established about one thing by another, both the judging and the judged being in continual change and motion."[37] Note that here rolling is associated with flow and dispossesses us radically.

The flow and the voluntary act are perpetually inceptive [*inchoatif*] movements, which remain forever incomplete, at some distance from their goal. In passive relaxation, our dispersal and dissolution never end; in active enthusiasm, we seek solidity, stability, ponderous and certain rigidity, but we never finally achieve these ends. Note, moreover, that both movements elicit and provoke their contrary. This is what happens, as we saw earlier, when Montaigne withdraws from the world. He hopes to "stay and settle in himself" but finds that his mind is like a "runaway horse," for it "gives birth to so many chimeras and fantastic monsters, one after another, without order or purpose."[38] By contrast, reflecting on his inner "mobility" gives Montaigne the opportunity to "engender in [himself] a certain *constancy* of opinions."[39] Thus as soon as he feels himself being passively carried away at a dizzying rate, he immediately feels the need to bring all his energies to bear to counter the force that hurries him along: "Look into yourself, know yourself, keep to yourself; bring back your mind and your will, which are spending themselves elsewhere, into themselves; you are running out, you are scattering yourself, concentrate yourself, resist yourself; you are being betrayed, dispersed, and stolen away from yourself."[40]

To march—to be carried; to seize—to be dispersed; to resist—to flow. Not only does Montaigne alternately "essay" first one kind of movement, then the other, but he judges each according to different standards, sometimes preferring one, sometimes another. Now he will issue a call to action and resistance, now he will praise complacent passivity as far less vain and foolish. One must *seize* control—but to do so is to try to draw up a "fistful of water." One must give in to manipulation—but how weak one is, to be at the mercy of every wind.

These same oppositions and reversals of value also apply to material qualities: e.g., the pairs *full/empty* and *heavy/light*, which are closely related to the images of motion. In Montaigne's metaphors densities vary as objects move. Depending on whether an object causes movement or is moved, it becomes heavy or light, it vanishes like smoke or takes on bulk. Flow invariably lightens. Water becomes lighter the faster it flows, and Montaigne moves easily from water to wind, which is pure "emptiness," without constant mass, direction, or current. At the extreme of lightness, flow becomes intangible agitation: the movement that destroys being itself disintegrates in stationary disorder, weightless entropy. Did the flow originally have a direction, an orientation? Perhaps, but only to end in this meaningless weightlessness. One step further and we come to the perfect vacuum. At the other extreme is voluntary initiative, waiting to take shape, to define itself, to consolidate its strength until it is capable of surmounting any obstacle. Energy, as it gathers, acquires mass, weight, fullness. But the ponderous, like the weightless, can be either good or bad.

When good, fullness and weight always evoke contact, actual possession: the hand seizing hold of a solid object, which allows itself to be grasped. Proper fullness is a quality shared by the possessed object and the exploring body. When Montaigne refers to pleasure "firm and full," firmness and fullness are mixed values that belong jointly to the grasp and to the external object seized. As hand and body heft the object, they are in such close contact with it that they become more fully aware of their own form. As a result, the object becomes internalized, a part of the action that depends upon it, that incorporates and penetrates it. Fullness is not a property of action or of the world but emerges and comes to fruition at the junction between the two.

The quest for plenitude is usually the act of an ego that turns inward upon itself as privileged object to be held as tightly as possible. The mind, at first alienated, a spectator, considers its own life as a part of the objective world, yet it cannot rest until the compromised unity is restored. When it has taken hold of its object it exerts its weight to abolish the division between ego-subject and ego-object, in order to put an end to the reflexive split. "Meditation is a powerful and *full* study."[41] Immediately thereafter, the nature of that fullness is specified in terms of action and workmanlike effort: "A powerful and full study for anyone who knows how to *examine and exercise himself* vigorously. I would rather *fashion* my mind than furnish it."

Weight and fullness can also be bad, however, when they take the form of inertia, paralysis, or encumberment. "I am nearly always in place, like heavy and inert bodies."[42] And a "well-made" head, Montaigne tells us, will always be better than a "well-filled" head.[43] Fullness here no longer connotes actual possession but merely a passive filling up with foreign matter, with pedantic baggage. Speaking out against such heaviness, Montaigne declares himself to be empty, light, forgetful, apt to let things escape from his mind and be lost forever. It is the privilege of God alone to be "all fullness." For our part, we must accept our "imperfect essence" and recognize that "we are all hollow and *empty*." In warning against the temptations of glory, Montaigne adds: "It is not with wind and sound tht we have to fill ourselves; we need more solid substance to repair us."[44] For he knows from experience how emptiness calls forth language: "wind" and "sound" offer themselves as a first compensation, woefully inadequate. Montaigne says as much in "Of glory," where he mocks the way we try to inflate our names with meaningless grandeur. But can we hope for anything more substantial and firm? Is "more solid substance" within our reach? Or is it wisdom perhaps to accept our emptiness? This is what Montaigne thinks when he asserts that a soul that is "open, docile, and with little presumption" possesses "the principal qualities for the preservation of human society."[45]

Certainly emptiness is a perilous condition. We are at the mercy of anyone who wishes to foist some opinion upon us: "The more a mind is empty and without counterpoise, the more easily it gives beneath the weight of the first persuasive argument."[46] Ignorance therefore makes us liable to credulity. What is to be done? For one thing, we can preserve our gaping emptiness and not attempt to fill it at the first opportunity. Moreover, if "sound" and "wind" must be allowed in, then we should take care to ensure that that sound is at least our own, that the image that fills the void emanates somehow from our own depths. Recall Montaigne's explanations (or excuses) for starting to write the *Essays*. This sentence has been cited before, but rereading it now we are in a better position to appreciate the importance of the image of emptiness: "And then, finding myself entirely destitute and void of any other matter, I presented myself to myself for argument and object."[47] This is a curious antithesis: the finding of emptiness precedes and provokes the act of self-examination. Contrast this with the case of Descartes: Montaigne, upon discovering that he is an empty vessel, realizes that he will make a fine model for a life-size portrait, whereas Descartes, making the same discovery, immediately draws the simple conclusion "I think, therefore I exist," and that is all.

To speak about oneself is to fill a void. At the beginning of the chapter "Of friendship" (1:28) Montaigne makes a well-known comparison between his own work and that of a painter who fills the empty space around his frescoes with grotesque images. He thus lik-

231

ens his writing to a *marginal* filler. We know that he had hoped to honor La Boétie by placing his work in the central position. Unable to publish *Contr'un*, Montaigne at first included twenty-nine of La Boétie's unpublished sonnets. Later, however, he eliminated these and resigned himself to leaving a hole in the middle of his work, a hole whose dimensions would give a precise measure of his own *inadequacy:*

> (A) As I was considering the way a painter I employ went about his work, I had a mind to imitate him. He chooses the best spot, the middle of each wall, to put a picture labored over with all his skill, and the empty space all around it he fills with grotesques, which are fantastic paintings whose only charm lies in their variety and strangeness. And what are these things of mine, in truth, but grotesques and monstrous bodies, pieced together of divers members, without definite shape, having no order, sequence, or proportion other than accidental? . . . I do indeed go along with my painter in this *second* point, but I fall short in the *first* and better part; for my ability does not go far enough for me to dare to undertake a rich, polished picture, formed according to art.[48]

The empty central panel calls forth a proliferation of undisciplined shapes on its periphery; the bareness brings out a mad "strangeness." Emptiness in fact turns out, paradoxically, to be quite fecund, in that it somehow gives rise to a whole "fantastic" growth of shapes and figures that fill it and give it life. Yet it fails to satisfy the need for substantial riches: "the polished picture, formed according to art," will remain undone. But because it does remain undone the marginal decoration is happily free to expand, yielding that very special form that comes from taking advantage of the absence of form.

Thus heaviness and lightness, fullness and emptiness can be either desirable conditions or infirmities, depending on the circumstances. There is euphoria in fullness, there is reassuring solidity, yet a body that is too dense and heavy inhibits the spirit and imprisons us in an invisible armor. Believing the quarry to be firmly in hand, the act of will becomes caught in its own ponderous coils. Its very energy may carry us beyond its goal, where it bogs down of its own excess, in passive immobility. By contrast, lightness is a marvelous privilege: the blithe spirit is never captive and can float effortlessly from sensation to sensation. But lightness soon loses itself in its own ubiquity; it holds no power, it watches as its identity and boundaries are eroded, it ebbs into insignificance, it dwindles to a paltry, unsteady breeze. In Montaigne's imagination, the bad forms of lightness and heaviness are both misfortunes involving the loss of energy: on the one hand there is complete immobility, the inability to overcome inertia; on the other, total dissipation. The one is the culmination of passivity, the other of voluntary action. Both states are extremes, in which movement either comes to a halt or runs wild. Fortunately, though, the closer we come to either extreme, the more powerful the force tending to move us in the opposite direction.

Montaigne often sees this opposition in terms of the contrast between the soul (which is too fluid) and the body (which is too heavy). The body is a mass subject to inertia; the soul is a scene of perpetual agitation. Body and soul can assist each other, however. Montaigne believes in the possibility of an association of the heavy and the light, a reconciliation in which one tempers and moderates the other. He imagines the union of body and soul in dynamic terms: their difference is not metaphysical but physical. Here there is no problem (as there will be for Descartes) of making the body act on the soul or vice versa. The movement of each can easily be harmonized with the movement of the other. Under the right conditions the least dense and the most dense of substances can be made to mix. The happy man knows the intimate connection between weight and lightness. To separate them is to "tear apart a living man."[49] In his rhetorical justification of bodily existence, Montaigne does not settle for the traditional theme of a marriage (or brotherhood) between soul and body and of the mutual services they perform for one another. He feels the need to describe these in dynamic terms. And it is to the kinesthetic sensibility that he turns for images to illustrate the reconciliation of opposites in the tempered relationship that exists between body and soul:

> (B) To what purpose do we dismember by divorce a structure made up of such close and brotherly correspondence? On the contrary, let us bind it together again by mutual services. Let the mind arouse and quicken the *heaviness* of the body, and the body check and make fast the *lightness* of the mind.[50]

Montaigne's fundamental concern is to bring opposites into harmony. It is of little importance to him to establish a constant association between mind and lightness, body and heaviness. Indeed, it suits his purposes just as well if the attributes are reversed, so long as the opposition and at the same time the possibility of reconciliation are

233

respected. In the following passage, for example, the mind is characterized by *heaviness* and "tension." At issue are our imagination and our will, which exaggerate the burden of "loads" that come from outside:

> (B) For the body receives the *loads* that are placed on it exactly according as they are; *the mind often extends them and makes them heavier* to its cost, giving them the measurements it sees fit. We do like things with different degrees of effort and tension [*contention*] of the will.[51]

The will is a faculty of the mind, and Montaigne, by ascribing to it energy metaphorically represented by images of tension (*contention*, *intention*), is now conferring upon the mind a dangerous power to heap burdens upon itself. Thus the mind seems to bear responsibility for any *overburdening*, which carries a negative connotation. In Montaigne *tension* is an ambiguous state: should it run to excess and clench in the act, it becomes a harmful force, inimical to man's vital interest. He regards tension as a good thing only if it does not paralyze the ability to move.

There is more to Montaigne's imagination of motion than movement-as-flow and movement-as-act. He also imagines their sum, a composite in which two contrary kinds of experience mix and mingle with one another. When Montaigne declares that the Pyrrhonist sage "is bound to follow [circumstances] and to let himself be swayed by appearances,"[52] he draws a close parallel between an active movement (*to follow*) and a passive assent (*to let himself be swayed*). Here the two movements are joined together and oriented in the same direction, almost identified with one another. The active movement does not resist the passive, and passivity does not prevent action. The harmony thus created can be seen as a kind of suppleness, a deft adaptation of the body to the flow that carries it along. Now, a supple maneuver is one in which the body uses its freedom in a manner compatible with the forces impinging on it. The body can easily back out of the maneuver if it wishes, without undue stress: "The best of my bodily qualities is that I am *flexible* and not very stubborn. I have inclinations that are more personal and customary, and more agreeable to me, than others; but with very little effort I *turn away* from them, and easily *slip* into the opposite habit."[53] This flexible slipping from one habit to another is the positive, ideal form of this type of "composite movement." Montaigne likes to express the euphoria this causes him by using normally intransitive verbs in transitive constructions: *couler la vie, glisser la vie* [literally: to flow life, to slip life]. This admittedly involves abandonment, but abandonment of a kind that immediately transforms the impinging forces into an act. Passivity turns into activity, in which the simple *passage* of time becomes an object upon which the will can exert itself. The willful spirit rejoins and mingles with laxity and confident abandon. A decision is necessary to slip from one inclination into another: this requires only the slightest effort. It practically ceases to be an action and becomes merely a controlled slide: "I slip easily."

Montaigne speaks at times of a less smooth kind of composite movement: movement where by deliberate exertion one resists being passively dragged along by the current (so that progress becomes irregular, fitful) and yet where the current is violent enough to prevent the goal of the action from being attained. First drifting, then struggling against the current, the body is constantly trying to regain the passive state: it does not want to abandon itself to the current altogether, but it cannot successfully resist. So it lurches, totters, stumbles, spins, limps, sways (Montaigne is never at a loss for colorful verbs of motion). The body moves like a drunkard, unable to control its actions; it loses control of its direction and can no longer "be sure of its goal." Unlike the supple motion described a moment ago, this lurching motion is fitful, discontinuous: from one moment to the next it exhausts its energy only to generate a fresh supply. That this unsteadiness and recovery from the brink of disaster may have an erotic value is reflected in what Montaigne has to say about the love of the "cripple" (3:11).

In the system of metaphors for describing motion, to totter is not always to *fall*. "Tottering" is a middle term between proceeding straight ahead and falling. To go straight to the truth of things is the dream of philosophical knowledge; but there is always a truth closer to home that philosophy neglects, and Montaigne feels "grateful to the Milesian wench who, seeing the philosopher Thales continually spending his time in contemplation of the heavenly vault and always keeping his eyes raised upward, put something in his way to make him *stumble*."[54] The fall is punishment for the presumptuousness of self-neglect. Moreover, the person who does attend to himself is obliged to follow an irregular, unpredictable, labyrinthine path. He requires a great deal of strength to maintain his course, for old age is itself a kind of fall.[55]

Vagabondage remains: "I seek out change indiscriminately and tumultuously. My style and my mind alike go roaming."[56] "Have I left something unseen behind me? I go back; it is still on my road. I trace no fixed line, either straight or crooked."[57]

To be flexible is the ideal, but not just any kind of flexibility will do. Montaigne is unwilling to let anything get away from him: he wants to experience what it is like to *go after* things as well as the intoxication of *being carried away*. A proper synthesis maintains intact the differences between the contrary elements it subsumes. If opposites are too intimately fused, the result is mere moderation, a mediocre form of wisdom, a pliable prudence; notwithstanding a widely believed legend to the contrary, Montaigne's philosophy is nothing of the kind. What he wants is flexibility in dealing with contrasts; he wants heaviness and lightness to remain distinct, to form a couple in which "mutual services" are required of and performed by both sides. Body and soul, united in "close and brotherly correspondence,"[58] find in their continuing duality the essential prerequisite for a rich dialogue and harmonious tension. This "correspondence" is precious because it must be achieved despite the ever-present threat of divorce and dissension: "Those who want to split up our two principal parts and sequester them from each other are wrong. On the contrary, we must couple and join them together again."[59] Our dual nature perpetuates a risk of conflict. Our only way of dealing with this risk is to make use of our ability to sustain dynamically opposed qualities: we experience activity against a background of passivity and passivity in the very thick of action. The happy man, the harmonious individual, does not occupy a place midway between two extremes, part active and part passive. He is not one who refuses to experience contradiction, who does not wish to know fullness or emptiness, heaviness or lightness. He is rather a person who gives himself simultaneously to all extremes, without allowing himself to be torn apart. He is a person in whom a sudden grace brings about a paradoxical marriage between passive abandonment and active striving, acquiescence and effort. He accepts the unfolding of the movement through all its various keys.

So, against a background of completely passive motion, an act stands out, rich in significance and fully voluntary. Activity and passivity do not ignore each other, nor is one simply superimposed upon the other without reciprocity; each must wrap around and implicate the other. Active intent implies full acquiescence in passive involvement, and conversely, passive flow can be channeled by action. The tension of the act and the relaxation of the flow accentuate one another, and the individual draws strength from the feeling of dissolution.

The same harmonious division governs the relationship between Montaigne's judgment and his natural manner, so nearly identical and yet so far apart. The judgment is characterized by tension, the natural manner by fluidity. Thus self-knowledge and abandonment to nature can be made compatible. A vigilant attention turns toward the evasive and fuzzy flow so as to translate it into a conscious sensation: *"We must really strain our soul to make it feel how it is ebbing away."*[60] The soul is likened both to a fluid and to a stretched spring. The act of *feeling* occurs at the point of contact between these two forces, represented by images of opposite sign. It comes at the point where *straining* and *being carried away* coexist in a fugitive fullness, i.e., in a fullness that lightness and flow "awaken and vivify." Now, this feeling, which is a momentarily enlivened heaviness, as also lightness made temporarily weighty. Perceptible fullness emerges when action "holds and fixes" an infinitely light substance, namely, life, thereby giving it weight long enough to be perceived. Thus the effect of the tension of judgment, of its active vigilance, is to *hold back* that which in any case continues to ebb away:

> (B) Especially at this moment, when I perceive that [my life] is so brief in time, I try to increase it in *weight*; I try to *arrest* the speed of its *flight* by the speed with which I *grasp* it, and to compensate for the haste of its *ebb* by my vigor in *using* it. The shorter my possession of life, the deeper and *fuller* I must make it.[61]

If the immediate experience is one of flight, of ebbing away, the reflexive consciousness is not simply a distant mirror in which images of that experience are reflected. It is an activity of capture; it bestows an imaginary weight upon what is weightless. This produces intense yet tranquil pleasure, in which the individual samples both emptiness and plenitude, weakness and strength, the poverty of one who has nothing and the wealth of one who has everything in his possession.

Repeatedly, in expressions such as "to let oneself go," "to let oneself be manipulated," "to let onself be carried away," we see signs of this two fold movement: passivity dominates, but not without active acquiescence in that passivity, not without a relaxation and voluntary surrender of the soul, which might have refused simply to drift, might have balked at being dragged along. For to allow oneself to be carried away is not simply to be carried away: it is to submit willingly to the current, even though resistance would not have been impossible. It is to know that one has the power to struggle and yet to refrain from doing so. Such renunciation is not cowardice: it serves the "pleasure principle"; it derives the greatest possible advantage from the experience of the moment. We have already seen how, after his fall from the horse, Montaigne was not merely a passive victim of delirium: he deliberately surrendered to it, he *let* himself slip into it, not without "pleasure." With what tenuous consciousness he still possessed, he gave his consent that his life should ebb and drain away. Even when Montaigne accepts the extinction of consciousness and the abolition of feeling, he states his own annihilation in a sentence governed by a reflexive verb representing a reflexive act of the will:

> (B) I plunge [*je me plonge*] head down, stupidly, into death, without looking at it and recognizing it, as into a silent and dark abyss which swallows me up at one leap and overwhelms me in an instant with a heavy sleep free from feeling and pain.[62]

Even at the twilight of consciousness, Montaigne must draw his energy from the decision to "plunge himself" into death. Again, this imaginary notion is accompanied by "some pleasure." A few pages later, he tells us that he would prefer to die while on a trip, far from his family. He will then be able to be more attentive to dying. For the ideal death is an active death, a "directed" death, in which the mind tries to surprise an event taking place in the depths of the body, which will put an end to it: "It is only an instant; but it is of such gravity that I would willingly give several days of my life to go through it in my own way."[63] Death is the absolute escape yet still available to the ideal grasp. It "unbinds" us, and up to the final moment we can "construct" it and look upon it as though it were our own work. To be sure, death is a kind of sleep, but Montaigne was never willing to separate sleep entirely from acting or feeling. "Simply to act costs [the mind] so little that it is acting even in sleep."[64] Montaigne had himself awakened so that he might catch a "glimpse" of sleep; similarly, he expresses the wish that he might be allowed to catch a glimpse of death, and to measure its weight.

The masterpiece of living

But this reconciliation of *grasp* and *abandon*, of activity and passivity, this reflective acquiescence in what must inevitably be endured, has the opportunity first to manifest itself in life—each of whose moments can be illuminated by this doubling.

Nothing is easier than living, and nothing is more difficult. Everything is given, and there is nothing to seek out; but everything is to be done. It is not simply a matter of acquiescing, accepting, letting oneself go. We must also undertake to "live this life naturally and well," to "live appropriately," and there is no other "knowledge so arduous": this is "our great and glorious masterpiece."[65] To live, then, is what is given to us, prior to all our reasons for acting: but living is also the act and the work par excellence, a purpose that transcends all our other acts and works. It is both a matter of fact and a task. Our existence is assigned to us, yet it remains a never-ending job. Thus the mind that applies itself to living must immediately accept itself and at the same time gain the distance necessary to construct itself as a *masterpiece*. The very idea of life implies that we cling to ourselves from the first and yet aim perpetually at "living" as at a far-off goal, a goal remote but not external, since what we hope to conquer is the territory that surrounds us, a perceptible plenitude.

At each moment life offers itself as *already there* in the spontaneous welling up of consciousness and the surrounding world. All that remains is to "perfect" it. Now, as Montaigne gains more experience, the moment when life manifests itself will take on the quality of a *final* moment: a moment of grace, an unexpected reprieve, capping a life that has run its course. Life is *already there* because it has already taken place. All the cards have been played. Concern for the future no longer affects it. In this fragile final moment, plenitude and emptiness coexist. Everything comes down to the most tenuous consciousness of being *still* alive, while in retrospect everything is full, everything has received its final form: the body that has known so many pleasures and that soon will feel nothing more; the now fixed series of past acts and words; life's irreversible and precarious course.

"Yes, it is all over. . . . My good man, it is all over."[66] Completion, perfection in imperfection—Montaigne is there with all his maladies, his habits, and his faults. To accept life, for him, means to accept having lived and to come to terms with himself as the years have made him. It is all over. It is too late. Let no one ask him to mend his ways. Montaigne can tell about himself only as he is, i.e., as life has made him and as illness is destroying him. But telling about himself now becomes an endless task, contradicting the apparent immobility of the assertion "It is all over." Nothing is stable. For to tell about oneself is to prolong, in the duration peculiar to language, the life and movement that one had thought ended. Thus Montaigne corrects his portrait and transforms himself by means of constant addition, even as he declares that he is incapable of changing his ways. In the thirteenth chapter of book three, after everything had seemed to come to a halt in the "It is all over," he exhorts us to construct our lives as masterpieces and then observes: "Thus do I melt and slip away from myself."[67] Thus, after everything is said to be over comes the call to formative action and the resignation of life's perpetual ebbing away: everything remains to be done, even as everything is coming undone. "Life is an uneven, irregular, and multiform movement."[68] What could be more marvelous than to experience this simultaneous clinging and ebbing, this impossibility to be other than oneself while also striving endlessly to *take our distance*: each moment—the one in which we cling, the one in which we take our distance—will by turns strike us as a weakness or a desirable goal, as proof of the power or the impotence of the living mind.

"I customarily do wholeheartedly whatever I do, and go my way all in one piece. I scarcely make a motion that is hidden and out of sight of my reason."[69] Montaigne here proclaims his unity, his inner unanimity. But no sooner is unity affirmed than it splits into *movement* and *reason*: a movement that exhibits itself quite openly, and a reason that acquiesces in the movement that unfolds before it. Division and unity: this antithetical pair has yet another dimension in which to unfold. On the threshold of death, movement and reason reveal their final meaning. Movement is movement toward death, and reason has recognized that life is "perishable by its nature." Acquiescence in death is but the necessary counterpart of a total conversion to life. When the distance posited by the mind implies an absolute break with life, i.e., death, the intimacy that the mind discovers by turning inward gives palpable evidence of life. In the present case, distance and intimacy are of course only thoughts, mere objects of consciousness: death does not actually occur, and life remains incompletely possessed. But in any case the gaze encounters limits that it cannot transcend. The mind then conceives of absolute distance and absolute intimacy, and conceives of them as inextricably intertwined: that it can *combine* the two thoughts in itself and make distance contribute to the advent of presence is perhaps the mind's true victory over death, a victory that will always remain incomplete, like the conquest of the self.

To the onslaughts of disease and the threat of imminent death Montaigne responds with praise for our *bodily condition*. He knows now better than before the good fortune of having a body, and the value of health, that "blaze of gaiety."[70] Here is what seems to be a banal truth, a perennial commonplace: misfortune gives renewed zest to the good fortune of the past. The Latin poets said it in a thousand ways, and Montaigne has cited their maxims. But it is not past good fortune that illness and disease now reveal to Montaigne: it is present good fortune, current happiness.

"When I dance, I dance; when I sleep, I sleep."[71] Here Montaigne clings

to himself utterly: the *act* of dancing and the *relaxation* of sleep are moments in time that coincide exactly. The repetition [*redoublement*] of the verb is here a consequence of the reflexive split [*dédoublement*], but what is ascertained by the reflexive consciousness is the perfect repetition, the pure and simple reaffirmation of the action that Montaigne is performing. The absolute identity of the repeated verbs manifests the fact that he is fully in accord with himself, with no second thoughts or reservations. The writer thus savors his own fullness; he sees himself as he is, he immediately approves what he sees, and he makes this fact known to his reader. Now, such exuberant clinging to the lived moment is possible only because the mind has finally accepted the fact that "death mingles and fuses with our life throughout."[72] In order to find absolute fullness in a fleeting instant, it is first necessary to break with life, if only in thought. In order to discover life's riches, one must be willing to lose them all. It is when all ties have been undone that the grip is strongest and the pleasure most enjoyable.

> (C) Henceforth I think of nothing but making an end; I rid myself of all new hopes and enterprises; I take my last leave of every place I go away from, and dispossess myself every day of what I have.[73]

> (C) I unbind myself on all sides; my farewells are already half made to everyone except myself. Never did a man prepare himself to leave the world more utterly and completely, nor detach himself from it more universally, than I propose to do.[74]

> (B) In my travels I hardly ever come to my lodgings without the question passing through my mind whether I could be sick and dying there in comfort.[75]

The thought of death brings about a total disengagement, but at the same time it intensifies one's attention to each minute and each object that life still has to offer. Montaigne goes beyond the lesson of the Stoics, who taught that life should be lived as though each moment were the last. For the disengaged mind life has already come to an end, and the world has been left behind forever. Meanwhile, a reprieve, an act of pure grace, has postponed the moment of death, and henceforth life's moments can be savored as though they were to be *returned* after death. They are given as a bonus, as an inestimable favor, the favor of the simple life, the life shorn of all regret for the past and worry about the future. Since the break has already been

241

made, each moment is seen as an immediate and gratuitous gift. The shadow of death does not darken the joy of life. Grasping things, seeing them straight, becomes easier. Destitution and dispossession give rise to a delightful superfluity. The sheer presence of things would not be so full or so substantial if granted to a consciousness that had not already taken its leave. Mystics who practice this sort of farewell to the world never go back to it; their pleasure comes from God alone. But Montaigne, having taken his leave, is able to see *human* life and *this* world in a new light: while still alive he enjoys a posthumous pleasure.

How many contradictions are then cleared up, as opposing terms reveal their necessary complementarity! Montaigne had told us that he began writing his book in a "melancholy humor" and that "there is nothing with which I have occupied my mind more than with images of death, even in the most licentious season of my life."[76] But he is no less sincere when he describes his soul as "not only free from disturbance but full of satisfaction and gaiety—as it usually is, half by nature, half by design."[77] First the soul has to imagine its death as a *storm*: "(B) I enter into familiar terms with dying. I wrap myself up and nestle in this *storm*, so that it must *blind* me and sweep me away furiously with a sudden and numbing attack."[78]

But this blindness makes possible a new vision, and the anticipated storm turns into the *calm skies* that are the recompense of reason:

> (B) Wherever she [the soul] casts her *eyes, the sky is calm around her:* no desire, no fear or doubt to disturb the air for her, no difficulty, (C) past, present, or future, (B) over which her imagination may not pass without hurt.[79]

Lack of being, appearances that deceive, man's nothingness, and the futility of life—transcending all of these, simple existence is restored to us, and our perishable bodies become the place where a truth is revealed: my truth, humble but absolute; unique but sustained by universal nature; incommunicable yet implicit in every human consciousness. We have lost the *essential*, but relative and *phenomenal* existence has been restored. We have accepted poverty only to acquire greater riches. Being is both what is most hidden and what is immediately perceptible. Our senses lie to us when they speak of being, yet now being has come to dwell in our lives and among our senses. Being reveals itself constantly but with each revelation immediately snatches away what it discloses. It is, it appears, and it hides itself almost simultaneously. We must assent to the fulness and the emptiness (which we carry within us and discover outside). We must espouse the movement that ends in disintegration. We must plunge in, and discover in plunging a perceptible plenitude, a joyful, healthy body alive to the pleasure in its own act. At once tense and relaxed, active and passive, indestructible yet subject to time, passionate yet indifferent, we trust in what is given to us and content ourselves with the little that we can apprehend of it. This is a small treasure compared to what philosophy claimed to possess and know. Yet it is actually far greater, for what we now possess is the instrument with which all things can be represented or negated, affirmed or denied, brought near or relegated to the distance: our consciousness, which possesses nothing but knows its poverty and thereby surpasses itself. "My theme turns in upon itself."[80] Consciousness *is* because it *appears to be*. But it cannot appear to be except by bringing forth a world with which it is intimately involved. It needs room and if necessary will create it, thereby assuring itself the power to approach its objects freely, or to withdraw. Consciousness seeks itself among things, and also flees from itself. It exists to ascertain its difference from the world and to establish ties thereto, to endure and to will, to impugn its own emptiness and to fill itself with experience. It establishes itself in estrangement from God (in whom it places its trust) and in the presence of the world, in the horizon of death and in intimacy with life. It confronts its end and discovers in itself the strength to begin again and again, indefatigably.

SEVEN

Concerning «public affairs»

From sympathy to criticism

The magistrate who fled the servitude of Parlement and sought repose "in the bosom of the learned Muses" found instead endless movement. We now know that this movement, though not ruled by any order or subject to any rhetorical "arrangement," is governed by a kind of meaning. We have seen, in several different connections, an enemy of appearances (i.e., of masks) reconcile himself to those same appearances and resort to fiction and representation. His adventures, begun by bidding farewell to appearances, end with a return to their infinite diversity—a diversity made acceptable by reflection, which henceforth knows what to believe. He who wanted to depend on no one so that he might grasp the truth about himself discovers the necessity of "compromise" and the need, if he hopes to paint himself, to accept "relations with others." Though words and language may be a "commodity so vulgar and so vile," it is with their help that books are made: a singular vitality breathes life into materials thought to be so poor in quality and unworthy of our confidence. If words are but sound and wind, if they fail to attain essences, fail to capture immutable being, it is nevertheless true that a single person, a man in the midst of constant change, can splendidly reveal himself in the words of which he builds his book. The expressive success compensates for the "referential" failure: the impossibility of telling the truth about the world becomes a means of telling the truth about oneself. Language, itself caught in the slick and slippery web of appearances, is nevertheless capable of giving adequate expression to changeable feeling, to the act that would complete itself in "grasping and holding." The more it uses metaphors, or "transplants" of meaning, the more likely it will be to capture the mutability that Montaigne feels in his body and mind. Our language is limited, as are our senses: both can do no more than articulate the law of a world of which they themselves are a part. They can declare their allegiance to nature and, if they cannot know her, can at least swear fidelity from the depths of artifice. Our language is powerless if what we expect from it is revelation of a truer world, but it offers us fullness if we agree to live in it, in this primary world of trouble, pleasure, and suffering. Being eludes us and doubt has the final word, but our hands are not empty, we are not in exile. We are at home in this world of unstable appearances whose legitimacy we once challenged and whose lawful participants we now discover in everything that exists. Appearances deceive us, but they are not counterfeit coin: no better money exists.

"Pure phenomenalism" (or *mobilisme*) is the way Thibaudet characterizes Montaigne's philosophy.[1] Supported by innumerable citations, this definition tends to make that philosophy a kind of precursor of Bergsonism. It also attributes to it systematic coherence, something Montaigne himself always denied that it had. More cautiously, Merleau-Ponty speaks as a phenomenologist about Montaigne but without making Montaigne a disciple of Husserl. Yet he cannot help noticing in this philosophy of consciousness elements that will make a kind of phenomenology possible: "Skepticism is movement toward the truth."[2] Merleau-Ponty, who shows himself so eager to *go back* to the fundamental "chiasmus" that links man to the world, has no difficulty discerning the *return* motion of which Montaigne offers us so many examples: "To *rediscover* naturalness, naïveté, and ignorance is thus to rediscover the grace of *primary certainties*, in the doubt that encompasses them and makes them visible."[3] "Superficial appearances" are by no means an inferior substitute for true being; although we thought we could turn our back on them at the beginning, they are still there waiting for us at the end.

Appearance regained in this way takes on a new aspect: admittedly, it yields no general law, but in the absence of any comprehensible law it makes us understand that nothing else is ever revealed; it exculpates the act of feeling, with its natural limitations and imperfections. At the same time, all our other natural faculties (imagination, memory, reason, and judgment), all of which depend on the senses and share their imperfections, are reduced to their proper "scope" and assigned new, legitimate ends: not to take possession of being but rather to savor the act of living and to put that experience down in words, in the hope of evolving a philosophy adapted to our common existence (which is also existence *proper*). To feel, to work with language: the moral project unfolds between the *aesthesis* of immediate existence and the *aesthetics* of writing the *Essays*. Instead of an ontological legitimation, therefore, Montaigne is content to settle for aesthetic legitimacy, in both senses that the term aesthetic has taken on in the modern philosophical vocabulary. The feelings and the work are both involved: the feelings put to language. Immersed in the constantly changing world of appearances, consciousness is mistress only of that finite region where, with each passing moment, it exercises its judgment and its sensory powers. Combining the finite and the infinite, it manages to make wealth coincide with utter destitution. It never finishes accepting life's pleasures and "giving proper thanks . . . to him who grants [them] to us."[4] Self-consciousness is never more fully in possession than when it abandons itself, than when it *perceives itself* abandoning itself in order to set down the "form" of that possession and abandonment in the pages of a "ledger" that always remains open, a ledger whose very margins are constantly being filled, for the reader's sake, with new writing.

In order to awaken the reader's sympathies in the realm of the sensible, Montaigne is obliged to follow the whole long path that leads from feeling to the work of language. For the life of the senses of which Montaigne speaks is buried by the text itself in the obscurity that shrouds that portion of his life that predates his writing. For the reader, the sensory awakening comes only upon contact with the already formulated message. This is the aesthetic effect of the written page—with its deft shifts from topic to topic, its hammering on certain points, its alliterations, its puns, its rhythm, its antitheses and paired words, its play of figures, its verve, and its surprises—the page that not only represents but also brings to life (for us) the primary sensory experience. To be sure, this involves a new sensible order connected with the words themselves, with their phonic texture as much as their intelligible meaning. But this new sensible order, produced by art (and by that higher form of art that consists in the eschewing of art), does not merely offer us its own values, words that we take pleasure in "ruminating" as Montaigne does with the verses of Virgil and Lucretius; it also brings us back to the preverbal experience of feeling, to which it lends renewed flavor. The sympathy that exists between the raw materials of the essay and the act of writing helps to develop a complicity that reinforces our belief in the conceptual content.

Recall that Montaigne once described himself as having an "aping and imitative nature." As a reader, he is so overwhelmed by sympathy for the authors he reads that their styles come to inhabit him. Identification leads to metamorphosis:

> (B) When I used to dabble in composing verse (and I never did any but Latin), it clearly revealed the poet I had last been reading. And of my first essays, some smell a bit foreign. (C) In Paris I speak a language somewhat different

than at Montaigne. (B) Anyone I regard with attention easily imprints on me something of himself. What I consider, I usurp: a foolish countenance, an unpleasant grimace, a ridiculous way of speaking. Vices even more: once they prick me, they stick to me and will not go away without shaking. I have been observed to swear more often by imitation than by nature.[5]

But Montaigne's "wish to make a show only of what is [his] own,"[6] his concern to escape from the influence of the great authors he admires, enables him to throw off the dependence that makes his voice an echo of others. Then, having become an author himself, he is able to ascertain his own influence on the language of others, as people begin to imitate him:

(A) I want the substance to stand out, and so to fill the imagination of the listener that he will have no memory of the words. The speech I love is a simple, natural speech, the same on paper as in the mouth; a speech succulent and sinewy, brief and compressed, (C) not so much dainty and well-combed as vehement and brusque. . . . Strength and sinews are not to be borrowed; the attire and the cloak may be borrowed. Most of the people who frequent me speak like these Essays; but I don't know whether they think like them.[7]

Every reader of Montaigne has experienced this influence. This explains Ranke's remark: "How many people we see fall into his manner merely from talking about him." Hugo Friedrich, who cites Montaigne's remark, is willing to have it applied to himself: "I wouldn't take it for a reproach."[8] Except for those hostile to Montaigne (a point on which Valéry[9] is for once in accord with Pascal), it is not easy for interpreters to avoid imitating Montaigne's style (some more closely than others); in so doing they reformulate what he has to say in the terminology of another age, inevitably oversimplifying and oversystematizing his ideas. When he wants to speak of the human condition, Montaigne uses "we," and the reader finds himself caught up in that "we": the interpreter will confidently occupy the same position. Montaigne wins assent or acquiescence and infects the reader with his own gestures largely by the way he manipulates feeling: he educes feelings mimetically, not by means of an affective "sentimental" rhetoric like Rousseau but through the energy of a language abundant in material metaphors, rich in phonic effects, and handled with perfect freedom and agility.

This series of shared sentiments attests to a power of generalization and universalization that grows out of the uniqueness of sensory experience. Even before he formulates any moral precepts, Montaigne feels spontaneous sympathy for animals and men he sees suffering and in torment:

> (C) The sight of other people's anguish causes very real anguish to me, and my feelings have often usurped the feelings of others.

> (A) For myself, I have not even been able without distress to see pursued and killed an innocent animal which is defenseless and which does us no harm.[10]

No sooner does spontaneous sympathy enter consciousness than it states its law, that of "mutual obligation": this is the first ethical consequence of the reinstatement of appearances and the restoration of legitimacy to the sensible world. The issue clearly has implications broader than the power of a style and its communicative effects. Compassion is one of the features that define Montaigne's moral attitude toward the events of his day: war, torture, and the persecution of heretics, witches, and Jews. Prior to all political theory, moreover, compassion is one of the enduring characteristics of the background against which Montaigne presents pell-mell his ideas concerning the relations between the state (that is, the Prince) and the individual.

Sympathy gives rise to a conviction of similarity. It effaces differences and greets all suffering with our agonized "displeasure." Now, identification of this kind, which is wholly spontaneous and in which Montaigne sees only the effects of a "childish innocence,"[11] immediately establishes the possibility of a *refusal*. Compassion is not merely suffering shared with the victim; it is a declaration that the persecutor's act is unacceptable, and it is an uncompromising repudiation of cruelty.[12] This is the main count in Montaigne's indictment of the fanatical leaders who transformed religious controversies into bloodbaths as well as in his criticism of the conquerors of the New World.

Yet this enemy of cruelty seems tolerant of the evocation of evil. Montaigne describes numerous scenes of horror, expressing his distaste as he does:

> I could hardly be convinced, until I saw it, that there were souls so monstrous that they would commit murder for the mere pleasure of it; hack and cut off other men's limbs; sharpen their wits to invent unaccustomed torments and new forms of death, without enmity, without profit, and

for the sole purpose of enjoying the pleasing spectacle of the pitiful gestures and movements, the lamentable groans and cries, of a man dying in anguish.[13]

Reading any number of such bloody scenes in the *Essays* might lead one to suspect some hidden sadistic tendency on Montaigne's part.[14] Repelled as he was by cruelty, Montaigne knew from experience that compassion is not a pure sentiment: "For in the midst of compassion we feel within us I know not what *bittersweet pricking of malicious pleasure* in seeing others suffer; even children feel it."[15] It is to the credit of Montaigne's "good faith" that he recognized this fact, that identification with the victims can go together with an obscure complicity with their torturers: in other words, perverse forms of sympathy also exist. To be sure, the "maliciousness" and "bitterness" of those sympathies contradict the benign and sweet disposition that Montaigne generally exhibits. But those qualities accord well with one of the three stages of "relations to others" that we have learned to identify, namely, the second stage, which I earlier called the "desire for non-dependency." Self-sufficiency is not compassionate; the sword turned against oneself is its main defense. (One of Freud's most accurate intuitions is the connection he sees between the sadomasochistic personality and the way in which an isolated individual achieves self-discipline.)

Sympathy, or feeling in its expansive form, makes the moral requirement of equal treatment for all a very basic aspect of human development, prior to the effects of art and reason. Montaigne's sympathies extend to animals (to the deer at bay, to the dog that entertains his master or the cat that teases hers), to the cannibals of America, to the peasants and other "poor people," to the child tormented by his tutor, to all who are held in contempt or oppressed in the name of a presumptuous form of knowledge.

Montaigne does not stop simply at feeling compassion for these "inferior" creatures, however; going beyond the usual humanist toying with *paradox*, he is prepared to recognize the moral and intellectual superiority of the alleged inferiors. Animals outstrip us in many respects. Cannibals are more humane than we are, even in war, and perceptive enough to see the abuses in our political system. The social distance between peasants and nobles is immense: "Look at the difference between the life of my manual laborers and my own. The Scythians and Indians are in no respect more remote from my powers and ways."[16] Yet in the face of illness and death, the peasant and "the poor beggar at [his] door" are more serene than the philosopher.

Montaigne admired the behavior of simple folk during an epidemic of plague: "A whole nation was suddenly, by habit alone, placed on a level that concedes nothing in firmness to any studied and premeditated fortitude."[17]

Thus sensuous participation, with its power to bring about identification with the other, creates a bond among living beings, a bond in which unpremeditated community is quickly reinforced by conscious notions of solidarity. What virtue sought to achieve through upward striving is thereby achieved in "life below." Together Montaigne and La Boétie had sought the good in their joint masterpiece, their uncommon friendship; is that same good not present, though more obscurely, in the general society of "common" people, to whom we are tied by "some mutual obligation?"[18] On this point Montaigne's diction sheds a good deal of light. In speaking of his friendship with La Boétie, Montaigne writes: "We went *halves* in everything."[19] And from a conversation he has in Rouen with three American savages he remembers this: "They have a way in their language of speaking of men as *halves* of one another."[20] This universalized sympathy and friendship also enable the "cannibals" to detect at a glance inequalities in French society, as Montaigne is at pains to report: "They had noticed that there were among us men full and gorged with all sorts of good things, and that *their other halves were beggars at their doors*, emaciated with poverty; and they thought it strange that these needy halves could endure such an injustice, and did not take the others by the throat, or set fire to their houses."[21] In Montaigne's thinking, the universal bond that the simplest soul forms through feeling establishes a moral criterion that legitimates the indignant repudiation of anything that contradicts the "natural" feelings of solidarity. To cling to the life of the senses, and then through sympathy to extend that loyalty beyond the limits of personal life, is to live a life of nonviolence, or at any rate of the *least possible* violence. Montaigne is convinced that "presumption" plays a greater role than "feeling" in brutal persecution, even if, unlike Rousseau, he is not prepared to believe that the goodness of "our mother nature" is reflected in a supposed "natural goodness" of man. Therein lies a paradox: the scandalous inequality that the Indians rightly criticize in France is bound up with ancient institutions of which Montaigne does not fully approve; yet he prefers that those institutions not be overthrown by violence, for fear that something worse will take their place. For it is the nature of violence not to recognize limits and not to foresee the consequences of destroying one thing, which leads to the destruction of other things, and so on, *ad infinitum*. Montaigne manages to accommodate both critique and "conservatism."

Disillusioned obedience

The bonds of society can be tightened if proper attention is paid to fundamental human sensibilities: beneath the superstructure of religion, politics, and custom there is a humble but firm solidarity that binds us together. This natural sympathy can be extended to create an ethical system in which virtue and goodness are defined in terms of social existence: these moral qualities then become a part of our living relationships, a consequence of our finiteness. In short, spontaneous sympathy (dependent relationship) must take on the *form* of law and moral rules (disciplined relationship). (Rousseau, who fleshes out and develops suggestions that Montaigne scatters throughout the *Essays*, describes compassion as "the first relative sentiment to touch the human heart, according to the order to nature";[22] elsewhere he says that "from this one quality derive all the social virtues."[23])

Nature is the sovereign judge. If her judgment is available only through man's immediate conscience (and in the first place through the almost animal feeling he has for his own life), then it is our duty not to do violence to the conscience of another person on any pretext. But it is also our duty to exhort him, through persuasion, to free himself from the belief that distorts his conscience and keeps him from abandoning himself to his fugitive spontaneity—that "fluctuating and various" spontaneity (like our own) that makes each of us differ from every other and that, by our very capacity for dissimilarity, makes all of us alike. Furthermore, we are obliged to recognize that, no matter how much we would like to rid ourselves of "prejudices" and unfounded opinion these pervade our thoughts. Hence we can form bonds of sympathy with people whom we presume to be similar to ourselves only by overcoming endless obstacles and misunderstandings. Full sympathy is not always realized in an actual community; it often remains a mere abstract standard or idea, against which we can judge the imperfections of the world we live in.

For Montaigne, this thought has well-known consequences in the political sphere. Once one has resolved to reject illusions and masks, no institution can withstand the skeptic's indictment: no social rule can prove that it is founded on an absolute standard of justice. The application of what Sextus Empiricus calls "the tenth way of the *epoche* (or suspension of judgment)"[24] shows that institutions, laws, customs, and convictions all contradict one another. But once doubt has wiped the slate clean, the mind finds nothing capable of establishing a higher authority. The standards used to justify "reform" in any area stand or fall with the dogmatic, formalistic assumption that rational coherence can justify a political theory. In the face of abuses, cruelty, and torture, surely we must heed the protest of our natural sensibility. But no one holds the secret that will cure a sick age if Fortune inclines the world to ruin. The way to minimize the damage is to turn back from current abuses to prior custom, to usages and conventions justified by venerable age and long obedience. Perhaps there isn't time enough: perhaps the corruption has become so general that no return to a once-respected order is possible. While it is still permissible to fall back on custom and convention, this should be done without illusions as to what is arbitrary and perishable in tradition. With benevolent irony toward those who persist in placing all their "faith" in the past, Montaigne turns back to custom with his eyes open, seeing it for what it is: for him it is enough simply to feign respect, since it is only the outward form that matters. Acceptance of the legal conventions currently in force is analogous in the political sphere to phenomenalism in the cognitive sphere. Laws must be obeyed "not because they are just, but because they are laws."[25] On this point Pascal agrees with Montaigne, as many commentators have noticed; similarly, Descartes, in his "provisional ethics," approved formal obedience until such time as morality and politics could be based on certainty (how long did he propose to wait?). For all three men, formal respect for the law is justified by an immediately beneficial result: public tranquillity. It is worth noting that this notion, while it is generally adduced as grounds for accepting the status quo, is according to Montaigne useful only in relatively stable situations. When violent conflict has overturned all legality, conservatism, which treats only the symptoms, gives way to the feeling that the disease is incurable. From his reading of the historians Montaigne is well aware that in some situations there is "no remedy"[26] that a decent man can accept. But despite the chaos that looms on the horizon, and even as he prepares for the worst, Montaigne does not lose hope that arguments favorable to life may regain the upper hand and that, faced with the threat of general destruction, adversaries may find some ground of common understanding, if for no other reason then to assure their own survival. We must do and say whatever we can (if we make ourselves heard above the din) to make men understand that peace is the most precious of all goods, and that old laws (or simply respect for the law) that once assured tranquillity may yet be not totally devoid of efficacy. Thus skeptical criticism may dissolve the bonds of belief without leading to indifference. What Montaigne has brought to light is a "duty of humankind," a "mutual obligation" that applies to all who share the same experience of the senses, even though it is impossible to state any positive law that is not open to debate and controversy: the sense of felt *similarity* justifies the repudiation of violence. The apparent paradox is that *acquiescence* in the inherited order is based, for the enlightened mind, on the infinite *variety* of usages and customs, among which no criterion of superiority enables one to choose: no criterion, that is, except for that of public tranquillity and the survival of the community. Yet the convention to which the war-weary skeptical mind rallies is unlike the convention it earlier denounced: it is the same in appearance but henceforth deprived of the foundation it once claimed, and which guaranteed it a timeless, not to say transcendent, authority. What had been the object of attack and criticism, and what continues to be held suspect, is the "mystical" authority that the civil and religious order had claimed. What is finally recognized is the *usage* (the living moral order) that *appears* to best serve the general welfare. A loyalism becomes possible. If there is no longer any hidden essence, then there is no further need to attack a hiding power. There is no hidden norm, and the norm that might have been thought illusory because it wrapped itself in venerable justifications becomes useful and beneficial because of its effects. In the political and moral world the rule is just the publicly successful relationship, the peaceful exchange of "mutual services." What is recommended, then, is the act of obedience as such, carried out in full awareness of the fact that the rules being followed can claim nothing more than formal legitimacy. But form in itself is of value insofar as it preserves the social bond. Laws, which vary from one country to the next—what Montaigne calls "special, national justice, constrained to the need of our governments"—certainly have nothing in common with "justice in itself, natural and universal."[27] Yet we can do no better than to comply with such laws. Montaigne has chosen to do his duty and serve the king, but he keeps his eyes open:

> (A) For the most plausible advice that our reason gives us in the matter is generally for each man to obey the laws of his country, (B) which is the advice of Socrates, inspired, he says, by divine counsel. (A) And what does reason mean by that, unless that our duty has no rule but an accidental one? Truth must have one face, the same and universal.[28]

(B) What I myself adore in kings is the crowd of their adorers. All deference and submission is due to them, except that of our understanding. My reason is not trained to bend and bow, it is my knees.[29]

For Montaigne, there is nothing sacred about the person of the king: it is enough that others think the royal person sacred. The antiquity of the law deserves to be taken into account when men are accustomed and attached to it. But apart from the *principle* of legality, the law must not arouse any particular reverence. The majesty of the law is assured by the seductiveness of what is hidden (again). It is easy to mistake the meaning of the following lines, in which Montaigne seems to attribute divine origin to the most ancient laws. If God did not promulgate those laws himself, at least His will has enabled them to survive:

(C) In all things except those that are simply bad, *change is to be feared:* change of seasons, winds, food, and humors. And no laws are held in their true honor except *those to which God has given some ancient duration*, so that no one knows *their origin* or that they were ever different.[30]

Montaigne's thought reveals itself more fully, however, in the following passage:

(A) The laws take their authority from possession and usage; it is dangerous to trace them back to their birth. They swell and are ennobled as they roll, like our rivers: follow them uphill to their source, it is just a little trickle of water, barely recognizable, which thus grows proud and strong as it grows old.[31]

The *past* no more justifies the laws that derive from it than it justifies exemplary figures. Montaigne cannot admit that ancient laws by themselves possess unshakable respectability. Rather, he fears the harmful effects of "change." That is why he doesn't think it urgent to move the "vulgar" or "common herd," who, "not having the faculty of judging things in themselves, let themselves be carried away by chance and by appearances."[32] In religious matters, Montaigne readily admits that the people remain attached to articles of faith and superstitions by which he himself sets no store; he reverts to such things only because he sees nothing better capable of taking their place. "We who deprive our judgment of the right to make decisions look mildly on opinions differing from ours; and if we do not lend them our judgment, we easily lend them our ears. Where one scale of the balance is totally empty, I let the other vacillate under an old woman's dreams."[33] If the best use we can make of our reason ends in the determination that the plate is empty, then we possess no truth with which to counter dogmatism and superstition. Our nonknowledge does not give us the right to adopt a strategy of "two truths" like the Paduans and their disciples, for such a strategy requires that true knowledge be obtainable by purely human means. Skepticism yields to all positive doctrines, but the advantage it concedes is ruinous and risible. All positive doctrines are equivalent, because in their contradictory diversity they go beyond the *nothingness* to which rigorous thought has retreated. Montaigne, by declaring that he is not in competition with established beliefs, in effect abandons the field to them, yet grants them authority only insofar as they are socially useful and exert effective power over individual imaginations. What is more, he is perfectly sincere. He is not feigning when he professes his faith in God or his adoration of kings: he obeys, he says, because these are the *established* authorities. Thus he makes no mystery of his "formalism [34] (which can also be regarded as a flexible form of "conventionalism," a far cry from the systematic conventionalism of Hobbes). In this way he can satisfy the authorities, who in time of strife and dissension are content with a mere *act* of submission in lieu of firmer commitment. But for the exponents of a living faith (the Jansenists, Pascal, Malebranche, etc.), Montaigne will be a "dangerous" author, a subversive in the guise of a believer whose faith has no rational foundation (and which will later receive the name "fideism"). More recently, the exponents of reformist or revolutionary political action (inspired in their own way by an act of faith) have leveled the opposite charge at Montaigne's political philosophy: namely, that it lacks audacity and sanctions a conservatism less beneficial to the general welfare than to the private comfort and "individualist" leisure of a fairly wealthy nobleman whose only concern is to survive unscathed in an age of unrest.[35]

The fact that both lines of criticism have long been directed against Montaigne shows that his "conservatism" cuts two ways. For if he accepts the established order (insofar as any sort of order and benevolent authority remain in the midst of general collapse), he does so while denying it any supernatural source of authority or sacred foundation, and, what is more, on the express condition that the established order reduce the prevailing level of violence: "(B) Not all things are permissible for an honorable man in the service (C) of his king, or (B) of the common cause, or of the laws."[36] Rooted in sympathy's opposition to violence and convinced of the impossibility of establishing a political system superior to the one being criticized, Montaigne's "conservative" acquiescence remains conditional. His negative vigilance remains intact. His submission to the law, to the Catholic party, and to the monarchy as bulwarks of social cohesion is not exclusively formal. Its limits are defined solely by the dictates of individual moral consciences. Here again, Montaigne adopts *simultaneously* attitudes that he had previously described as opposites: he does not want to stand apart from nature, which governs the movements of universal sympathy, and yet he does not repudiate art, usage, custom, and private justice, for all that he has criticized them in the past. He describes himself as a man of mixed character, a composite of nature and custom. The compromises that he accepts in regard to the life of the body can also be applied to political life:

> (B) If what Nature flatly and originally demands of us for the preservation of our being is too little . . . then let us grant ourselves something further: *let us also call the habits and condition of each of us nature;* let us rate and treat ourselves according to this measure, let us stretch our appurtenances and our accounts that far. For in going thus far we certainly seem to me to have some justification. Habit is a second nature, and no less powerful. (C) What my habit lacks, I hold that I lack.[37]

The truth about man is not what remains when art, convention, and custom have been taken away; rather, it lies in the power that man has to *add* to his "nature" in ways that augment it, contradict it, and render it precarious and mutable.

Calm action

From the standpoint of faith, it is perfectly justifiable to look upon Montaigne as an author who, having humbled human reason, "acted as a pagan" (as Pascal puts it) rather than submit to the arguments of religion. Faith acknowledges the authority of a prior Word: the world and human life are legible only *secundum scripturas*. By contrast, Montaigne makes out a variety of discourses in the past, both religious and philosophical. He is astonished by them and admires some, but he is even more struck by their contradictions: the question of authority remains undecidable. Faced with a multiplicity of religions and customs, he indicates no intellectual preference. If he does frame a choice in favor of Catholicism, it is for reasons of *present* utility and opportunity, and he yields none of the privileges of the onlooking intelligence. That intelligence occupies none of the worlds that men of faith have constructed: it comprehends and compares those worlds, the better to maintain its own distance from them. If authority exists, it resides in the *present* exercise of judgment, of a judgment conscious of its limitations and inadequacy but also of having found its foundation within itself. That foundation, though it may be no firmer than the foundations claimed by various religions, at least coincides with the moral primacy of what is *properly mine;* it coincides with the origins of Montaigne's *authorship* and thus supports the *authority* of his self-representation: "(A) This capacity for sifting truth, whatever it may amount to in me, and this free will not to enslave my belief easily, I owe principally to myself."[38] Hardly an attitude of submission to the faith! What pride in independence we find in this mind contemptuous of human reason, a mind that remains deaf to the revelation that has been transmitted down through the ages and blind to the light it is supposed to recognize in the Book or to receive by the Grace of God!

This attitude is so obvious that many commentators have seen it as one of the main aspects of the religious influence of the *Essays.* For Cassirer, Montaigne reduces all religion, "in its empirical manifestation," to nothing more than "the reflection of a dominant tendency of our will. Human nature, in all its anthropological and ethnographic diversity, constitutes the 'natural foundation' to which religion is reduced." Furthermore, Cassirer continues,

> if in ethics . . . despite the relativity of external formulations, it has proved possible to find a generally valid internal criterion, this outcome here remains closed to us: for by what resource would self-consciousness be capable of assuring and guaranteeing that a being in the mind is *transcendent?* Admittedly, positive dogmas are nowhere subjected to examination by Montaigne. But this way of dismissing them is actually the sharpest form of ironic criticism. For they are shown to belong to the solid conventional mass of 'customs,' to which the individual is obliged to submit.[39]

Hence it cannot be argued that Montaigne's reserve is not active: criticism is a form of action. But it does not create worlds; it awakens individuals. In Cassirer's view, this action is not of the same order as that which built the edifice of religion: religion was the work of human *will,* and Montaigne, for his part, does not appeal to the will. This, according to Cassirer, is

> the inner limit of *skepsis.* The new values that it elaborates remain confined to the thinking subject: they determine and guide the individual's judgment without involving his

257

will. Any effort to transfer to the outside world what has been created inside is avoided, and no attempt is made to transform the external situation to conform to the new criterion. It is the negative side of the principle of doubt that is here demonstrated: for precisely where *skepsis* resigns itself to submit to the established social and political powers the notion of moral self-consciousness is not capable of maturing and achieving its full development.[40]

In other words, even if Montaigne's thought is not devoid of active force, Montaigne himself is not capable of making the transition to action. But here a very important observation needs to be made: namely, that in order for any philosophy to entail action and to attempt, after transforming the subjective consciousness, to transform the world as well, what is required is not merely the audacity to act. It is also essential that a mind eager to impress upon external reality the stamp of its "new criterion" see the possibility of a *future* receptive to its work. Now, with Montaigne it is not lack of initiative that determines the lack of a future. It is rather the lack of a future that discourages action and initiative. If this were merely a matter of personal psychological makeup, a mood linked with "old age" or with the very volubility of his mind, then it would be possible to agree that there was an occasional interedependence between the inner experience of time and the inner experience of action: a person who does not believe in the future is likely to "husband his will." Conversely, because he husbands his will, his projects will not aim to achieve results beyond the short term (for it is concern with the present that dominates his mind). But beyond this subjective individual disposition (which Montaigne, in his teasing, depreciative manner calls *nonchalance*), it is important to bear in mind that in Montaigne's time the ideas of a "historical" future and of action directed toward the future were not current among people generally or even among intellectuals; these ideas did not begin to become widespread in Europe until the end of the eighteenth century.

With this in mind, let us reread "Of husbanding your will" (3:10). This chapter does indeed contain a plea in favor of personal life, reserve, and living "close to home," but a corrective twist is applied to this thesis from the very first lines: "(B) In comparison with most men, few things touch me, or, to put it better, hold me; for it is right that things should touch us, provided they do not possess us."[41] Thus right from the start, Montaigne declares his "middle-of-the-road" attitude. He is perfectly willing to remain in contact with things. He has no wish to stand apart from them, but he does not wish to belong to them either. He continues as follows:

> (B) I take great care to augment by study and reasoning this privilege of insensibility, which is naturally well advanced in me. I espouse, and in consequence grow passionate about, few things. . . . As much as I can, I employ myself entirely upon myself. . . . But the passions that distract me from myself and attach me elsewhere, those in truth I oppose with all my strength. My opinion is that we must lend ourselves to others and give ourselves only to ourselves. . . . Those who know how much they owe to themselves, and for how many duties they are obligated to themselves, find that nature has given them in this a commission full enough and not at all idle. You have quite enough to do at home; don't go away.[42]

This might seem to express such a decided preference for private life, such predominance of one's *own* existence, as to discourage any externally directed action, any "busyness" in public affairs. It is true, moreover, that Montaigne is primarily concerned about his personal freedom, but not so as to keep it safe by disuse or by solely private use. His purpose is in fact "to mortgage it [i.e., his freedom] only on the right occasions."[43] Thus in the political and religious sphere we find the same reconciliation with the *outside* and *alien* as we discovered earlier in various aspects of Montaigne's "relations with others."

Montaigne sees mortal danger in actions that involve undue self-neglect. To be sure, this danger, as he sees it, does not lack for nobility: his father, in serving as mayor of Bordeaux, gave himself to the job with marvelous abnegation, "truly heedless of his life, which he nearly lost." Yet Montaigne objects: "This course, which I commend in others, I do not love to follow, and I am not without excuse. He had heard it said that we must forget ourselves for our neighbor, that the individual was not to be considered at all in comparison with the general."[44] For himself, he sensed that too great an involvement in public affairs would lead to his own destruction:

> If my will happened to be prone to mortgage and attach itself, I would not last: I am too tender, both by nature and by practice. . . . If I were to bite off as much as others do, my soul would never have the strength to bear the alarms and emotions that afflict those who embrace so much; it

would be put *out of joint* from the start by the inner agitation.[45]

Ardor in action, which in his father "sprang from a great goodness of nature," from a "kindly and public-spirited soul," Montaigne feared in himself as an entanglement in which he would quickly have lost control of any movement into which he might cast himself headlong. The paradox to which he calls attention is this: that the man of action commonly becomes a man of passion; he is no longer his own man, ruled as he is both by others and by his inner turmoil. Both are reasons for passivity:

> (B) Men give themselves for hire. Their faculties are not for them, they are more for those to whom they enslave themselves; their tenants are at home inside, not they. . . . See the people who have been taught to let themselves be seized and carried away: they do so everywhere, in little things as in big, in what does not touch them as in what does; they push in indiscriminately wherever there is business (C) and involvement, (B) and are without life when they are without tumultuous agitation. . . . (C) They seek business only for busyness. It is not that they want to be on the go, so much as that they want to be on the go, so much as that they cannot keep still; no more nor less than a stone that has started falling, and that does not stop until it comes to rest. Occupation is to a certain manner of people a mark of ability and dignity. (B) Their mind seeks its repose in movement, like children in the cradle.[46]

To act in this way is to waste one's energy imprudently: external action is interpreted as a loss of the self and a form of slavery. We think we are *doing* when in reality we are *surrendering* to our inner disarray. Montaigne sees just two possible results of impassioned action. Most people who allow themselves to be carried away fairly quickly end up like rolling stones or, still more absurdly, like children in their cradles, lulled to sleep by "movement." Paradoxically, it is inertia that triumphs after a brief spasm of agitation. For a few deserving individuals the reward will be glory and honor and lasting renown. But such an outcome is exceptional. Usually, the more passionately an action is undertaken, the more ineffective it will turn out to be. Awareness of inner danger is thus Montaigne's *first* reaction to the imperative of action.

The idea of "giving oneself only to oneself" is a *second* reaction, which corresponds to the wish to protect oneself against the threat of *dislocation.* If we isolate the statements that correspond to this second stage, we can construct an image of man as concerned only with his own comfort and accuse Montaigne of being a man of privilege whose only ambition is to take refuge in lukewarm privacy and cultivated pursuits. This is what is done, for instance, by a leading figure of the Frankfurt School, Max Horkheimer, in a curiously ill-tempered study. If Horkheimer is right, Montaigne was unable to live up to the requirements of "active humanism": "However benevolent toward man and animals, the central logical focus of Montaigne's thought is still inner repose and the security of his empirical self."[47] Since inner repose is in fact an aspect of his ethics, Montaigne is not unaware that this ideal is determined in part by the political conditions of his time and by the disposition of his own mind. There is no inner repose without public tranquillity, even if it is assumed that the wise man and the courageous warrior are capable of remaining calm through the worst of storms. Montaigne's intellectual abstention (the skeptical *epoche*) entails neither political abstention nor refusal to act nor a desire for security at any price, even if action, in order to win Montaigne's approval, should be undertaken with the least possible passion. After taking steps to protect himself against the personal dangers of overcommitment, Montaigne clearly moves on to a third phase: temperate action. Statements like the following are not unusual in Montaigne's writing:

> (B) To keep oneself wavering and half and half, to keep one's allegiance motionless and without inclination in one's country's troubles and in civil dissensions, I consider neither handsome nor honorable. . . . (C) That may be permitted in regard to the affairs of our neighbors. . . . It would be a sort of treason to do this in our own domestic affairs, in which (B) one must (C) necessarily (B) *take sides by deliberate plan.* . . . Nevertheless, even those who espouse a cause completely can do so with such order and moderation that the storm will be bound to pass over their heads without harm.[48]

We must therefore take sides and act in consequence. But Montaigne proposes what amounts to a hygiene of action, prescribing that inner "repose" and serenity be maintained not only in the interst of the individual but also to be sure that the action itself will be just and effective. The third attitude, which Montaigne here adopt reconciles the requirements of active life with those of private life, not by confounding the two (which would be impossible) but by separating them in such a way that the individual does not fail either in his social duty or in the "friendship that each man owes to himself."⁴⁹ The primacy that Montaigne undeniably grants private values does not exclude political ones: the problem is to establish the correct relationship between moral life and political life. Man realizes his potential in moral life, but he cannot do so unless political institutions afford him the possibility. Hence it is wise for him to manage his will, to "husband" it (in the "economic" sense that the word had in Montaigne's time), in accordance with what is possible and desirable in the sphere of collective life. Inevitably, this leads to engaging in political struggle, or better still, in political negotiation, if one hopes to achieve the conditions necessary to leading a moral life. Montaigne's diversions and "desertions" (such as his travels in Germany and Italy) are only temporary: the excuses that he gives for them prove in the first instance that he felt the need to excuse himself. Everyone is obliged to accept certain "political" duties and responsibilities of public life. Furthermore, the more one is capable of maintaining in oneself a center of calm impervious to the shocks and surprises of political action, the more effective that action will be. Montaigne's almost solemn tone in the following passage attests to the strength of his conviction:

> (B) He who knows [the duties of the friendship that each man owes to himself] and practices them, he is truly of the cabinet of the Muses; *he has attained the summit of human wisdom and of our happiness.* This man, knowing exactly what he owes to himself, finds it in his part that he is to apply to himself his experience of other men and of the world, and, in order to do so, *contribute to public society the duties and services within his province.* (C) *He who lives not at all unto others, hardly lives unto himself. . . .* (B) The main responsibility of each of us is his own conduct; (C) and that is what we are here for. (B) Just as anyone who should forget to live a good and saintly life, and think he was quit of his duty by guiding and training others to do so, would be a fool; even so he who abandons healthy and gay living of his own to serve others thereby, takes, to my taste, a bad and unnatural course.⁵⁰

Bear in mind that a "good and saintly life" requires the fulfillment of a social "obligation," which cannot be shifted onto others who act in our place. It would be foolishness for us to neglect this obligation; but to neglect the need for "healthy and gay living"—i.e., to preserve our inner health and happiness—would be to commit the opposite mistake. Montaigne constructs his sentence in such a way as to formulate a double precept in a perfectly balanced manner. (It is important to remember this attitude, which respects man's integrity, in an age when totalitarian ideology, in the name of the collective interest, is impugning the legitimacy of private life and seeking to eliminate it.)

Thus it is desirable both to engage in action and to preserve one's calm against external temptations and internal emotions:

> (B) I do not want a man to refuse, to the charges he takes on, attention, steps, words, and sweat and blood if need be:
>> To die for what is dear,
>> Country or friends, I do not fear.
>>> —Horace
> But this is by way of loan and accidentally, the mind holding itself ever in repose and in health, not without action, but without vexation, without passion. Simply to act costs it so little that is acting even in sleep.[51]

With this condition, he who had recommended that "we lend ourselves to others and give ourselves only to ourselves,"[52] came eventually (with an insertion in the 1595 edition) to exhibit much more generosity toward others: "I have been able to take part in public office without departing one nail's breadth from myself, (C) *and to give myself to others without taking myself from myself.*"[53]

Here it is not simply a question of Montaigne working out for himself an attitude designed to protect his private existence. He can cite others who have shared a similar attitude. He has recognized and admired this same mixture of inner repose and firmness in action in men who have shouldered responsibilities considerably more extensive than those of the mayor of a large city—men who "make history" (as people say nowadays). Here is the way the king of Navarre appeared to Montaigne:

> (B) He sees the gravity of accidents like anyone else, but in those that have no remedy he at once makes up his mind to bear them; in the others, after making the necessary provisions, which he can do promptly thanks to his quick-wittedness, he *composedly* [*en repos*] awaits what may ensue. In truth, I have seen him at work, maintaining a great nonchalance and freedom in his actions and countenance throughout very great and thorny affairs.[54]

Clearly, the coexistence of inner repose and other activity (in both the mayor of Bordeaux and the future Henry IV) reinstates a kind of *duplicity*, which can now be legitimated both by the duty to discharge public responsibilities and by the need to preserve one's equanimity for the sake of the action itself. "Mask and appearance," if not used for purposes of treason or self-interest, merely reflect the impersonal code that governs the "offices" of social life. Insofar as it is superficial, the mask ensures that the functions required by the social institution or "discourse" are carried out to the minimum degree necessary. But precisely by remaining superficial, it guarantees the continued integrity of the inner self; it prevents the absurd identification of the individual with the temporary social role that he has agreed to take on. The passages in which Montaigne denounces the comedy of the world (some of which are cited at the beginning of the present work) also reveal a partial and conditional acquiescence in the rules of social life:

> (B) Most of our occupations are low comedy. . . . *We must play our part duly, but as the part of a borrowed character*. Of the mask and appearance we must not make a real essence, not of what is foreign but what is our very own. We cannot distinguish the skin from the shirt. (C) It is enough to make up our face, without making up our heart. (B) I see some who transform and transubstantiate themselves into as many new shapes and new beings as they undertake jobs, who are prelates to their very liver and intestines, and drag their position with them even into their privy. I cannot teach them to distinguish the tips of the hat that are for them from those that are for their office, or their retinue, or their mule.[55]

In condemning the mask or *persona* Montaigne held that it was responsible for *dispossessing* the individual. When the mask is reinstated and receives Montaigne's approval, he makes precisely the opposite argument: namely, that the mask marks the boundary between the public role and private existence. These two moments of thought— *condemnation* in the name of truth, *rehabilitation* in the name of the need for a social style governed by collective signs—arise in rapid succession. We have analyzed them in slow motion, because it was important to show how appearance and custom first represent what the individual must reject in the hope of *being* himself, and later come to constitute the dividing line that enables him to understand and *determine* himself both as a subject and as an actor in the world subject to the constraints of reality. Once the mask is accepted, it comes to stand for external reality as such; it is the criterion that determines the distinction between "giving oneself to others" and "giving oneself to oneself," thereby saving this double gift from being contradictory. It delineates and protects an inner realm wherein, ideally, an individual can enter fully into possession of himself, without external influence or emotional turmoil. The name for this inner realm is "consciousness" *(conscience)*, meaning not only self-consciousness or the inner dialogue but also the moral conscience or judgment, which is concerned to protect its independence and competent to intervene in any matter that comes before the mind.

To "conserve and endure"

"I had nothing to do but *conserve and endure*, which are noiseless and imperceptible acts. *Innovation* has great luster, but it is forbidden in these times, when we are hard pressed and have to defend ourselves mainly against *innovations*."[56] These are the terms in which Montaigne explains the principles that guided him as mayor of Bordeaux. The very words of this declaration shed all the light that one could wish on what has been called Montaigne's "conservatism." In Montaigne's political lexicon "to conserve" is defined as the opposite of "to innovate." Conservation takes its lexical "value" from the contrast with innovation and novelty. This semantic pair, which was common in the sixteenth century in French as well as in most other European languages, is quite different from the now current contrast between the concept of "conservatism" (itself a recent development) and the notions of "progress" or "progressivism," in the sense that these have taken on since the end of the eighteenth century (although "innovation" still stands as an antonym to "conservation" and helps to determine its "value"). The current semantic system can hardly help ascribing to "conservatism" a function essentially antithetical to historical "progress," or to theories of such progress, which generally view innovation in an a priori favorable light.

A *modern* interpretation of Montaigne and his times is certainly entitled, at its own risk and peril, to attempt to identify where "the path of progress" lay at the end of the sixteenth century, what the progressive "factors" were, and so forth. But it is illegitimate to judge the men of that era as though they consciously decided what to do by reference to an idea that was not yet part of their intellectual repertoire. For to do so would be not only to commit an anachronism, a sin against the elementary rules of historical method, but also to propose an invalid interpretation, an interpretation wholly at odds with what it claims to explain. To regret the Montaigne declared his loyalty to an idea contrary to that of progress (even if we call it, as Horkheimer does, by a different name, such as "active humanism") is to fall victim to a logical fallacy or pious wish, which is easy enough to formulate four centuries after the fact and in the arrogant certainty that, as a modern intellectual, one is well versed in the "dialectics of history." Oddly enough, it is the adepts of History who are often the first to forget that the modern notion of history as the *collective* development of a people or nation or of mankind in general came into being in the eighteenth century, at the same time as, and in some sense as a complement to, the modern idea of progress. Montaigne had no inkling of History or Progress. Neither had yet been *invented*. When he uses the word history (*histoire*) in the singular, it is to refer either to the study of the past (the "science of History") or to the history, or story, of a particular individual (as in the title of 2:23, "L'histoire de Spurina," or "The Story of Spurina"). Otherwise he speaks of *histories* in the plural, which shows that what he had in mind was not a unique and providential interpretation of the past that would hold within it the key to the future. To Montaigne the past is a spectacle of diversity and difference. When we compare ourselves to the men of the past, he says, we feel different, and exposed to dangerous innovations, but in no way superior or better or wiser. What is more, our knowledge of the past is incomplete and full of gaps. Books and documents preserve only a small portion of what has happened:

> (B) Even in these vanities [the games of the circus] we discover how fertile those ages were in minds *different* from ours. It is with this sort of fertility as with all other productions of Nature. This is not to say that she then put forth her utmost effort. *We do not go in a straight line; we rather ramble, and turn this way and that.* We retrace our steps. I fear that our knowledge is weak in every direction; we do not see very far ahead or very far behind. It embraces little and has a short life, short in both extent of time and extent of matter. . . . Even if all that has come down to us by report from the past should be true and known by someone, it would be less than nothing compared with what is unknown. And of this very image of the world which glides along while we live on it, how puny and limited is the knowledge of even the most curious! Not only of particular events which fortune often renders exemplary and weighty, but of the state of great governments and nations, there escapes us a hundred times more than comes to our knowledge.[57]

What we call human history is for Montaigne a collection of "particular events" or vicissitudes that plunge into a vast "whirl" those collective entities known as *polities and nations.* These exist in the world and undergo change; they are subject to the decrees of nature and for- tune. The empires and kingdoms about which the histories tell us are a part of that larger world whose causes the scholars seek in vain and whose "mutations" and "agitations" shape human destinies. Our ig- norance of the totality of historical events is of the same order as our ignorance of the totality of physical reality. A similar state of igno- rance once enveloped the courageous heroes who lived before Agamemnon and even now (as Montaigne writes) envelops the un- known lands where civilizations, religions, and states of splendid or modest mien are flourishing and of which we have no more idea than we have of the creatures that nature has brought forth in other climes. The infinite diversity of human events is but one aspect of the infinite diversity of nature, whose abundance is beyond our ken. Yet nature, in its fertile ubiquity, remains the same even as it undergoes meta- morphosis. Montaigne speaks frequently of the *ordinary progress* of nature: by this he means, on the one hand, the power that guides creatures, generation after generation, from birth to maturity, and then to decay and destruction, and on the other hand the variable influence of place and "time" on individuals. The subordination of events to natural causes that vary over time means that the historian and the philosopher are interested in the same subject. Consider the following passage from the "Apology," in which Montaigne sketches out a physically deterministic theory of history (which is said to be governed by the climate, the heavens, etc.), from which he immedi- ately draws the following consequence: that what we say, what we think we know, is no more valid than what men in other times and places have said and thought. We are no less mistaken today than were the men of the past:

> (A) If nature enfolds within the bounds of her ordinary progress, like all other things, also the beliefs, judgments, and opinions of men; if they have their rotation, their sea- son, their birth, their death, like cabbages; if heaven moves and rolls them at its will, what magisterial and permanent authority are we attributing to them? (B) If we feel palpably by experience that the form of our being depends on the air, the climate, and the soil where we are born—not only the complexion, the stature, the constitution and counte- nance, but also the faculties of the soul . . . so that just as fruits are born different, and animals, men too are born more or less bellicose, just, temperate, and docile—here subject to wine, elsewhere to theft or lechery; here inclined

to superstition and elsewhere to unbelief; (C) here to freedom, here to servitude; (B) capable of one science or of one
art, dull or ingenious, obedient or rebellious, good or bad,
according to the influence of the place where they are situated—and take on a new disposition if you change their
place, like trees; . . . if we see flourishing now one art, one
opinion, now another, by some celestial influence; such-
and-such a century produce such-and-such natures and in-
cline the human race to such-and-such a bent; the minds of
men now lusty, now lean, like our fields; what becomes of
all those fine prerogatives on which we flatter ourselves?
Since a wise man can be mistaken and a hundred men, and
many nations, yes, and human nature according to us is
mistaken for many centuries about this or that, what assurance have we that sometimes it stops being mistaken,
(C) and that in this century it is not making a mistake?[58]

The plant and animal similes that dot this passage ("like cabbages,"
"just as fruits . . . and animals," "like trees," "like our fields") show
the degree to which "the progress of nature," as Montaigne conceives of it, differs from the modern notion of "historical progress."
Thus, leaving aside nature's obvious productive power, no "opinion"
can claim "magisterial" *authority* (and in the passage cited above,
Christianity is not explicitly exempted from natural causality). Moreover, it is clear that Montaigne shared with many other men of the
Renaissance the belief that the course of history is determined by the
heavens and parallels the course of the stars—though Montaigne
doubts that it is possible to calculate or predict what that course is, as
the "mathematicians" and astrologers claim to be able to do. We can
do no more than take note of the growth and decline of empires and
"beliefs," much as we watch trees and fruits prosper or wither according to the year and the "climate." As Montaigne sees it, history
shows only this, that *historical* individuals and groups lead a limited
and dependent existence; the corollary of this is on the one hand that
historical knowledge is fragmentary, short-sighted, and inevitably
partial and on the other hand that human will is for the most part
powerless to alter the course of events. Do we even know what
events would be advantageous to us?

(A) Among other tokens of our imbecility, it seems to me
that this does not deserve to be forgotten: that even
through desire, man does not know how to find what he
needs; that not by enjoyment, not even by imagination and
wish, can we agree about what we need for our content-
ment. . . . (C) And the prayer of the Lacedaemonians,

public and private, was simply that good and beautiful things should be granted them, referring to the divine discernment the choice and selection of these. . . . (A) And the Christian prays God that his will be done, so as not to fall into the mishap that poets invent about King Midas.[59]

It is apparent that Montaigne's fideism pertains not only to the object of belief but also to the object of desire and will, or in other words, to the ends of human action. Man has no hold on his destiny, and when he obtains what he wanted he discovers that like Midas he is "overwhelmed beneath the enjoyment of his desire and endowed with an unendurable privilege."[60] When innovation brings men what they thought their needs required, they find themselves in something like Midas's position. It is better to leave the initiative to God.

It is apparent, then, that in developing arguments in favor of his conservatism, Montaigne almost always uses traditional organic metaphors in which states are compared to immense living bodies, periods of unrest to diseases, and reforms or political decisions to attempts at therapy. Using this system of metaphors he is able to describe, without illusions, the state of affairs preceding the wars of religion. The malady had already begun:

> (A) The diseases and conditions of our bodies are seen also in states and governments: kingdoms and republics are born, flourish, and wither with age, as we do. We are subject to a useless and harmful surfeit of humors. . . . [61]

> (C) The state of health from which we started was such that it is itself a solace for the regret that we should have for it. It was health, but only in comparison with the sickness that followed it. We have not fallen from very high. The corruption and brigandage that enjoy dignity and established status seem to me the least endurable. We are robbed less wickedly in a forest than in a place of safety. There was a universal conjunction of members, each individually vying in rottenness with the others, and most of them afflicted with age-old ulcers which no longer admitted of cure or asked for it.[62]

Ruin and destruction would inevitably prevail but for the fact that the diseases that afflict the body politic (which, like that body, are thought of as natural entities) are themselves limited in duration and destined to die out:

> (B) Troubles have their life and their limits, (C) their illnesses and their health. The constitution of diseases is pat-

terned after the constitution of animals. They have their destiny, limited from their birth, and their days. He who tries to cut them short imperiously by force, in the midst of their course, prolongs and multiplies them, and stimulates them instead of appeasing them.[63]

It is therefore better to let the disease follow its natural course, at the end of which the suffering individual will be cured. Medicine errs by ignoring this lesson of experience and insisting upon inappropriate remedies. Now, in diseases of the body, most cures are worse than the disease. The same is true of the diseases that afflict societies, particularly when the cure involves violence or violation of the basic rules of morality:

> (B) But is there any disease in a government so bad that it is worth combating with so deadly a drug? Not even, said Favonius, the usurpation of tyrannical authority over a state. (C) Plato likewise does not consent to have the repose of his country violated in order to cure it, and does not accept an improvement that costs the blood and ruin of the citizens, ruling that it is the duty of a good man in that case to let everything alone and merely to pray God to lend extraordinary aid. . . . How great an impiety it is to expect no help from God that is simply his own and without our cooperation. I often doubt whether among so many men who meddle in such a business a single one has been found of so feeble an understanding as to have been genuinely persuaded that he was moving toward reformation by the worst of deformations; that he was heading for his salvation by the most express ways that we have of very certain damnation.[64]

It is of course true that Montaigne many times declared himself in favor of the status quo, because the present, relatively stable evil is still a lesser evil than those that will be brought on by any attempt at innovation. For Montaigne, change always wreaks havoc:

> (A) Our morals are extremely corrupt, and lean with a remarkable *inclination toward the worse;* of our laws and customs, many are barbarous and monstrous; however, because of the difficulty of improving our condition and the danger of everything crumbling into bits, if I could *put a spoke in our wheel and stop it at this point,* I would do so with all my heart. . . . The worst thing I find in our state is instability, and the fact that our laws cannot, any more than our clothes, take any settled form. It is very easy to accuse

a government of imperfection, for all mortal things are full
of it. It is very easy to engender in a people contempt for
their ancient observances; never did a man undertake that
without succeeding. But as for establishing a better state in
place of the one they have ruined, many of those who have
attempted it have achieved nothing for their pains. (C) I
give my prudence small share in my conduct; I readily let
myself be led by the general way of the world. Happy the
people who do what they are commanded better than
those who command, without tormenting themselves
about the reasons, who let themselves roll relaxedly with
the rolling of the heavens. Obedience is not pure or tranquil in a man who reasons and argues.[65]

Two spatial metaphors (which may in fact form a single metaphor)
here describe the course of human affairs: *inclination* ("toward the
worse") and the circular, rolling motion of the *wheel*. On the one hand
Montaigne would like to halt the catastrophic spread of corruption,
abolish time, put things on a even keel, and stop the rolling wheel
short of imminent disaster. On the other hand, since this wish clearly
cannot be fulfilled, he favors obedience ("I readily let myself be led"),
which by way of submission to "those who command" connotes acceptance of the "rolling of the heavens" and the great cosmic cycles.
Let time stop! Or else "roll relaxedly with the rolling of the heavens"
and follow a human cycle that merely mimics, on a less grand scale,
the cycle of the stars! Here, then, we have two ways of opting for the
pure *present*: one is to accept the paradoxical immobility of circular
motion, which is the motion of the worlds that constitute the universe; the other is to choose one of the infinite series of similar moments that constitute time. To endure is to perpetuate the present.

It is easy enough to accuse Montaigne of proposing "ideological"
justifications for the status quo: a suspicious critic might argue that
anyone with a personal stake in preventing change will ingeniously
discover any number of arguments against action. To this objection it
is at the very least worth responding that Montaigne does not view
the cosmic order as a justification for the existing political order. This
commonplace conservative argument is foreign to him: how could he
adduce the order of the world as a justification, when he knows nothing about it? He openly recommends submission to "those who command" not because "the general way of the world" is harmonious but
because sublunary affairs, earthly life, invariably involve an element
of disorder. It is not given to us to do anything about it, whether by

solitary rebellion or general upheaval. Montaigne's skepticism, by casting doubt on the hierarchical model of a geocentric universe—a closed, circular world—prevents him from arguing that the harmonious proportions of the great Whole justify the social hierarchy and the necessary obedience that it implies, as Ulysses does in a famous tirade in the first act of Shakespeare's *Troilus and Cressida* (lines 75–137). Montaigne's resigned submission can also be seen as a consequence and counterpart of La Boétie's relentless analysis of the mechanisms of tyranny in *Contr'un*. Better to have an imperfect monarchy than a perfect tyranny. Montaigne certainly harbored no illusions on this score. Submission is preferable, he believed, only because it recognizes a *present* authority, and because no other authority, either past or future, appeared to him to carry as much force. Those who were attacking the state in the name of the *reformation* of religion and morals proudly based their claims on Scripture, i.e., on a revelation granted to mankind some fifteen centuries earlier and since then abused and misused in a variety of ways, including the assertion of the pope's primacy, which to the reformers seemed so many "novelties" to be cast aside: their proposed cure was to recover the purity of an *earlier* authority of unquestioned validity, from which mankind should never have departed in the first place. Even though Montaigne declares himself ready to bow before the revelation, he does not refrain from pointing out that it can become a rule of conduct only by way of an *interpretation* that brings it up to date,[66] and in any such interpretation the arbitrariness and weaknesses of the human mind will make their influence felt. At best, therefore, the Christian faith can be respected as the customary religion that it has become, failing more certain proof. For it is impossible to recover that faith as it was, all pristine and fresh, through the tradition of the Church, much less through the personal "fancies" of those who pretend to have understood the original message of the Gospels better than the Church.

As for the future of this world, no one in Montaigne's time proposed any motives for worldly action other than those rejected in the essay "Of husbanding your will" (3:10): namely, *avarice*, or the will to acquire, and *ambition*,[67] or the desire to impose one's name (as well as one's progeny and renown) upon future generations. We have seen, in any case, that men did not hope for durable improvement in the human condition to sustain, guide, and justify action in the present. To be sure, there were political issues at stake in the wars of religion: such matters as the distribution of power among the pope, the king, the religious orders, the princes, the nobles, and individual consciences were contested. But changes in human institutions were justified only by the need to order the terrestrial city in such a way as to permit men to seek their *eternal* salvation more effectively. Even utopias were not, in this period, set in the future. The utopian literature described the imaginary practices and customs of a world apart, far from our own, and often situated in the past. It was a commonplace of courtly poetry to use a marriage or a birth as an occasion to herald the return of a golden age. Montaigne was little given to this kind of dreaming: in reporting descriptions he has read of the newly discovered societies in America, he does of course paint them in the idyllic colors of a golden age (as in "Of cannibals"), or again, as places of marvelous wealth and luxury (as in "Of coaches"). But these are "infant worlds," whose attraction can only be one of nostalgia: for us their blandishments lie in the past, to one side, as it were, of actual existence. What is more, these are worlds that have already been destroyed by the barbarity of their European conquerors.

Since men have no hold on the future (which is decided by the "rolling" bodies of the heavens), it is impossible to base a claim for authority on the idea of a better "polity," a social and political order *yet to come*, to which men offer obedience in anticipation. Montaigne's explicit reservations as to "evil means employed to a good end" (the title of 2:23) and injustices committed for reasons of state (3:1) show how little he is willing to dispense with immediate ethical requirements in exchange for supposed future improvements in the general welfare. The future is not within the compass of our knowledge or our will. God decides, or fortune. Apart from the Last Judgment, at which time our actions and feelings will be weighed (and upon which it is true that Montaigne's thoughts scarcely dwell), and apart from the names of a few exceptional men, whose renown will endure through the ages (and among whom Montaigne does not count himself), it is ridiculous for us to focus our attention on a far-off future. Our "everyday" actions deserve nothing better than oblivion:

> (B) Ambition is not a vice for little fellows and for undertakings such as ours. . . . [Alexander] would not have wanted to enjoy the empire of the world softly and peacefully. . . . This malady is perhaps excusable in so strong and full a soul. When these dwarfish and puny soullets behave like vain baboons and think to spread their name for having rightly judged an affair or continued the order of the guards at a city gate, the more they hope to raise their head, the more they show their tail. These minute good works have neither body nor life: they vanish at the first telling and travel only from one street corner to the

next. . . . Renown does not prostitute itself at so cheap a
rate. The rare and exemplary actions to which it is due
would not endure the company of the innumerable crowd
of *petty everyday actions.* Marble will exalt your titles as
much as you please for having had a piece of wall patched
up or a public gutter cleaned out; but men who have sense
will not.[68]

It is not to be expected that petty actions will be talked about for
long. When Montaigne examines why our lives are so agitated, he
begins by noting the futility of the *causes* that serve as pretexts for
action. In a paragraph of this same essay ("Of husbanding your will")
he lists derisory causes that have triggered great events. Charles the
Bold incurred disaster "because of a quarrel about a cartload of sheep-
skins."[69] And was not Sulla's decision to engrave a seal "the first and
principal cause of the most horrible upheaval [i.e., Sulla's conflict
with Marius—Trans.] that this machine [i.e., the earth] has ever
suffered?"[70]

> (B) And I have seen in my time the wisest heads in this
> kingdom assembled, with great ceremony and public ex-
> pense, for treaties and accords of which the real decision
> meanwhile depended in all sovereignty on the talk in the
> ladies' boudoir and the inclination of some little woman.
> (C) The poets understood this well who put Greece and
> Asia to fire and sword for an apple. (B) See why that man
> goes off to risk his honor and his life with his sword and
> dagger; let him tell you whence comes the source of this
> quarrel; he cannot do so without blushing, so frivolous is
> the occasion of it.[71]

There has been no dearth of great events over the centuries: empires
have collapsed and whole peoples been wiped out. But were these
events willed as they actually turned out? Were they the fulfillment of
some definite plan, hatched by some exceptional individual? Alexander and Caesar did exist, to be sure. But recent experience had
taught Montaigne that great "effects" are often produced by mere
whims or mean rage. No one's desires or anticipations seem to have
been fulfilled. For the actions that we undertake tend to get out of
hand once they are under way. This is the point that Montaigne
makes in the remainder of the passage from which we have been
citing; he uses it, moreover, to justify abstention unless exceptional
resources are in hand:

(B) At the beginning only a little reflection is needed; but once you are embarked, all the ropes start pulling. Then you need great resources, much more difficult and important. (C) How much easier it is not to go into it than to get out of it![72]

Once again Montaigne will resort to a simile with plants, which he uses to represent the pace of action: furiously begun, it is not long before it slows down:

(B) Now we should proceed in the opposite way from the reed, which on first shooting up produces a long, straight stem, but afterward, as if it had grown languid and out of breath, comes to form frequent thick knots, like so many pauses, which show that it no longer has this first vigor and constancy. We must rather begin gently and coolly, and save our breath and our vigorous efforts for the thick and culmination of the business. We guide affairs at their beginnings and hold them at our mercy; but afterward, when they are under way, it is they that guide us and carry us away, and we have to follow them. . . . I find some who enter the lists heedlessly and furiously, and slow up in the charge. . . . He who enters a quarrel lightly is apt to get out of it just as lightly. This same difficulty that keeps me from cutting into it would spur me on when I was once stirred up and heated. It is a bad habit: once you are in it, you must go through with it or burst. (C) "Undertake softly," said Bias, "but pursue hotly."[73]

Clear-sighted perseverance is rare. A fundamental antithesis has action ("we guide affairs") turn into passivity ("it is they that guide us and carry us away"). Yet Montaigne does allow for one positive exception, it, too, controlled by an antithesis: we should enter into affairs *coldly* so as to conserve sufficient energy, i.e., *heat*, to carry them through to a conclusion. Our vital heat is precious and must not be wasted. A discipline of action is therefore not inconceivable, and it would be false to believe that the skeptic's denial of knowledge and repudiation of curiosity had compulsory inaction as their corollary. For all his nonchalance, Montaigne is too susceptible to feelings of responsibility to resign himself to perpetual inactivity. As mayor he says that he dispensed with actions that were merely ostentatious but not with those that seemed necessary:

(B) I was prepared to work myself a bit more roughly if there had been any great need of it. For it is in my power to do something more than I do or than I like to do. I did not leave undone, as far as I know, any action that duty genuinely required of me.[74]

Still, he maintains that he has no aptitude for undertakings requiring sustained effort. If he sets about doing something, it is always with the expectation of quick results:

> (B) I have a lively way of acting, wherever my will carries me along. But this eagerness is an enemy to perseverance. If anyone wants to use me according to my nature, let him give me tasks in which vigor and freedom are needed, tasks that require *direct, brief,* and even hazardous conduct; in those I can do something. If it has to be long, subtle, laborious, artificial, and tortuous, he will do better to apply to someone else.[75]

Thus Montaigne, despite his "habitual languor," is in no way unfit for action, provided it does not involve him in lengthy calculations and strategies. He commits himself "with difficulty," but under certain conditions he does commit himself. In all things Montaigne likes to consider only the *near future*.[76] And if he refers so frequently to his age, his sickness, and his impending death, the reason is perhaps that these justify his preference for the present and for activities that do not require him to detach himself from it. Here I think it justifiable to make two somewhat contradictory assertions. Montaigne invokes his impending death because he has chosen to live in the present; because he has little time left to live, he must make do with what he has now:

> (B) I am no longer headed for any great change or inclined to plunge into a new and untried way of life, not even a better one. . . . (C) I, who am on my way out, would readily resign to anyone who came along what wisdom I am learning for dealing with the world. Mustard after dinner. I have no use for a good thing of which I can make no use. . . . (C) The end is found of itself at the conclusion of every task. My world is done for, my form is emptied; I belong entirely to the past, and I am bound to recognize it and conform my departure to it. . . . Time is forsaking me; without it nothing can be possessed. . . . (B) In short, here I am in the act of finishing up this man, not of making another out of him.[77]

A man who has little future ahead of him resigns himself to that fact all the more readily if he feels that his country is headed for ruin at the same pace; society, too, has but a brief future ahead of it:

(B) He who desires the good of his country as I do, without getting ulcers and growing thin over it, will be unhappy, but not stunned, to see it threatened either with ruin or with conditions of survival no less ruinous. Poor vessel, which the waves, the winds, and the pilot pull about with such contrary purposes.[78]

If the effectiveness of public action promises to be so limited, what can be said about the effectiveness of the work, the book to which Montaigne has entrusted his form, his "fancies," and his mutations? Does he expect it to have a better fate? Might it be the bearer of another future, a future more assured than that of the institutions of government? It will, of course, outlive its author. But by how much? Here again (and no doubt with a touch of flirtatiousness in his humility) Montaigne expects the future to be brief. He knows full well, moreover, that the French language is rapidly being transformed:

(B) I write my book for few men and for few years. If it had been durable matter, it would have had to be committed to a more stable language. In view of the continual variation that has prevailed in ours up to now, who can hope that its present form will be in use fifty years from now? (C) It slips out of our hands every day, and has halfway changed since I have been alive.[79]

In the sphere of political action, the narrow expanse of time that is given to us ultimately coincides with the limited region of space whose boundaries moral wisdom enjoins us not to overstep. Complete inaction is incompatible, as we saw earlier, with the project of "living unto oneself."[80] But as for "engaging oneself to the quick,"[81] like those ancient heroes who "obstinately determine to see resolutely and without perturbation the ruin of their country, which possessed and commanded their entire will," that is not possible in the contemporary world: "For our common souls there is too much effort and harshness in that."[82] This still leaves open the possibility (examined several times already) of action that turns back on the actor himself, action in which the actor abandons himself only in order to find himself again. To make this idea palpable Montaigne uses the image of reflection, which he conflates with the image of circularity:

(B) The range of our desires should be circumscribed and restrained to a *narrow limit* of the nearest and most contiguous good things; and moreover their course should be directed not in a *straight line* that ends up elsewhere, but in a *circle* whose two extremities by a *short sweep* meet and terminate in ourselves. Actions that are performed without this *reflexive* movement, I mean a searching and genuine reflexive movement—the actions, for example, of the avaricious, the ambitious, and so many others who run in a *straight line*, whose course carries them ever *forward*—are erroneous and diseased actions.[83]

In other words, besides the semipassive form of circular motion, in which one allows oneself to be carried along by the "rolling of heavenly objects," there is another kind of circular motion, a circular motion that is deliberately engaged, whose range is but a "short sweep," and whose purpose is not to "change the world." Within the ambit of reflexive action it is tempting to see the spirit of the Renaissance at work, reproducing on a human scale the same movement that animates the "objects of the heavens," a perfect revolution in miniature and the equivalent, in this fallen world, of the movement of the spheres in the macrocosm. We must be wary, however, of overemphasizing this connection, even though Montaigne at times draws a parallel between the harmony of the world and the harmony that ought to govern our lives: if man and the world are similar, their similarity lies in their common diversity, in *concordia discors* and not in regularity of motion. Montaigne accuses science of having concocted identical fictions to describe the world and to explain the human body. The only objective connection between the two is in the similarity of the interpretive models, which is always reason for caution; the "short sweep" of reflexive action has nothing in common with the circles that presumptuous science traces in the heavens or in our bodies: Science

> (A) gives us in payment and as presuppositions the things that she herself teaches us are invented; for those epicycles, eccentrics, concentrics, which astrology calls to its aid to conduct the movement of its stars, it gives us as the best it has succeeded in inventing on that subject. . . . It is not to heaven alone that she sends her ropes, her machines, and her wheels. Let us consider a little what she says of ourselves and our make-up. There is no more retrogradation, trepidation, accession, recession, reversal, in the stars and heavenly bodies, than they have fabricated in this poor little human body. Truly they had good reason therefore to call it the little world [i.e., the microcosm—Trans.], so many pieces and facets have they used to plaster it and build it.[84]

We know nothing of the world, except that Nature and Fortune there reign in their own element, opening up an infinity of possibilities over which we have no control. The circularity of human reflection is not *guaranteed* by the rotation of the planets. On the contrary, it is a result of the lack of any such guarantee. Man, with his feelings, his needs, and his conscience, knows only that he is part of nature, but that at any moment, especially when he hurries "straight ahead," "forward," or "in a straight line," he runs the risk of being unfaithful to nature and of paying for that infidelity in misfortune—the memory of which the historians do well to preserve.

The refusal of "credit": The thinness of time and the "great picture"

To "conserve and endure"[85] is the only way to counter the ravages that time brings to human institutions, the only response to disease, so far as it is in our power to respond at all. But is it possible to conserve and endure when the law of the world is "movement" and change? How can we be sure that tomorrow will not topple all that is standing today? And why is Montaigne unwilling to accept change in the political order when he is willing to accept it in himself? How can "polities" endure when generations pass and when "stability itself is nothing but a more languid motion?"[86]

To endure is to make sure that the passage of time spares what is precious to us today. To endure, for Montaigne, is not so much to perpetuate a mythical status quo as it is to keep faith with the present by refusing to anticipate as well as by refusing to submit to domination said to be justified by the past. In the realm of knowledge, Montaigne emphasizes the superiority of "present knowledge," thus stating a preference that carries over to all other realms as well: "We are, I believe, learned only with present knowledge, not with past, any more than with future."[87] It was in the name of the present that Montaigne initially developed his critique of appearance, opinion, and "presumption." The present is the only temporal category that neither hides nor is hidden. Nature and God, when Montaigne invokes them, are certainly the masters of an unknown, but the territory of eternity that they share extends into the present, in which they are able to make themselves manifest through their powers of intervention. Man must open himself up to their intervention by ridding himself of the desire to secede from time. For if a "universal law" exits, it is decreed in the present, and each individual confirms that law by obeying it in his present existence. When Montaigne speaks of *present pleasure,* he sees the tightening of the knot that ties body to soul, sensual existence to reasoned thought: "(C) I am unable to keep myself from *grossly* pursuing the *present pleasures* of the general human law—intellectually sensual, sensually intellectual."[88] "I am unable to keep myself": here again we see the acceptance of passivity, the giving in to *present* incitement, with no other purpose than to achieve, under the watchful gaze of the conscience, the greatest possible fulfillment—to the point of "grossness." As for "competence," Montaigne maintains that he has wished for it only "to serve my *present and essential* advantages, not to lay up a stock and reserve for my heirs."[89] Montaigne of course likes to reinforce his meaning by pairing adjectives: "essential" lends to "present" its higher ontological status. What is also significant, however, is an addition in the Bordeaux manuscript that links "present" and "natural": "(B) My philosophy is in action, in *natural (C) and present* practice."[90] What is natural can only be present. Conversely, what is present bears nature's obvious stamp. Furthermore, what is present *in us* fulfills the requirement of presence in an incomparably more complete manner than what attempts to impose itself upon us from *outside,* even if this happens concurrently, at the same point in time. This explains why Montaigne rejects all extrinsic authority. What is external is always weighted down by a past and destined to a future. Montaigne's rejection of extrinsic authority is particularly apparent in his statement of educational principles: "(B) Our mind moves only *on faith* [à crédit], being bound and constrained to the whim of others' fancies, a slave and a captive under the authority of their teaching."[91] Healthy pedagogy focuses on that faculty whose field of action is situated in the present moment: the faculty of judgment, whose function is to make free discriminations, here and now. Montaigne reminds the tutor of this: "(A) Let the tutor make his charge pass everything through a sieve and lodge nothing in his head on mere *authority* and *trust* [à crédit]."[92] The word *crédit* [faith, trust, credit] is linked, in both of the above passages, to "authority": the word implies credulous submission to authoritarian indoctrination; it suggests that faith is given without appropriate guarantees. In its economic sense, "credit" refers to acceptance of a deferred payment, of a note drawn on the future. External authority is built upon collateral and the promise of future profit: it does not settle all its accounts on the spot. In order to discredit credit, with which individuals *mortgage* their freedom (to use a term that is used frequently by Montaigne), the *Essays* constantly emphasize the prevalence of the present as made real in the act of conscience, in the fine point or fine mesh of judgment. Montaigne uses the image of a "sieve" [*estamine*], an instrument used for separation and sorting, a finer-meshed cousin of the [French] *crible* [from the Latin *cribrum*, sieve—Trans.], whose etymological influence is felt in the word *criticism* (from the Latin *crisis* and the verb *crinein*, to separate or discriminate—J.S.).

But what objects fall under the jurisdiction of criticism? Surely internal events—passions, feelings, sensations—are readily available for the evaluation and recording that judgment requires. Moreover, when judgment is required to render a moral verdict as to one's own actions and the actions of others, it can rely on its ability to distinguish between what is "honest" and what is "dishonest" even while acknowledging that custom and usage make access to any kind of "essential" justice impossible. In empirical life and ethical judgment the individual therefore remains in control of his own present; his own authority is fully legitimate, and he is justified in opposing any intrusion by outside forces. This dual realm is inalienably his own. It is a question here of judgment as applied in the private sphere. Nothing prevents the individual from extending his scrutiny to the public sphere as well. But will he be justified in proposing a politics based on the values of "the present" and "judgment" instead of "credit" and "authority," before which most people bow down?

For "present knowledge," in this domain especially, is knowledge of nonknowledge. After traveling around the entire reflexive circle, judgment comes into possession of itself just as it discovers how limited and vulnerable it is, and how little capable of settling on its own the ecclesiastical and theological questions that bear so heavily on the problems of the social order. Now, "we must live among the living"[93] and with an eye to the survival of the community. Sympathy and compassion are necessary but not sufficient. We must take part in the political and religious debate, in which many of the disputed points are closely linked to symbols not within our jurisdiction, indeed, not within the compass of human reason. How can a man who has concluded that human capacities are inadequate and human knowledge doubtful—a man who has refused to give credit—rally to a cause and support a party that claims to possess certainty and authority worthy of credit? But no one can escape the obligation to choose, even one who in the name of intellectual integrity points out that the questions at issue exceed the competence of individual critical judgment. Criticism's final act is to point out that political and religious choices are beyond the scope of criticism and yet must be made. Rather than adopt a subversive strategy of "two truths," Montaigne once again indicates—critically—that there is a sharp division between private convictions and public professions of faith. Does this mean that we are again "on the wheel" and that, after reconciling himself with appearance and custom, Montaigne is to some extent willing to grant the credit that he had refused? As we saw earlier, he is willing, since one pan of the scale is "entirely empty," to let the other slip "beneath the dreams of an old woman." In one of the clearest statements of his religious conservatism, Montaigne both accepts the authority of a "learned man" (commentators have suggested the name of the Jesuit Maldonat) and seems to abdicate his right to criticize:

> (A) We must either submit completely to the *authority* of our ecclesiastical government, or do without it completely. It is not for us to decide what portion of obedience we owe it. Moreover, I can say this for having tried it. In other days I exercised this freedom of personal choice and selection, regarding with negligence certain points in the observance of our Church which seem more vain or strange than others; until, coming to discuss them with learned men, I found that these things have a massive and very solid *foundation*,[94] and that it is only stupidity and ignorance that make us receive them with less reverence than the rest. Why do we not remember how much contradiction we sense even in our own judgment? How many things were articles of faith to us yesterday, which are fables to us today?[95]

The sequence of ideas in this passage is highly revealing. Montaigne began by exercising his judgment, as he recommended doing in the pages where he rejects opinions accepted "by mere authority and on credit." He passed religion through the sieve, using his own "freedom of personal choice and selection." Submission did not at first come easily. It was not obvious. Yet after conferring with experts Montaigne comes to the decision that the authority that he himself had contested must be reinforced. This was at a time when Catholics were making "partial surrender of their beliefs" and yielding "to their opponents some of the articles in dispute."[96] A solid foundation must be reestablished, a way must be found of dealing with the general confusion caused by unchecked exercise of individual judgment. Now, what is a foundation if not a remnant of the past and support for a now tottering structure? In other words, something of a synthesis between the present need for political solidity and the authority of the past, which is finally accepted as a possible bulwark against the threat of chaos? Do we not find here, as in the figures of Montaigne's father and his friend La Boétie (and as in all "relations with others") the "third condition" that restores what had been removed by death and reinstates rights that had been denied in the accusatory urge to unmask?

But Montaigne's argument is not limited to restoring a "massive and very solid foundation" where at first he had seen none. Indeed, it overshoots its objective. In order to discredit "our judgment" and thus the "personal choice and selection" that judgment presumes to make, Montaigne emphasizes the vulnerable and transitory nature of our beliefs: "How many things were articles of faith to us yesterday, which are fables to us today?" This reflection on the mutability of our beliefs is immediately turned against secondary authority, against the renewal of the credit accorded to the observances "of our Church." The passage from "yesterday" to "today" and the metamorphosis of "articles of faith" into "fables" are not likely to reassure anyone as to the solidity of the foundations that Montaigne swears he now acknowledges. As in the "Apology for Raymond Sebond," the attack on the enemies of the faith quickly proves destructive of the faith itself. The argument ultimately reinforces the objections against religion and reactivates uncertainty. Here we see how relative and vulnerable was the fideism in which Montaigne sought refuge. It is in insecurity[97] that Montaigne returns to the dogmas and practices he had abandoned.

Today is but a moment; soon it will be called yesterday. Other lives and indeed our own deaths are somehow obscurely implicated in the present moment. To be sure, Montaigne tries to hold on to those fleeting "images of life" that are perpetually eluding his grasp. And yesterday's preferences persist in him in the customs and practices that with each passing day become a more and more intimate part of his existence. But are those images and persistent preferences enough to establish the present on a solid foundation, firmly rooted in the past? In many places in the *Essays* Montaigne speaks of the present as the slimmest of moments, sustained solely by the evidence of its instantaneity and receiving no support at all from the past. And when he discovers that the present—his own and society's—is subject to the general decline that affects all things, his only recourse, paradoxically, is to turn his mind exclusively to the here and now, to everything that coexists with him in this moment of time. Peering down from the heights of the present, he broadens his gaze to take in a wider sweep of the landscape below. He finds this comforting, because it reveals that he is not alone in his decline; the whole world is falling with him: "(B) Nothing falls where everything falls."[98] Yet there is also something consoling in another discovery of rather contradictory import. Gazing still farther into the distance reveals that the present collapse is but a brief moment in the history of the world, only a small portion of which is affected: worse things have happened before, and even now there are other places more fortunate:

> (A) Seeing our civil wars, who does not cry out that this mechanism is being turned topsy-turvy and that the judgment day has us by the throat, without reflecting that many worse things have happened, and that ten thousand parts of the world, to our one, are meanwhile having a gay time.[99]

In Montaigne's mind the meagerness of the present is coupled with the magnitude of the universe. The present is our only resting place, and it is from the vantage of the present that we discover the immensity of space and the diversity of time and destiny. We are able to look upon other places and past times as a contemporary spectacle as soon as we cease to look to them as places of happiness and sources of authoritative examples. Other places and past times fill the horizon with signs, enabling us to take stock, to gauge the value of the present moment, which is so important for us and yet so absurdly insignificant compared with the rest of the known world and the vastly larger unknown worlds. By now our gaze has broadened as much it can: in his statements on education, Montaigne emphasizes the need to hold up before the student an image of the world as a vast *synoptical portrait*, in which all the accidents of history, held fast, become almost contemporary with us and subject to interpretation in terms of what they can do for us *now*. And the first thing they can do is to teach us something about the relativity of our situation:

> (A) But whoever considers *as in a painting* the *great picture* of our mother Nature in her full majesty; whoever reads such universal and constant variety in her face; whoever finds himself there, and not merely himself, but a whole kingdom, as a dot made with a very fine brush; that man alone estimates things according to their true proportions.
> This great world, which some multiply further as being only a species under one genus, is the mirror in which we must look at ourselves to recognize ourselves from the proper angle. In short, I want it to be the book of my student. So many humors, sects, judgments, opinions, laws, and customs teach us to judge sanely of our own, and teach our judgment to recognize its own imperfection and natural weakness, which is no small lesson. So many state disturbances and changes of public fortune teach us not to

make a great miracle out of our own. So many names, so many victories and conquests, buried in oblivion, make it ridiculous to hope to perpetuate our name by the capture of ten mounted archers and some chicken coop known only by its fall. The pride and arrogance of so many foreign displays of pomp, the puffed-up majesty of so many courts and dignities, strengthens our sight and makes it steady enough to sustain the brilliance of our own without blinking. So many millions of men buried before us encourage us not to be afraid of joining such good company in the other world. And likewise for other things.[100]

The immensity of the great painting makes our meager present look even more ridiculous. But it is the fact that we are looking, now, in the present, that causes the picture to unfold and to raise, behind us and all around us, its jumbled planes and masses. Not until we have cast our eyes upon this "great picture" do we realize that we are carried along by the moving crest of the present. That realization is enough to dampen all presumption, in keeping with the ideal of a *theoria* that now seeks not to grasp the nature of things but rather to strengthen the learned ignorance of the contemplator.

Nothing in the "great picture" is complete. The ancients surpassed us in technique, but can it be said that nature "then put forth her utmost effort?"[101] The moderns have discovered a new continent, but "who will guarantee that it is the last of its [i.e., 'our' world's] brothers?"[102] In any case, incompleteness is not incompatible with repetition or even regression. Not only knowledge but also civilization is governed, in Montaigne's world, by obscure vicissitudes. What nature may have accomplished in one place is counteracted by decline in another place: in one of the rare passages in which he uses the future tense, Montaigne (again speaking of America) sees the emergence of new life and the movement toward death as compensating each other so precisely that the result is immobility:

> (B) This other world will only be coming into the light when ours is leaving it. The universe will fall into paralysis; one member will be crippled, the other is in full vigor. I am much afraid that we shall have very greatly hastened the decline and ruin of the new world by our contagion, and that we will have sold it our opinions and our arts very dear.[103]

Again, the metaphor of rotation dragging along the great circle of the stars will win out over that of the straight line and straightforward progression. The fate of Rome is an important example, a gift of nature, which illustrates everything that can possibly befall a political community:

> (B) The stars fatally destined the state of Rome for an example of what they can do in this way. In it are comprised all the forms and vicissitudes that affect a state: all that order can do, and disorder, and good fortune, and misfortune. What state ought to despair of its condition, seeing the shocks and commotions by which Rome was disturbed, and which it withstood?[104]

Endless change means endless starting over: nothing resembles a circular motion more than another circular motion; nothing resembles the growth and decline of a living being more than the growth and decline of another living being. The new continues to roll in, but the new is also the return of the old. If the rotation of the stars governs revolutions on earth, what can be said about the cycles in human opinion concerning the laws of celestial motion, and whether the sun is fixed in one place or moves? Montaigne is not unaware of the fact that the widely accepted geocentric theory had recently been challenged by the heliocentric theory of Copernicus. But in his eyes the Copernican theory was merely the resurrection of the theory of Cleanthes, which had already been "refuted" by Aristotle and Ptolemy; all signs pointed to the likelihood that yet another new doctrine, no less vulnerable than the old, would one day supplant the two current antagonstic theories:

> (A) The sky and the stars have been moving for three thousand years; everybody had so believed, until it occurred to (C) Cleanthes of Samos, or (according to Theophrastus) to Nicetas of Syracuse, (A) to maintain that it was the earth that moved, (C) through the oblique circle of the Zodiac, turning about its axis; (A) and in our day Copernicus has grounded this doctrine so well that he uses it very systematically for all astronomical deductions. What are we to get out of that, unless that we should not bother which of the two is so? And who knows whether a *third opinion*, a thousand years from now, will not overthrow the preceding two?[105]

In this speculation, where Montaigne once again risks guessing the future, there is not the slightest hint of any notion of scientific progress. This is just one more argument to dissuade us from clinging to any "opinion" whatever. Following a citation from Lucretius concerning the vagaries of honor and scorn, the text continues as follows:

(A) Thus when some new doctrine is offered to us, we have great occasion to distrust it, and to consider that before it was produced its opposite was in vogue; and, as it was overthrown by this one, there may arise in the future a *third invention* that will likewise smash the second.[106]

One invention or opinion follows another in a regular circular pattern, as our minds are passively moved by various external influences:

(A) The result of that would be that all the common herd— (C) and we are all of the common herd—(A) would have its belief *as easy to turn as a weathercock*; for their soul, being soft and without resistance, would be forced to receive incessantly more and more different impressions, the last one always effacing the traces of the preceding one.[107]

Here, the "third invention" is not, as in other three-part patterns noticed earlier, the synthesis that transcends an opposition. It is yet another variation in a series of equivalent variations. Montaigne adds it (before the fact) to the synoptic spectacle of the human world, characterized by presumptuousness and infirmity (because of which men are prone to violence). This extrapolation does not indicate a road to follow; it merely suggests the likelihood that a new opinion will some day gain currency even though it has no greater grasp of reality than its predecessors. Such an opinion cannot yield any program of action, whether to increase our knowledge or to enhance our domination over the forces of nature. For Montaigne, wisdom is trusting obedience: while he tries to take a broad view, he is unwilling to abandon the present in order to constrain nature by means of effective artifice. "I ignorantly and negligently let myself be guided by the general law of the world."[108] Our lot is to obey that law, not to make use of it or to actively modify it: "My knowledge could not make it change its path; it will not modify itself for me."[109] What we think we know of causal processes is insufficient to make any prediction: "And vain is the undertaking of him who presumes to embrace both causes and consequences and to lead by the hand the progress of his affair."[110] Thus Montaigne denies that with knowledge comes effective technology that might to some extent enable us to gain control over the future: for him the only possible knowledge is self-knowledge, present knowledge in which what the books of the past have to teach surely survives, but only insofar as we assimilate and incorporate their lesson into ourselves, so that it becomes part of the very rhythm of our breathing and the cadence of our style. The benefits of knowledge are measured by the quality of this act of presence: "Knowledge" must "improve [the mind's] imperfect state."[111] "Any other knowledge is harmful to a man who has not the knowledge of goodness."[112] Its purpose is to "govern the movements of the soul": what is required is an art of movement, a style of going places relieved of the worry of an itinerary. The authority of the present is therefore based on the impossibility of drawing support from the past or of laying down ambitious practical plans for the future. As soon as time's other dimensions are stripped of their authority, the present life of the self stands revealed as the least vain of all vanities. But the present is precariously balanced between the past and the future. It is full only because we have divested ourselves of our investment in the future and reduced the past to a "great picture" that has no power to serve as an example for the present. No voice from the past speaks with absolute sovereign authority except for that of Socrates, confessing his ignorance.

By making himself an author, by writing the *Essays*, Montaigne was of course establishing a new kind of authority: that of the work in which an individual "records" himself. But that authority is negative; it claims no credit and imposes nothing: "I have no authority to be believed, nor do I want it."[113] The literary work is that authority which speaks when all authority other than that implicit in the power to denounce one's own "inadequacy" is placed in suspense. The present, i.e., the point in which the full force of nature makes itself felt, is also the point in which the mind experiences both itself and the world as fleeting shadows. Labile, the present contains that which is "in being" [*en estre*], the palpable presence of which is fleeting. The present is our dwelling place, as eternity is God's. It is up to us to make our humble abode as sumptuous as we can.

After Montaigne

Before long, however, the European mind brought forth a new idea: namely, that knowledge grows with time, as does the range of actions that can be carried out with the aid of scientific calculations and predictions. Montaigne resigned himself to "ceaselessly revolve." The new project, which first saw the light in the generation following Montaigne's, literally involved breaking out of the circle and making progress. Listen to Bacon: "Sed instauratio facienda est ab imis fundamentis, nisi libeat perpetuo circumvolvi in orbem, cum exili et quasi contemnendo progressu."[114] Montaigne was willing to submit to the "general law" of nature without asking nature for anything more. Bacon wants obedience to nature to be a means of dominating it and establishing man's empire: "Hominis autem imperium in res, in solis artibus et scientiis ponitur. Naturae enim non imperatur, nisi parendo."[115] And when he comes to giving a synopsis of what he knows about the world, he sets aside, in advance, a place for knowledge yet to come, knowledge that will still further augment and enhance man's powers. The tableau of the world is no longer a confused composition of countless lives and deaths succeeding one another down through the ages; rather, it is an orderly array of sciences and arts (each corresponding to one of our faculties). And that array is not yet complete: gaps due to our ignorance are destined one day to be filled in by objects that have yet to be named and classified. No longer is any reproach made to desire that looks to the future as the time when it will possess what it now lacks (*desiderata*). The exploration of the world by the mind (*inquisitio*) is no longer rejected as *idle curiosity*. Contrast this attitude with that of Montaigne, whose denunciation of idle curiosity extended both his skeptical critique of anything that threatens the soul's repose and his religious critique of worldly temptations that divert the soul from its supernatural goal.

When, moreover, the Montaignian moment of the "I feel" turns, with Descartes, into the moment of intellectual certainty, the moment of the "I think," subjective evidence becomes the point of departure for a new method that places its confidence in calculation and geometry, and proposes using these tools to explain all the manifestations of "extended substance" in "mechanical" terms, thus opening the way to predictable action. Descartes of course wanted to use this mechanical knowledge, which he thought nearly complete, to change the world in very specific ways: to lighten the burden of labor, to conquer disease, to extend life. The promise of the future, the hope of achieving a better lot for man, gave scientists reason to work.

What Montaigne had seen as merely another variant in an endless series of opinions (e.g., Copernican heliocentrism) or another illustration of nature's inexhaustible fecundity (the discovery of the New World, which he believed to be but another fragment of an infinite world that man would never fully explore) now became figures of decisive progress, assuring the moderns of lasting superiority over the ancients and holding out the promise of further discoveries. What Montaigne had believed to be impossible, namely, to escape from the "whirl" of opinions and move decisively forward, now became the essence of the possible; and science has not ceased to multiply man's possibilities ever since.

Montaigne had reconciled himself with the phenomenal world. At first he had declared that world to be false and unstable. But since stable and true *being* remained inaccessible behind appearances, he ultimately abandoned himself, with full awareness of what he was doing, to the ceaseless flow that our senses report yet somehow fail to grasp, that is imperfect and yet replete. But his successors were not satisfied with this phenomenalist solution, which brings the mind back to its starting place, disappointed in its first hope but compensated by the friendlier eye now cast on man's natural condition. Starting from the same critique of appearances, the same initial doubt, these later thinkers would sweep away all "idols" and wipe the slate clean; using the language of mathematics (verified by constantly improved experimental methods and techniques), they would construct the laws that for all practical purposes give us control over the material world. Henceforth doubt would be a mere preliminary (though always active) critical precaution, prior to the real work of writing down equations and making observations. Henceforth the development of modern science would be accompanied by a constant polemic against the illusions to which sensory perception and the undisciplined imagination are prone. Moreover, scientific criticism would not stop at the conclusions drawn by Montaigne, who limited the mind's understanding to itself, destitute and changeable as it is. The progress of knowledge would strengthen man's confidence in the powers of the mind, equipped with the tools of mathematics and the experimental method. One may as well use the future indicative to say that science will not cease its development and that man will be able to count on science to dominate nature's adverse forces.

For "modern" science the phenomenal world cannot be taken just as it appears. It is subject to causal interpretation based on general laws. Those laws, quantitative in nature, are products of the mind [*pensable*], and are framed in terms of a small set of fundamental or basic processes. The phenomenal world, which in experimental procedures is constituted both by our natural perception and by the current state of cultural practices, is the starting point of scientific reflection. Depending on the interests of the "researcher," critical analysis of experimental results may reveal problems that require the elaboration of new explanatory models. At one extreme, i.e., in experimental work guided by theory, sense data again play a modest role: they indicate, via some measuring device, the response of the object under study. Every experiment is designed not only in conformity with some conceptual model but also in such a way as to reveal to us a *perceptible* result through some recording instrument. But these sense data are not the sense data of "naïve" perception: they are the mere sensory residue; perception serves merely to verify scientific

thought, whose purpose is to grasp, behind appearances, the reason for those appearances.

Sensory experience cannot be erased, however, for it is primary. Even as "logical truth" triumphed in the eighteenth century, the philosophical vocabulary therefore had to make room for a new category, that of "aesthetic truth," so as to afford some legitimacy (of a lesser order, to be sure, than logical truth) to what nature and art make available directly to our senses. Supreme authority as to the nature of things continued to be vested in objective knowledge and mathematical method, which pointed the way to the future. But it was deemed appropriate to make a place for aesthetic knowledge (alongside or beneath scientific knowledge), since the triumphant language of science could not accommodate it.[116] Just as the "Copernican" approach to physical reality concluded its triumph over all challengers, *literature* acquired what has ever since been its characteristic feature: namely, its ability to attest to "inner experience," to powers of imagination and feeling over which objective knowledge has no hold. The literary work is a private estate in which feeling and perception may legitimately prevail as "personal" truths. Contemporary civilization has become used to the coexistence of two mutually exclusive yet complementary languages: the mathematical language of science, which progresses by tirelessly subjecting to rational criticism anything that tends to become fixed in "appearances," and the language of art, whose task is essentially to organize the uniquely personal material produced by the artless activity of our sensibility.[117] If Montaigne's doubt was the inspiration for the Cartesian "clean slate" and the initiator of the scientific method, it is also true that his skeptical retreat to transitory sensory experience, his aesthetic conversion, and his steadily growing interest in creating a portrait of himself make him a *writer* in the modern sense of the word—possibly one of the first. (In this connection, let me simply list some of the ways in which Rousseau, who extended Montaigne's influence, was indebted to him: namely, for his denunciation of appearances and of man's subjugation to the opinions of others, for his criticism of the vanity of knowledge, for his ideas about pedagogy, and for the idea of a work of self-description.)

Now, the scientific ideal, and with it the notion of the future, wherein the possibilities opened up by science find their proper application, did not limit itself simply to the achievement of technical mastery over the material world. A new ambition emerged, to extend to the "moral world" the methods that had made it possible to establish the laws of the "physical world": some people turned their attention to developing an objective psychology and ethics, to uncovering the impulses and energies that make men act as they do and that morality praises or blames under the names "vice" and "virtue." It was hoped that these impulses and energies could be weighed and analyzed by the scientific method with the same rigor that had made it possible to understand the behavior of matter and that had revealed hidden laws inaccessible to the senses. For this, it was necessary to apply to the "thinking substance" an experimental approach analogous to the one that had proved so fruitful in the investigation of "extended substance." The dream was to discover, to *lay bare*, laws and regularities of individual and social behavior equivalent to the laws and regularities that mechanics had established in its proper sphere: the goal, in other words, was to establish in the "moral" order a principle as general, as neutral, as quantifiable, and as measurable as force or acceleration. Accordingly, it was no longer sufficient merely to discover "vice" beneath the mask of virtue. All the hidden vices that moralists thought they had unmasked up to now were only illusions: "vice," "corruption," and the like were mere verbal entities, derived from the language of theology—a kind of second mask, this time due not to man's malice but to the imperfect knowledge of the moralists. The point was now to penetrate behind the mask to lay bare a primary substance or cause: self-love, the instinct of self-preservation, desire, interest, need. The names were various (and the nineteenth century would add a few more to the list, such as "psychic energy" and "libido") but the ambition remained the same: to construct a mechanics (or psychology) of the feelings and passions, treated as things in accordance with a model loosely based on the mechanics of solids or fluids (including electricity). In the nineteenth century the scope of this kind of investigation would be broadened still further, from individual psychology to history and the study of society, which came to be seen as explicable in terms of the effects of "real forces" unknown to the actors themselves and previously ignored (so it was believed) by historians. There developed a social "physiology" that aimed to compete if not with the exact sciences then at least with the sciences of nature; in some cases the social sciences were seen as extensions of the natural sciences, as theories of social progress were grafted onto theories of the evolution of living things. Thus in the future that scientific investigators dreamed of bringing nearer, ontological unmasking and ethical/political unmasking tended to be combined in a single causal *science*, which became the conscious justification for action whose explicit purpose was to give mankind control over its destiny.

After at first rejecting custom, Montaigne for want of anything better ultimately reconciled himself to it: since the present is the only place in which man can dwell, it is unwise to shake its foundation. Now, in the ethical and political sphere Montaigne's movement describes the same full circle as in the ontological sphere. In fact, he frequently combines two indictments: one of our pretension to penetrate the secrets of the natural world, the other of indulgence of pretense in the moral world. Vain ostentation and refusal to bow before the mysteries of nature are both aspects of a single "presumptuousness," a single unwillingness to accept our finite condition. At this point Montaigne's wisdom sounds the retreat: the only thing wrong with our presumptuousness and unwillingness is that we are unaware of our affliction. Man must know that he is a limited being destined to be always saddled with opinions and fancies. He must let the changes that nature brings about within him and all around him run their course, and refrain from attempting to stem the tide by making what he believes to be necessary changes in the natural and institutional order, when in reality he can never be sure whether his undertakings will bring improvement or ruin. This resignation (which, as we have seen, is in no way incompatible with firm opposition to injustice) is diametrically opposed to what has been, right up to the middle of the twentieth century, the modern attitude: extrapolating from the example of science and technology, where results are predictable, man has developed a fondness for the idea that he can *shape* his own destiny. And to be sure, political and economic action can in many areas be made more effective through the use of scientific methods. Man can thus cease to be a mere plaything of Fortune. He possesses the means to mobilize large numbers of people and vast industrial resources with which he can construct a world whose functioning can to a large extent be planned. What has changed as a result is not merely the number or nature of the purposes toward which man may reasonably direct his efforts but, even more, the importance that those purposes, remote though they may be, claim within the context of our present behavior and thinking. Whether the concern has been to increase man's material wealth or to extend his freedom, the modern age has increasingly directed its efforts toward a future from which all present dissatisfactions will have been abolished. Modern man knows (or imagines) that he can have whatever he sets his mind to obtain, no matter what unforeseeable contigencies may arise (the assumption being that any obstacle can be dealt with by manipulating the equations that presumably govern all that happens in the world). But he must be willing to pay the price. Now in moving from the idea that in the future science will enable men to do things that cannot be done at present to the myth that human happiness will be achieved with the aid of science, a considerable enlargement of ambition has occurred. It is increasingly common to forget that it was men living in the present who conceived of the future as a time that would cure man's present woes. Invested with an almost sacred value, the future has become the supreme authority—the standard of comparison, the source of legitimacy, the ideal that moves men to action. The work on behalf of the common good, the investment in the future, has become a major conceptual category, an organizing principle that shapes all other ideas and attitudes.[118] To modern minds imbued with such convictions, and the zeal that they justify, Montaigne's philosophy, wholly preoccupied with the present and always careful to take the short view, has seemed old-fashioned, overly cautious, and wanting in generosity. Given all that the modern spirit holds can and should be changed, Montaigne's conservatism no longer appears to be the choice of the lesser evil; indeed, it has been called a philosophy to protect the privileges of the nobility. Some commentators have questioned Montaigne's "good faith," even when he says that his aim is to find the best possible compromise between individual tranquillity and the welfare of all. Some commentators have even forgotten that Montaigne's paramount concern was never to lose his self-respect, and that he therefore combined his conservatism with an ethics of *refusal*. (This is one of the important lessons the chapter entitled "Of the useful and the honorable," 3:1.) Today, many people believe that they have found grounds for hope that Montaigne, in an age of fear, plague, war, and religious persecution, was never able to find either within himself or in the world around him.

And surely it is here that illusion makes a triumphant comeback. For if the laws of nature as revealed by mathematical physics are subject to the test of experiment and technological application, the same cannot be said for moral or historical "reality." And yet those who claim to be enemies of the "mask" pretend to be able to read that reality behind all appearances, and to reveal its hitherto unperceived inner workings.

The age of the human sciences has witnessed the birth of a new dream: the dream of a knowledge that would demystify and unmask.

But new masks and new myths have insinuated themselves into the very heart of the new sciences. Some were immediately recognized as myths, but others were accepted as articles of faith. The "scientific" interpretation of moral and historical phenomena is supported by little more than its own powers to persuade and mobilize, its own ability to move individuals and societies to give *credit*, to subscribe to a cause. But the pursuit of proof in pragmatic effectiveness brings us back to the old couple, *mask* and *belief*. What had been denied or repressed here makes its return, this time not in an allied sphere (that of aesthetics) but within a discourse that claims to describe real forces and hence to determine a new psychic or social order.

To cite one example from a hundred possibilities, consider the ambiguity inherent in the word "ideology." Marx used it to stigmatize false consciousness, but Lenin cleansed it of all pejorative connotations and applied it to the world view that he believed ought to be instilled into the masses in order to induce them to work more zealously toward their own "liberation."[119] Thus Lenin had no compunctions about describing his doctrine as a new ideology, albeit an ideology worked out in full consciousness of the laws of history and free of the obscurity and deception that marked earlier forms of "ideological discourse." Thus a new danger enters the scene, wrapped in the shining garb of what is proclaimed to be ultimate knowledge: the stage is set with new scenery, no less deceptive than the old. Compared with Montaigne's avowed reconciliation with appearance and custom, of whose relativity he was perfectly well aware, what we have here is a reinstatement of the presumption of true knowledge. The ultimate illusion is the belief that one has escaped illusion, that one has come close to the truth of being, that one has found the way to weed out falsehood and error. More precisely, the illusion consists in the belief that one has moved beyond the uncertain realm of ethical decision and into the realm where certain knowledge can be infallibly applied.

This is not to say that illusion of this kind—this new mask of knowledge that replaces the old mask of ideology—is without pragmatic effectiveness. But historical success is no proof of epistemological superiority. It proves merely that belief in the power of knowledge to dispel illusion can be a powerful mobilizing force. Montaigne knew this already: "Every opinion is strong enough to make people espouse it at the price of life." We encountered this judgment once before, when we were considering Montaigne's indictment of false appearances. The importance of that indictment is only amplified now that the dubious claims of self-styled sciences have superseded other dubious claims based on authority and tradition. As for the heroism of the new believers, the reader of Montaigne will object that their sacrifice proves the intensity and not the truth of their beliefs: "How many of them have been seen patiently letting themselves be burned and roasted for opinions borrowed from others, unknown, and not understood! . . . It seems to each man that the ruling pattern of nature is in him; to this he refers all other forms as to a touchstone. The ways that do not square with his are counterfeit and artificial. What brutish stupidity."[120] With such convictions Montaigne certainly did not go to martyrdom like the founders of the Church. But neither did he send anyone else to martyrdom. Inhumanity and cruelty outraged him; but he had little belief in sin and hence cared little about setting forth, and imposing upon others, rules for earthly or spiritual salvation.

In a striking reversal, this absence of historical hope, which for so long made Montaigne seem a writer from another era, today, owing to the crisis in modern thought, makes him seem remarkably up to date. The crisis to which I refer can be defined as a crisis of confidence in the future—a premature disenchantment stemming from fear of the "perverse effects" of changes originally undertaken for the noblest of reasons and carried through with the most powerful of means. This century's malaise is due in large part to the fact that the future has exerted undue influence over the present: exercising dictatorial powers, the future has triumphed by obscuring the fact that it is manipulated in the present by men who inevitably treat other men as objects, offering as compensation the prospect of future happiness and wealth. But more and more people are unwilling to be bled white today in the hope of achieving something better tomorrow. What is being asked in the way of "commitment," of a "mortgage" on the future, has reached such proportions that it is as though the present were being wished away, as though life here and now were being exchanged, in the words of Reinhart Koselleck, for a "blank check drawn on the future."[121] Today we are increasingly wary of making such investments without collateral. It is no guarantee of success that such dreams are secularized versions of the theological virtue of hope, particularly since such secularization frequently tends to displace another theological virtue that used to exert some influence in this fallen world, namely, charity. What has happened can be seen with particular clarity in industrial societies that have adopted totalitarian forms of government: the effort to "end alienation" in the future has led to extreme and undeniable alienation in the present. To a lesser extent the same thing is true wherever an excessive emphasis

on "growth" has led to neglect of the present in favor of an anticipated future. When the promise of future justice is used to excuse
present injustice, or when a promised golden age does not mate-
rialize and people begin to disbelieve in renewed promises of a better
tomorrow, the authority of the future begins to pale. Disillusionment
and rebellion have vigorously asserted themselves, so much so that
some people have lost hope of ever restoring the balance and reestablishing a just relationship between present existence (centered in
the individual identity and will) and remote ends. The retreat into the
present—in the form of physical self-indulgence, intoxication, and
hedonism of all kinds—has proceeded much farther with some of our
contemporaries than it ever did with Montaigne. Whatever the importance Montaigne the skeptic ascribed to momentary happiness, he
continued to believe in the value of exercising judgment, and therefore in the individual's right to survey the future, even if changing the
future by his own action was out of the question. For Montaigne, the
mind is constantly engaged in dialogue with the images of the past;
but many contemporary adepts of immediacy repudiate not only the
siren song of tomorrow's utopia but also the entire cultural heritage of
the past. Their present is thus reduced to such meager proportions
that it suggests a mere animal existence—a form of life upon which
Montaigne bestowed paradoxical praise when he repeated the Pyrrhonian condemnation of human anticipation: "The philosopher Pyr-
rho, incurring the peril of a great storm at sea, offered those who
were with him nothing better to imitate than the assurance of a pig
that was traveling with them, and that was looking at this tempest
without fear."[122]

The retreat to the present, which in Montaigne can be considered
the expression of a premodern state of mind, recurs in a more pro-
nounced form in a "postmodern" situation. This return to sense certainty can surely appear *regressive* (compared with such modern
values as evolution and progress), for it is indicative not only of rebellion against the tyranny of the future but also of a generalized anxiety about purposeful activity of any kind. The immediate goal
becomes to "find oneself" in body or spirit, and this goal must be
achieved at all cost, even if it means giving up any systematic plans
for the future. To "conserve and endure" are no longer matters that
are taken into account. Today, the restriction of an individual's interest to his present condition often means that attention is concentrated exclusively on the body: between anxiety and the search for
pleasure, between hypochondria and hedonism, attention to the
body has almost supplanted older religious concerns. The cult of the

body has taken over the seriousness, the importance, and the ritualized character of religious devotion. And for anyone who looks to the past in search of "precursors," Montaigne immediately comes to mind as the most striking example. What other author dwelt at such length on his "bodily conditions?" And isn't the body the main focus of the *experience* that is the subject of the final essay (3:13)? But how different Montaigne's attitude is from today's narcissism! For him, physical life was one important aspect of life among others. He does not make a fetish of the body. If the body, the imperative of health, is the focus of sustained attention, that attention is exercised by a faculty of *judgment* that "plays its game apart"[123] and that observes from a distance, with affectionate irony. Montaigne's interest is not so wholly absorbed in the life of the body that he forgets about "relations with others." It is true that one of his last recommendations is that we should be at one with ourselves: "It is an absolute perfection and virtually divine to know how to enjoy our being rightfully."[124] Yet this self-absorption (remotely patterned after Aristotle's God) immediately becomes a way of making contact with others. A few lines later Montaigne says: "(B) The most beautiful lives, to my mind, are those that conform to the common (C) human (B) pattern, (C) with order, but (B) without miracle and without eccentricity."[125] The conciliatory middle term between the *personal* concern for health and the need for communication is set under the sign of the god of the Muses, invoked by Horace in the following lines:

> Now old age needs to be treated a little more tenderly. Let
> us commend it to that god who is the protector of *health*
> and *wisdom*, but *gay and sociable* wisdom:
>> Grant me but health, Latona's son,
>> And to enjoy the wealth I've won,
>> And honored age, with mind entire
>> And not unsolaced by the lyre.
>
> —Horace[126]

The simultaneous insistence on one's relation to oneself (to be perfected through that inner cultivation whose goal is *wisdom*) and on one's relations to others (through that sociable *gaiety* that is intimately connected with the "art of discussion") delivers Montaigne from the narcissistic temptation that threatened to entrap him (and that does entrap so many of our contemporaries, when they turn upon themselves the energies that they no longer devote to a future world). To say that experience should bear fruit of an objective as well as a subjective kind, Montaigne likes to use the image of a "concert" of instruments, as in the following late addition to "The art of discussion" (3:8):

> (B) The fruit of a surgeon's experience is not the history of his practice and his remembering that he has cured four people of the plague and three of the gout, unless he can derive from that experience the means of forming his judgment and can make us aware that he has become wiser in the practice of his art. (C) So in a concert of instruments we do not hear a lute, a spinet, and the flute; we hear a rounded harmony, the effect of the various elements joined into a whole.[127]

If there is such a thing as the "authority of experience,"[128] for Montaigne this has to do both with our active grasp of external realities and our inward reflection of that activity, which becomes our wisdom and our conscience. If the present plays a preponderant role in Montaigne, it is a polyphonic present, which like music is carried along by the beat of time and which acquiesces in, even as it transcends, its own disappearance. The breadth and variety of the present are compensation for the short span of the future to which Montaigne resigns himself. A forerunner of the commonplace contemporary interest in savoring the existence of the body in each fleeting moment, Montaigne is not a prisoner of that interest; for him the present also includes the duties of "civic" and political life. The question of how much of life should be set aside for private pursuits is so important to Montaigne only because private life must coexist with a public life that cannot be shirked. The only issue is how much importance to assign to each. Montaigne's polyphonic demands remind us of such early musical forms as the motet or the madrigal, but in many respects it must be admitted that, compared with the meager and transitory rewards of hedonism and the illusory rewards promised by technology and various political dogmas, this vision represents our best hope for the future, our still-uncompleted task.

Acceptance of the body implies in the first place acceptance of the sensory message. It does not give us access to ideal essences, or certain knowledge. But we must live among men and create a human community, taking into account the sensory world that is our point of contact with others. Just as we must "duly play our role" in the "low comedy" of ordinary occupations, so must we stop criticizing "common usage in language" and subscribe to it.[129] So, too, must we recognize the validity of "superficial ceremonies and appearances," even if these are precisely what prevents us from grasping profound truths. Thus the enemy of masks comes round to praising appearance and outward show, at least insofar as these are politically effective:

> (B) These senses act as the proper and primary judges for us, and they perceive things only by their external accidents; thus it is no wonder that in all the functions that serve the welfare of society there is always such a universal admixture of ceremony and outward show that the best and most effective part of a government consists in these externals. It is still man we are dealing with, and it is a wonder how physical his nature is.[130]

This is the justification given for Montaigne's reproach to the Protestants whose wish it was to abstract from the sensible world and "construct . . . a system of religious practice that is all contemplative and spiritual," so much so that "religion would have melted away and slipped through their fingers." To be sure, Montaigne remains sensitive to all the abuses of authority that stem from deception: "(B) I hate every sort of tyranny, both in words and in acts. I am inclined to resist with all my mind these vain externals that delude our judgment *through the senses.*"[131] He therefore refuses to let himself be duped by "the gravity, the gown, and the fortune" of those with whom he has dealings. But if their "words" and "grimaces" don't inspire confidence, he nevertheless expects to judge the qualities of an individual on the basis of some outward appearance. Thus *appearance* again takes on an essential function: "(B) If travels and offices have improved them, this ought to *show* [faire paraître: literally, to make appear— Trans.] in their increased understanding."[132] The metaphorical richness of Montaigne's style is the product of this imperative to *faire paraître*, to show.

Appearance is not distinct from essence. Hegel would later make the same point in a language all his own: "Essence can only *appear.* The act by means of which essence appears is in itself the act by which essence suppresses itself in order to become immediacy. . . . Essence therefore does not lie *behind* or *beyond* the phenomenon, but, by virtue of the fact that essence is that which exists, existence is phenomenon."[133]

Despite Hegel's warning and Montaigne's experience, numerous writers have more recently repeated the attack on "masks" and embarked anew on a quest for essences *behind* or *beyond* appearances. "Suspicion" is directed first of all at that which *dissimulates,* whether in the sphere of ontology (i.e., the phenomenon) or in the ethical-social sphere (language, conventions, "ideologies," myths): in the end it becomes apparent that that which dissimulates is also that which *expresses* and therefore must be not suppressed or circumvented but respected and interpreted. It is possible to show that many writers, at many different times, followed an identical trajectory in this regard. They were not merely repeating one another, however. Their trajectories merely *appear* to be the same owing to a certain schematization or abstract reductionism that fails to take into account the many issues that criticism of appearances involves. It may be because this trajectory has been so insistently repeated in such a variety of ways in the recent literature (and in literature which, though still fairly recent, has already achieved "classic" status) that I have been able to discern a similar course in Montaigne's development. Differences also stand out sharply. Montaigne, no matter how much he resigns himself to relativism, never gives up insisting on the need for truth. He is at pains to preserve the full measure of truth that the human condition allows: even if we renounce the pride of knowledge, we still know that a benevolent Nature stands ready to meet our needs and deserves our docile obedience. This residue of ontology or metaphysics is not to the taste of modern writers. When they attack masks or alienation, they not infrequently fall back on rhetoric and subterfuge quite as conventional as anything they are attacking: the code that is ultimately approved differs from the code that was initially denounced only in that the former is openly admitted to be a deliberate artifact. The new code is held to be liberating because it has not been imposed or "reproduced" by teaching, tradition, or lazy consensus—but no claim is made that it is the language of truth. Rather, it proclaims itself to be artifice. "Values" have no other foundation than the decrees of an arbitrary will. Aestheticism frequently goes hand in hand with a sometimes openly acknowledged penchant for nihilism. The enemy of the sort of ordinary hypocrisy that is a common part of everyday life becomes the apologist for a more deliberate form of hypocrisy carried on at a higher level of consciousness: he admires the tactics of ambition (Stendhal), or extols the stratagems of disguise (Baudelaire), or adopts an elaborate style (Flaubert), or praises obligatory convention (Valéry), or makes himself the apologist of the gratuitous act (Gide). As for the individual who rebels against the seductive beauty of a world that is a purveyor of death, what else can he do when he can no longer hold out but give himself passionately to that same mortal world and its superficial pleasures; there is nothing with which to ward off its blandishments, nothing to substitute for or transcend them, for below the surface of the world is the void (Camus). Men live lives of inauthenticity and bad faith, but, incapable as they are of instituting any concrete form of authenticity, there is no choice but to adopt a voluntarist ethics, which sweeps away recalcitrant facts to impose a liberating interpretation of history, an imposed interpretation in which the ruse of the mask triumphs, by a freak of fate and unbeknownst to the "authentic" writer (Sartre). Ordinary language is a web of mythologies, a code "fixed" to favor the powers-that-be. But when all is said and done, there is nothing but codes, and none can claim the warrant of truth: this disillusionment leaves us free to enjoy the rhetoric of the signifier, alert for opportunities to free ourselves from its rules as well as to arrange them to our liking (Barthes). The case for appearances was stated in a modest form, a consoling pragmatist version, by Santayana: "When life draws to a close and the world has vanished in smoke, what are the realities that our minds can still, without illusion, claim as their own, if not the very form of the illusions we once attacked."[134] Nietzsche, who admired Montaigne's "loyalty" and "gaiety" and who claimed "to have in mind and—who knows?—perhaps also in body something of Montaigne's impetuosity [*Mutwille*],"[135] was the first to turn back to appearances, with enthusiasm, and his example has been widely followed in this century:

> The "apparent" world is the only one; the "true world" is merely a superfluous lie.[136]

> It is nothing more than a moral prejudice that truth is worth more than semblance; it is, in fact, the worst proved supposition in the world. *So* much must be conceded: there could have been no life at all except upon the basis of perspective estimates and semblances; and if, with the virtuous enthusiasm and stupidity of many a philosopher, one wished to do away altogether with the "seeming world"—well, granted that *you* could do that—at least nothing of your "truth" would thereby remain! Indeed, what is it that forces us in general to the supposition that there is an essential opposition of "true" and "false"? Is it not enough to suppose degrees of seemingness, and as it were lighter and darker shades and tones of semblance— different *valeurs*, as the painters say? Why might not the world *which concerns us*—be a fiction?[137]

> What is it that is now "appearance" to me! Verily not the antithesis of any kind of essence—what knowledge can I

assert of any kind of essence whatsoever, except merely the predicates of its appearance! Verily not a dead mask which one could put upon an unknown X, and which to be sure one could also remove! Appearance is for me the operating and living thing itself; which goes so far in its self-mockery as to make me feel that here there is appearance, and Will o' the Wisp, and spirit dance, and nothing more—that among all these dreamers, I also, the "thinker," dance my dance, that the thinker is a means of prolonging the further terrestrial dance, and in so far is one of the masters of ceremony of existence. [138]

It should come as no surprise that, in restoring to appearances the primacy that Montaigne had earlier bestowed upon them, Nietzsche almost simultaneously rediscovered, in the form of what he called "eternal recurrence," the "wheels" that Montaigne believed responsible for the revolving course of history. [139] But for Nietzsche the play of appearances was not simply the pretext for a "dance," or rather, dance, as Nietzsche interprets it, is merely a metaphor for the exuberance of the will. [140] Following shortly after the passage cited above from *Beyond Good and Evil* is another passage (section 36), this one "panvoluntarist" in character, which, while contesting Schopenhauer's metaphysics, carries it to an extreme: what is "given" to us as real is simply "our world of appetites and passions." What prevents us from asking "whether that which is 'given' does not *suffice*, by means of our counterfeit understanding, for the understanding even of the so-called mechanical (or 'material') world?" What is to prevent appearance from assuming the status of reality in the full sense of the word? The *world* in all its various aspects would then be simply the diverse forms of a single passion or will present in its most primitive state:

> Granted, finally, that we succeeded in explaining our entire instinctive life as the development and ramification of one fundamental form of will—namely, the Will to Power, as *my* thesis puts it; granted that all organic functions could be traced back to this Will to Power, and that the solution of the problem of generation and nutrition—it is one problem—could also be found therein: one would thus have acquired the right to define *all* active force unequivocally as *Will to Power*. The world seen from within, the world defined and designated according to its "intelligible character"—it would simply be "Will to Power," and nothing else.

This sketch of a totalizing anthropology-cosmology is vaguely reminiscent of certain philosophies of the Renaissance. I say vaguely reminiscent because with the exception of Paracelsus none of the philosophers in question moved from inner experience, subjective emotions, to a speculative model of all reality. As far as Montaigne was concerned, such intoxication with totality would have seemed the very height of presumption. It would have figured as one more opinion in the infinite variety of opinions that lay motionless in the balance of skepticism, measured by the question, "What do I know?" Concerned to "*husband* [*mesnager*] his will," Montaigne set forth the principles of an economy of the will (and remember that in sixteenth-century French, the word for "economy" was *mesnager*): far from feeling himself in harmony with some sort of "will to power" supposedly implicit in every aspect of his nature and every stage of his evolution, he feels instead that this will, whenever it takes the form of desire and commits itself "with fierceness and violence" in the outside world, "hinders more than [it] serves."[141] The will to power, as Montaigne witnesses it at work in avarice and ambition, fails to bear fruit. To achieve its goal, the will must give way to another faculty, namely, judgment.

> (B) We never conduct well the thing that possesses and conducts us:
>> (C) Passion handles all things ill.
>>> —Statius
> (B) He who employs in it only his judgment and skill proceeds more gaily. . . . In the man who is intoxicated with a violent and tyrannical intensity of purpose we see of necessity much imprudence and injustice; the impetuosity of his desire carries him away. These are reckless movements, and, unless fortune lends a great hand, of little fruit. . . .
> (B) As in precipitancy—more haste, less speed [Quintus Curtius]—haste trips itself up, hobbles and stops itself.[142]

The will finds its limit in what brings it close to appetite and passion. It is up to *judgment*, Montaigne believes, to make proper use of appearances. It is judgment that teaches us that in public life we must "play our part duly, but as the part of a borrowed character."[143] And therefore it is judgment that prevents desire (i.e., individual or collective "will") from interfering with political affairs. It must be granted that Nietzsche's philosophy lent itself to interpretations that extended the domain of the "will to power" into the sphere of collective life: these interpretations viewed the individual as the agent of an impersonal but unique and universal energy that pervaded and exalted all his actions. Force, naked power, was then able to impose itself upon nothingness as appearance transmuted into triumphant reality. The aesthetic option (that which favors, over the Montaignian ideal of the *portrait*, that of the "dance") is then able to move toward action, to turn from aestheticism into activism. Action for action's sake (for the beauty of posture and step) then supplants Montaigne's "artificialist" prudence and judicious conventionalism.

Now, Montaigne's thought does not suffer as Nietzsche's does from the possibility of totalitarian interpretation. Whatever unifying role Nature plays in Montaigne's philosophy, nothing authorizes the interpreter to diminish the variety of faculties, "humors and conditions," and physical actors. It may be that a stubborn duality persists in Montaigne's thought not simply because the world is in fact dualistic but also because of an imperative need to protect the life and liberty of the individual. In 3:10 *will* and *judgment* are said to be distinct faculties. More than that, the specification of the respective jurisdiction of each makes it possible to draw a sharp dividing line between the sphere of private life (of subjective desire and reflection, of "the friendship that each man owes to himself"[144]) and the obligations of "public society":[145] "The mayor and Montaigne have always been two."[146] But this relationship through its very exclusiveness establishes a kind of interdependence between the two terms, which define each other reciprocally. Similarly, in 3:1 the "useful" and the "honorable" are values that serve to distinguish between, on the one hand, what the prince and the law can rightfully require and, on the other hand, what comes under the jurisdiction of conscience. The pairing of these terms implies that contradiction between them is possible; hence opposition and refusal are also possible: our services may be required by reasons of state (the "useful"), but we may give them only if no violence is done to our inner sense of what is "honorable." Disobedience is justified (at our peril) because utility is not the only, or the highest, value. As we have now had repeated opportunities to observe, antagonistic terms often serve Montaigne as the starting point for an argument that leads to reconciliation in a higher synthesis. But this is not always the case. Such terms can also serve to ground choice, wherein freedom affirms itself, if need be, by *denying* what threatens it, by refusing to submit to tyrannical coercion. This power of negation through free thought (which is also a power of liberation through refusal) is what Montaigne retains from his initial revolt against mask and appearance even after his reconciliation with them is complete. Reconciliation *knows* that it follows on negation. One of the most tenacious features of Montaigne's thought is that he perpetuates, in a generalized, internalized form, the injury that gave rise to all the agitation recorded in the essays, even as the mind, made wiser by experience, casts a new light on what had initially been rejected as inessential but is now rehabilitated. Montaigne had originally wished to free himself from the world's comedy. Then he refused to give in to the seductive dogmatism of a philosophy of hidden essences. And finally, he was quite unable to reinstate appearances without preserving some memory of the distance traversed. By struggling constantly against his own movement he succeeds finally in acquiescing in a condition that is made more precious by having been rejected at the outset. Along the way he does not shrink from finding fault with the most cherished parts of himself; he does not spare himself:

> (B) Let us always have this saying of Plato in our mouths: (C) "If I find a thing unsound, is it not because I myself am unsound? (B) Am I not myself at fault? May not my admonition be turned around against me?" A wise and divine refrain, which scourges the most universal and common error of mankind. (C) Not only the reproaches that we make to one another, but also our reasons and arguments in controversial matters can ordinarily be turned against ourselves; and we run ourselves through with our own weapons. . . . I do not mean that no man should criticize another unless he is clean himself, for then no one would criticize; nor indeed that he must be clean of the same sort of fault. But I mean that our judgment, laying upon another the blame which is then in question, should not spare us from judging ourselves.[147]

Montaigne admits that an indictment can always be *turned back* on itself, even as he writes, in another addition to the third book, that "my conscience is content with itself—not as the conscience of an angel or a horse, but as the conscience of a man."[148] This "reversion" of the accusation is also seen in one of the essential duties of friendship: "to admonish one another" (*monere et moneri*). It also figures in Montaigne's condemnation of excessive borrowing and citation: "To criticize my own faults in others seems to me no more inconsistent than to criticize, as I often do, others' faults in myself. We must denounce them everywhere and leave them no place of refuge."[149] Though he proudly declares that he "rarely" repents, Montaigne leaves open the possibility that he will turn against himself the accusations that he first leveled at the world. Criticism, he believes, is equitable only if it is directed both ways, inward as well as outward. The serene statement that "I rarely repent" and the vigilant exercise of internal judgment are the two components of Montaigne's inwardness. And this *inwardness* in turn takes on its true value through its complex relationship with the outer sphere, the sphere of *public* life: the inner life stands apart, but not without acknowledging that public life must be given its due, and not without awareness that its own intimate value can be achieved only through communication and externalization: "In favor of the Huguenots, who condemn our private and auricular confession, I confess myself *in public*, religiously and purely."[150] It would be impossible to give a clearer statement of the connection between subjectivity and the "outside" world, which Montaigne needs equally to oppose and to observe. The free mind is not a solitary mind. It is opposed to the world and yet it lives in the world. It is opposed to itself and yet it "broods over [its] thoughts."[151] Montaigne is undoubtedly one of those writers most responsible for fleshing out our Western notion of individual existence. But he warns us to be on our guard: the individual comes into possession of himself only through the image of himself reflected by others—all others. He must first be friend and citizen (and, for his father's sake, mayor of Bordeaux) before he can belong to himself in all his variety, in all the free flow of his language—language which, in the pages of the "ledger" first opened out of idleness, becomes action.

Notes

Chapter One

1. Montaigne, *Essais*, ed. P. Villey (Paris: Presses Universitaires de France, 1965), 2:18, p. 666. For the convenience of the reader, page references to Montaigne's *Essays* will be given not only to the Villey edition, but also to the Pléïade edition of the complete works of Montaigne prepared by Albert Thibaudet and Maurice Rat (Paris: Gallimard, 1967). Where the English translation has been used, a reference will also be given to *The Complete Works of Montaigne*, trans. Donald M. Frame (Stanford: Stanford University Press, 1957). The Thibaudet-Rat edition will be abbreviated TR, the Frame translation F. Thus the current reference would be:

2:18, 666; TR, 649; F, 505,

indicating book 2, essay 18, page 666 of the Villey edition, page 649 of the Thibaudet-Rat edition, and page 505 of the Frame translation. This format will be used throughout. Where a reference is made to something found in one of the editions but not the others, the initials will identify which edition is being referenced. Montaigne uses italics only for citations. Any other italicized words in passages from Montaigne have been italicized by me to emphasize a word or phrase that seemed relevant to the issues being discussed.

2. 3:1, 795–96; TR, 773; F, 604. Or again: "Each man labors to defend his cause—but even the best of them resort to dissimulation and lying" (3:9, 993; TR, 972; F, 760).

3. *Polycraticus* 3.8: "Comoedia est vita hominis super terram, ubi quisque sui oblitus, personam exprimit alienam. . . . Non duco contentionis funem dum constet inter nos quod fere totus mundus, juxta Petronium, exerceat histrionem." The attribution to Petronius cannot be confirmed from extant texts. Concerning the *topos* of the actor, one of the most striking and least-known examples is found in the Hippocratic treatise *Of the diet* 1.34.3. [Professor Starobinski cites the French translation of this by R. Joly (Paris, 1967), which I have rendered into English as follows: "The art of the actor deceives the spectators. They say this and think that; they enter one way and exit another. It is quite human, also, to say one thing and to do another, to be the same and not the same, to think this at one moment and that at another."] Concerning the fundamental division between being and saying, see also the classical texts cited in my study, "Je hais comme les portes d'Hades," *Nouvelle Revue de psychanalyse* 9 (Spring 1974): 7–22.

4. 3:10, 1011; TR, 989. As Pierre Villey points out, Montaigne borrowed this citation from Justus Lipsus, *De constantia* 1.8.

5. Shakespeare, *As You Like It* 2.7.138–65. Concerning the connections between the *Essays* and Shakespeare, see the excellent study by Robert Ellrodt, "Self-consciousness in Montaigne and Shakespeare," *Shakespeare Survey* 28 (1975): 37–50.

6. 3:8, 935, TR, 913; F, 714.

7. 1:9, 37; TR, 38; F, 24.

8. 1:14, 53; TR, 52; F, 35.

9. 3:10, 1013; TR, 991; F, 775. And, in the same chapter: "Not the thing but the appearance pays them" (1021: TR, 999; F, 781). The list of occurences of this theme is far from exhausted by the examples cited.

10. Cf. Jean Rousset, *La Littérature de l'âge baroque en France* (Paris, 1953). On what may link Montaigne to mannerism and the baroque, see R. A. Sayce, *The Essays of Montaigne: A Critical Exploration* (London, 1972), pp. 313–26; and I. Buffum, *Studies in the Baroque from Montaigne to Rotrou* (New Haven, 1957). The earlier work of Morris W. Croll is still important; it may be found in J. M. Patrick and R. O. Evans, eds., *Style, Rhetoric and Rhythm* (Princeton, 1966).

11. 2:17, 647; TR, 630; F, 491. A few lines further on, we also find this: "It is a craven and servile idea to disguise ourselves and hide under a mask, and not to dare to show ourselves as we are. In that way our men train for perfidy; (B) being accustomed to speak false words, they have no scruples about breaking their word."

12. 2:18, 666; TR, 649; F, 595.

13. 3:1, 795; TR, 772; F, 603.

14. Latin synonyms for *parrhesia* are *licentia* and *oratio libera*. Quintilian makes the following pertinent remark: "What is less figured than true liberty? In this guise flattery is frequently hidden, however" (*Oratory art* 9.2.27). The questions debated as late as the seventeenth century were whether *ostentatio libertatis* should be included among the figures (or *schemata*) of rhetoric and what proportion of simulation it involved.

15. As Henri Gouhier pertinently reminds us: "It is always from within an ideology that one casts discredit upon ideology." See his "L'idéologie et les idéologies," in E. Castelli, ed., *Démystification et idéologie* (Paris, 1973), p. 89.

16. 3:5, 846; TR, 823; F, 642.

17. 3:5, 845; TR, 822; F, 642.

18. 3:12, 1061; TR, 1039.

19. 3:10, 1011; TR, 989; F, 773.

20. 1:50, 303; TR, 291; F, 220–21.

21. In the *Letters* (Hippocratic apocrypha), Democritus explains to his visitor from Cos: "I am writing about madness. . . . What would I write about other . . . than its nature, its causes, and the means of treating it? The animals that you see opened up, I have opened . . . because I am seeking to discover the nature and seat of the bile; for as you know, it is usually, when it is superabundant, the cause of madness." Hippocrates, *Oeuvres complètes*, trans. E. Littré (Paris, 1861), 9:355. Later (p. 375), after apostrophizing Hippocrates, Democritus expresses his desire to lift all veils, in much the same

voyeuristic manner as Asmodée will actually accomplish in Lesage's *Le Diable boiteux:* "Would that I had the power to uncover every house, to sweep away the veils that cover the things within, and to see what goes in within those walls."

22. *Hamlet* 2.2.554.

23. Sigmund Freud, "Trauer und Melancholie," *Gesammelte Werke* (London, 1946), 10:432.

24. 3:9, 961; TR, 938; F, 734.

25. 2:18, 666; TR, 649; F, 505.

26. On this point see Michael Baraz's discussion in the first part of his important work, *L'être et la connaissance selon Montaigne* (Paris, 1968).

27. 3:9, 973; TR, 951.

28. For the full Latin text, see the Villey edition of the *Essais*, p. xxxiv (French translation on p. xxxi) or the Thibaudet-Rat edition, p. xvi. In English: "In the year of Christ 1571, at the age of thirty-eight years, on the eve of the calends of March, the anniversary of his birth, Michel de Montaigne, long since disgusted with the slavery of the court of *parlement,* and still feeling fit, came away to repose on the breast of the learned virgins in calm and security; there he will pass the days that he has left to live. Hoping that destiny will allow him to perfect this residence, this sweet paternal retirement, he has consecrated them to his freedom, his tranquillity, and his leisure."

29. 2:3, 828; TR, 806–7; F, 629.

30. 2:8, 401; TR, 383; F, 293.

31. Hugo Friedrich, *Montaigne* (Berne, 1949), pp. 22–23 (pp. 21–23 of the French translation by R. Rovini (Paris, 1968)). This work remains the best general study of Montaigne's thought and art.

32. The largely conjectural Latin text of the second inscription is here translated into English based on the French translation in the Thibaudet edition: "Deprived of the sweetest, dearest, and most intimate friend, the best, most learned, and most perfect friend our century has seen, Michel de Montaigne, wishing to consecrate the memory of this mutual love with a unique token of his gratitude, and unable to express it in any better way, has dedicated to that memory this studious work that is his delight."

33. Montaigne explains himself in the first paragraph of the chapter "Of friendship" (1:28).

34. 1:39, 241; TR, 235–36; F, 177–78.

35. See the opening pages of my *Jean-Jacques Rousseau: la transparence et l'obstacle* (Paris, 1957). Revised version published by Gallimard.

36. 1:3, 15; TR, 18; F, 8.

37. 3:2, 814–15; TR, 793; F, 710–11.

38. 3:4, 834; TR, 812, F, 633: "Our thoughts are always *elsewhere.*" If there is a synthetic term in Montaigne's writing, it is the adverb "elsewhere," which derives its force from its indeterminancy. Its locative value allows it to signify all our dislocations.

39. 2:12, 549; TR, 531; F, 411.

40. 1:39, 241; TR, 235; F, 177.

41. I am referring here to a moral doctrine that combines features from various schools and that was given wide currency in the diatribe. See André Oltramare, *Les Origines de la diatribe romaine* (Geneva, 1926).

42. 1:39, 239; TR, 234; F, 176.

43. 1:39, 245; TR, 239–40; F, 208.

44. 1:39, 246; TR, 241; F, 182.

45. 3:13, 1115; TR, 1096; F, 856.

46. In the chapter "Of solitude," an addendum to the Bordeaux manuscript sets forth the principles of a division of life between activity and solitude: "Solitude seems to me more appropriate and reasonable for those who have given to the world their most active and flourishing years, following the example of Thales" (1:39, 242; TR, 236; F, 178).

47. Friedrich, *Montaigne*, p. 19 and *passim*; French translation, p. 19.

48. 1:26, 158; TR, 157–58; F, 117. Cf. Joachim Ritter, "Die Lehre vom Ursprung und Sinn der Theorie bei Aristoteles," *Metaphysik und Politik* (Frankfurt, 1977); Hans Blumenberg, *Schiffbruch mit Zuschauer* (Frankfurt, 1979).

49. 3:12, 1046; TR, 1023; F, 800.

50. 1:39, pp. 247–48; TR, 242; F, 183. Concerning the "pragmatic" function of the exemplum, see Karlheinz Stierle, "L'histoire comme exemple; l'exemple comme histoire," *Poétique* 10 (1972): 176–98. The Latin citation is from Cicero, *Tusculan Disputations* 2.22.

51. 2:17, 659; TR, 643; F, 500.

52. Albert Thibaudet, *Montaigne* (Paris, 1963), p. 62. Michel Butor, *Essai sur les Essais* (Paris, 1968), pp. 42–44.

53. Friedrich, *Montaigne*, chap. 4. Stierle, "L'histoire comme exemple."

54. 1:21, 105; TR, 104; F, 75. In most of the texts of the last period, including the one cited here, Montaigne casts doubt on the factual truth of the exemplary event. Only the moral reflection for which the alleged event serves as pretext has any validity: "Fabulous testimonies, provided they are possible, serve like true ones" (ibid.).

55. 3:13, 1070; TR, 1047; F, 819. The chapter "Of experience" (3:13) is primarily a sustained reflection upon the notion of *exemplum*.

56. 3:13, 1079; TR, 1056; F, 826.

57. 1:39, 247; TR, 242; F, 182.

58. 1:8, 33; TR, 34; F, 21. The Latin citation is from Lucan: "Ever idle hours breed wandering thoughts" (*Pharsalius* 4.704).

59. 2:8, 385; TR, 364; F, 278.

60. See Owsei Temkin, *Galenism* (Cornell: Cornell University Press, 1973). The subject will be treated more fully in chapter 4.

61. See R. Kilibansky, E. Panofsky, and F. Saxl, *Saturn and Melancholy* (Nelson, 1964). Cf. 2:8, 392; TR, 372.

62. 2:27, 784; TR, 764; F, 596.

63. 2:12, 492; TR, 472; F, 363.

64. 2:8, 385; TR, 364; F, 278.

65. 2:18, 665; TR, 648; F, 504.

66. 2:17, 641; TR, 624; F, 487. Elsewhere Montaigne says: "I am by nature not melancholy but dreamy," 1:20, 87; TR, 85; F, 60.

67. 2:12, 566; TR, 549; F, 425.

68. 2:9, 964; TR, 941; F, 736.

69. 1:39, 248; TR, 242; F, 183.

70. 1:39, 247–48; TR, 242; F, 183.

71. 3:9, 981; TR, 959; F, 749–50. A little earlier in the same essay we find: "I feel this unexpected profit from the publication of my behavior, that to some extent it serves me as a rule."

72. 2:6, 378; TR, 358; F, 273. This passage is part of a concluding section belatedly added to the essay "Of exercise." The 1580 text excluded *"autrui"* (others): "This is not the lesson of others, it is my own." The ultimate addition reintroduces the *"other"*: "What serves me may by accident serve another."

73. 2:8, 400–402; TR, 380–83; F, 291–93.

74. 3:9, 983; TR, 961; F, 751. The presence of the verb *démentir* (to give the lie), which is so important in this passage, suggests that we reread 2:18, "Du Démentir" ("Of giving the lie").

75. 2:37, 784; TR, 764–65; F, 596.

76. Pascal, *Pensées* (Paris: Sellier, 1976), p. 322.

77. 3:2, 805; TR, 782; F, 611.

78. 3:9, 982; TR, 960–61; F, 751.

79. 3:1, 790; TR, 767; F, 599.

80. 3:9, 983n.4; TR, 961n.3; F, 752n.14 (1588 text). Thibaudet offers some very penetrating remarks on the role of La Boétie and his memory in *Montaigne* (Paris, 1963) 52–54 and 142–53. Maurice Merleau-Ponty goes straight to the essential point: "It is clear that Montaigne's friendship with La Boétie, far from being an accident of his life, was what gave life to the author of the *Essais*, and that for him, to exist was to exist in the eyes of his friend" ("Lecture de Montaigne," *Signes* [Paris, 1960], p. 262). Cf. M. Butor, *Essai sur les Essais*, and R. L. Regosin, *The Matter of My Book: Montaigne's "Essais" as the Book of the Self* (Berkeley, 1977), 7–29.

81. 1:28, 193; TR, 192; F, 143.

82. *Journal de Voyage*, TR, 1270; F, 989.

83. 2:8, 396n.1; TR, 376n.1; F 286n.3.

84. 1:28, 188; TR, 187; F, 139. Worthy of note here are the equal syllabic quantities and parallel syntactic structures (*isocola*) that form an alexandrine divided exactly in the center by the caesura! The almost twinlike quality of the pair of friends received this emblematic expression only in a rather late edition (1595).

85. TR, 1360; F, 1056.

86. TR, 1360–61; F, 1056.

87. 2:12, 439–40; TR, 416; F, 320.

88. 2:12, 439; TR, 416; F, 320.

89. 3:9, 951; TR, 928; F, 726.

90. On the book as substitute for a male heir, cf. Antoine Compagnon, *Nous, Michel de Montaigne* (Paris, 1980), pp. 194ff.

91. TR, 1361–62; F, 1057.

92. TR, 1364; F, 1059.

93. TR, 1365; F, 1060.

94. Ibid.

95. 1:50, 303; TR, 291; F, 220.

96. TR, 1364; F, 1059.

97. Ibid.

98. TR, 1350; F, 1048: "And then, my brother, perhaps I was not born so useless as not to have the means of doing some service to the commonwealth."

99. TR, 1364; F, 1059.

100. TR, 1365; F, 1060.

101. TR, 1366; F, 1061–62.

102. TR, 1368; F, 1063.

103. TR, 1368–69; F, 1063–64.

104. TR, 1369; F, 1064.

105. Ibid.

106. Ibid.

107. TR, 1370; F, 1065.

108. TR, 1371; F, 1065.

109. Ibid.; F, 1066.

110. TR, 1359–60; F, 1055–56.

111. 1:18, 183; TR, 181–82; F, 135.

112. 3:10, 983; TR, 961; F, 752.

113. 1:28, 189; TR, 187; F, 139. Total opening of one's heart or insides, without dissimulation, was from the beginning a part of the *topos* of perfect friendship: *"Quid in amicitia fieri oportet, quae tota veritate perpenditur? in qua nisi, ut dicitur, apertum pectus videas tuumque ostendas, nihil fidum, nihil exploratum habeas; ne amare quidem aut amari, quum, id quam vere fiat, ignores."* In translation this reads: "What must take place in friendship, which rests entirely on truth? If your soul does not show itself naked, as it is said, if you do not read into that of your friend, there is no longer confidence, no longer abandon. You love no longer, you are no longer loved, once you cease to know what is going on in the depths of the heart" (Cicero, *De amicitia* 26). But it is even more to the Neoplatonic philosophy of love that this text refers. Cf. Marsilio Ficino, *Commentary on Plato's Symposium* 2.8.

114. Jean-Jacques Rousseau, *Du contrat social*, book 1, chap. 6 (*Oeuvres complètes*, vol. 3 of the Pléiade edition [Paris, 1964], p. 361).

115. In *La Nouvelle Héloïse*, the society of noble souls marks the intermediate stage between friendship *à deux* and popular sovereignty. The concepts used by Rousseau to define the society of contract are *liberty* and *equality*. The re-

publican motto, which adds to these *fraternity,* gives prominence to a notion that the Rousseauist theory of popular sovereignty "repressed" or contained in a latent form. The contract theory was formulated as a specimen of pure reasoning without an emotional component. But the *gift* of oneself at the crucial moment indicates clearly enough that friendship was taken for a model—and "generalized."

116. 1:28, 190; TR, 189; F, 141.

117. 1:28, 191; TR, 190; F, 141.

118. 1:27, 189; TR, 188; F, 140.

119. Ibid.; F, 140–41.

120. Ibid.; F, 140.

121. 1:28, 189–90; TR, 188; F, 140.

122. 1:28, 191; TR, 190; F, 142.

123. 1:28, 193–94; TR, 192; F, 143.

124. 2:12, 553; TR, 534; F, 414: "Man is possessed by an extreme concern with prolonging his existence."

125. 3:9, 983; TR, 961; F, 752.

126. 3:9, 977; TR, 955; F, 746–47. Somewhat earlier in the same essay we read: "I know that friendship has arms long enough to hold and join from one end of the world to the other; and especially this kind, in which there is a continual interchange of services that reawaken the bond and memory of it. The Stoics indeed say that there is so great a tie and fellowship between the sages that one who dines in France feeds his comrade in Egypt. . . . Count up your daily musings, and you will find that you are most absent from your friend when he is in your company; his presence relaxes your attention and gives your thoughts liberty to absent themselves at any time and for any reason" (3:9, 975; TR, 953; F, 745).

127. "I know well that I will leave behind no sponsor anywhere near as affectionate and understanding about me as I was about him. There is no one to whom I would be willing to entrust myself fully for a portrait" (1588 text: 3:9, 983; TR, 960; F, 752n.14). A psychoanalyst would say that La Boétie had become an "internal object." Cf. Masud Khan, "Montaigne, Rousseau, and Freud," *Le Soi caché,* trans. C. Monod (Paris, 1976), p. 137.

128. "To the reader," 3; TR, 9; F, 2.

129. 1:28, 184; TR, 182; F, 135.

130. Ibid.; F, 136.

131. 2:6, 380; TR, 360; F, 274.

132. 2:8, 396; TR, 376; F, 287.

133. 3:9, 996; TR, 975; F, 763.

134. 1:28, 184; TR, 182; F, 136.

135. La Boétie, *Oeuvres complètes* (Paris, 1892), pp. 53–54. The theme is treated by Cicero in chapters 15 and 24 of *De amicitia.* On this point of the *Contr'un,* see the essay by Claude Lefort, "Le nom d'Un," in La Boétie, *Le Discours de la servitude volontaire* (Paris, 1976), pp. 247–307.

136. TR, 1352. In the *Discours* La Boétie speaks of friendship as a "sacred

thing," and Montaigne, in the dedicatory letter to Michel de L'Hospital, describes La Boétie as the person with whom he "practiced" the rights and duties of "sacred friendship." No doubt this is a standard formula, but Montaigne's insistence is significant.

137. Cicero, *De amicitia* 25.

138. La Boétie, *Oeuvres complètes*, p. 235.

139. 1:28, 185; TR, 183–84; F, 137.

140. TR, 1347–48; F, 1046.

141. 1:28, 189; TR, 188; F, 140.

142. La Boétie, *Oeuvres complètes*, p. 225 ll. 10–11.

143. 1:28, 184; TR, 182; F, 136.

144. 1:28, 189; TR, 187; F, 139.

145. 1:28, 192; TR, 191–92; F, 143.

146. 1:28, 194; TR, 193; F, 144.

147. 1:28, 192; TR, 191; F, 143.

148. 1:28, 190; TR, 188.

149. 1:28, 188–89; TR, 187; F, 139.

150. 1:28, 188; TR, 186; F, 139.

151. 2:17, 635; TR, 618; F, 481.

152. 3:2, 805; TR, 782; F, 611.

153. 3:12, 1055; TR, 1033; F, 808.

154. 2:17, 650; TR, 634; F, 493–49.

155. 1:10, 40; TR, 41–42; F, 26–27. And Montaigne adds: "I will have tossed off some subtle remark as I write. . . . Later I have lost the point so thoroughly that I do not know what I meant; and sometimes a stranger has discovered it before I do. If I erased every passage where this happens to me, there would be nothing left of myself."

156. La Boétie, *Oeuvres complètes*, p. 226.

157. Ibid., pp. 210–13.

158. TR, 1347. Montaigne, in return, promises La Boétie to take him as an example: "I said to him . . . that up to then I had thought that God gave us no such great power against human calamities, and I had had difficulty believing what I had come across on this subject in the histories; but that having felt such a proof of it, I praised God that this had been in a person by whom I was so loved and whom I loved so dearly; and that this would serve me as an example, to play this same part in my turn" (TR, 1353; F, 1050).

159. 3:9, 978; TR, 955; F, 747.

160. 2:17, 653–54; TR, 637; F, 496. Concerning the "scar" that Montaigne mentions here, see Philip P. Hallie, *The Scar of Montaigne* (Wesleyan University Press, 1966), pp. 130–33.

161. 3:2, 805; TR, 782; F, 611.

162. 2:29, 705; TR, 683; F, 533.

163. Ibid.

164. 1:37, 229–30; TR, 225–26; F, 169–70. The first citation is from Cicero:

"There are men who praise nothing except what they are confident they can imitate" (*Tusculan Disputations* 2.1). The second is from Horace: "They think that virtue's just a word, and a sacred grove mere sticks" (*Epistles* 7.6.31–32). The third is again from Cicero: "[Virtue] is something they should revere even if they cannot understand it" (*Tusculan Disputations* 5.2).

Chapter Two

1. 2:12, 487; TR, 467; F, 359.
2. 1:23, 117; TR, 116; F, 84.
3. 1:23, 116; TR, 115; F, 84.
4. 1:23, 117; TR, 116; F, 85.
5. 2:6, 378; TR, 358; F, 273.
6. 3:11, 1029; TR, 1006; F, 787.
7. "There is the name and the thing. . . . " Here, all of chapter 2:16, "Of glory," should be cited.
8. "We receive things in one way and another, according to what we are and what they seem to us" (2:12, 598; TR, 583; F, 452).
9. 2:12, 553; TR, 535; F, 415.
10. 1:30, 197; TR, 195; F, 146.
11. 2:13, 610; TR, 594–95; F, 462.
12. 2:11, 424–25; TR, 403; 308–9. The first citation is from Cicero, *Tusculan Disputations* 1.30. The second is from Horace, *Odes* 1.37.29.
13. 1:19, 79–80; TR, 78–79; F, 55. The citation is from Lucretius, *De natura rerum* 3.57–58.
14. 1:20, 81–96; TR, 79–95; F, 56–68.
15. 2:20, 675; TR, 656; F, 511.
16. 1:14, 51; TR, 50; F, 50. This is the famous saying, "Qui potest mori non potest cogi."
17. 1:20, 96; TR, 94; F, 68.
18. 1:20, 84; TR, 82; F, 57.
19. 1:19, 80; TR, 78–79, F. 55.
20. 1:20, 96; TR, 94; F, 67.
21. 1:20, 95; TR, 95; F, 66; and 1:14, 56; TR, 56; F, 38.
22. 1:20, 96; TR, 94; F, 68.
23. 3:12, 1051; TR, 1028; F, 804.
24. 1:19, 80; TR, 79; F, 55.
25. 2:11, 425; TR, 404; F, 308. The following celebrated passage is also worth rereading: "It seems to me that death is indeed the end, but not therefore the goal, of life; it is its finish, its extremity, but not therefore its object. Life should be an aim unto itself, a purpose unto itself; its rightful study is to regulate, conduct, and suffer itself" (3:12, 1051–52; TR, 1028–29; F, 805). As Villey remarks, this is the final riposte to the "Stoic" assertion that I cited earlier: "The aim of our career is death; it is the necessary object of our aim."
26. 2:11, 425–26; TR, 404–5; F, 310.

27. 3:12, 1055; TR, 1032; F, 867; and 3:2, 805; TR, 782; F, 611.
28. 3:12, 510; TR, 490; F, 378.
29. 2:12, 604; TR, 589; F, 457.
30. Ibid.
31. 2:12, 601; TR, 586; F, 455.
32. 2:12, 500; TR, 479–80; F, 369.
33. 2:12, 518; TR, 499; F, 385.
34. 2:12, 506; TR, 486; F, 375.
35. Ibid.
36. 2:12, 568; TR, 551; F, 427.
37. 2:12, 527; TR, 508; F, 392.
38. "We do not go; we are carried away, like floating objects, now gently, now violently, according as the water is angry or calm" (2:1, 333; TR, 316; F, 240).
39. 2:12, 601; TR, 586; F, 455.
40. 2:12, 527; TR, 508; F, 392.
41. Ibid.
42. Ibid., F, 393.
43. Cf. Marcel Raymond, "L'attitude religieuse de Montaigne," *Génies de France* (Neuchâtel, 1942), pp. 50–67. Also, cf. Richard H. Popkin, *The History of Scepticism from Erasmus to Descartes* (Assen, 1960), pp. 44–65.
44. Cf. Ernst Cassirer, *Das Erkenntnisproblem*, 3d ed (1922), reprinted by Wissenschäftliche Buchgesellschaft, Darmstadt, 1971; vol. 1, pp. 172–200. See also Leon Brunschvicg, *Descartes et Pascal lecteurs de Montaigne* (Paris and New York, 1944).
45. 2:12, 506; TR, 486; F, 374.
46. Ibid.
47. 2:12, 553; TR, 535; F, 415.
48. 2:12, 510; TR, 490; F, 378.
49. 2:12, 493; TR, 473; F, 364.
50. 2:12, 524; TR, 504; F, 389.
51. 3:12, 1057; TR, 1034; F, 809.
52. 3:13, 1107; TR, 1087; F, 849.
53. 2, 1, 332; TR, 315; F, 239.
54. Title of 1:38.
55. 1:38, 233–35; TR, 229–31; F, 272–73. The citation is from Publius Syrus.
56. 1:38, 235; TR, 231; F, 174. Cf. Rachel Bespaloff, "L'instant et la liberté chez Montaigne," *Deucalion*, 3, (Neuchâtel, 1950), pp. 65–107.
57. 1:38, 236; TR, 231; F, 174.
58. 3:13, 1076–77; TR, 1054; F, 824–25. The "arrangement into bands" is particularly striking in the "Art of Memory: cf. Frances A. Yates, *The Art of Memory* (London, 1966).
59. 2:12, 596: TR, 580–81; F, 451.
60. 3:13, 1089–90; TR, 1068.

Chapter Three

1. 3:9, 968–70; TR, 946–47; F, 740–41.
2. 3:9, 968; TR, 945; F, 739.
3. 3:9, 966; TR, 943; F, 738.
4. 3:9, 966; TR, 944; F, 738.
5. 3:9, 968; TR, 946; F, 739–40.
6. 3:9, 955; TR, 932; F, 729.
7. Ibid.
8. 3:2, 807–8; TR, 785; F, 613.
9. 3:9, 991; TR, 970; F, 758. This sentence (the final phrase of which reads, in French, "selon le temps, selon les hommes, selon les affaires"—Trans.) gives cause to reflect upon Montaigne's use of the word *selon*, as a preposition that establishes a relationship between one who wields authority or power and one who docilely carries out orders, in thought or action.
10. 1:23, 118; TR, 117; F, 86.
11. 3:10, 1021; TR, 999; F, 781; and 2:16, 629; TR, 613; F, 477.
12. 3:2, 807–8; TR, 785; F, 613.
13. 3:8, 942; TR, 921; F, 720.
14. 3:9, 963; TR, 940; F, 735.
15. 1:28, 184; TR, 182; F, 136.
16. 2:17, 631–32; TR, 614; F, 478.
17. 3:13, 1073; TR, 1050; F, 821. "We are much better if we let ourselves be led without inquisitiveness in the way of the world" (2:12, 506; TR, 486; F, 375).
18. 3:2, 805; TR, 782; F, 611.
19. 2:18, 665; TR, 648; F, 504.
20. Ibid.; TR, 647–48; F, 504.
21. 3:11, 1028; TR, 1005; F, 786.
22. 2:18, 666–67; TR, 650; F, 505.
23. 3:5, 847; TR, 824; F, 643.
24. Ibid.; F, 643–44.
25. 3:5, 845; TR, 822–23; F, 642.
26. 3:9, 980; TR, 958; F, 749.
27. 2:16, 626; TR, 610; F, 474–75.
28. 1:26, 157; TR, 156; F, 116.
29. 3:9, 973; TR, 950; F, 743.
30. Ibid.
31. 3:9, 975; TR, 953; F, 745. The same was true, as we saw earlier, in Montaigne's relationship with La Boétie.
32. 3:7, 919; TR, 897–98; F, 702. Total involvement is a precondition of plenitude: "[My soul] cannot ordinarily apply itself unless it becomes wrapped up in a thing or be employed unless with tension and with its whole being" (3:3, 809; TR, 796; F, 621).
33. 3:3, 821; TR, 799; F, 623.

34. 3:13, 1068; TR, 1045; F, 818.
35. 3:3, 820; TR, 797; F, 622.
36. 3:3, 823; TR, 801; F, 625.
37. 3:9, 986; TR, 965; F, 754.
38. 3:3, 823; TR, 801; F, 625.
39. 3:4, 834; TR, 812; F, 633.
40. The manner in which this problem is dealt with in 3:10 will be examined in chap. 7 below.
41. 3:9, 946; TR, 923; F, 722.
42. Ibid.; F, 721.
43. 2:11, 435; TR, 414; F, 318. Thibaudet, in *Montaigne* (Paris, 1963), p. 135, was fond of emphasizing the "external origins of Montaigne's inner life." See also B. Wojciehcowska Bianco, *Nel Creposcolo della coscienza: Alterità e libertà in Montaigne* (Adriatica, Lecce, 1979).
44. 1:26, 146–47; TR, 145; F, 167.
45. 1:26, 147; TR, 145; F, 107.
46. 1:26, 148; TR, 147; F, 108.
47. 1:26, 148; TR, 146; F, 108.
48. 3:12, 1055; TR, 1033; F, 808.
49. 3, 5, 874; TR, 852; F, 666.
50. "I allow myself to add, since it (i.e., my book) is only an ill-fitted patch-work, some extra ornaments" (3:9, 964; TR, 941; F, 736).
51. 3:5, 875; TR, 853; F, 667.
52. Ibid.
53. 3:5, 875; TR, 852–53; F, 666.
54. 3:12, 1055; TR, 1033; F, 808.
55. 2:10, 408; TR, 388; F, 297.
56. 1:26, 151–52; TR, 150–51. See also 1:25, 137, 140; TR, 136, 139.
57. 1:26, 152; TR, 151; F, 111–12.
58. 1:26, 152; TR, 151; F, 112.
59. 2:10, 508; TR, 387–88; F, 296–97.
60. 3:5, 880; TR, 858; F, 671.
61. Ibid.
62. 2:10, 408; TR, 387; F, 296.
63. 3:12, 1056; TR, 1034; F, 809.
64. Ibid.
65. 2:26, 147; TR, 146; F, 108.
66. 2:17, 658; TR, 641–42; F, 499.
67. 2:18, 666; TR, 648–49; F, 505.
68. 3:12, 1055; TR, 1033; F, 808.
69. 3:9, 964; TR, 941; F, 736.
70. 1:26, 175; TR, 175; F, 130.
71. 1:26, 173; TR, 172–73; F, 128.
72. 1:26, 173; TR, 173; F, 128–29.
73. 1:26, 174; TR, 174; F, 129.

74. 1:26, 175; TR, 175; F, 130.
75. Ibid.
76. Ibid.
77. Ibid.
78. 1:26, 176; TR, 176; F, 131.
79. 1:26, 148; TR, 146; F, 108.
80. 1:26, 146; TR, 144; F, 107.
81. 1:25, 136; TR, 135; F, 100.
82. 1:14, 62; TR, 63; F, 43.
83. Ibid.
84. 1:14, 64; TR, 64–65; F, 44.
85. 1:14, 65; TR, 66–67; F, 45–46. At the end of essay 1:26 Montaigne speaks in this vein about "laziness" (*paresse*). See 1:26, 175–76; TR, 175–76; F, 130–31.
86. 3:6, 898ff.; TR, 876ff. This chapter has been much commented upon, in particular by Marcel Raymond, "Montaigne devant les sauvages d'Amerique," *Etre et dire* (Neuchâtel, 1970), pp. 13–37, and Etiemble, "Sens et structure d'un essai de Montaigne," *C'est le bouquet!* (Paris, 1967), pp. 101–15.
87. 3:6, 901; TR, 878; F, 687.
88. 3:6, 912; TR, 891; F, 696.
89. 3:9, 975; TR, 953; F, 745.
90. 2:12, 488; TR, 467. See also 2:16, 619; TR, 602.
91. 2:12, 520; TR, 501; F, 387.
92. 3:10, 1005; TR, 982; F, 768. "For my part I commend a gliding, obscure, and quiet life" (3:10, 1021; TR, 999; F, 782).
93. 3:9, 988; TR, 967; F, 756.
94. 3:2, 806; TR, 784; F, 612.
95. 2:12, 604; TR, 589; F, 457.
96. Ibid.
97. 3:9, 945–46; TR, 922; F, 721.
98. 3:2, 790; TR, 767; F, 599.
99. 3:13, 1088; TR, 1066; F, 834.
100. Montaigne's commentators, carried away by this ternary rhythm, have had a penchant for seeing three philosophical stages in his work: a stoic phase, a skeptical phase, and finally a "personal" phase.
101. By Antoine Compagnon, *Nous, Michel de Montaigne* (Paris, 1980), pp. 38–39.
102. Without raising again the question of the "three sorts of situation"—i.e., the three attitudes toward money—that Montaigne describes in 1:14 ("That the taste of good and evil depends in large part on the opinion we have of them"), it is clear that the succession of three stages—the endurance of dependence, the desire for independence, and finally acceptance of dependence (which, because it is accepted calmly and deliberately, ceases to be experienced as subjugation), is a pattern that recurs in various areas of Montaigne's life. It is not the only ternary pattern we find, however. Besides tem-

poral successions of three *moments,* we also find static classifications consisting of three *categories.*

103. 2:12, 502; TR, 482; F, 371.

104. 2:12, 506; TR, 486; F, 375.

105. Ibid.

106. 2:12, 558; TR, 540.

107. Villey, in his edition of the *Essays* (p. 438), ascribes broader scope to the preamble, which he sees as containing the responses to both objections. But he sees the remainder of the text as divided into three parts (vanity of man; vanity of knowledge; vanity of reason) followed by a conclusion.

108. 2:12, 604; TR, 588–89; F, 457.

109. Ibid.

110. Socrates is described as follows: "(A) In the movement of his virtue I cannot imagine any difficulty or any constraint. I know his reason to be so powerful and so much the master in him that it would never so much as let a vicious appetite be born" (2:11, 423–24; TR, 402; F, 308).

In the essay "Of physiognomy" (3:12, 1058; TR, 1035; F, 810), Montaigne challenges (in an insertion that appears in the 1595 edition) the *topos* according to which Socrates' ugliness as indicative of a wicked nature that the philosopher was able to correct "through training": "So excellent a soul was never self-made." But Montaigne himself introduced this *topos* into the essay "Of cruelty" (2:11, 429; TR, 408; F, 313): "Socrates admitted to those who recognized in his face some inclination to vice that that was in truth his natural propensity, but that he had corrected it by discipline."

111. 2:11, 424; TR, 402; F, 308.

112. 2:11, 426; TR, 405; F, 310.

113. 2:11, 423; TR, 402; F, 308.

114. 2:11, 427; TR, 406; F, 311.

115. 2:11, 428; TR, 407; F, 311.

116. 2:11, 429; TR, 408; F, 313.

117. In fact, the essay began with a dichotomy: "It seems to me that virtue is something other and nobler than the inclinations toward goodness that are born in us." After a lengthy introductory paragraph the example of Socrates is introduced to justify the final division into three categories.

If goodness (as opposed to virtue) is a property of "naturally regulated and wellborn" souls, is it reasonable to persist in ascribing to such souls an "accidental and fortuitous . . . innocence"? Doesn't scholastic terminology permit us to call the qualities of a wellborn soul *essential* qualities? Montaigne himself seems to have found this idea attractive. An insertion in the Bordeaux manuscript reads as follows: "Might it be that to be good in fact we must be good by virtue of some occult, natural, and *universal* property, without law, without reason, without example, as by an inexplicable quintessence of our natural being?" But Montaigne seems later to have regretted invoking this "quintessence." He deleted the final phrase in the 1595 edition, where the sentence ends "without example." (See the "Municipal Edition," vol. 2, Bordeaux, 1909, pp. 128–29.) The *property* alleged here is closely connected with the "natural and *universal*" character of the individual, as is the name Michel de Montaigne under which the author of the *Essays* intends to convey his "*universal* being." If it is "good," it is as a physical object might be good, a production of nature, and not as the result of an art developed through "long practice." The "occult property" to which Montaigne refers is analogous to the occult properties of certain plants, stones, drugs, etc. It is in no sense the product of the soul's labors.

118. Rousseau would later make extensive use of the opposition between innocence and virtue. See, in particular, the second *Dialogue*, where he paints the portrait of Jean-Jacques: "Our man will not be virtuous because he will be weak, and virtue is a property only of strong souls" (*Oeuvres complètes*, Paris: Gallimard, 1959), 1:624.

119. 2:11, 428; TR, 407; F, 312.

120. Ibid.

121. 2:11, 428; TR, 407–8; F, 312.

122. 2:11, 424; TR, 402–3; F, 308.

123. 2:11, 429–30; TR, 408–10; F, 313–14. I shall have more to say in chap. 7 about the significance of sympathy in Montaigne's thought. It will then emerge that sympathy plays a part in his political choices.

124. 2:17, 657; TR, 640–41; F, 498.

125. 3:3, 829; TR, 807; F, 629.

126. Ibid.

127. Ibid.

128. Thibaudet, *Montaigne*, p. 79. For Thibaudet (p. 61), "the *Essays* represent . . . [Montaigne's] *third* attitude, one that he adopts after two failures." He fails twice in the active live "in order to know himself, to filter himself, to develop himself."

129. 3:3, 828; TR, 807; F, 629.

Chapter Four

1. 3:8, 924; TR, 902; F, 705.

2. 2:17, 649; TR, 632; F, 492.

3. 3:5, 846; TR, 824; F, 643.

4. 3:5, 847; TR, 825; F, 644.

5. 3:5, 888; TR, 866; F, 677.

6. 3:5, 877; TR, 855; F, 669.

7. Thibaudet, *Montaigne*, p. 162.

8. 1:3, 18–19; TR, 22; F, 11.

9. 2:15, 614; TR, 598; F, 465.

10. 2:15, 612–13; TR, 596; F, 464–65. The same argument occurs in 3:5, 854; TR, 831; F, 649: "The liberality of the ladies is too profuse in marriage, and blunts the point of affection and desire." I shall come back to this subject in the next chapter.

11. See, among others, Hippocrates, *L'Ancienne Médecine*, trans. A.-J. Festugière (Paris, 1948); Louis Bourgey, *Observation et expérience chez les médecins de la collection hippocratique* (Paris, 1953); Ludwig Edelstein, "Empiricism and Skepticism in the Teaching of the Greek Empiricist School," in Owsei and Lilian C. Temkin, eds., *Ancient Medicine* (Baltimore, 1967), pp. 195–203.

12. 3:12, 556; TR, 538; F, 417.

13. Recall the tremendous importance of *prognosis* in Hippocratic thought and the entire subsequent tradition. Ludwig Edelstein has written a fine essay on the subject, "Hippocratic Prognosis," in Temkin and Temkin, eds., *Ancient Medicine*, pp. 65–85. Montaigne attempts to show that it is dangerously illusory both to predict the consequences of a disease and to seek to trace its causes.

14. 2:37, 764; TR, 742; F, 579.

15. 2:37, 764; TR, 742–43; F, 579.

16. 2:37, 760; TR, 738–39; F, 575–76.

17. 3:13, 1073; TR, 1051; F, 822.

18. 2:37, 770; TR, 749; F, 584.

19. 2:37, 760–61; TR, 739; F, 576–77.

20. 2:37, 761n.2; TR, 739 and n. 2; F, 576. This passage was published during Montaigne's lifetime.

21. 2:37, 762; TR, 740; F, 577.

22. 2:37, 773; TR, 752–53; F, 586.

23. See the excellent study by Owsei Temkin, "Health and Disease," in *The Double Face of Janus* (Baltimore, 1977), pp. 419–40. On Renaissance medicine, see Charles Sherrington, *The Endeavour of Jean Fernel* (Cambridge, England, 1946); for a more general account, see Pedro Lain Entralgo, "La medicine del renacimento," in *Historia de la Medicine moderna y contemporanea* (Barcelona, 1963), pp. 5–116; Pedro Lain Entralgo, ed., *Historia Universal de la Medicina*, 7 vols. (Barcelona, 1973), 4:1–189; and Allen G. Debus, *Man and Nature in the Renaissance* (Cambridge, 1978).

24. Ambroise Paré, *Les Oeuvres* (1561), book 1 of the introduction to surgery, chap. 25: "Des indications." The cited passage is taken from the eighth edition (Paris, 1628), p. 40.

25. Ibid.

26. Ibid.

27. 3:13, 1087; TR, 1065; F, 833.

28. 2:37, 781–82; TR, 761–62; F, 594.

29. 2:37, 782; TR, 762; F, 594.

30. Ibid.

31. Gustave Lanson, *Les Essais de Montaigne* (Paris, undated), pp. 278–81.

32. 2:37, 782; TR, 762; F, 594.

33. 2:37, 782; TR, 762–63; F, 594–95.

34. 2:37, 782–83; TR, 763; F, 595.

35. 2:37, 764; TR, 742; F, 579.

36. 3:13, 1065; TR, 1041; F, 815.

37. 3:13, 1073–74; TR, 1051; F, 822.

38. 3:13, 1081; TR, 1059; F, 828.

39. 2:37, 782; TR, 763; F, 595.

40. 3:13, 1079; TR, 1056; F, 826.

41. 3:2, 805; TR, 782; F, 611.

42. "The scholars distinguish and mark off their ideas *more specifically* and in detail. I, who cannot see beyond what I have learned from experience, without any system, present my ideas *in a general way*, and tentatively" (3:13, 1076; TR, 1054; F, 824).

43. 3:13, 1072–73; TR, 1050; F, 821.

44. 3:13, 1095; TR, 1074; F, 840.

45. 3:13, 1075; TR, 1052.

46. 3:13, 1076; TR, 1054.

47. 3:13, 1077–78; TR, 1055.

48. 3:13, 1079; TR, 1056; F, 826.

49. 3:13, 1114; TR, 1094; F, 855.

50. 3:13, 1107; TR, 1087; F, 850.

51. 2:17, 639; TR, 622; F, 484.

52. 2:17, 640–42; TR, 623–25; F, 484–86.

53. 2:17, 642–59; TR, 627–43; F, 487–500.

54. 2:17, 642–43; TR, 625–62; F, 487.

55. 3:13, 1077; TR, 1055; F, 825. It is a question of a friendly favor. On Montaigne's refusal to be a flatterer of princes, see my "Sur la flatterie," *Nouvelle Revue de psychanalyse* 4 (Fall 1971): 131–51.

56. 2:6, 379; TR, 359; F, 274.

57. 3:8, 943; TR, 922, F, 827. Bodily consciousness in Montaigne is carefully examined in Glyn P. Norton, *Montaigne and the Introspective Mind* (Mouton, 1975), pp. 153–70.

58. 3:13, 1079; TR, 1057. Cf. W. G. Moore, "Montaigne's Notion of Experience," in *The French Mind: Studies in Honour of Gustave Rudler* (Oxford, 1952), pp. 34–52; M. Baraz, "Sur la structure d'un essai de Montaigne (3:13, 'De l'experience')," *Bibliothèque d'Humanisme et Renaissance* 13 (Geneva, 1961): 265–81; J. Brody, "From Teeth to Text in 'De l'experience,' A Philological Reading," *L'Esprit Créateur* 20, no. 1 (Spring 1980): 7–22.

59. 2:6, 379; TR, 359; F, 274.

60. 3:13, 1079; TR, 1056–57; F, 826–27. This argument is one that medical writers have sought to refute ever since the beginnings of medical science in Greece, seeking thereby to establish the superior powers of the health specialist. An important part of the Hippocratic treatise *On Ancient Medicine* is devoted to this purpose. Neither individual experience nor even wisdom is as certain as a *technē*. Only the physician, who has compared large numbers of cases, is able to draw inferences from the similarities and differences and to identify the substances that make up the human body. Medicine is reasoned experience, *tribe meta logou*. Socrates, in the *Phaedrus* (270b–270e), praises the Hippocratic method.

61. 1:31, 207; TR, 205; F, 153. Rousseau develops these ideas in the first part of the *Discours de l'inégalité* and in book 1 of *Emile*.

62. 2:12, 491; TR, 470–71; F, 362.

63. 2:37, 767; TR, 745. On these ideas, see A. O. Lovejoy and G. Boas, *Primitivism and Related Ideas in Antiquity* (Baltimore, 1935; New York, 1965).

64. 2:37, 772; TR, 751; F, 586. Scholars themselves were fond of noting contradictions between different medical treatises. Cf. Jerome Cardan, *Contradicentium Medicorum libri duo* (Paris, 1564–65).

65. Marcel Raymond, *Jean-Jacques Rousseau: la quête de soi et la rêverie* (Paris, 1962), p. 10.

66. Cf. Walter Pagel, *Paracelsus* (Basel–New York, 1958), especially the second part, devoted to the philosophy of Paracelsus; and Allen G. Debus, *The Chemical Philosophy: Paracelsian Science and Medicine in the Sixteenth and Seventeenth Centuries* (New York, 1977).

67. The most prominent document in this regard is probably Diderot's *Le Rêve de d'Alembert*.

68. 3:13, 1079; TR, 1056; F, 827.

69. 3:13, 1080; TR, 1057; F, 827.

70. 3:13, 1080; TR, 1057; F, 827. Note that here Montaigne writes *souvenance* rather than *mémoire*. [In view of this distinction, I have translated the former as "remembrance" and the latter as "memory" throughout this section—Trans.] This is not by chance. Montaigne generally associates "memory" with what is learned from books, hence he needs another word to refer to personal reminiscences. On this point, see Michel Beaujour, *Miroirs d'encre* (Paris, 1980), pp. 113–31.

71. Paré, *Les Oeuvres*, book 1 of the introduction to surgery, chap. 17, p. 29.

72. 3:2, pp. 816–17; TR, 795–96; F, 620–21.

73. Paré, *Les Oeuvres*, chap. 15, p. 26. Fernel, for his part, speaks of necessary causes ("quae necessario nobis ferendae sunt, et sine quibus vivere non liceat"), *Universa Medicina* (1567), "Pathologia," 1.12.

74. Paré, *Les Oeuvres*, chap. 17, p. 29. The ancient source is Hippocrates, *Aphorisms* 2.50. "Custom, second nature" is an expression that goes back at least as far as Cicero, *De finibus* 5.25.74 ("consuetudine quasi alteram quandam naturam effici"). But the idea is already clearly expressed by Aristotle in his *Rhetoric* (1.11.1). Pascal would later put it more dramatically: "Custom is a second nature, which destroys the first."

75. 3:13, 1080; TR, 1057–58; F, 827.

76. In the chapter "Of husbanding your will" (3:10) Montaigne makes this point even more explicitly: "If what Nature flatly and originally demands of us for the preservation of our being is too little . . . then let us grant ourselves something further: let us also call the habits and condition of each of us *nature*; let us rate and treat ourselves according to this measure, let us stretch our appurtenances and our accounts that far. For in going thus far we certainly seem to me to have some justification. Habit is a second nature, and no less powerful. (C) What my habit lacks, I hold that I lack" (F, 772). Custom

becomes acceptable, but only by virtue of an appropriation that makes it cease to be an alien influence. It becomes "my own," my "appurtenance."

77. 3:13, 1083–84; TR, 1061–62; F, 830–31.

78. Paré, *Les Oeuvres,* chap 17, p. 29.

79. 3:13, 1085; TR, 1063; F, 832.

80. 2:37, 773; TR, 752–53; F, 586.

81. 2:37, 763; TR, 741; F, 578. Fernel writes: "Quocumque enim morbo quum generat tenetur, eum semine transfert in prolem" *Universa Medicina* (1567), "Pathologia," 1.

82. 3:13, 1088; TR, 1066; F, 834. Montaigne is here borrowing, as Villey has pointed out, an idea put forward by Plato in the *Timaeus* (896): "Diseases unless they are very dangerous, should not be irritated by medicines, since every form of disease is in a manner akin to the living being, whose complex frame has an appointed term of life."

83. Ibid.

84. 3:13, 1084; TR, 1062; F, 831.

85. 3:13, 1104–5; TR, 1084; F, 848.

86. 3:9, 994; TR, 973; F, 761.

87. 3:13, 1085; TR, 1064; F, 832.

88. According to the medical system, sexuality can be classified either as one of the "appetites" or, more trivially, as one of the *excreta,* or again as one of the "passions of the soul." I shall say more about this when I come to examine 3:5, "On some verses of Virgil," which is entirely devoted to the memory of love. In "Of experience," Montaigne discusses his sexual life in the course of an argument intended to prove that anything that is the object of a desire, whether food or amorous gratification, could not possibly be harmful to the body. It is worth noting that the most indiscreet confessions are couched in Latin citations inserted into a lengthy sentence (1086: TR, 1064). The same is true of 3:5, as we shall see later.

89. 3:13, 1099; TR, 1078; F, 843.

90. 3:13, 1100; TR, 1080; F, 844.

91. 3:13, 1102; TR, 1082; F, 846.

92. 3:13, 1103; TR, 1082–83; F, 846.

93. 3:13, 1103; TR, 1083; F, 847.

94. 3:13, 1104; TR, 1084; F, 847.

95. 3:13, 1104; TR, 1084; F, 848.

96. 3:13, 1087–88; TR, 1065–66; F, 834.

97. 3:13, 1095; TR, 1074; F, 840.

98. 3:13, 1096; TR, 1075; F, 841.

99. 3:13, 1096; TR, 1075; F, 840–41.

100. 3:13, 1105; TR, 1085; F, 848.

101. 3:13, 1105; TR, 1085; F, 848.

102. 3:13, 1105–6; TR, 1085–86; F, 848–49.

103. 3:13, 1106; TR, 1086; F, 849.

104. 3:13, 1097; TR, 1076; F, 842.

105. 3:13, 1097–98; TR, 1077; F, 842.

106. 3:12, 1058–59; TR, 1036; F, 835–36.

107. 3:13, 1085; TR, 1063; F, 831.

108. As we shall see later, the activity of recording, by which the *Essays* are put together, occasionally partakes of the excremental metaphor. This is a rhetorical device associated with *humilitas*.

109. 3:13, 1089; TR, 1067–68; F, 835.

110. 3:13, 1090; TR, 1068; F, 835–36.

111. Ibid. The citation that Montaigne addresses to himself occupies pages 1090–95 of the Villey edition (TR, 1068–75; F, 836–40).

112. 3:13, 1091; TR, 1069; F, 836–37.

113. 3:13, 1092; TR, 1071; F, 837.

114. 3:13, 1095; TR, 1073; F, 839.

115. 3:13, 1092; TR, 1071; F, 837.

116. Ibid.; F, 838. This "paper memory" is present in almost every page of the *Journal du voyage*. Montaigne there records what he drinks, what he urinates, the gravel that he eliminates, etc.

117. 3:13, 1093; TR, 1071; F, 838.

118. 3:13, 1095; TR, 1071–72; F, 838.

119. 3:13, 1075–76; TR, 1053; F, 824.

120. 3:13, 1094–95; TR, 1072–73; F, 839.

121. 3:13, 1095; TR, 1073–74; F, 839–40.

122. 3:13, 1095; TR, 1074; F, 840.

123. 3:5, 946; TR, 875; F, 721. The comparison was suggested by Terence Cave, *The Cornucopian Text* (Oxford, 1979), pp. 293–94.

124. 2:6, 374; TR, 354; F, 270. Concerning this impression of "sweetness," see the remarks of Michael Baraz, "L'integrité de l'homme selon Montaigne," in *O un Ami: Essay on Montaigne in Honor of Donald M. Frame*, R. C. La Charité, ed. (Lexington, Kentucky, 1977), pp. 20–21.

125. 2:6, 374; TR, 354; F, 269.

126. 2:6, 377; TR, 357; F, 272.

127. See François Rigolot, "Le langage des *Essais*, référentiel ou mimologique?" in *Cahiers de l'Association internationale des études françaises* 33 (May 1981): 19–34.

128. 3:13, 1091; TR, 1069; F, 836.

129. Ibid.

130. 3:9, 997; TR, 957; 748.

131. 3:13, 1091; TR, 1069; F, 836.

132. Ibid.; F, 837. The prosopopoeia of "mind" should be compared with the prosopopoeia of Nature in 1:20, 92–96; TR, 91–94.

Chapter Five

1. 1:28, 186; TR, 184; F, 137.

2. 3:5, 841; TR, 818; F, 638–39. Unless otherwise indicated, all notes to this chapter refer to chapter 3:5 of the *Essays*; only the pages will be indicated.

3. Ibid.
4. Ibid.
5. Ibid.
6. Ibid.
7. 842; TR, 819; F, 639.
8. Ibid.
9. Ibid.
10. Ibid.
11. Ibid.
12. 841; TR, 818; F, 638.
13. 843–44; TR, 821; F, 640.
14. 842; TR, 819; F, 639.
15. 844; TR, 821; F, 641.
16. Ibid.
17. Ibid.
18. 844; TR, 822; F, 641. Recall that the final words of the *Essays* mention once again a "gay and sociable wisdom," placed under the patronage of Apollo.
19. 845;TR, 822; F, 642.
20. 845–46; TR, 822–23; F, 642.
21. 847; TR, 824; F, 643.
22. 845; TR, 822–23; F, 642. Whence a particular definition of the unconscious *avant la lettre*. The unconscious is not defined as a lack of self-knowledge introducing distortion into one's relations with others. It is rather a suspicious closing oneself off from others that leads to ignorance of the self. "To see one's vice and study it" does not run up against any intrinsic psychological obstacle, notwithstanding the difficulty we sometimes encounter in observing the "inner folds" of our mind. The unconscious is the result of a failure of communication: "Those who hide [their vice] from others ordinarily hide it from themselves" (845; TR, 823; F, 642).
23. 847; TR, 825; F, 644.
24. Ibid.
25. Ibid.
26. Ibid.
27. 847–48; TR, 825; F, 644. Cf. 2:12, 583n.13; TR, 568n.2 and text p. 1577: "And that decency and reverence, as we call it, of covering and hiding some of our natural and legitimate actions, of not daring to call things by their name, of fearing to say what we are permitted to do—wouldn't they [the ancients] have said, rightly, that this is rather an affectation and indulgence invented in the very boudoirs of Venus to pique and heighten pleasure? Isn't it an enticement, a blandishment, a stimulus to pleasure? For experience makes us clearly aware that ceremony, shame, difficulty are matches and kindling for those fevers?" On this subject it is also worth rereading all of chapter 2:15, "That our desire is increased by difficulty."
28. 849; TR, 826; F, 644–45.

29. 880; TR, 858; F, 671.

30. 873; TR, 850–51; F, 665. Note that, in order to characterize this style, so reserved and yet so effective, and to celebrate its complete referential success, Montaigne himself makes use of a style in which sexual metaphors abound. On this point see D. G. Coleman, "Montaigne's 'Sur des vers de Virgile': Taboo Subject, Taboo Author," in R. R. Bolgar, ed., *Classical Influences* (Cambridge, 1976), pp. 135–40; B. C. Bowen, "Montaigne's anti-*Phaedrus*: 'Sur des vers de Virgile' (*Essais* 3:5)," *Journal of Medieval and Renaissance Studies* 5 (1975): 107–21; and especially the chapter devoted to Montaigne in the important work of Cave, *The Cornucopian Text*, pp. 271–321.

31. 873; TR, 851; F, 665.

32. Ibid.

33. 880; TR, 859; F, 671.

34. 881; TR, 859; F, 671–72.

35. 2:12, 493; TR, 473; F, 364.

36. 855; TR, 833; F, 650.

37. 855; TR, 864; F, 675.

38. 1:28, 186; TR, 184; F, 137.

39. 885; TR, 864; F, 675.

40. 857; TR, 834–35; F, 652.

41. 871; TR, 849; F, 663.

42. 877; TR, 855; F, 668.

43. 877–78; TR, 855–56; F, 668–69.

44. 878–79; TR, 856–57; F, 669–70.

45. 880; TR, 858; F, 671.

46. Ibid.

47. 884; TR, 862; F, 674.

48. 874; TR, 852; F, 666.

49. 875; TR, 853; F, 667.

50. 875; TR, 852; F, 666.

51. 875; TR, 853; F, 667.

52. 876; TR, 854; F, 668.

53. Ibid.

54. 876–77; TR, 854–55; F, 668. Elsewhere Montaigne explains: "I seldom dream, and then it is about fantastic things and chimeras usually produced by amusing thoughts, more ridiculous than sad. And I hold that it is true that dreams are faithful interpreters of our inclinations; but there is an art to sorting and understanding them" (3:13, 1098; TR, 1077; F, 843).

55. 850; TR, 827; F, 645–46.

56. 851; TR, 829; F, 647.

57. 852; 829; 648.

58. 852; TR, 830; F, 648.

59. 852–53; TR, 830; F, 648.

60. 851; TR, 829; F, 647. The difference between love and marriage is described by a metaphor involving heat. In the chapter "Of friendship" we find

the following: "In friendship it is a general and universal warmth, moderate and even, besides, a constant and settled warmth, all gentleness and smoothness, with nothing bitter and stinging about it." What is more, Montaigne, who at this point is extolling virile friendship above all else, adds that this emotion, superior as it is to love, is not found in "marriages" any more than in amorous affairs: "During the reign of this perfect friendship those fleeting affections once found a place in me. . . . Thus these two passions within me came to be known to each other, but to be compared, never; the first keeping its course in proud and lofty flight, and disdainfully watching the other making its way far, far beneath it" (1:28, 186; TR, 184; F, 137).

61. 891; TR, 869; F, 680.

62. 3:3, 824–25; TR, 802–3; F, 626.

63. 3:10, 1014; TR, 991; F, 776.

64. 3:5, 891; TR, 869; F, 680.

65. 874; TR, 851; F, 663.

66. 889; TR, 867; F, 678.

67. 882; TR, 860; F, 672–73.

68. 3:5, 835; TR, 813; F, 634.

69. 3:3, 825; TR, 803; F, 626.

70. 3:3, 825–26; TR, 803–4; F, 626–27.

71. 3:5, 891; TR, 869; F, 680.

72. 866; TR, 843–44; F, 659.

73. 889–90; TR, 867–68; F, 679.

74. 889; TR, 868; F, 679.

75. 887; TR, 866; F, 677.

76. 894; TR, 872–73; F, 682.

77. 892–93; TR, 871; F, 681. On this point comparison should be made between the concluding pages of 3:13, "Of experience," and the injunction to "couple and join together again" "our two principal parts" (2:17, 639; TR, 622; F, 485).

78. Ibid.

79. Ibid.

80. 893–94; TR, 872; F, 682.

81. 895; TR, 873; F, 683.

82. 886; TR, 865; F, 676.

83. 893; TR, 871; F, 681.

84. 887; TR, 865–66; F, 677.

85. 860; TR, 837; F, 654.

86. 874; TR, 851–52; F, 665–66.

87. 873; TR, 850; F, 665.

88. 875; TR, 853; F, 667.

89. 874; TR, 851; F, 665–66. It is hardly necessary to point out that it had long been traditional, in antiquity as well as the Middle Ages, to express the "capture" or "conquest" of the beloved in terms of the vocabulary of warfare and the hunt.

90. 875; TR, 853; F, 667. The imperfection of the *Essays* is thus excused on the grounds of fidelity of reference. On the preceding page Montaigne praises Horace's perfect art, made legitimate, we are told, by his concern to "represent" the *thing* described as accurately as possible: "Horace is not content with a superficial expression; it would betray him. He sees more clearly and deeply into the thing. His mind unlocks and ransacks the whole storehouse of words and figures in order to express itself; and he needs them to be beyond the commonplace, as his conception is beyond the commonplace." Cf. F. Rigolot, "Le langage des *Essais*, référentiel ou mimologique?" *Cahiers de l'Association internationale des études françaises* 33 (May 1981): 19–34.

91. 842; TR, 819; F, 639.

92. 891–92; TR, 870; F, 680.

93. 3:4, 837; TR, 815; F, 636.

94. 3:9, 978; TR, 956; F, 748. As Montaigne points out in the *Apology for Raymond Sebond*, it was the doctrine of the "Cyrenaics" that "only that was perceptible which touched us by internal *touch*, like pain and pleasure" (2:12, 587; TR, 571; F, 443).

95. 892; TR, 870; F, 680–81.

96. 892; TR, 871; F, 681. The same assertion occurs in "Of vanity": "As natural comforts fail us, let us sustain ourselve with artificial ones" (3:9, 977; TR, 955; F, 747).

97. 893; TR, 872; F, 681–82. As is well known, Chateaubriand is responding to these lines in the episode of the Occitanian woman: "My poor Michel, you say some charming things, but at our age love doesn't bring us what you seem to suppose. We have but one thing to do, and that is to get ourselves entirely out of the way" (*Mémoires d' Outre-Tombe*, part 3, book 10, 1).

98. 895; TR, 874; F, 683.

99. 896–97; TR, 875; F, 684.

100. Virgil, *Georgics* 3.98–100.

101. 897; TR, 875; F, 684–85.

102. Montaigne experienced physical love at a very early age: "It is certainly distressing and miraculous to confess at what a tender age I first chanced to fall under its subjection. It was indeed by chance, for it was long before the age of choice and knowledge. I do not remember about myself so far back. And my lot may be coupled with that of Quartilla, who had no memory of her maidenhood" (3:13, 1086–87; TR, 1064–65; F, 833). Again Montaigne compares himself to a woman (in this case, to a character in Petronius's *Satyricon*).

103. 897; TR, 875–76; F, 685. In the eighth of the *Neuf matinées* of Cholieres (1585), we read "que la poêle ne se moque du fourgon" (Jouaust edition, 1879, p. 297). According to Le Roux's *Dictionnaire comique* (1735), the expression "applies to two equally ridiculous individuals who make fun of each other." In Montaigne's time *fourgonner* was one of the metaphors for the sexual act used by the authors of ribald stories.

Chapter Six

1. 2:12, 601; TR, 586; F, 455. Cf. chap. 2 above.
2. 2:12, 520; TR, 501; F, 387.
3. 2:8, 386; TR, 366; F, 279.
4. 3:12, 1019; TR, 1036–37; F, 811.
5. Ibid.
6. Ibid.
7. 3:12, 1049–50; TR, 1026–27; F, 803.
8. 2:12, 580; TR, 564–65; F, 438.
9. 2:8, 387; TR, 366; F, 279–80.
10. 1:26, 149; TR, 148; F, 109.
11. Cf. the sentence cited above in chap. 4: "It is for habit to give form to our life" (3:13, 1080; TR, 1058; F, 827).
12. 3:10, 1011; TR, 988; F, 773.
13. 2:8, 386–87; TR, 366; F, 279.
14. 2:37, 784; TR, 764; F, 596.
15. Remember the peremptory statement: "I am less a maker of books than of anything else" (ibid.).
16. 3:6, 903; TR, 881; F, 689.
17. 2:16, 619; TR, 603; F, 469.
18. Ibid.
19. 3:8, 942; TR, 921; F, 720.
20. 3:13, 1074; TR, 1052; F, 822.
21. Ibid.
22. Ibid.
23. 2:6, 379; TR, 359; F, 274.
24. 2:8, 386–87; TR, 366; F, 279.
25. 2:3, 350; TR, 330; F, 251.
26. 3:13, 1081; TR, 1059; F, 828.
27. 3:13, 1112; TR, 1092; F, 854.
28. 1:50, 302; TR, 290; F, 219.
29. 2:17, 657–58; TR, 641; F, 499. In the commentary that follows, I return to topics treated in chap. 1 in connection with essay 1:8 and the spatialized representation of the ego.
30. 1:39, 241; TR, 235; F, 177.
31. 3:1, 792; TR, 769; F, 601. In context this sentence does not deal with deliberate action, but it can be interpreted more broadly.
32. 3:9, 988; TR, 966; F, 755.
33. 1:38, 236; TR, 231; F, 174. See above, chap. 2, section entitled "The happiness of feeling: Between wakefulness and sleep." Thibaudet, in his *Montaigne* (which, though not a finished book, is a fine collection of reader's notes), compiles an impressive catalogue of images of motion in Montaigne (see pp. 505ff.).
34. 1:4, 22; TR, 25; F, 14: "So it seems that the soul, once stirred and set in

motion, is lost in itself unless we give it something to grasp; and we must always give it an object to aim at and act on."

35. 2:1, 333; TR, 316; F, 240.

36. 2:1, 337; TR, 321; F, 244.

37. 2:12, 601; TR, 586; F, 455. These lines, from the conclusion of the *Apology*, are preceded by the following sentence: "Finally, there is no existence that is constant, either of our being or of that of objects."

38. 1:8, 33; TR, 34; F, 21.

39. 2:12, 569; TR, 553; F, 428.

40. 3:9, 1001; TR, 979; F, 766.

41. 3:3, 819; TR, 797; F, 621.

42. 3:2, 811; TR, 789; F, 615. In the *Apology* Montaigne refers to himself as "being of indolent and sluggish disposition" (2:12, 568; TR, 552; F, 428).

43. 1:26, 150; TR, 149; F, 110.

44. 2:16, 618; TR, 601; F, 468.

45. 2:12, 408; TR, 477; F, 368.

46. 1:27, 178; TR, 177; F, 132.

47. 2:8, 385; TR, 364; F, 278.

48. 1:28, 183; TR, 181–82; F, 135.

49. 3:5, 892–93; TR, 871; F, 681.

50. 3:13, 1114; TR, 1094–95; F, 855.

51. 3:10, 1007; TR, 984; F, 770.

52. 2:12, 506; TR, 486; F, 374.

53. 3:13, 1083; TR, 1061; F, 830.

54. 2:12, 538; TR, 519; F, 402.

55. 1:39, 242; TR, 237; F, 178.

56. 3:9, 994; TR, 973; F, 761.

57. 3:9, 985; TR, 963; F, 753.

58. 3:13, 1114; TR, 1094; F, 855.

59. 2:17, 639; TR, 622; F, 484. Or again: "We are built of two principal essential parts, whose separation is the death and destruction of our being" (2:12, 519; TR, 500; F, 386).

60. 3:13, 1105; TR, 1085; F, 848.

61. 3:13, 1111–12; TR, 1092; F, 853.

62. 3:9, 971; TR, 949; F, 742.

63. 3:9, 984; TR, 962; F, 752.

64. 3:9, 1007; TR, 984; F, 770.

65. 3:13, 1108; TR, 1088; F, 851.

66. 3:13, 1089; TR, 1067; F, 835.

67. 3:13, 1101; TR, 1081; F, 845.

68. 3:3, 819; TR, 796; F, 621.

69. 3:2, 812; TR, 790; F, 616.

70. 3:5, 844; TR, 821; F, 641.

71. 3:13, 1107; TR, 1087; F, 850.

72. 3:13, 1102; TR, 1082; F, 846.
73. 2:28, 703: TR, 681–82; F, 531–32.
74. 1:20, 88–89; TR, 87; F, 61.
75. 3:9, 983; TR, 961; F, 752.
76. 1:20, 87; TR, 85; F, 60.
77. 3:13, 1098; TR, 1077; F, 842.
78. 3:9, 971; TR, 949; F, 742.
79. 3:13, 1112; TR, 1093; F, 854.
80. 3:13, 1069; TR, 1046; F, 818.

Chapter Seven

1. Thibaudet, *Montaigne*, p. 368.
2. Maurice Merleau-Ponty, *Signes* (Paris, 1960), p. 262.
3. Ibid., p. 261. About chiasmus, Merleau-Ponty, in *Le visible et l'invisible* (Paris, 1964), p. 319, writes: "The idea of *chiasmus*, i.e., the idea that every relationship to being is simultaneously one of taking and being taken, of apprehension apprehended: apprehension is *inscribed*, and inscribed in the same being that it apprehends." Furthermore, on the subject of language he writes, in *La Prose du Monde* (Paris, 1969), p. 26: : "To say that thought, which is its own mistress, always refers back to a thought mixed up with language is not to say that it is alienated, cut off by language from truth and certainty. It is essential to understand that language is not an impediment for consciousness, that for consciousness there is no difference between the act of apprehending and the act of expressing itself, and that language in its nascent and vital form is the act of recovery that brings me back into touch with myself and others. We can conceive of consciousness only *in* the vicissitudes of language, impossible without its contrary."
4. 3:13, 1113; TR, 1092; F, 854.
5. 3:5, 875: TR, 853; F, 667.
6. 3:12, 1055; TR, 1033; F, 808.
7. 1:26, 171–72; TR, 171–72; F, 127–28.
8. Hugo Friedrich, *Montaigne*, trans. E. Rovini (Paris, 1968), p. 10.
9. See Paul Valéry, *Cahiers* (Paris: Gallimard, 1973), p. 206: "I opened a *Montaigne*. A few minutes later I put it aside. It oppressed me. Everybody can write such things." Cf. Jean Hytier, "Lecteur de Montaigne?" in "Reminiscences et rencontres valéryennes," *French Studies* 24 (1980): 179–80.
10. 1:21, 97; TR, 95; F, 68; and 2:11, 430, 432; TR, 409, 412; F, 316.
11. 2:11, 429; TR, 408; F, 313.
12. Montaigne never wavered in his reproach: "inhumanity, cruelty, and treachery" are for him "the worst kinds of vice" (3:9, 956; TR, 934; F, 730). "The horror I feel for cruelty throws me back more deeply into clemency than any model of clemency could attract me to it" (3:8, 922; TR, 900; F, 703).
13. 2:11, 432; TR, 411–12; F, 315–16.
14. Jean Paulhan, "Portrait de Montaigne," in Montaigne, *Oeuvres complètes*

(Paris, 1969), 4: 309–11, detects such a tendency in a portrait of Montaigne but at the same time asks himself how much faith once can place in the interpretation of a picture.

15. 3:1, 791; TR, 768; F, 599. Montaigne has just called cruelty "so unnatural a vice." But immediately afterwards he cites these famous lines of Lucretius: " 'Tis sweet, when the sea is high and winds are driving / To watch from shore another's anguished striving."

16. 3:13, 1082; TR, 1060; F, 829.

17. 3:12, 1049; TR, 1026; F, 803.

18. 2:11, 435; TR, 414; F, 318.

19. 1:28, 193; TR, 192; F, 143.

20. 1:31, 214; TR, 212–23; F, 159.

21. Ibid.

22. Jean-Jacques Rousseau, *Emile*, book 4. *Oeuvres complètes* (Paris: Gallimard, 1969), 4:505.

23. Jean-Jacques Rousseau, *Discours de l'origine de l'inégalité. Oeuvres complètes*, 3:155.

24. Sextus Empiricus, *Hypoyposes* 1.14, trans. C. Huart, at 1725, p. 70: "The tenth way belongs mainly to moral things, as being taken from establishments, customs, laws, fabulous convictions and dogmatic opinions."

25. 3:13, 1072; TR, 1049; F, 821. Cf. 2:12, 578–79; TR, 562–63; F, 436.

26. 3:1, 799; TR, 777; F, 607.

27. 3:1, 796; TR, 773; F, 604.

28. 2:12, 578–79; TR, 562; F, 436.

29. 3:8, 935; TR, 913; F, 714. Or again: "The souls of emperors and cobblers are cast in the same mold" (2:12, 476; TR, 454; F, 350).

30. 2:43, 270; TR, 261; F, 198.

31. 2:12, 583; TR, 567; F, 440.

32. 2:12, 439; TR, 416; F, 320.

33. 3:8, 923; TR, 901; F, 704.

34. The term is used by Hugo Friedrich, who recalls a penetrating remark of Valéry's: "Doubt leads to form."

35. See especially Max Horkheimer, "Montaigne und die Funktion der Skepsis," *Anfänge der burgerlichen Geshichtsphilosophie* (Frankfurt: Fischer Verlag, 1971), pp. 96–144.

36. 3:1, 802; TR, 780; F, 609.

37. 3:10, 1009–10; TR, 987; F, 772. Pascal, as is well known, radicalizes this idea: "Custom is a second nature that destroys the first. But what is nature? Why is custom not natural? I greatly fear that nature itself may be only a first custom, as custom is a second nature."

38. 2:17, 658; TR, 641; F, 499.

39. Ernst Cassirer, *Der Erkenntnisproblem* (1922; repr. Darmstadt: Wissenschaftliche Buchgesellschaft, 1971), 1:190. See also the chapter that Eric Weil devotes to *intelligence* as a category and attitude in *Logique de la philosophie* (Paris, 1950), chap. 11, pp. 263–81.

40. Cassirer, *Der Erkenntnisproblem*, p. 189. Cassirer's remarks are in part the source of Max Horkheimer's much less even-handed critique of Montaigne.

41. 3:10, 1003; TR, 980; F, 766.

42. 3:10, 1003–4; TR, 980–81; F, 766–77.

43. 3:10, 1004; TR, 981; F, 767.

44. 3:10, 1006; TR, 983; F, 769.

45. 3:10, 1003–4; TR, 980–81; F, 767.

46. 3:10, 1004; TR, 981; F, 767.

47. Horkheimer, "Montaigne," p. 116. In criticizing Montaigne, Horkheimer was actually attacking (without naming any) the skeptics of his own time (1938), who refused to take a firm stand against totalitarian movements of the right. He is quite wrong, in my view, when he argues that Montaigne's moderate neutrality in the war between the Huguenots and the Guise "took the form of retreat into his library" and of travels "in enemy territory." Horkheimer is, however, at pains to draw one distinction: "The obedience that Montaigne as a good skeptic preached was obedience to a monarchy struggling against reactionary forces. The obedience to which today's skeptic lends himself is submission to barbarism" (p. 124). Yet Montaigne, even as he proclaimed his loyalty and fidelity to the legitimate monarch, was without illusion as to the state of affairs that had preceded the civil war: "The state of health from which we started was such that it is itself a solace for the regret that we should have for it. It was health, but only in comparison with the sickness that followed it. We have not fallen from very high. The corruption and brigandage that enjoy dignity and established status seem to me the least endurable. We are robbed less wickedly in a forest than in a place of safety. There was a universal conjunction of members, each individually vying in rottenness with the others, and most of them afflicted with age-old ulcers which no longer admitted of cure or asked for it" (3:12, 1047; TR, 1023–24; F, 801). Montaigne's favorite metaphors are those of sickness and health, and secondarily stability and fall; the metaphors that Horkheimer uses are governed by the image of forward motion (progress) and its contrary, reaction. The only thing that Montaigne and his modern critic have in common is that both use terms of moral judgment ("barbarism," etc.)—which is not insignificant. The argument that Horkheimer uses to link Montaigne's individualism to the market economy would, if applied to Horkheimer himself, link his "active" (Marxist) humanism to Stalinism and the gulag. In his last years, of course, Horkheimer became a resolute foe of Stalinist dictatorship.

48. 3:1, 793; TR, 770; F, 601–2. The story of Spurina, who mutilated his handsome face in order not to arouse the passions of others and cause them to sin elicits the following comment from Montaigne: "Those who evade the common duties and that infinite number of thorny and many-faceted rules that bind a man of precise probity in civil life, achieve, in my opinion, a fine saving, whatever point of especial rigor they may impose on themselves. It is

337

in a sense dying to escape the trouble of living well. They may have some other prize; but the prize of difficulty it has never seemed to me they had, nor do I think there is anything more arduous than keeping oneself straight amid the waves and rush of the world, loyally responding to and satisfying every part of one's charge" (2:33, 734; TR, 712; F, 555). On the equilibrium between private life and public life, see the excellent analysis of 3:10 by Hugo Friedrich, *Montaigne*, pp. 262ff.

49. 3:10, 1006; TR, 984; F, 769.

50. 3:10, 1006–7; TR, 984; F, 769–70.

51. 3:10, 1007; TR, 984; F, 770.

52. 3:10, 1004; TR, 980; F, 767.

53. 3:10, 1007; TR, 985; F, 770.

54. 3:10, 1008; TR, 986; F, 771.

55. 3:10, 1011–12; TR, 989; F, 774.

56. 3:10, 1023; TR, 1001; F, 783.

57. 3:6, 907–8; TR, 885–86; F, 692–93.

58. 2:12, 575; TR, 559; F, 433–34. This "climatic theory," which originates with Hippocrates ("Of airs, waters, and places"), includes the idea that planets and celestial bodies affect changes in opinion (i.e., in religion). On the idea of astral determination of religious eras, see F. Boll, C. Bezold, W. Gundel, *Sternglaube und Sterndeutung* (1931; reprinted Darmstadt, 1961), pp. 200–205. This notion could hardly fail to arouse the suspicions of the Church. Jean Bodin and later Montesquieu paid close attention to the relationship between climate and social institutions.

59. 2:12, 576; TR, 560; F, 434.

60. Ibid., 434.

61. 2:23, 682; TR, 662–63; F, 516–17.

62. 3:12, 1047; TR, 1023–24; 801. Cf. n. 44 above.

63. 3:13, 1088; TR, 1066; F, 834.

64. 3:12, 1043; TR, 1019–20; F, 797.

65. 2:17, 655; TR, 639–40; F, 497–98. On the history of the idea of decline, the best summary may be found in the collection of essays by Reinhart Koselleck and Paul Widmer, *Niedergang: Studien zu einem geschictlichen Thema* (Klett-Cotta, 1980).

66. See especially his critique of interpretation at the beginning of 3:13, "Of experience."

67. Avarice and ambition are frequently closely connected in Montaigne, but only verbally. Of all the passions these are the ones that alienate us from ourselves the most, the ones that cause us to "think elsewhere" and dupe us with the hope of future benefits. The anticipated gain can never compensate us for the loss of self-presence. Even in the material sphere Montaigne still belonged to an age in which agricultural income was annual and commercial exchange was short-term. Although he was adept at judiciously increasing his land holdings, he hardly ever mentions, much less approves of, long-term

investments, labor that will bear fruit only in the distant future. This is not simply the wisdom of an old man who lives "from day to day."

68. 3:10, 1022–23; TR, 1000–1001; F, 782–83.

69. 3:10, 1018; TR, 995; F, 779.

70. Ibid.

71. Ibid. The fact that the causes we know explain nothing has as its corollary the idea that it is futile to explore unknown causes. Nothing is easier than "forging reasons for all sorts of dreams" (3:11, 1034; TR, 1012; F, 791).

72. 3:10, 1018; TR, 996; F, 779.

73. 3:10, 1018–19; TR, 996–97; F, 779–80.

74. 3:10, 1021; TR, 999; F, 781.

75. Ibid.

76. It is of course quite different with Rousseau, who values the future as a time of *rehabilitation*. He counts on the passage of time to dispel the slander that he feels unable to refute in the present. The idea of reparation requires a future and imperiously calls one forth.

77. 3:10, 1010–11; TR, 987–88; F, 772–73.

78. 3:10, 1016; TR, 994; F, 777–78.

79. 3:9, 982; TR, 960–61; F, 751. The same assertion occurs in the letter to Mme de Duras: Montaigne wants "to lodge [these same traits and faculties] (but without alteration or change) in a solid body that may last *a few years, or a few days*, after me" (2:37, 783; TR, 763; F, 595).

80. 3:10, 1007; TR, 984; F, 769.

81. 3:10, 1015; TR, 993; F, 777.

82. Ibid.

83. 3:10, 1011; TR, 988–89; F, 773.

84. 2:12, 537; TR, 518–19; F, 401. On the image of the circle and the idea of circular motion in the Renaissance, cf. Georges Poulet *Les métamorphoses du cercle* (Paris, 1979), pp. 25–69; Alexandre Koyré, *From the Closed World to the Infinite Universe* (Baltimore, 1957).

85. 3:10, 1023; TR, 1000, F, 782.

86. 3:2, 805; TR, 782; F, 610.

87. 1:25, 136; TR, 135. F, 100.

88. 3:13, 1107; TR, 1087; F, 850.

89. 2:37, 784; TR, 764; F, 596.

90. 3:5, 842; TR, 820; F, 635.

91. 1:26, 151; TR, 150; F, 111.

92. Ibid.

93. 3:8, 929; TR, 907; F, 709.

94. The foundation image is also found in a famous statement of political conservatism: "Nothing presses a state hard except innovation; change alone lends shape to injustice and tyranny. When some part is dislocated, we can prop it up; we can fight against letting the alteration and corruption natural to all things carry us too far from our beginnings and principles. But to under-

take to recast so great a mass, *to change the foundations of so great a structure,* that is a job for those (C) who wipe out a picture in order to clean it, (B) who want to reform defects of detail by universal confusion and cure illnesses by death" (3:9, 958; TR, 935; F, 731).

95. 1:27, 182; TR, 181; F, 134–35.

96. 1:27, 181; TR, 180–81; F, 134.

97. Cf. Marcel Raymond, "L'attitude religieuse de Montaigne," in *Génies de France* (Neuchatel, 1942), pp. 50–67.

98. 3:9, 961; TR, 938; F, 734.

99. 1:26, 157; TR, 156–57; F, 116.

100. 1:26, 157–58; TR, 157; F, 116.

101. 3:6, 907; TR, 885; F, 692.

102. 3:6, 908; TR, 886; F, 693.

103. 3:6, 908–9; TR, 887; F, 693.

104. 3:9, 960; TR, 937; F, 733.

105. 2:12, 570; TR, 553; F, 429.

106. 2:12, 570; TR, 553–54; F, 429.

107. 2:12, 570–71; TR, 554; F, 429.

108. 3:13, 1073; TR, 1050; F, 821.

109. Ibid.

110. 3:8, 934; TR, 912; F, 713.

111. 1:25, 140; TR, 139; F, 103.

112. 1:25, 141; TR, 140; F, 103.

113. 1:26, 148; TR, 147; F, 109.

114. Francis Bacon, *Novum Organum*, in *Works*, 7 vols. (London, 1857–59), 1:162. Translation: "But an instauration must be made starting from the deepest foundations, so as not to be carried along in a perpetual circle with scant and almost imperceptible progress."

115. Ibid., p. 222. Translation: "Man's domination over things can be established only by the arts and sciences. Nature can only be ruled by obedience to her laws."

116. Here I can do no more than mention the emergence of the idea of aesthetics, marked by the publication of Baumgarten's *Aesthetica* (1750). On this subject, see Ernst Cassirer, *Die Philosophie der Aufklärung* (1932), chap. 7; Joachim Ritter, "Landschaft," In *Subjektivität* (Suhrkamp. 1974), pp. 141–63.

117. Cf. the highly simplified treatment of the problem in my "Langage poétique et langage scientifique," *Diogène* 100 (1977):139–57.

118. On the function of the future in modern political thought, and on the crisis affecting the notion of the future, see Krzysztof Pomian, "La crise de l'avenir," *Le Débat* 7 (December 1980):5–17.

119. On this point, see the survey article by Leonard Shapiro in M. Cranston and P. Mair, eds., *Ideology and Politics* (Stuttgart, Brussels, and Florence: Alphen, 1980), pp. 75–92. See also the essays in E. Castelli, ed., *Démythisation et idéologie* (Paris, 1973), as well as the Summer 1979 issue of *Daedalus* devoted to "Hypocrisy, Illusion and Evasion." Another good survey

of the topic may be find in the R. Romberg and V. Dierse, "Ideologie," in J. Ritter and K. Grunder, eds., *Historisches Wörterbuch der Philosophie* (Basel, 1976), vol. 4.

120. 2:32, 724–25; TR, 702–3; F, 548. "It is unfortunate to be in such a pass that the best touchstone of truth is the multitude of believers, in a crowd in which the fools so far surpass the wise in number" (3:11, 1028; TR, 1005; F, 786).

121. Reinhart Koselleck, *Kritik and Krise* (Frankfurt, 1973), p. 157.

122. 2:12, 490; TR, 470; F, 361. The anecdote is also cited in 1:14, 54; TR, 54; F, 36.

123. 3:13, 1074; TR, 1052; F, 823.

124. 3:13, 1115; TR, 1096; F, 857.

125. 3:13, 1116; TR, 1096; F, 857.

126. Ibid.

127. 3:8, 931; TR, 909; F, 711.

128. Ibid.

129. 3:1, 796; TR, 774: F, 604.

130. 3:8, 930; TR, 908–9; F, 710.

131. 3:8, 931; TR, 910; F, 711.

132. 3:8, 931; TR, 909; F, 711.

133. G. W. F. Hegel, *Encyclopedie,* sec. 131. See also the concluding pages of the preface to the *Philosophy of Law.*

134. Cited without reference by Henry Matthews in *Bulletin Poésie,* Arc, Paris, third year, no. 40, p. 159. "To cling deliberately to the surface of things," writes Michel Leiris to define what is distinctive about the most valuable aspects of modernity. Leiris, in *Le Ruban au cou d'Olympia* (Paris, 1981), p. 244, is also the author of the following lines, one of the most splendid of all eulogies of appearances and the present: "To find a heaven on the suface of the earth, to confer eternal value upon a moment lived in full lucidity, these are the joys granted on occasion by the modern demon of negation to those who, unwilling to take black for white, no longer set store by any time but the present—by what is direct, immediate, and without memory or anticipation—and who can be satisfied only by that which, in isolation from any theory or project, directly creates a dazzling sensation of presence—not the presence of something ordinarily imperceptible suddenly manifesting itself through appearance, but presence of that very appearance that needs nothing other than its own radiance to shine forth."

135. Friedrich Nietzsche, *Ecce Homo,* "Why I am intelligent," 3.

136. Friedrich Nietzsche, *The Twilight of the Gods,* "Reason in philosophy," sec. 2.

137. Friedrich Nietzsche, *Beyond Good and Evil,* trans. Helen Zimmern (New York: Random House, 1954), sec. 34, p. 420.

138. Friedrich Nietzsche, *The Joyful Wisdom,* trans, Thomas Common (New York: Ungar, 1960), sect. 54, pp. 88–89.

139. With the desire (held by Montaigne to be illusory) to see the wheel

come to a stop. Remember the metaphorical wish: "If I could put a spoke in our wheel and stop it at this point, I would do so with all my heart" (2:17, 655; TR, 639; F, 497).

140. Montaigne praises not dance but an unfettered gait: "At dancing, tennis, wrestling, I have never been able to acquire any but very slight and ordinary ability. . . . I have a soul all its own, accustomed to conducting itself in its own way. Having had neither governor nor master forced on me to this day, I have gone just so far as I pleased, at my own pace" (2:17, 642–43; TR, 625–26; F, 486–87).

141. 3:10, 1007; TR, 985; F, 770.

142. 2:10, 1007–8; TR, 985; F, 770–71.

143. 3:10, 1011; TR, 989; F, 773.

144. 3:10, 1006; TR, 983; F, 769.

145. Ibid.

146. 3:10, 1012; TR, 989; F, 774.

147. 3:8, 929–30; TR, 907–8; F, 709–10.

148. 3:2, 806; TR, 784; F, 612.

149. 1:26, 147; TR, 146; F, 108.

150. 3:5, 846; TR, 824; F, 643.

151. 1:20, 88; TR, 86; F, 61.

Index